BORN-AGAIN
DEIST

Born-Again Deist

Beth Houston

New Deism Press • Florida

Beth Houston, MA, MFA, has taught creative writing, literature, and/or composition at San Francisco State University; University of California, Berkeley; University of California, Santa Cruz; Eckerd College; University of Central Florida; University of South Florida; University of Tampa; Polk Community College; and Manatee Community College/State College of Florida. She has published six poetry books and nearly three hundred works in literary and professional journals.

ISBN 978-0-9719190-7-5

Printed in Canada

FSC

Mixed Sources
Product group from well-managed
forests and other controlled sources

Cert no. SW-COC-003438
www.fsc.org
© 1996 Forest Stewardship Council

CONTENTS

Chapter 1

The Coming of Age of Deism

Have you ever had one of those Aha! moments when suddenly you just got it? If you have, perhaps you too have noticed that when perspective shifts, so does self-definition. A significant spiritual epiphany can trigger sine waves that rattle pretty much every facet of your life.

Those paradigm shifts can be painful. But in my experience, truth is always cathartic and often catalyzes a spiritual high.

Of course not all epiphanies happen in a flash. Something dawning on us can fade in like morning emerging from twilight—which, if you've ever sat still and closely observed the process, really does take some time. It's hard to pinpoint the threshold moment when anyone would agree that day has dawned. But day does dawn.

For me, most spiritual insights occur gradually as I'm thinking about something I've read, heard, or experienced. "Thinking about" can take place over a period of hours, weeks, even years, especially when a new insight necessitates a recalibration of prior knowledge and experience, not to mention relinquishment of a cherished assumption. But eventually the fog clears and the obvious truth stands there grinning at me quite matter-of-factly.

That kind of crystallization process took me from being spiritually inclined to born-again Christian to progressive Christian to disillusioned agnostic to delighted Deist. The crystal clear truth of Deism has been a potent epiphany generating joy that's like being born-again again.

Although this book is a kind of spiritual memoir, it's more a distillation of realizations rather than a recounting of events (though there's that, too). Chronologically, at least, I embraced Deism first because of all religions it made the most sense. In fact, I can't imagine a religion making more sense. And shouldn't religion be, above all else, *true*, and doesn't true mean *sensible*?

But conversion engages both intellect and spirit. I reached the threshold state of conviction because the principles of Deism that dawned on and in me provided the most direct encounter with God, both theologically and spiritually. Reaching that state took as much unlearning as learning.

Most people today probably remember Deism from junior high or high school history class as an antiquated philosophy held by some of America's Founding Fathers and other Enlightenment intellectuals in Europe. Merely a fringe worldview that resembled scientific determinism or pagan nature worship more than any of the major world religions, Deism had something to do with a Clockmaker God who wound up the universe and left it to run on its own like a ticking clock.

The pop quiz definition, with its impersonal God and mechanical Creation, is a modern misconception of a thriving, immensely popular religion that pervaded American society during the eighteenth and nineteenth centuries—a religion as thoroughly understood by early Americans as it is misunderstood by most Americans today.

It's true that traditionally Deism presented a common sense, nature centered spiritual perspective that didn't necessarily claim to be a bona fide religion. Many Deists were suspicious of and even hostile toward organized religion, which for centuries had plagued the world with bloody, superstition-driven crusades, inquisitions, and pogroms. But at the same time, some Deists remained Christians.

Some Deists rejected all religion, while a number embraced Deism itself as the one true religion, and others considered Deism to be an elevating complement to any religion. Was there, and is there, then, such a thing as one universal *Deism*?

In my view, yes. Commonsense truth has always been the essential foundation and final touchstone for any version of Deism. And as the name implies, De-ism—de from *deus*, meaning God—is centered in God, and only God, whether the focus be on theory or practice or a fusion of both. The defining tenet of God-ism is that the scope and elegance of Creation—both as noun and verb—necessitates a Creator that transcends that Creation.

(A Creator actively Creating could also be to some extent immanent in Creation—but not in the sense of being a human or other material component of Creation. God purely and truly Creates—is "in" Creation as ultimate source and process of Creation—yet is wholly other than—transcends—all Creation. God can't *be* Creation any more than a human poet is a word or line in a poem or the form and content of the poem as a whole. But unlike a human poet, whose poetry is always derivative, God Creates something from nothing.)

The updated rendition of Deism presented in this book stems from the original version initiated in the early seventeenth century by British philosopher Edward Herbert, later First Baron Herbert of Cherbury. Brother of the well-known religious poet George Herbert, the Father of Deism was himself a metaphysical poet and literary scholar, besides being a diplomat, soldier, courtier, and historian.

Edward Herbert's seminal works on the nature of truth, the bedrock of Deism, include *De Veritate* (On Truth), *De Causis Errorum* (On the Causes of Errors), *De Religione Laici* (On the Religion of the Laity), *De Religione Gentilium* (On the Religion of the Gentiles), and his *Autobiography*. In his treatises, Herbert proposes that all humans since the beginning of time have held five innate, God-given religious ideas: belief in God, in the need for worship, in virtue as the ultimate form of worship, in the need for repentance, and in rewards and punishments in the afterlife. How these five concepts expressed as private beliefs and the fundamental beliefs of institutionalized religions determined whether the religion would be humane or barbarous.

Subsequent Deist thinkers—the list includes Charles Blount, John Toland, Anthony Collins, Conyers Middleton, Matthew Tindal, Thomas Chubb, Thomas Woolston, Voltaire, Hermann Samuel Reimarus, Elihu Palmer, and Thomas Paine—modified and expanded Herbert's ideas. Considerations by skeptics like Montaigne, Pierre Bayle, Montesquieu, and many other freethinking philosophers and poets further legitimized Deism.

Though some Deists and political philosophers like John Locke argued that Deism need not contradict basic Christian beliefs, conservative Christianity begged to differ, and seeing it a grave threat, set about discrediting Deism, deeming it unorthodox, if not heretical. Though equated with paganism, the intelligent, progressive naturalistic theology quickly spread.

Though Deist ideas were rooted in ancient understandings, most notably those of the Greeks, centuries of Church constriction had smothered the principle of universal beliefs beneath the edifice of compulsory Christianity. The premise that religious ideas were innate was radical in its time—and still is today. If religion is innate to us all, we don't need organized religion and its hierarchy of sanctified insiders to instill religion within us or bestow its blessings upon us. There is no, and can be no, intermediary between an individual and God. No doubt unwittingly, Herbert planted the seed of a truly democratic religion that would help fuel major secular movements like the French and American Revolutions.

Probably most of us contemporary Americans don't really appreciate the extent to which Deism informed the basis of our Constitution and our nation. Some of our most illustrious Founding Fathers, such as Thomas Jefferson, George Washington, John Adams, John Jay, and Benjamin Franklin, as well as other famous thinkers in America and on the Continent, were proponents of the popular new "natural religion," Deism. Like most Americans of that era, our Founders learned about Deism primarily via Thomas Paine, whose books critiqued organized religion, especially Christianity, and espoused revolution, both spiritual and political; his *Common Sense* inspired our Declaration of Independence, and *Age of Reason* most directly prompted our Constitution's ideals of freedom of religion and separation of church and state, as well as the notions of justice and basic human rights upon which our laws and governing institutions were constructed. Although Paine's religious affiliation was Quaker, a sect for which he continued to hold great respect, he adopted many of the Deist ideas he first encountered in France and brought them with him to America.

Just as important to the development of American Deism was Elihu Palmer's *Principles of Nature, or A Development of the Moral Causes of Happiness and Misery among the Human Species.* A Baptist clergyman, Palmer was driven from the pulpit for preaching against the divinity of Christ. He wrote his monumental work after being left blind, widowed, and unemployed following a bout of yellow fever, an epidemic that plagued the early Republic. It was Palmer's *Principles* that were most often read and discussed during meetings of early Deist societies.

Conservative Christianity demonized Deist ideas during the eighteenth-century Enlightenment just as it had in the previous century. Many of us Americans were taught in our history classes that Thomas

Paine was atheist or agnostic, and that the Deists' Clockmaker God was obviously no longer engaged with nature or humanity, making God, in effect, the absent Father. But in fact Paine was a passionate believer in a dynamically creating, actively virtuous God, and Clockmaker God was a term coined by reactionary Christians who wanted to discredit the Deists and their rational theologies.

Still today conservative religionists tout Deism as "humanism," the error of well-meaning agnostics or the heresy of demonic pagans, depending on which conservative you talk to. But humanism is the expression of commonsense virtue, and heresy, like "paganism," is simply a spiritual difference of opinion.

What most upsets conservatives is the Deist claim that religious truth is not received through special revelation or exclusive insider knowledge of a religious body or sacred text. In the opening of *Age of Reason*, Paine makes this still very relevant point about privileging any particular revealed religion:

> Every national church or religion has established itself by pretending some special mission from God, communicated to certain individuals. The Jews have their Moses; the Christians their Jesus Christ, their apostles and saints; and the Turks their Mahomet, as if the way to God was not open to every man alike.
>
> Each of those churches show certain books, which they call revelation, or the word of God. The Jews say, that their word of God was given by God to Moses, face to face; the Christians say, that their word of God came by divine inspiration; and the Turks say, that their word of God (the Koran) was brought by an angel from Heaven. Each of those churches accuse the other of unbelief; and for my own part, I disbelieve them all.
>
> As it is necessary to affix right ideas to words, I will, before I proceed further into the subject, offer some other observations on the word revelation. Revelation, when applied to religion, means something communicated immediately from God to man.
>
> No one will deny or dispute the power of the Almighty to make such a communication, if he pleases. But admitting, for the sake of a case, that something has been revealed to a certain person, and not revealed to any other person, it is revelation to that person only. When he tells it to a second person, a second to a third, a third to a fourth, and so on, it ceases to be a revelation to all those

persons. It is revelation to the first person only, and hearsay to every other, and consequently they are not obliged to believe it.

It is a contradiction in terms and ideas, to call anything a revelation that comes to us at second-hand, either verbally or in writing. Revelation is necessarily limited to the first communication—after this, it is only an account of something which that person says was a revelation made to him; and though he may find himself obliged to believe it, it cannot be incumbent on me to believe it in the same manner; for it was not a revelation made to me, and I have only his word for it that it was made to him.

For a Deist, in the eighteenth century and now, truth supersedes myth, no matter how steeped in tradition that myth might be. Any myth, be it of a talking devil-serpent or man-God or God-breathed text or man living in the belly of a whale, is derivative and unverifiable. That doesn't prove it to be false; the point is that a myth cannot be proved to be true and therefore should not be deemed absolute sacred truth. This is especially the case for a myth that is clearly impossible besides being primitive and/or childish.

To curb scrutiny, the high priests of organized religions and less organized cults transmute their myths into "revelation." The great "revelation" of a Christ/Bible is, to be quite honest, a man-made myth wearing a paper halo. (If that image offends you, ask yourself this: If your cherished assumptions were proven to be false, would you have the integrity to give them up? If the proof were valid and true, would you not agree that even refusing to hear the argument would be both dishonest and cowardly?) As I will prove beyond a shadow of a doubt (which used to mean something in this country), neither Christ nor Bible is God or divine or "truth" in the way the fundamentalist means it.

The focus of Deism is on God as truth—and on truth as *true*. That Deism is not the mythic "special revelation" bestowed upon a chosen spiritual elite but is a universally inclusive natural religion available to anyone via innate, God-given faculties such as reason, conscience, and intuition continues to pose a threat to the privileged position of Church and Bible and their equivalents in other religious traditions.

Although immensely popular in the era of our Founders—Paine's books were major bestsellers, and tens of thousands more copies were distributed among the poor by political clubs at their own expense—

Deism gradually faded, in large part due to misunderstandings deliberately spawned by Christian conservatives throughout the eighteenth and nineteenth centuries and by fundamentalists during the early twentieth.

I believe that we have reached a critical threshold when Deism will be—indeed *must* be—brought to the fore again. Deism is the only theology intent on transcending the myths of ancient religions by following the map of common sense on the universal quest for God. Only by following the map together, with mutual respect for each other's differences replacing the violent urge to destroy them, can we halt our battle march toward extinction.

In a sense, Deism is the world's most authentic religion. Prominent in any dictionary definition of religion is the word "belief," or "beliefs"; few would not agree that religion is a set or system of beliefs.

But probably most of us would acknowledge that typically, the more religious a person is, the more he asserts his "beliefs" as absolute fact. The religious extremist replaces faith in certain beliefs with a claim to *know* ultimate truth with certainty.

Deism, on the other hand, truly maintains its faith in *beliefs* and respects any belief that does not contradict common sense. One might even argue that common sense itself is the high priest of Deism.

Deism critiques religion, including itself, for the sake of truth. Like other religions, Deism is rooted in a belief in the Divine. But Deism honors God and only God rather than honoring a religion *about* God. And Deism acknowledges that God is inscrutable—tentatively deduced via common sense, experienced via a kind of spiritual intuition, but never perfectly "known" in the sense maintained by organized religion. For the Deist, God is not an absolute fact "proven" by an absolute text conferred by an absolute human divinity confirmed by specially ordained priests. Enlightenment is not a stasis of having arrived but is a process of improvement via increased understanding. God is not contained in a box on the altar of any religion. The Deist deeply respects the transcending Mystery of God.

Deism is perhaps the only religion invested in its own evolution rather than in upholding its traditions. The only "ultimate assumption" in Deism—and even that is recognized to be a belief deduced via common sense—is that God is the Creator and Sustainer of existence as we know it.

Deism is a progressive spiritual perspective informed by honest reflection. It rejects the arrogance of religious absolutism in favor of a more humble lifelong quest for the absolute truth that is God. The quest never ends, because God, being boundless and unbounded, who transcends all Creation down to the essence of each minute detail, is ultimately inscrutable. Religious claims to a full authoritative knowledge of God are just plain absurd.

My Deist beliefs represent one particular perspective among many others. While my rendition is similar to the Enlightenment version popularized by Thomas Paine, its focus is more decidedly a spiritual outlook rooted in a belief—operative word *belief*—in a Creator God who is both transcendent and immanent and with whom one has a perpetual relationship, whether or not it registers as an encounter with the Divine. When it does register, one's awareness is Deist—unless or until it is appropriated by organized religion.

No one can prove that the spiritual exists. What I'm relying on here is the intuited understanding that I believe we all have but don't all cultivate—the understanding of a very specific faculty, the spirit.

If you are spiritually inclined, you will understand what I mean when I assert that spirit exists. If you are unspiritual or anti spiritual, if you don't experience the spiritual yourself (or don't register spiritual experience as spiritual) or assume that spiritual experience is impossible, you will likely reject my claims without even considering them, like the cynic who has never been in love (or more likely, has been rejected) argues that there is no such thing as love.

Here lies a major problem with any discourse about spirituality: Actual spirituality requires a discerning spirit, and spirit, just like mind, body, or any other faculty, needs to be cultivated. Some won't cultivate spirit because they believe it doesn't exist. Others cultivate spirit the wrong way. As I will show, religion rooted in belief-as-fact, which inevitably becomes "organized religion" for its own sake, is ultimately a detrimental way to cultivate spirit. In fact, throughout history, more people have been persecuted, tortured, and murdered by organized religion for the sake of belief-as-fact than by any other cause on earth.

New Deism—which is a theology of God and only God—holds as its fundamental tenets (*beliefs*) that God exists; that God is one; that God is Creator; that God is both transcendent and immanent in Creation; that

God is all-knowing, omniscient, and omnipotent; that God is good; that God is just; that God transcends the limits of human knowledge, goodness, and justice; that God spiritually engages with human individuals; and that no human or text or material or immaterial object is God or embodies God or fully or accurately represents God: This version of Deism is extreme in its rejection of idolatry.

Deism critiques fundamentalism for espousing belief in one transcendent (heavenly) spiritual Deity while in reality it is a religion of text worship. This is the case not just for Christian fundamentalism. Fundamentalist sects of the major religions have their own roots and beliefs, but each venerates a divine text, be it book (Bible, Koran, Torah, Sutras...), or prophet (Jesus, Mohammad, Moses, Buddha...) or leader (Paul, pope, mullah, rabbi, Dali Lama...) embodied in writings, as its ultimate source of truth; worship of a divinely inspired infallible text—a text that incarnates the divine Word—is what makes a sect radically fundamentalist.

The version of Christian fundamentalism prevalent in the U.S. today stems from an ultraconservative, anti-Enlightenment Protestant movement that arose in late nineteenth-century America to combat higher criticism—the historical-literary study of the Bible—and to thwart attempts to reconcile traditional Christian beliefs with contemporary experience and scientific knowledge. The fundamentalists, as they called themselves, transfigured the words of the Bible witness into God's infallible Word, elevating the Bible to the status of full equality with God.

This mystified "Word" not only justifies God's authority, but by extension, it confirms the fundamentalist's own authority. Most of us have heard at least one evangelist claim to be speaking and/or acting "in the full authority of God." The evangelist's word (i.e., his interpretation of the Bible) equals God's Word equals God.

Deism, on the other hand, is a truly democratic religion with a universal text of existence itself, which is available to anyone. Not a religion for "chosen" elite worshippers of a cultural or regional god, Deism is the ideal religion for people who truly believe that God is One.

And when all the myths of religion and anti-religion have been demystified, who wouldn't believe that?

Chapter 2

A Philosophical Basis for Deism

Commonsense Truth and Humanism

New Deism—the twenty-first-century version descended from Thomas Paine that I present here—is an experiment with non-institutional, judicious spirituality that advocates reality-as-truth and embraces the process of educated inferring. It is rooted in the premise that true religion is a set of reasons that exist in the real world, not in the world of antiquated codes derived from opinions colored by superstitions certified by myths.

Like traditional Deism, new Deism acknowledges the self-evident existence of a Creator, presumed to be one God that is good, omniscient, and eternal. Deism is humanism that includes belief in God, as opposed to atheistic humanism. When fundamentalists use the slur "humanism," they usually mean atheism.

The charge that humanists are necessarily atheists is false. Most humanists are fundamentally Deists, though they might not use that term. Most religionists, however, worship some false *representation* of God, making them idolaters (by those religions' own definitions) or dishonest atheists. The disagreement isn't really over the existence of God. The rift between humanism and religion is the difference between speculative and absolutist faith, between active revelation and static indoctrination, between humble and self-righteous assumptions about God.

Contrary to the claims of religionists, Deism's natural humanism doesn't erase or displace God. But organized religion does, by deifying itself and its validating "God-breathed" texts; it elevates antiquated human knowledge to the status of absolute divinity while it denigrates human scientific and philosophic explorations of God's natural Creation.

Humanism simply admits that at the center of all human concern stands the human being. It can't be otherwise. Our experience even of objective fact is always subjective. We see with human eyes, reason with human minds, feel with human emotions, act with human wills. The universe is ordered in such a way that we truth-seekers known as humans can catch a glimpse—but only a fragmentary glimpse—of its countless mysteries.

In contrast to religious absolutism, humanism humbly acknowledges that every glimpse is finite, temporal *human* interpretation. Theories, experiments, exploration, deductions, and accumulated data can culminate as facts, but even facts can be updated and revised. Absolute truth might exist (and common sense tells us it does), but human knowledge is tentative.

Subjective Objectivity

Even the most basic assertions about God are always beliefs and as such are subject to revision based on new information. Christians, Muslims, Jews, Buddhists, Hindus, agnostics, pagans, and atheists feel confident asserting 2+2=4 as absolute fact, but should we be as confident contending that God exists or does not exist, or that God is good or beyond good and evil? Observation and mathematical reasoning confirm that gravity behaves exactly the same way everywhere in the universe. But on what basis can we assert that God is one, is transcendent and/or immanent, or is the creator and sustainer of the universe? Can there be true knowledge of God, the fundamental basis of religion, and if so, how do we *know* that our knowledge is absolutely true?

Our need for a sense of security often makes us unwilling to concede that even "absolute facts" are beliefs. We thought it absolute fact that the shortest distance between two points was a straight line, but then Einstein demonstrated that because space is curved (or rather curving, since space is still expanding), the shortest distance between two points is a curve, and in fact, a perfect straight line doesn't exist anywhere in nature, it only exists as a mental construct in the human mind. Knowledge is a *process* of coming to know; what we come to know is an *aspect* of reality.

It's hard for most of us to wrap our very human minds around the possibility that the shortest distance between two points *isn't* a straight line. Maybe Einstein was wrong, maybe the shortest distance *is* a straight line. Or maybe, as scientists explain, it depends on context, in this case, the extreme macro or micro dimensions of space-time; in the everyday world, the shortest distance between two points would still be a straight line when you're buying wallpaper or building a deck.

Regardless of any objective truth, each and every one of us can only know that truth subjectively. We call a red sweater red when in fact the sweater is all colors except red. Red is the wavelength of light reflected off the sweater rather than absorbed by it along with the other colors. Our retinas absorb that reflected wavelength, and our brains interpret it as red. Although we believe that the sweater is red, in actuality (in a sense), red is the color the sweater is not.

Deists assume that God is not a static précis of reductive human knowledge but is the exuberant Creator that keeps us humans on our toes. Nature—all space-time existence—is the field where God engages with humans. Humans are that part of nature that humans are closest to; each human mind is the temple of knowledge, understanding, and experience of God, limited as it is.

We take 2+2=4 to be an objective fact that is true whether or not we believe it. Granted, but its truth is not dependent on observation alone but requires interpretation via internal logic. For a time, Plato considered mathematics to be ultimate objective truth. But still, it is the preprogrammed human mind that subjectively judges the equation 2+2=4 to be true. Mathematical concepts, Aristotle reminded Plato, are mental generalizations of concrete reality—concepts that we all understand because we all share the same innate mental capacity to grasp generalizations about a common reality we all experience.

THE WILL TO THINK

Collectively we are human, but we are also human individuals. We are born with our learning apparatuses—our inherent faculties—but we must participate in the process of learning. Early in life we seem to catch on to many lessons instinctively, but later, more sophisticated learning requires our active, willful participation. According to many experts, we are all wired to be geniuses. Most of us are not geniuses because we lack focus and flow; creativity and imagination to think outside the box; critical listening/observing learning skills; and persistent expression by which we engage in feedback loops. Geniuses are actively engaged in creation, synthesis, and articulation; non-geniuses—let's just be honest—tend to be passively receptive mockingbirds. Genius is not about superiority; it is about thinking. We've all got good physical brains. It's the way we use them, the way we think, that transforms our brains into intelligence. According to scholars in the field of accelerated learning, anyone can learn to think as a genius.

Thinking is not instant recognition of truth. It is a willful process of weighing, evaluating, reasoning, and tentatively concluding. Sometimes there is that Aha! moment of recognition, for instance when a kid first realizes that if A equals B, and B equals C, then A equals C. But higher thought is always open-minded, which is another way of saying creative; it always admits the possibility of new information that leads to different conclusions. The earth is not flat. The sun and planets do not revolve around the earth. The shortest distance between two points is not necessarily a straight line.

Fallacies of thought and semantic misinterpretations are as common as misinformation. One might assume that if A is B, then B is A. But just because God is love does not mean that love is God. That a car is red does not mean that red is a car. Even basic equations have to be thought through. *Through* implies evolution via process. In fact, evolution is process, and process evolution. Creation *is* process.

Doubt as Spiritual Necessity

Doubt (here meaning open-minded tentativeness) must be admitted as a legitimate and necessary condition of subjective truth-seeking and subsequent subjective apprehension of truth. Machines can be programmed, but humans need to understand. In this life, at least, doubt is a component of knowledge and knowledge a component of understanding. By denying doubt, we admit absolutist petrifaction; we deny active engagement in truth-seeking—thinking—and therefore in living human consciousness itself. Only humans know Creation as *creation*. Creation is a perpetual coming into existence. Static absolutism is the real heresy against the Creator.

Doubt is the natural consequence of two important subjective emotions that absolutists usually claim to own but don't—humility and faith. It is doubters, skeptics, truth-seekers that humbly admit that no human mind or institution is the perfect receptacle of absolute truth. The human pea-brain is enormously limited in what it can and does know about our immense universe, not to mention its possible meaning. Perfect knowledge of anything can be perfectly doubt-free knowledge only if the knower perfectly knows everything. If we cannot and do not know the existence, means of existence, and operative substance of every minute particle and every mathematical dimension of every universe (just for starters), then there *might* be an exception or an unknown context for *anything*, even something as simple and obviously true for us non rocket scientists as the straight line being the shortest distance between two points.

The humble knower is denigrated and often demonized by the arrogant knower, the knower who rejects new ideas and updated information, who burns heretics at the stake for dark arts like flying on broomsticks, copulating with devils, or acknowledging that earth is neither flat nor the center of the universe—nowadays translated as Harry Potter, gays, and evolutionists. This arrogant knower "obediently" clings to the "authority" of myths, legends, and superstitions generated by unknown authors in an age steeped in similar myths, legends, and superstitions, and calls that the "Word of God." This is the imperfect knower who calls blind faith divinely inspired absolute truth.

The Perfect Knower

The perfect knower, it seems, can only be God. The reasonable assumption is that only the One who actually creates it all, knows it all. And that One necessarily stands "above" it all to some extent. (The Creator that creates existence can't not yet exist). Because the perpetual coming-into-existence of a universe as elegantly complicated as ours must be known by something ultimately intelligent, we can deduce the existence of an ultimate knower/creator God still actively creating our perfectly synchronized universe—which does not preclude the possibility of another God creating another universe or more than one God creating ours. But the transcendent creating Divinity is one in creating one elegantly coherent Creation.

SPIRITUAL TRUTH VIA GOD-GIVEN FACULTIES

To assert the a priori reality even of God requires faith that our limited inherent faculties are capable of accurately apprehending and/or deducing God's existence just like anything else. Understanding this is crucial to dispelling the myths of absolutism.

Again, faith necessarily includes doubt, because in order to believe anything else, first and foremost we must believe in the ability of our faculties to apprehend and experience; we must trust our faculties as our ultimate guide, yet we must acknowledge that our faculties are limited.

Despite the limitations of our own faculty of reason, it is—it *must* be—by that faculty of reason that we can deduce from the massive evidence of our universe that at least one Creator exists (or that multiple Creators must be "one" in the process of creating one cohesive Creation). Even if we don't realize it, we are also trusting in our innate faculty of aesthetic sensibility, which apprehends that this universe is consistently elegant, coherent, and magnificent beyond total human comprehension. Even just a glimpse of its sublimity inspires a quality of awe in many of us that can properly be called spiritual. That experience of awe is sometimes sufficient to persuade us of the necessity of a Creator, which tradition has named God/Gods.

Furthermore, our faculties — intuition, conscience, aesthetic sensibility, reason, and all our other "registers"— are endowed upon us by something that necessarily transcends those faculties. Whether we believe that something to be Nature or God or some cosmic energy, we just have to trust that our endowed apparatuses are trustworthy—which further puts us in the logically precarious position of having to trust the trustworthiness of our ability to trust. It is possible that we have been deceived. To believe that we have not been deceived, to trust the trustworthiness of our faculties, we must also trust that what endowed us is trustworthy, and furthermore, that trustworthy is good, good being that which ultimately benefits. We can choose to believe that we have been deceived, but that would lead to a kind of existential madness, which seems to be a kind of built-in aversion response diverting us away from naturally repugnant nihilistic thinking that ultimately harms rather than benefits us, and ultimately destroys rather than gives life. That instinctive response appears to be beneficial in averting anxiety, depression, inertia, and suicide. A beneficial response mechanism would most likely have been implanted in us by a benevolent Inventor.

That is an opinion, a belief. But can we *know* that God is benevolent? Couldn't God as logically be sadistic and deceiving? The ultimate sadistic deception, then, would be the (false) "revelation" of a good God.

Can we *know* that the universe, or the powers of reason, or God truly exists? Can our belief that a Creator exists, can our register of sublimity, can our understanding that 2+2 was designed to be always 4 properly be called *knowledge*? Only if our definition of knowledge includes doubt, the kind of doubt that allowed us to reconsider the "fact" of a flat earth. We know what is, in part in contrast to what it is not.

Skepticism

Skepticism is the Golden Mean between the two extremes of absolutism—fundamentalism and atheism, both of which deny the possibility of truth that contradicts presumed knowledge.

At this point in my life, my understanding is that absolutist beliefs that God is "out to get us" or that there is no God and thus life is ultimately meaningless stem in part from paranoid thinking. The absolutist Pollyanna belief, on the other hand, is that God is exactly what the believer thinks He is, that God won't let anything bad happen to her, that God is her personal genii, who, if she rubs her Bible or rosary (or Koran, or tassel, or talisman) hard enough, if she says the right abracadabra and prays loud enough with her hands extended to heaven, God *must* grant her every wish and serve her best interests. That is primitive/infantile thinking, the kind of non-thinking exploited by TV evangelists. Absolutist paranoid thinking and absolutist primitive/infantile thinking are both examples of blind faith. Both shut out skepticism and its critiques. Perhaps you too have noticed that paranoid and primitive/infantile thinkers tend to be know-it-alls.

The problem with absolutists is that they land on an insight (often someone else's that they claim as their own), stamp it as conclusive, codify it as absolute, and refuse to budge. They stop thinking. They stop seeking. They refuse to admit any data that doesn't fit into the prefab little box of "truth." Absolutists are the direct antithesis of truth-seekers.

Knowledge is not blind faith. One can and should—and must—have faith in that which in us registers what we call truth, one's own inherent faculties, including reason, conscience, intuition, experience, emotions (emotional intelligence), and the aesthetic (aesthetic sensibility, which registers beauty and the sublime). But even absolutists know how easy it is for these faculties to be ignored, misinterpreted, or deluded. When biblical infallibility has been proven beyond any shadow of a doubt to be false, to continue "believing" in infallibility requires that the believer reject the discerning of his God-given faculties in favor of a hand-me-down opinion that cannot possibly be proven true.

Blind faith is no faith at all; it is the rejection of truth for a myth of truth. We only have authentic faith in that which appears most clearly true in that all our faculties concur. To "believe" as truth that which clearly is *not* true is the opposite of truth; it's a lie. Today as always, religious myths like Noah's Ark or the parting of the Red Sea are asserted as truth only by the ignorant, those in denial, the gullible, or purposeful deceivers. One is entitled to one's opinions, religious or otherwise, but intent to deceive is not opinion. Absence of thought is not opinion. Belief that contradicts one's inherent faculties is not opinion; it is the negation and displacement of faculty-generated opinion by indoctrination.

That the Bible is not infallible and that religion is mythic at least in part does not prove that God does or does not exist, nor does it prove that religion is devoid of truth, meaning, or value. But belief in biblical infallibility or religious tradition is not the same as belief in one's own ability to register truth. Our faculties are all we've got to stand on; that is the foundation of humanism. To reject our inherent faculties is a kind of spiritual suicide. If we reject our faculties, we have nothing left by which to judge if anything is true. Enter Big Brother to program the lobotomized herd.

The validity of any claim is only possible if we have the capacity to know that it is or is not. If we deny the validity of our faculties—say, in order to affirm a belief in biblical infallibility—we have nothing left by which to confirm that our belief is valid. We could believe absolutely anything. Meaning nothing. If we believe that 2+2 could equal 5 or 12 or 0 or red or insurance because the Bible says so, then there is no truth, only absurdity. Truth is what it is only in contrast to what it is not. Every biblical jot and iota has to be weighed and judged by our God-given faculties. In matters of faith, by refusing to discern between what is and what is not, fundamentalists reduce themselves to unthinking windup dolls.

Of course, a human being is more than a collection of interconnected faculties. Our faculties are contained in a body, itself a faculty, and most of us believe that that body houses or embodies not only our interior faculties but also our spiritual essence, our core being. The spirit is the part of us that is most uniquely our own discrete self. Ironically, it's the part that is most capable of "oneness" with others.

I can't prove that the spirit exists, or for that matter, that our faculties and bodies exist. I have no choice but to believe that they exist, because all my faculties concur that this is so and because I choose to be honest.

MEANING AS KNOWLEDGE OF GOD'S EXISTENCE

Why do some people deny the existence of God while others "just know"? I agree with many religions that God "touches" some of us in the sense that most "touched" believers mean they have had a concrete spiritual experience of God. "Touched" doesn't quite name it. We are limited to our space-time language, which is never adequate to describe something that transcends space-time. The atheist would argue that nothing transcends space-time; certainly nothing in space-time transcends space-time. But a great work of art, to offer but one example—its metaphors and symbols, its meaning, its aesthetic qualities—transcends the sum of its material parts.

Truth that transcends the material realm and its space-time-bound language we apprehend metaphorically, by analogy, through the imagery of our material life. God the Father and God the Mother, for instance, allow us to intellectually understand and express by analogy our spiritual experiences. But they are legitimate metaphors only if we recognize that metaphors are not specifically the realities they represent. God is not male or female; God is not human. Belief in a literal male/female human God is primitive and childish, the product of minds lacking the sophistication to grasp the symbolic, or of hearts craving the security of a surrogate trans-parent to rescue us from chaos and death.

Like all things symbolic, religion is subject to interpretation. My interpretation is my opinion, which might or might not accurately name actual reality. Opinions are guesses. My guesses about the existence and nature of God are educated, but that doesn't make them correct. But our educated guesses are all we have to go on. And by educated I mean not only formal study at a university but also the natural education that comes via attentive reflection upon life itself. Like all opinions, guesses about religion are part of a process of adjustment to new information. In a sense, the meaning of life is revision, which is what it means to really "get educated."

My current guess regarding life's ultimate meaning is that our religions, arts, and dreams provide us with mythic representations of transcendental truth. Even if there was no literal Edenic "fall," we might be fallen in a transcendental sense, a real state that the myth of the fall unconsciously represents.

Unlike many of my postmodern colleagues, I don't believe that our myths represent attempts to create meaning out of life materials that are in themselves meaningless. Nor do I believe that our religious myths simply mirror the psyche or represent some other purely space-time experience. Many myths contain transcendental material or are themselves transcendental. They provide a conduit between our space-time existence and a transcendent "heavenly" dimension.

THE GOD OF GESTALT

My notion of gestalt accepts that reality is fragmented like the frames of a movie and acknowledges that the frames are themselves representations of gestalts that convey only fragmentary material, but I do not accept that the resulting unified gestalt is an illusion created by humans who long for a unity that does not exist. A movie, or a discrete frame or picture, is lacking everything but one very limited perspective that is itself (in the picture example) limited to the visual. Life experience is "infinitely" more rich and complex.

My guess is that meaning is not simply constructed of infinitely reductive materials that are inherently non-meaningful in themselves. I believe that everything down to its every minute particle is objectively meaningful, and I believe this because what I intuit makes sense to my rational and other faculties. Like a multitude of other people, I intuit that there is one unifying Creator, the unifier represented with the designator "God." Is God the unifier created in our own image, or are we created in the image of the unifier? Of course, there are other possibilities, but do they make sense? Something in us wants either-or choices. Good v. evil. Is God a moral Creator that wants us to separate out the fragments of good and evil? What would it mean if God were *not* a moral Creator?

I believe a case for morality can be made on the basis of unity. This contradicts the elitism of religions that seek to demonize good represented in other religions—that seek to demonize good as evil rather than unifying in the cause of universal good. The fragmenting of unifying good is exactly what makes religions dangerously evil. Good is that which benefits; evil is that which harms. All major religions lift up love as one of its highest ideals, because love is a condition that ultimately benefits because it ultimately unites while preserving independent uniqueness; it is, in the view of many, the consummate good. When religion prevents a black person from marrying a white person, a Muslim from marrying a Christian, a Catholic from marrying a Protestant, a young person from marrying an older person, a rich person from marrying a poor person, a respectable person from marrying a bohemian, or two gay persons from marrying, religion creates fragmentation of the good rather than unity of the good. It fosters harm rather than the beneficial good of love, and isn't that the definition of evil?

The seemingly infinite fragments of what we perceive to be existence are really our fragmentary experiences of aspects of a unified reality. Through contemplation and communion we are able to deepen our understanding of the unity. It's an overgeneralization to say that contemplation is the method of the pure rationalist while communion is the more direct method of the sensitive. Contemplation and communion are present together in nearly all of us, and certainly in the wise. The truly wise don't make the mistake of dehumanizing humans by relegating them to convenient categories, like the thinking-type, feeling-type, creative-type, etc. We are far too complex to be represented accurately as cartoons. We are pieces—fragments—but those pieces constitute a unified whole.

God is the source of unity but is not the unity itself—indeed, cannot be. The poem is not the poet, nor is the poet the poem, though something of the poet will always be in the poem, even if negatively. Shakespeare, for instance, is negatively "in" *Macbeth*; Macbeth represents what Shakespeare is not, what he despises, what he warns us against becoming. God, I believe, is to some extent negatively in existence in that the unity contains evil (what God is not, what he despises, what he warns us against becoming), and in that humans possess the free will to choose to do and be evil. But that does not make good and evil absolute polarities. They are discrete ingredients that have been tossed into the space-time blender. We can—and most of us would say *should*—attempt to separate those ingredients, to pursue the good and eliminate the evil. But it's a fatal mistake to assume that those ingredients are ever truly separated in this space-time realm or that what we believe to be good is actually good. We remind ourselves of that ignorance via our myths and symbols—the poison apple, for instance, or even an ordinary, seemingly good apple offered by a venomous serpent initiating poisonous consequences.

Because I guess that God is one, good, transcendent ("above" and "outside of" Creation), and the Creator of this space-time unity of "infinite" discrete entities (I think that space-time is not itself infinite/eternal, if only because it is still coming into existence), and because I guess that God is a nonhuman, non-bodily "person" that is actively engaged from within ("immanent") in the process of creation, my opinion is that the highest meaning of life is that life is inherently meaningful and it is our job to discover actual meaning. There is one meaning (and again, this is just my opinion), but there are infinite possible ways to represent that meaning. Our myths, arts, and dreams—indeed, human life itself—represent discrete, limited, individual interpretations of comprehensive meanings of meanings expanding outward with the Big Bang cosmos and inward to the Taoist still point in the turning wheel.

TRANSCENDENTAL TRUTH

Everything I have just said, of course, is itself a representation of a guess.

My guess is that religions, arts, and dreams collect mythic representations of transcendental truth. Religions, arts, and dreams are themselves collections. Unfortunately, many people believe that the interpretive collections are themselves objective reality and ultimate reality. Fundamentalism is the misinterpretation of collected religious material as absolute God-breathed fact.

For instance, the myth of the fall in the Garden of Eden is an ancient archetypal myth found in one form or another in numerous cultures and their religions throughout the world. The Judeo-Christian version represents a transcendental truth of moral misjudgment, estrangement from the Creator, awakening to a need for redemption, and rebirth into the quest for the redemptive solution. This paradigm is told and retold in numerous myths of various religions. One could argue that the myth represents the core essence of religion itself.

Milton represented it dramatically with the fall of Satan, the temptation of Eve and Adam, the principle of evil working to thwart redemption, and the coming of a redemptive hero to assist Eve and Adam in fulfilling their quest—in fact, to fulfill it for them. In this version, Eve and Adam lack the free-will power of Satan.

My current interpretation of the subtext of Milton is that it reveals a primal belief—really a fear—that the power of evil transcends the power of good, and that Milton is confessing the primal hope that some higher power of good, represented by Christ, will prevail. Milton's glorification of Satan, the real protagonist in *Paradise Lost* (which Christ in *Paradise Regained* never matches), exposes his doubts about the divinity (even by adoption) of humanity and the efficacy of the Christian religion to save us by granting continued life.

That Christianity has elevated Christ to the status of man-god exposes humanity's doubt about its own ability to establish—or regain—communion with God as represented by the lost Paradise or hoped-for Promise Land, Heaven. It is a childish wish to hand over to a parental figure all personal responsibility and spiritual hard work of the experienced quest for meaning. My guess is that religious absolutism is an archetypal juvenile excuse to remain immaturely mediocre. Clean your room. Do your homework. No way, says the spoiled brat glued to his computer game. Mom or Dad or the housekeeper will do it for me.

This guess about the universally represented myth of a transcendental fall informs my other guesses about reality and meaning. I further guess that we are truly fallen from some pre-space-time (transcendental) communion with God. But I could be wrong; sometimes I agree with many that life is a test rather than a quest for redemption.

All religion represents this kind of guesswork, and to assert otherwise exposes the person's unwillingness to get his hands dirty in the necessary cultivation of his own life, his own meaning. But like a cultivated garden, we dig and water, but, as the saying goes, God gives the growth. We create, yes, but even our creation is intimately in communion with "discovery" of inherent existence and its meaning.

REPRESENTATIONS OF GOD

Christianity, Islam, Judaism, any religion can provide powerful representations of God, which authentically resonate and clarify when they are understood to be *representations*. At their best, religions aesthetically initiate focus and facilitate access to communion with God—keeping in mind that there are as many ways to commune with God as there are communers. Religions simply provide approaches that can be shared. But a good approach does not exclude other approaches from being equally good or better. Religious elitism is never good, because it is based on a fallacy of inherent superiority; it plays God.

Religions tend to reduce God to a representation. Each religion pretends that its representation is God and that this God is the revelation of God by God. But it is easy to show how mainstream religions have borrowed freely from the so-called pagan religions. Christian, Muslim, Jewish, and other worshippers of the anthropomorphic image of a legalistic, jealous, vengeful, violent male god are primarily modern remnants of the primitive cult of Zeus or some other patriarchal head of a familial pantheon. If it is idolatry to worship Zeus or any other anthropomorphic father-god, it is idolatry to worship the Judeo-Christian "God the Father," that anthropomorphic old geezer with a cosmic voyeur ego leaning over the lip of the universe and perpetually wrecking havoc on innocent mortals—a representation naively worshipped as actual to this day. There are legitimate uses of aesthetic, mythic representations of the divine, but surely their worship is not among them.

To worship God is to seek God. To have faith in one God is to consider all fundamentalist religions to be idolatry. Deism seeks God as God, the actual God, not superstitions, not self-righteous projections of our own shadow, not the schizophrenic God of sectarian wars. Deism seeks peace through love and love through truth. Perhaps only the truth-path of Deism can demystify humanity's "sacred" path of self-destruction and establish unity for the benefit of love.

Chapter 3

Born-Again Deist

Deism is a religion of commonsense truth. But it can also be an experience of immanence, which many call communion with God, or being in the Spirit.

My beliefs, like anyone's, have been derived through personal experience. The reality of the spiritual dimension is something I personally can't deny. As a very young child—no older than five or six—I had spiritual "feelings" that I couldn't understand. And by *feelings* I mean something quite tangible; and by tangible I mean something intimately "one" with the natural Creation—nature. Deep emotions accompanied the sensation but were responses to the visceral, sensual experience of some kind of "Presence" in nature.

Many people have feelings of being "one" with nature. What is that sense of oneness if not an experience of immanence, the presence of the Creator actively creating, creative Eros, life-force itself? In my experience, the people who say "No" to that explanation are people who have never experienced that oneness. And most of them conclude that the experience therefore does not and cannot exist.

I've talked with many people who had similar feelings of immanence as young kids, though for most, their authentic spiritual experiences were squelched by some contrary religious doctrine.

I remember one grade school friend abruptly warning me matter-of-factly, as if suddenly remembering something in the middle of our long conversation about "something" in nature, "You better not say that; that's the devil." The devil—now that was a new concept. To me the devil had been nothing but a fake-scary Halloween costume. Was that all he thought of my feelings?

My mystical feelings persisted, as did my need to understand them (and by "mystical" I mean a sense of Presence, and a heightened sense of life's depth, for lack of a better way of putting it). In high school I tried to articulate my intuited understanding verbally and in journals, but the right words escaped me. I tried to find evidence of what I felt in religious books, including the Bible, but everything I read was boringly esoteric if not downright silly, and all of it colored by jargon derived from my immediate world's specific religious tradition. None of it jived; none of it cut to the quick. It was all irrelevant.

And that was the root of a big problem for me that was felt long before it could be intellectually understood. I felt something spiritual, and though "secular" writers like Thoreau, Frost, and Whitman twanged that nerve, I still felt my naïve ignorance about *real* religion, which translated emotionally as frustration, and by my teen years as depression and even anger. By the time I hit college, I was suffering from an acute need to *know*.

My spiritual quest kept butting against a common dilemma, which back then was sensed rather than articulated: Regardless of our religious backgrounds and beliefs and our unique personal experiences, all Americans have been indoctrinated to think, judge, and act according to certain narrowly defined Judeo-Christian mores codified as part of our nation's socio-political infrastructure. Independent mysticism is typically not part of the program. Organized religion had long ago supplanted spirituality with its agenda of knowing *about* via indoctrination rather than *coming to know* via personal experience, although it claimed to absolutely know and to be able to "force" that knowledge upon another. The irony is that religion's agenda of knowing *about*, which is always indirect, is asserted as ultimate and intimate knowledge.

Luckily, my family was not strictly religious. My parents were self-proclaimed agnostics who were raised by devout, but not aggressively dogmatic Protestants. My mom's family was Lutheran, my dad's Presbyterian (though only in the most vague, abstract way were Luther and Calvin my spiritual ancestors). My siblings and I were baptized in one or the other church, went through the catechism process in both churches, and took the catechism vows to become members of the Beecher Presbyterian Church.

Although sometimes my aunt, the church organist, recruited me to sing in the choir, church attendance was always my choice. My parents rarely attended church (I don't recall my dad ever being in a church except for weddings and funerals), but they had no problem with God, only with the church's behavioral dictates and the judgmental attitudes that came with them. My parents were very sociable people who became close friends with their neighbors and co-workers. They laughed and smoked and drank socially, and both had been professional jazz musicians—hardly candidates for piety. I occasionally went to church with my grandmother, who attended regularly and to whom I was quite close. If she influenced me at all, it was by the quiet force of her nature, which was truly morally pure and loving, but not in a way that I would call religious. She never mentioned doctrines or anything about religion at all, though she did sometimes recall good times with my grandpa's best friends, the then local minister and his wife, but my grandpa died when I was five or six and the minister's family had long ago moved away.

Church was a profound bore for me, as it was for most kids I knew. But that didn't keep us from staying up all night discussing serious questions about the meaning of life and God. It makes perfect sense to me that a charismatic religious leader could quell a person's spiritual anxiety with exciting answers and promises of "The True Way." Certainly it makes sense that intelligent adults who have dismissed their early spiritual sensations as make-believe or inappropriate could have those hidden memories triggered by just about any authority, even a charlatan, who affirms those experiences as valid. Surely acceptable, mainstreamed recontextualization of primal spirituality could help explain the enormous and dangerous appeal of obviously exploitive TV evangelists, cult gurus, and spiritual leaders calling for jihad, suicide bombings, and contributions of your life savings to bogus "missions" sweetened with promises of prosperity or salvation.

As a university teenager, I did buy into hard-line fundamentalism for a time. But like many progressive born-agains I knew, I refused to sacrifice my brains on the altar. Even during my initial born-again phase, I rarely went to church, and I never attended just one.

Ironically, it was probably due largely to my agnostic upbringing that I would not, in fact could not squelch my own personal spiritual experiences, which I knew were "mine" and not the church's. Even much later, during dry periods of limited sensations, the memories of Presence remained vivid in the back of my mind.

Back when I started college I was depressed and "mad at the world," frustrated by my unfruitful quest for answers.

Then suddenly I began to get them.

My college courses in literature, philosophy, and religion began to give shape to a spiritual interpretation of historical reality. Although I took classes in comparative religion and had a few liberal professors, my small Midwest buckle-on-the-Bible-Belt campus was Christian and so were most of my professors, including the handful who had taken time to engage with me in a serious way outside of class. My gestating concept of reality was shaping up into a decidedly Christian one. At age nineteen, I went through an initial born-again experience "alone" and for years insisted that it was completely independent of any influence. I realize now, of course, that that's not true—couldn't possibly be true.

Being born-again was a powerful spiritual and emotional experience, a gestalt moment when all that appeared to me as spiritual chaos suddenly took a dynamically coherent shape rooted in an imposing tradition that had existed since antiquity. Where had I been! I was overjoyed. I basked in Christianity's well-labeled tenets and in the loving fellowship and often deep friendship with those who accepted them as fact.

At the time, it never occurred to me that my personal born-again experience was very much a socially orchestrated event. In fact, social motivation would have been my last possible explanation for the powerful spiritual trans-figuration I was going through. And while I don't at all deny the spiritual nature of the experience, it is clear to me now that any person's born-again experience occurs within a socio-religious context that erroneously claims to be the source of the experience. God "came" to me, a good Christian. By the time God "came"—as if God had not been "coming" to me throughout my whole life—I had been thoroughly indoctrinated in the friendliest way by some of my closest friends and professors, and this was a small university in a town that boasted it had more churches per capita than any other town in the country, a small university where people were indeed very close. The closeness to smart, progressive people who were unabashedly spiritual was a blast of fresh air. As I read the Bible and went to Bible study groups and heard literature and philosophy courses and in effect all existence interpreted in a Christian context—all of it melded with time spent communing with likeminded Christian friends—my own spirituality was suddenly squeezed into a context of "having arrived." The pressure of gift-boxed answers and concentrated feelings produced the surge of joy and love that catalyzed the explosion classically termed a born-again experience.

This is not to say that being born-again is not authentically spiritual. It most certainly is, or was for me. But because it occurs within a constricted context, a small gift box called "the real thing," spirituality is squeezed into absolute definitions that are not accurate or even ultimately meaningful. It took awhile for me to come to my senses and acknowledge that God is not a Christian God and that religion appropriates authentic spirituality for its own dark and dangerous purposes at least as often as it worships Divinity or ministers to the human spirit.

The dark side of authoritarian religion was not the only problem. From the other extreme came disdain of atheistic Freudians for whom religious ecstasy was a projection of repressed sexual fantasy, or more likely, sexual abuse in the hands of a macho father-god—neither being the case for me—, and an equal distain of atheistic materialists, for whom matter was the be-all and end-all beyond which there was nothing.

In the midst of religious and anti-religious extremism, without even knowing it I began to follow a straight and narrow path down the middle of "God-as-such."

Being born-again had happened in a flash of acceptance accompanied by that old "feeling" of immanence. The closeness I felt with many of my comrades, mostly roommates and friends, might not have been as extraordinary as I assumed at the time. I have been an adjunct professor for twenty years and have taught at ten universities and colleges. I regularly pull students into "heavy" conversations, and the powerful spiritual epiphanies they share with me are not always religious. I have met young people in college, and older people in college, and all ages of people in other contexts whose lives were changed in ways that I would call born-again, but their experiences were within the non-Christian context of serving in the Peace Corps, or getting involved with environmental actions, or being immersed in the feminist anti-violence movement, or teaching kids on a reservation to read, or sharing mind-expanding ideas with kids from other traditions via online blogs, or being in-flow in music or writing or art, or getting immersed in non- or quasi-religious spirituality—any number of ways. Kids and adults alike feel the heightened sensation that comes with getting a new set of answers to the questions of life's meaning and new forms of communion in the deeply spiritual sense. Just because their experiences occur outside the jurisdiction of church or religion doesn't mean they aren't getting in touch with God.

In fact, I had gotten in touch with what most people call "God," or rather God had gotten in touch with me, outside any hard-line religious context. I was quite young and uneducated when I first started having those numinous feelings (I don't remember ever not having them). What the born-again experience gave me was the addition of seemingly rational answers and a sense of coherent tradition. It seemed that my quest had reached its goal. I accepted a biblically fundamentalist stance toward God and felt spiritually normal and acceptable for the first time.

But that confidence was short-lived. As I read the Bible and learned more about Christian history and got to know and know about "good Christians" who were anything but good, my religion began to deflate. Eventually I realized that of course religion was not spirituality. And Christianity was far from rational and its tradition anything but coherent.

When what I was being taught clashed with my sense of truth and decency, I had no choice but to deprogram myself—a painstaking, painful process. But in rejecting the rigid fundamentalist interpretations of Christianity, I was, like many "recovering Christians," being authentic and true to myself as a spiritual person. I was being faithful to my God-given reason, conscience, intuition, experience, and all my other inherent faculties.

Once I reached the other side, I realized that it's the social aspect of born-again spirituality that makes it hard for many well-educated, intelligent believers to doubt even obvious absurdities. Doubt became a cornerstone of my new-found truth. I never questioned the self-evident existence of God, but I did question religion and found it wanting.

In the meantime, it did gradually dawn on me that there were other possibilities besides the either-or choice between religion and agnosticism, or between Eastern and Western religion.

Once I had totally shaken the Christian identity, a new spiritual high overtook me. I felt elated realizing that God was not in any way controlled or embodied by religion. I experienced the same spiritual high that I had enjoyed as a Christian born-again.

Today, I see the Bible as America's golden calf. Extreme reverence for the Bible, initiated especially by Luther and other challengers of papal authority during the Reformation, has been amplified by fundamentalists into full-fledged Bible-worship. Because many fundamentalist adherents put faith above scholarship and reason, they don't usually bother to check to see if the views expounded to prove a pulpiteer's position are even actually biblical. Many of those faithful have been indoctrinated to be suspect of "liberal" scholarly exegesis, and even though the historical facts are easily accessible, they know little if anything about the contextual creation and recreation of the Bible in all its very fallible glory.

At its worst, Christian pulpiteers today use Bible-worship to persuade adherents to accept views that contradict fact, common sense, and decency. Ironically, on the Bible's own terms, fundamentalist text-worship is idolatry. Some high priests, like Benny Hinn, Jesse Duplantis, Oral Roberts, and Pat Robertson, claim to be prophets commanding direct access to God, thereby transcending even the Bible. They persuade because their prophecies mimic biblical stories and are couched in biblical rhetoric. Keep "God" on the tongue, and the text-worship fabricated by high priests provides an efficient means to program and exploit the obedient.

The modus operandi of too many successful contemporary evangelists and their political comrades is based on a model as ancient as the devil himself. Attract gullible sheep, locate a scapegoat, create a fictional menace, generate bigotry, justify it biblically, rile up the sheep, escalate bigotry into fear, then plead for money to help eradicate the cause of that fear, especially via rightwing political agendas. Support of political agendas, in direct defiance of church/state separation, is sometimes the sole justification for soliciting the contributions that make the evangelists and their tax-free churches filthy rich.

Globally, high priests of fundamentalism instigate wars, inquisitions, jihads, and exterminations of practitioners of versions of fundamentalism that differ from their own. Fundamentalism is the direct antagonist of the democratic ideals of equality, liberty, and freedom of conscience.

The truth is that no religion does, or can, dictate to us the absolute truth about God. Underneath all the pomp and circumstance, be it quiet exclusionism or violent authoritarianism, religion simply describes people's inferences and preferences about what God might be. Deism—the version Thomas Paine conveyed to Americans—considers most religions to be false, idolatrous religions because they replace the quest for God with truth-claims asserted to be absolute God-inspired truth, making those claims and therefore those religions equal to God. Each religion claims that because its inspired truth is the only absolute truth, anyone disagreeing with it is destined for the Christian equivalent of hell.

The pathetic hypocrisy of good Christians at times reaches a level of absurdity that makes me laugh. For instance, a few months before I moved from L.A. to San Francisco to begin graduate school, TV evangelists Jim and Tammy Faye Bakker hit the front of every tabloid rack in America. For years the couple's PTL (Praise The Lord) network had raked in millions from their fundamentalist viewers, most of them lower income, so the evangelists could themselves live in luxury. Jim Bakker had bribed Jessica Hahn, his church secretary, to keep quiet about his having drugged and seduced her, but he was headed for prison for his illegal pyramid business scheme. Meanwhile, Tammy Faye's obsessive lust for country singer Gary Paxton had broken up his marriage.

Jim lashed out at reigning evangelist Jimmy Swaggart, accusing him of publicizing the Jessica Hahn scandal so he could take over PTL. Swaggart, a notorious gay basher who took in $150 million a year policing the good seed and the bad, had been busted by Rev. Marvin Gorman for frequenting a prostitute, who eventually told the public about Swaggart's preference for ritual humiliation and abasement rather than the usual sex. Swaggart had gotten Rev. Gorman unfrocked for adultery, so Gorman got revenge by blackmailing Swaggart, who just said no. So Gorman "outed" Swaggart for his hypocrisy in viciously attacking him and other rival TV evangelists such as the Bakkers and Jerry Falwell.

When the Bakkers resigned from PTL, they left their assets, which included PTL and their tacky Christian theme park, Heritage USA, temporarily in the hands of Jerry Falwell, whose Moral Majority and "Old Fashioned Gospel Hour" had been steadily stealing Swaggart's client base. In no time, Bakker accused Falwell of trying to wrench control of PTL. Falwell called a press conference to make public the sworn affidavits he'd obtained from men who had had homosexual relationships with Bakker. Falwell also included Tammy Faye's list of demands she would exchange for quietly disappearing: $300,000 a year for Jim, $100,000 for her; royalties on all PTL records and books; their mansion, cars, security staff, and hefty legal and accountant fees.

In the midst of these tabloid scandals—I clearly remember Tammy Faye's massive mascara dripping down her remorseful face, her lips pouting seductively against her beloved microphone—I started grad school at San Francisco State, right about the time that mega-rich Christian Coalition tsar Pat Robertson announced his bid for the presidency, right about the time that the self-proclaimed God Jim Jones tested his disciples' faith with mass suicide via a communion of Kool-Aid and cyanide.

The Jonestown incident struck me as profoundly symbolic. I decided to become educated about the connections between psychopaths and cults, between religion and violence. In the process I uncovered a plethora of scandals involving the most famous TV evangelists, their lies, frauds, scams, adulterous trysts, lucrative business dealings with the world's most vicious dictators, and everyday rip-offs gleaning God's prosperity prophets millions—and in the case of Robertson, at least, billions—in profits for yachts, jets, and multi-million dollar mansions purchased with viewer contributions to bogus missions, and worse, with earnest investments of the truly needy in hyped promises of special prayers and healings.

I also discovered numerous studies documenting a clear statistical correlation between authoritarian religious beliefs and incidents of rape, molestation, murder, torture-as-punishment, and numerous lesser offenses such as theft, fraud, and even divorce. Once I saw the statistics laid out on the page (which I will discuss in depth in later chapters), it became clear to me that proponents of a "Christian America" were throwing up a smokescreen.

I thought I was well-informed by the time I got to grad school, but my education was only beginning. At least by then I understood that God was not religion and religion not God. In fact at times it seemed that God was as far from religion as from the devil. And perhaps even farther.

Chapter 4

Portrait of a Barbaric God

One thing that led me out of born-again Christianity, through progressivism and agnosticism, and "back" into Deism was that when I read the Bible, I saw a portrait of God that varied greatly from the God I had come to know.

Maybe "know" is a bit presumptuous. Should I use the more postmodern "understand"? How do we understand God if not through revealed religion?

How else but through our various faculties. I do think we put quite a bit of ourselves into our definitions of God. That doesn't mean that we create God in our own image, just that we represent our experience of God in our own language.

I've always found the Old Testament to be dark and disturbing: Treks through the desert, tribal wars, dusty prophets casting whole nations into the sulfurous pit of hell. Of course heroes were deified in the age of myths, and scapegoats demonized to explain tragedies like the grave injustice of a murdered or otherwise violated hero. The ultimate scapegoat, of course, was the idealized devil, an omniscient, all-powerful god, like the Satan who made visits to heaven and tricked God into ordaining evil upon Job.

I had to ask myself, which character really has more power in the Bible, God or the devil? Which character is more evil? Is the evil that the Bible attributes to Satan greater than the evil it attributes to God?

The Bible is steeped with the brutality of an anthropomorphic god known as God. That God reportedly (by whom, we don't know) spoke directly to Moses, telling him to muster an army of twelve thousand to invade and destroy the demonized Midianites. They killed all the males and took all the women and children captive, meaning they would become property available for rape (women and children as property was part of the family values of the era). All the towns were burned, although they took "all the spoil and all the booty, both people and animals." Moses was angry that the women had been allowed to live. He ordered all the women and all the male children to be slaughtered, "but all the young girls who have not known a man by sleeping with him, keep alive for yourselves." Child molestation was okay if it involved innocent children of non-invading "enemies" of God's chosen. Not surprisingly, a huge chunk of the spoils and booty went to Eleazar the priest.

In Genesis, God tests Abraham, the so-called "father of faith." "Take your son, your only son Isaac, whom you love, and go to the land of Moriah, and offer him there as a burnt offering on one of the mountains that I shall show you." Why would God, who knows and can do all things, resort to this kind of cruel testing? That Abraham didn't blink but instead obediently followed the orders of that voice in his head is deemed the ultimate gesture of "faith." Today we would likely call such a man schizophrenic. Abraham's god clearly was not a good, loving, mentally stable God. Yet today Jews, Christians, and Muslims still base their faith on Abraham's primitive god who orchestrated the revered sacrifice of Isaac, a truly sadistic mind trip reminiscent of the games of psychopaths. Sanctification of this kind of blind obedience could only have been invented by a control-driven priest or chieftain like Moses.

The Old Testament God was a god of human overkill. For instance, when Jacob's daughter Dinah was reportedly raped by Shechem, who "loved the girl, and spoke tenderly to her," and wanted her for his wife, Jacob and Shechem's father, Hamor, sought a peaceful resolution. Shechem had said, "Let me find favor with you, and whatever you say to me I will give. Put the marriage present and gift as high as you like, and I will give whatever you ask me; only give me the girl to be my wife." Dinah's vengeful brothers tricked Shechem and Hamor into believing that they would give Dinah to Shechem in marriage. The sons of Jacob demanded that all the males be circumcised, and they were. Shechem's gullible father told the people, "These people are friendly with us; let them live in the land and trade in it, for the land is large enough for them; let us take their daughters in marriage, and let us give them our daughters." The response of God's chosen? Absolute barbarism.

On the third day, when they [the circumcised] were still in pain, two of the sons of Jacob, Simeon and Levi, Dinah's brothers, took their swords and came against the city unawares, and killed all the males. They killed Hamor and his son Shechem with the sword, and took Dinah out of Shechem's house, and went away. And the other sons of Jacob came upon the slain, and plundered the city, because their sister had been defiled. They took their flocks and their herds, their donkeys, and whatever was in the city and in the field. All their wealth, all their little ones and their wives, all that was in the houses, they captured and made their prey. Then Jacob said to Simeon and Levi, "You have brought trouble on me by making me odious to the inhabitants of the land, the Canaanites and the Perizzites; my numbers are few, and if they gather themselves against me and attack me, I shall be destroyed, both I and my household." But they said, "Should our sister be treated like a whore?"

Barbarians have always created gods in their own image not only to explain life's injustices but also to sanctify their vicious behavior. Monotheistic barbarians are no different from their polytheistic neighbors, just more focused. Their one god's prophets cry out "His" (their) curses like madmen in asylums. If these were presented as human prayers for vengeance, we might have more tolerance. But divinely inspired promises of revenge on a people years and even centuries later for the crimes of their remote ancestors come from a mythical god powerless to institute justice in the moment against the guilty parties.

Priest parading as prophet is the oldest trick in the book. Prophet-priests hold the threat of God's wrath over the heads of their gullible congregations. Centuries after their deaths, prophets are credited with fulfilled prophecies that even biblically never actually occurred. Future events that have little to do with the original prophecy are force-fit as its "fulfillment." And of course prophecies fulfilled can easily be constructed after the fact.

Today, just like in the old days, prophecy is often a crapshoot. For instance, the first week of May, 2006, the History Channel first broadcast "Mega Disasters: West Coast Tsunami." On May 8, Pat Robertson prophesied, "If I heard the Lord right about 2006, the coasts of America will be lashed by storms," and on May 17 he warned, "There well may be something as bad as a tsunami in the Pacific Northwest."

Just as no authentic prophecy by a contemporary evangelist has been fulfilled, there is not a single prophecy in the Bible that can be substantiated as fact. Not one. But there are many prophecies recorded in the Bible that the Bible itself substantiates as having *not* happened the way the prophet prophesied. I will give an example, but first, I will offer a sampling of the terrors the Bible writers dangle over people's heads.

The kinds of wrath that the "great" prophets hoped for are reminiscent of the plagues that God brought down on Egypt.

Exodus 7 begins, "The LORD said to Moses, 'See, I have made you like God to Pharaoh, and your brother Aaron shall be your prophet.'" Isn't it dishonest of God to make Moses appear to be a god? According to the writer, God says to Moses, "You shall speak all that I command you, and your brother Aaron shall tell Pharaoh to let the Israelites go out of his land. But I will harden Pharaoh's heart, and I will multiply my signs and wonders in the land of Egypt."

How can Pharaoh be held accountable if God hardens his heart? What choice does Pharaoh have? He might as well be drugged and hypnotized.

God continues: "When Pharaoh does not listen to you, I will lay my hand upon Egypt and bring my people the Israelites, company by company, out of the land of Egypt by great acts of judgment." How ridiculous! God, who could bring the Israelites out by any means whatsoever, forces a hard heart upon Pharaoh, conning both him and the Israelites, making them all suffer. And this, "God" calls justice. "The Egyptians shall know that I am the LORD, when I stretch out my hand against Egypt and bring the Israelites out from among them." Yes, but what kind of evil, deceptive, unjust Lord will they know?

Now the magic tricks begin. Moses has Aaron throw down his staff; it becomes a snake, symbol of the devil; Pharaoh's magicians do likewise, though the snake of Aaron eats the other snakes. Only the credulous would believe this happened, now or then. "Then the LORD said to Moses, 'Pharaoh's heart is hardened; he refuses to let the people go.'" Well, duh. That's God's doing. What's the point of this silly display of sadistic machismo?

Now God turns the Nile to blood. The fish die, the river stinks, and the people have no drinking water—all the people, all the innocent people, not just God-hardened Pharaoh.

Next comes God's plague of frogs that swarm over land and water. But the magicians produce the same. Then God kills the frogs, and they stink.

Then "all the dust of the earth turned into gnats throughout the whole land of Egypt." When the magicians couldn't pull off this trick, they proclaim it produced by "the finger of God." God is proven by the greater display of *evil*. God is the great God of gnats. It is meant to be impressive that God brings life, even annoying life, out of lifeless dust.

Not satisfied, God causes Egypt to be "ruined" with swarms of flies, that classic symbol of rot and death. Then Pharaoh says he will let Moses and his people go into the wilderness to sacrifice to God, which was what God originally said He wanted. But God hardens his heart, and Pharaoh changes his mind.

The sadistic game continues. Because God refused to let Pharaoh let Moses and crew worship in the wilderness, which is what God said he wanted Moses and crew to do, God sends a fifth plague. The other plagues were suffered by the Israelites as well as the Egyptians. Now God causes just the Egyptian livestock to suffer pestilence disease and die.

But the sixth plague is for everyone. God tells Moses and Aaron to throw handfuls of soot from the kiln in the air so it can become a fine dust causing festering boils on humans and animals throughout the whole land. Ashes to ashes, dust to dust, and ashes to dust. Impressive.

Things are about to get much worse. Why? "This is why I have let you live: to show you my power, and to make my name resound through all the earth. You are still exalting yourself against my people, and will not let them go." Well, in all honesty, it's only the crooked maniacal god of Moses and Aaron that's exalting himself and refusing to let them go. (In the real world outside the text, this is probably a be-patient, muster-the-troops exemplum written by an elitist Hebrew whose "chosen" tribe was intent on destruction of territorial and religious rivals.)

Now lightning strikes with a vengeance and all hail breaks loose, utter destruction beating down on humans, animals, and crops everywhere but in Goshen, where the Israelites have battened down.

After God sends the plague of locusts, "Pharaoh hurriedly summoned Moses and Aaron and said, 'I have sinned against the LORD your God, and against you. Do forgive my sin just this once, and pray to the LORD your God that at the least he remove this deadly thing from me.' So he went out from Pharaoh and prayed to the LORD. The LORD changed the wind into a very strong west wind, which lifted the locusts and drove them into the Red Sea; not a single locust was left in all the country of Egypt." Pharaoh has repented. "But the LORD hardened Pharaoh's heart, and he would not let the Israelites go."

Instead, he causes "a darkness that can be felt" to spread over Egypt for three days. More repenting, more hardness of heart compliments of the God who is clearly projecting his own hardness of heart.

Then, one midnight, God strikes dead all the firstborn of all the Egyptians and their slaves and animals. Then Pharaoh summons Moses and Aaron in the night, and says, "Rise up, go away from my people, both you and the Israelites! Go, worship the LORD, as you said. Take your flocks and your herds, as you said, and be gone. And bring a blessing on me too!"

The text doesn't bother to tell us that God hardens Pharaoh's heart yet again, but it's implied by the fact that Pharaoh's entire army has followed, which Moses destroys by raising up the sea to drown everyone but the Israelites, who "walked on dry ground through the sea, the waters forming a wall for them on their right and on their left."

It's not hard to see how the writer has twisted and exaggerated the mishandled deeds of Moses—or a legend of Moses—into this gruesome children's story about the will of an abusive God who has deemed these people special. It's a classic allegory of an abusive father.

My interpretation of the subtext is that Moses was probably the illegitimate son of Pharaoh's daughter. Why else would she be allowed to raise Moses, the son of slaves, as her own son even though Pharaoh himself had decreed that all the male children born among the Hebrews should be put to death? Of course, this genesis of Moses is likely one of many folktales about a baby who escaped an ordained death, was hidden and raised by surrogate parents, and returned to fulfill his role as hero. Oedipus is perhaps the most famous example among Westerners. The Akkadian "Legend of Sargon" tells of a baby born in secret, placed in a basket of rushes sealed with pitch, floated down the Euphrates, retrieved by the water drawer who raised him as his own, and protected by the goddess Ishtar, under whose care he grew up to become a great king. This tale is clearly one prototype of the Moses legend.

Like all legends, Moses is subject to interpretation. Perhaps Moses, who was born an Egyptian, was ostracized and deemed "an Israelite" because he fled Egypt after killing an Egyptian who was beating an Israelite (Ex. 2:11-15). Moses would have been demoted to illegitimacy and would not be in line to succeed Pharaoh.

Seeing the incredible accomplishments of the Israelite slaves who were building and sustaining Egyptian society, and feeling incensed that he would be denied his rightful inheritance, Moses hatched a plot to seize for himself the labor force and its pack-and-carry infrastructure. Pretending to be one of them, he persuaded them that he would liberate their entire tribe. The well-educated Moses was no doubt impressive not only as a writer and presumably as a speaker; he had knowledge of magic that surpassed that of Pharaoh's royal magicians, as was demonstrated in the big magicians' poker game when he raked in all the chips. He who could not inherit Egypt left Egypt a king of multitudes.

The only problem was that he left behind all the luxuries, not to mention the tools, building materials, and engineering experts he would need to build his kingdom. The people had it pretty good in Egypt, but Moses led the Israelites out of Egypt into a desert wilderness. The Bible mentions God-given provisions of sweet water, manna, and pheasants, but the Israelites got tired of wandering and codependence. Rather than bring them into the Promise Land, the God of Moses set the Israelites to the task of invading other nations and stealing their provisions.

In Numbers 13, God tells Moses to send spies into the land of Canaan, which God says he is giving to the Israelites. Why couldn't God just give them the promised Promise Land?

Furthermore, why couldn't God, who knows everything, just tell Moses what to expect in Canaan without sending in spies? Perhaps because the barbarian god of the barbarian Moses is a god of stealth and subterfuge who likes to kick back and watch his subjects struggle.

Moses sends a large band "to spy out the land of Canaan," and says to them, "'Go up there into the Negeb, and go up into the hill country, and see what the land is like, and whether the people who live in it are strong or weak, whether they are few or many, and whether the land they live in is good or bad, and whether the towns that they live in are unwalled or fortified, and whether the land is rich or poor, and whether there are trees in it or not. Be bold, and bring some of the fruit of the land.'" Should

Moses be checking out the land that God already said he was giving to them, as if questioning whether it was good enough or not, or whether or not they could take it? Couldn't God have filled him in? Couldn't he have trusted God?

"Now it was the season of the first ripe grapes" when the spies arrived. They "spied out the land from the wilderness of Zin to Rehob, near Lebo-hamath. They went up into the Negeb, and came to Hebron; and Ahiman, Sheshai, and Talmai, the Anakites, were there. (Hebron was built seven years before Zoan in Egypt.) And they came to the Wadi Eshcol, and cut down from there a branch with a single cluster of grapes, and they carried it on a pole between two of them. They also brought some pomegranates and figs. That place was called the Wadi Eshcol, because of the cluster that the Israelites cut down from there." "Cut down" meaning *stolen*.

After forty days, they return to Moses with their report. "We came to the land to which you sent us; it flows with milk and honey, and this is its fruit. Yet the people who live in the land are strong, and the towns are fortified and very large; and besides, we saw the descendants of Anak there."

Caleb, the band leader, says, "Let us go up at once and occupy it, for we are well able to overcome it." But the men who had gone up with him disagree. "We are not able to go up against this people, for they are stronger than we." After all, the people there are giants, "Nephilim," they called them. (Whoops; never mind that all the Nephilim were killed during Noah's flood.) In comparison, the Israelites "seemed like grasshoppers."

Moses had said that God had said that they were being given this land. But now that Moses has the official report, which doesn't look promising, he blames the congregation of "complaining" against him, and changes his mind, or God's mind, saying that God now says that they won't take the land after all. For their concerns about attacking and subduing Canaan they have to suffer in the wilderness for forty years. And in the meantime, all the spies, except for Joshua and Caleb, are on the spot struck dead by plague.

The congregation responds by saying that they are perfectly willing to go to the place that God had promised, and they repent of their sin. But Moses says, "That will not succeed. Do not go up, for the LORD is not with you; do not let yourselves be struck down before your enemies. For the Amalekites and the Canaanites will confront you there, and you shall fall by the sword; because you have turned back from following the LORD, the LORD will not be with you." Mighty convenient prophecy, given the information provided by the spies. Those who try to fulfill God's promise by going out to the hill country are defeated by the Amalekites and the Canaanites, who pursue them as far as Hormah, proving God's promise to be false.

Moses had promised the Israelites the Promise Land, then reneged. By Numbers 16, "two hundred fifty Israelite men, leaders of the congregation, chosen from the assembly, well-known men . . . confronted Moses and his cohort, Aaron." Their complaint was just. "You have gone too far! All the congregation are holy, every one of them, and the LORD is among them. So why then do you exalt yourselves above the assembly of the LORD?" Moses responds to this challenge to his priestly superiority, "Is it too little for you that the God of Israel has separated you from the congregation of Israel, to allow you to approach him in order to perform the duties of the LORD'S tabernacle, and to stand before the congregation and serve them? He has allowed you to approach him, and all your brother Levites with you; yet you seek the priesthood as well!" They *were* the priesthood. Then as now, priests were protective of their rank and file.

Moses sends for their leaders, who refuse to come. "Is it too little that you have brought us up out of a land flowing with milk and honey [Egypt] to kill us in the wilderness, that you must also lord it over us? It is clear you have not brought us into a land flowing with milk and honey, or given us an inheritance of fields and vineyards." A valid complaint.

"Moses was very angry and said to the LORD, 'Pay no attention to their offering.'" It looks suspiciously like it's Moses who's on high, bossing around even God Himself. Moses orders the "complainers" to each bring a censer to put in the fire with incense. According to the story, the ground splits apart and swallows the worshippers. Their two hundred fifty censers, however, are spared. In fact, "the censers of these sinners have become holy at the cost of their lives. Make them into hammered plates as a covering for the altar, for they presented them before the LORD and they became holy," just like the tithes, sacrifices, pardons, dispensations, indulgences, and all the other holy-gilded spoils and relics of later Christian priests who damned complainers and burned witches as heretics.

When the people complain that Moses has "killed the people of the LORD," Moses and Aaron go to the tent of meeting, where "the cloud had covered it and the glory of the LORD appeared." One wonders what desert drug was being burned in those censers that produced a cloud believed to be God. Moses tells Aaron, "Take your censer, put fire on it from the altar and lay incense on it, and carry it quickly to the congregation and make atonement for them. For wrath has gone out from the LORD; the plague has begun." Atonement for what? For challenging the arrogance of a priest—a false one, from all indications? The atonement evidently didn't work very well. Moses "stood between the dead and the living; and the plague was stopped." But not until "Those who died by the plague were fourteen thousand seven hundred, besides those who died in the affair of Korah."

In these and many other texts, Moses comes across as a petty tyrant who has created a tribal god in his own image to sanctify his decisions and to justify his mistakes.

Christians rest their authority on this kind of Bible testimony. The belligerent use the biblical evidence of a belligerent God to justify their belligerence. But for most of us who actually *read* the texts, the unknown writers' testimonies to their belligerent God run against the grain of basic morality and common sense.

I have offered only a few examples, but the Old Testament is steeped in these kinds of stories. That the talking god speaks and acts like any jealous, macho, changeable *human* indicates that just like pagan myths, these stories were written by humans. These are qualities that we attribute to barbarians; and in fact, it was barbarians that attributed these qualities to God.

Historical books have no authority other than the *testimony*. Common sense tells us that if the testimony is anonymous, we should not blindly accept that testimony as authoritative, certainly not as divinely inspired. At the very least we should remain skeptical.

If the testimony presents the character of God in terms of human barbarity, common sense tells us that we should suspect that the testimony is likely manmade rather than blindly accept that testimony as the Word of God.

If a Bible passage has obvious links to already existing myths or legends, common sense tells us that we should err on the side of probability that the Bible passage has borrowed from that myth/legend and is therefore itself also fictional. Like most myths and legends, the Bible stories are probably often rooted in actual people and events or are composites that have been exaggerated, conflated, and embellished.

In the gospels, Jesus is presented as sometimes upholding the Old Testament law and sometimes challenging it. My guess is that some real "Jesus" was hated by the priestly Jews for challenging their Old Testament law and their authority and for accusing them of hypocrisy. Jesus was probably a brilliant philosophical teacher more like Socrates than the in-your-face rebel, John the Baptist. The gospel writers probably didn't want to alienate the Jewish status quo, so they watered down the words of Jesus and compensated by deifying their inspiring rabbi and arming him with validating miracles that rivaled those of other local gods. Thomas Jefferson expunged all the miraculous elements from the Bible, leaving us with a portrait of Jesus that is probably closer to the truth of the man than the gospel accounts give us. Unlike Jefferson, I am not saying the miracles could not have occurred; I am arguing that they *probably* did not. Just because something is in the Bible doesn't prove that it's true.

What *is* true is that if the Bible is not word-for-word perfect, it can't be the perfect Word of a perfect God. If the Bible is not word-for-word "God-breathed," then the authority of any Bible book is limited to the character of the writer or writers, and even a writer of good character might have gotten it wrong. But we don't even know who the Bible writers were.

Surely we dishonor God by calling a book the Word of God if it has an unknown origin; has been translated and changed; contains any self-contradictory material; portrays God as a mythological god with human qualities; contains words and deeds attributed to God that are contrary to the notion of a good and just God; describes God's character as changeable, vengeful, jealous, wrathful, and petty, and his intellect as inferior to the stratagems of devils and humans; demands unreasonable blind "faith" in a doctrine constructed upon the same kind of murder/suicide sacrifice common among some primitive religions; accepts convoluted explanations for this murder/suicide that are the opinion of one man (Paul, for instance, who was not present when the main action occurred, who had persecuted the followers of the man he later deified, and who was by his own report and the reports of other Bible writers, a person of questionable character).

Simply put, the Bible is not a valid authority on God's nature, activities, or will. But if people do accept Biblical infallibility, they can point to the portrait of a barbarian God as justification for their own barbarian behavior.

Which explains a great deal about the brutal history of the world.

Chapter 5

Biblical Misinterpretation

Most Christians would probably agree that religious leaders at times misrepresent biblical truth in the name of God. And why not? Certainly there is biblical precedence. If the Bible contains stories exposing God's questionable morals or his chosen's dubious "faith" in obeying, why shouldn't evangelists speak in the tongues of dead prophets? If the Bible writers misinterpreted texts or events in their attempts to explain the inexplicable, why shouldn't evangelists take the same liberties?

The problem is that believers accept the Bible as true, and that sets them up to believe anyone who supposedly represents the Bible. Until experience taught me to doubt, I too trusted the emissaries of truth. Even if I thought their reasoning was absurd, I still trusted their motives. Like many believers, I approached the Bible with reverence, and I looked for inspiration or insight into the meaning of a text I already accepted to be honorable and true. My focus wasn't critical. On the contrary. I passionately defended the Bible against critics.

Soon enough, though, I began to see flaws that couldn't be explained away. I couldn't keep trying to accommodate biblical "truth" to—well, truth.

When I realized that the barbaric biblical god was not God but was rather the projection of barbaric tribal leaders whose missions were steeped with not quite hidden agendas, the Bible was instantly demystified. But for a long time I kept trying to remystify the biblical god I occasionally glimpsed as the wise, loving God I had experienced especially during my born-again phase.

It took awhile for the Bible's numinous glow to fade, or rather for me to realize that the numinous sensation came from something other than the Bible itself. For a time I felt like a spiritual schizophrenic. I still felt a powerful sense of Presence at the same time that I began to see how Christians and the Bible writers themselves misinterpreted key sections of the supposedly infallible Word, until the Bible finally became irreconcilably self-contradictory.

Many believers are just as receptive to the truth of evangelists as they are naively trustful of the Bible. They have learned to rationalize, to doubt their own brains, to live in an illusory otherworld where Bible transcends reality. The evangelist justifies the Bible and the Bible sanctifies the evangelist.

At some point we just have to pinch ourselves awake, to differentiate the fictional theme of the story from the objective truth of the real world. I remember the first time I took a good hard look at the myth of Abraham and Isaac. Frankly, I'd always been quietly appalled by the notion that God would tell his faithful servant or anyone else to sacrifice his son on an altar. All the explanations about its symbolic meaning and how God never intended to let Abraham follow through just didn't ring true. But I kept hacking away at it, trying to fathom its truth. Then I heard a well-educated preacher explicate the text and thought I'd better have a closer look.

Good literature graduate that I was, I approached the account of Abraham's trial as if it were literal truth pregnant with transcendental meaning in need of my literary interpretation. I already knew what it meant. In a sense, Paul's explanation of the text was the foundation of the Christian faith as a religion. Part of me already "in faith" believed it to be true that God sacrificed His own son as propitiation for our sins, and reckoned as righteousness Abraham's faith in that future sacrifice. But another part of me was still trying to believe that God sacrificing His son for whatever reason wasn't as primitive, barbaric, and inefficacious as Abraham sacrificing Isaac. The Abraham story of primitive sacrifice just had that quality of a classic myth.

Finally I just had to be honest: It *was* a myth.

Once I had thoroughly deconstructed the text, I wondered, what was the source of its numinousness? The Spirit was present, in my opinion. That was my felt experience. But I realized then that although the Spirit was present in the experience of grappling with the text, the Spirit wasn't the text and the text wasn't God-breathed. I had reached a crossroads and had veered onto a path of truth—truth in the sense of just plain honesty. It was like suddenly growing up and feeling embarrassed about a comment I'd made about the stork.

I believe that many people have trouble letting go of their religions and their Bibles for the same reason that I had trouble: the numinous sense of Presence one gets when encountering the dynamic sacred. The feeling is good as long as one realizes that the object itself is not the source of the feeling. The object facilitates the feeling, but the feeling actually comes from the quest, the focus, the entering into a deeper dimension of truth that we can't exactly recognize because it's transworldly: not other-worldly—transworldly, because it's the transcendent aspect of this world.

It's like seeing the color of the world instead of only seeing black and white. We see in color, which is a kind of depth, but the world is still mysterious—even more mysterious, because now there's yet another layer of reality that is really quite beyond our comprehension even though it's our actual experience. Just because we can scientifically describe color doesn't mean we understand it. We know *about* it, but that's not the same as *knowing* it. Or put another way, knowing the scientific facts about color is not the same as being aesthetically *moved* by color.

Religion and the Bible ideally might help us know something about God, but they don't help us know God except in that they motivate the quest, the focus, the opening of a door to a deeper dimension. The spiritual is about deeper meaning. The numinous is the feeling of awe in the presence of deeper meaning.

Because literary analysis seeks to enter a deeper dimension, even in the most anti-religious hands it is still a spiritual activity. At that point in my life, my hands were anything but anti-religious. In a backhanded way, even the Abraham myth brought me to a spiritual understanding of what a religious text was *not*.

The back-story begins at Genesis 11:31, when Lot is migrating with his uncle Abraham and grandfather Terah from Ur of the Chaldeans toward Canaan. A quarrel breaks out between Lot's and Abraham's herdsmen (13:7), and Abraham suggests that he and Lot go their separate ways. Lot chooses to settle among the prosperous towns of the well-watered plains of Jordan. Abraham chooses Hebron, located about twenty miles from present day Jerusalem on one of Judah's highest mountaintops, where springs and wells provide an abundant water supply. Symbolically, by choosing to live on the mountaintop, the meeting or dwelling place of God in many religious traditions, Abraham demonstrates his desire to live closer to God. In contrast, Lot chooses to live down "in the valley of the shadow of death" among people whose lives demonstrate an utter disregard for communion with God.

In the next chapter, Lot has been taken captive in a battle between the five Jordan kings and four invading Mesopotamian kings. With only 318 men, the ever-peaceable Abraham defeats the invaders and rescues Lot and his belongings. We do not hear from Lot again until 18:23-33, and then indirectly, when Abraham pleads with God to spare Sodom and Gomorrah for the sake of any righteous people living there, including, presumably, his nephew.

But to get there, we need to back up to the beginning of Genesis 18, when the Lord and two other men appear to Abraham as he sits at the entrance of his tent in the heat of day. Abraham's tent is located near terebinths, which are trees of unknown species, here translated as oaks. Terebinths, and oaks, are sacred trees associated with pagan worship in that area and elsewhere throughout the ancient world. The text calls the Lord and the two angels "three men," which sounds quite pagan. Abraham runs to meet them, bows down, brings water for them to wash their feet, and invites them to rest under the tree. He hastens to Sarah, bidding her to make cakes using "three measures of choice flour," a bushel of their finest flour. Then he runs to the herd to hand-pick a choice calf, and gives it to a servant, who hastens to prepare it. He prepares the calf himself, and he himself sets the meat before them, along with curds and milk, and like a servant, he stands by them under the tree as they eat.

They all ask where Sarah is, and one of the men rewards Abraham for his hospitality with the promise that his old, post-menopausal wife would bear him a son. Sarah laughs to herself, saying, "After I have grown old, and my husband is old, shall I have pleasure?" Please note that pleasure is an assumed part of this undertaking. Sex is not just about procreation, according to Abraham's wife. And given that pleasure is still possible and often even better for post-menopausal women, Abraham no doubt had a bit of a performance problem, hence her laughing at the possibility of pleasure. The Lord responds to Abraham, not to Sarah. "At the set time I will return to you, in due season, and Sarah shall have a son."

This presents a space-time dilemma in that if God is omnipresent, how can he "return" to a specific place at a future point in time? How could it be that in the next verse, "the men set out from there, and they looked toward Sodom; and Abraham went with them to set them on their way"? Are God and angels men? Would God and angels need to "set out," implying a journey, and would Abraham need to "set them on their way"? What purpose would it serve to rather dishonestly go through the motions for Abraham's sake? God and angels here are old-fashioned pagan gods.

The Lord decides to reveal to Abraham his plans to destroy Sodom and Gomorrah so that Abraham can charge his children and his household to do what is righteous and just "so that the LORD may bring about for Abraham what he has promised him." In other words, the promise is only good if all the people of Abraham's household attend to righteousness and justice. God had not bothered to inform Abraham of this condition when the unconditional promise was given.

Then God, who has heard the great outcry against these two cities, says, "I must go down and see whether they have done altogether according to the outcry that has come to me; and if not, I will know." It is a natural tendency among primitives to anthropomorphize God. Most of us realize today, as no doubt many realized back then, that the omniscient God does not need to "go down" to "see whether" these claims have any validity. But here, God is more like a king or any of the pagan gods whose subjects came to him with accusations that God/the god (or goddess) needed to go verify in person.

Interestingly, the other two men head toward Sodom, but the Lord stays behind, with Abraham standing before him. This is where Lot comes in, possibly, and then only indirectly.

In this story, Abraham rather presumptuously challenges and even chastises God. "Will you indeed sweep away the righteous with the wicked? Suppose there are fifty righteous within the city; will you then sweep away the place and not forgive it for the fifty righteous who are in it? Far be it from you to do such a thing, to slay the righteous with the wicked, so that the righteous fare as the wicked! Far be that from you! Shall not the Judge of all the earth do what is just?" And the Lord said,

"If I find at Sodom fifty righteous in the city, I will forgive the whole place for their sake." Then the bargaining begins. The presentation of Abraham's plea to God uses a rhetorical style that today characterizes humor or stories for children. Suppose five of the fifty are lacking? Fine, I'll spare the city for the sake of the forty-five. And if only thirty righteous people are found? Fine—and so on down to ten, at which point God, who has had enough, "went his way"—which leaves open the possibility that if there were less than ten righteous people there, God would destroy the cities after all.

The Bible does not say that the angels went to Sodom to rescue Lot. When the angels arrive to destroy Sodom for its sins, Lot happens to be sitting at the gate. He invites the angels to stay with him, but they decline. He insists, they agree. According to the *New Revised Standard* translation of the Bible, which I am using throughout this book, Lot "made them a feast and baked unleavened bread." *The HarperCollins Bible Commentary* notes,

> Abraham the tent dweller provides refreshment characteristic of a pastoral nomad: cream and curds (18:8; cf. Isa. 7:21-22) and a choice steer. Lot is a city dweller who lives in a house in Sodom and meets the two strangers who arrive in the evening at the city gate. Abraham runs to greet the travelers and serves them himself; Lot stands and bows in greeting. In place of bread made from about a bushel of the finest flour (18:6), Lot offers unleavened bread to his guests. Such differences may serve to contrast Lot's entertainment of the guests with the greater generosity of Abraham.

In other words, Abraham runs to his guests, runs to make preparations, and serves his guests abundantly in the heat of the day, but Lot, who lives in prosperous Sodom, rises, bows, and invites his guests over for cheese and crackers.

The story never says or implies that the angels visit Lot in order that he might be spared from the impending doom. Lot is spared because he has shown hospitality, though on a lesser scale than Abraham had, and it would have been immoral for the angels to not reward him. Abraham's reward is a miraculous son. Lot's reward is his and his daughters' lives, and soon thereafter, two sons by abominable incest (the wife has been conveniently killed off).

When the men of Sodom notice the angels, i.e. "two men," they approach Lot aggressively, and for good reason; the men could well be imminent threats. Lot had bowed down to these men. Lot's uncle Abraham had not long before defeated those Sodomite clans in battle. Those angels could be Abraham's spies. The last time Abraham had let them off easy; maybe this time he would not. Rape was an efficient, traditional means of reducing men to the inferior, downright "nothing" status of women. The Sodomites were displaying power and sending back the message of aggression, and they were sending that message to Abraham via Lot.

These days, when we hear about "Sodom and Gomorrah" it's almost always in the context of a fundamentalist tirade against homosexuality. But the Sodom story clearly isn't about the evils of homosexuality.

The men, presumably all of them, and certainly not just the gay guys, collectively needed to conquer these two obviously powerful foreign men. The threatened gang rape of the two angels issued a formal communal warning. All "the men of the city, the men of Sodom, both young and old, all the people to the last man" had shown up to intimidate these two foreign men. If all the men were homosexual, which statistically is improbable, the old men would likely not have engendered the young men. Yet there they all are. The Sodom story is about the thwarting of male power—the attempted thwarting of the angels' power by the men of Sodom and the actual thwarting of the power of the men of Sodom by the angels.

Although the men of Sodom threaten Lot, it is to get to the angels. The men are not really after Lot; in fact, they order him to stand back. But Lot stubbornly refuses; it is his sacred duty to protect his guests. "Where are the men who came to you tonight?" the Sodomite men demand. "Bring them out to us, so that we may know them." One wonders why fundamentalists conveniently omit Lot's reply: "I beg you, my brothers, do not act so wickedly. Look, I have two daughters who have not known a man; let me bring them out to you, and do to them as you please; only do nothing to these men, for they have come under the shelter of my roof." In the dusty old days of road bandits and no criminal justice system, protecting male visitors had become a sacred duty. Lot instead offered his two virgin daughters to be raped. Women and girls, after all, were—as they have been nearly everywhere throughout almost all history—the chattel (property) of men that could be bartered, sold, and used as bribes.

The Sodomites' response is a bit incongruous. They tell Lot to stand back. Then they say, "'This fellow came here as an alien, and he would play the judge! Now we will deal worse with you than with them.' Then they pressed hard against the man Lot, and came near the door to break it down." It does not make sense to tell Lot to stand back, and then immediately call him an alien (foreigner) who is playing the judge, and then threaten him with worse than what they'll give the angels. Lot's negotiation tactics were wanting, so "the men [angels] inside reached out their hands and brought Lot into the house with them, and shut the door."

The angels answer the men's demand by striking them with blindness. This gives Lot a chance to slip out to warn the relatives. "But he seemed to his sons-in-law to be jesting." It is hard to believe that Lot's frantic pleading to escape impending doom would be taken as a joke, especially when he could have easily confirmed the sudden disappearance of all the men. And wait a minute—wouldn't Lot's sons-in-law be part of the category of "all" the men of Sodom that had shown up at Lot's house and were blinded?

Men, it seems, even Lot, can be defiant and disobedient, even to the orders of angels in crisis situations. When the angels say, "Get up, take your wife and your two daughters who are here, or else you will be consumed in the punishment of the city," Lot lingers. "So the men seized him and his wife and his two daughters by the hand, the LORD being merciful to him, and they brought him out and left him outside the city." Then they tell him, "Flee for your life; do not look back or stop anywhere in the Plain; flee to the hills, or else you will be consumed." After all the angels have done for him, Lot still does not trust them. Rather childishly he argues, "Oh, no, my Lords; your servant has found favor with you, and you have shown me great kindness in saving my life; but I cannot flee to the hills, for fear the disaster will overtake me and I die. Look, that city is near enough to flee to, and it is a little one. Let me escape there—is it not a little one?—and my life will be saved!" Doting on their spoiled child, the angels give in. "Very well, I grant you this favor too, and will not overthrow the city of which you have spoken. Hurry, escape there, for I can do nothing until you arrive there." So Lot heads for Zoar (Heb., "trifle").

Why were the angels not as generous with Lot's wife? Was it such an abomination to look back to the city that was her home, where her friends and relatives lived, where she had raised her children, where all her worldly possessions lay as kindling for a holocaust? Was glancing back one last time such an abominable crime? She had not argued with the angels, she simply instinctively turned, a human, humane response, a kind of "No!" to the horrors now afflicting her friends and relatives, her home, her history.

Or perhaps it was an instinctive response to an explosion. Scholars speculate that the rain of sulfur and fire was based on a story of an actual city destroyed by an earthquake caused by the release of combustible gasses.

That region has numerous salt pillars, some of which look eerily human to anyone with imagination. It is easy to see how the story took its next turn. The angels helped Lot and his family escape, but Lot's wife was turned to a pillar of salt for committing the horrific sin of glancing back.

Soon after Lot's wife had turned to salt, Lot's two daughters give birth to sons conceived by an incestuous liaison with him. Even back then the penalty for rape or incest was death. Why let Lot and his daughters off the hook? It's hard to believe that even after such a difficult day, Lot slept through the procreation process. But even granting the possibility of his innocence in the incest acts, he had nonetheless offered his daughters to be raped, and his daughters had committed incest without incurring the death penalty.

Though fundamentalists will tell you that the sin of Sodom and Gomorrah was homosexuality, the far more insightful Jesus clearly thought it was inhospitality (Matt. 10:5-15; Luke 10:1-12; Luke 17:28-30). The context of Luke 17 implies that the people of Sodom were simply going about their unspiritual business as usual when punishment descended.

The problem with Sodom, according to Ezekiel, is not homosexuality, which is not even mentioned (Ezek. 16:46-51), but the major abominations of pride, gluttony, prosperity, selfishness, and arrogance. The issue seems to be the poor and needy, not homosexuality.

Isaiah's take on the sins of Sodom and Gomorrah doesn't include homosexuality (Isa. 1:10-17). Judges 19 gives a much darker version of the story, the one that fundamentalists do not want you to read; it too fails to mention homosexuality.

One wonders why fundamentalists are preoccupied with interpreting this story as homoerotic.

But then, misinterpretation is biblical. Consider how in Galatians 4:22-26, Paul completely rewrites scripture by allegorizing probably the most important text (Gen. chapters 15, 16, 17) used to support his theology of justification by faith. By allegorizing he disregards the accepted assumption that the text was literally true.

> Tell me, you who desire to be subject to the law, will you not listen to the law? For it is written that Abraham had two sons, one by a slave woman and the other by a free woman. One, the child of the slave, was born according to the flesh; the other, the child of the free woman, was born through the promise. Now this is an allegory: these women are two covenants. One woman, in fact, is Hagar, from Mount Sinai, bearing children for slavery. Now Hagar is Mount Sinai in Arabia and corresponds to the present Jerusalem, for she is in slavery with her children. But the other woman corresponds to the Jerusalem above; she is free, and she is our mother.

The truth is that both sons were born of the flesh; Isaac was not a virgin birth. In saying that the story is allegory, Paul implies that it is not historical fact. The truth is that the full covenant had nothing to do, really, with either Sarah or Hagar. The covenant per se was with Abraham, and the promise was simply descendants: "Look toward heaven and count the stars, if you are able to count them.' Then he said to him, 'So shall your descendants be.' And he believed the LORD; and the LORD reckoned it to him as righteousness" (Gen. 15:5-6).

But the "law" (circumcision: sign of the covenant) was given from Sinai to the descendants of the freewoman, Sarah, through Isaac (Gen. 17:21) and not to the descendants of the bondwoman, Hagar, through Ishmael. The "everlasting covenant" (v. 19) was with Isaac, but Ishmael would also share in the covenant with Abraham (which promised descendants) in that he would be fruitful and exceedingly numerous even to the extent of becoming a great nation.

Hagar is Sinai is Jerusalem? Sarah is—what? And abstract Jewish heaven? It seems odd that Paul only mentions Hagar by name when

Sarah ("the other woman") is the main character of the actual "everlasting covenant" story. Could it be that Paul, a former persecutor of Christians and "untimely born" apostolic outsider (1 Cor. 15:8), feels like a bastard child? He wants to become the legitimate son of Sarah. He certainly spends ample ink inflating his legitimacy and authority. For instance, 2 Corinthians 11:5-6: "I think that I am not in the least inferior to these super-apostles. I may be untrained in speech, but not in knowledge; certainly in every way and in all things we have made this evident to you."

Within the context of guilt, it makes sense that Paul, a Jew, would make the rather outrageous assumption that those who respect and adhere to God-given law desire to be subject—slaves—to the law. It is law that makes him guilty, enslavement to law that makes him ashamed—and surely in the presence of the super-apostles, he must have felt ashamed of his past as a persecutor of Christians. It is ludicrous to claim that there are two covenants—keeping in mind that God, or anyone else in the Old Testament, never mentions two covenants and that the one covenant was not just one of God's many promises; this covenant with Abraham represented his obedience, not just his faith; it represented the very essence of what it meant to be Jewish.

The covenant is always referred to in the singular—except by Paul. And the law, which was given to Moses over four hundred years after the time of Abraham, did not annul the legal covenant made with Abraham. It's certainly a stretch to assume that Hagar represents Sinai, the place where the law was given to Moses centuries after Hagar's life and death.

Paul says (Gal. 3:16), "Now the promises were made to Abraham and to his offspring; it does not say, 'And to offsprings,' as of many; but it says, 'And to your offspring,' that is, to one person, who is Christ."

Of course, such stretching of the point is absurd. Nobody says "offsprings," or "seeds," as it is often translated, to refer to descendents. We—and that includes the Greeks and Hebrews—refer to descendents as offspring or seed. The only reference to offsprings or seeds referring to human offspring is Paul's use of the word. Throughout the Bible, the word used for offspring is offspring, or seed, not offsprings or seeds. This according to Bible translations that include *Young's Literal Translation, New Revised Standard Version, American Standard Version, Darby's New Translation, International Standard Version, King James Version* (Old and New), *New Living Translation, American Standard Version,*

The Message: The Bible in Contemporary Language, as well as reference books that include *HarperCollins Bible Dictionary*, *Brown-Driver-Briggs Hebrew Definitions*, *Easton's Bible Dictionary*, *Holman's Bible Dictionary*, *International Standard Bible Dictionary*, *Parsons Bible Dictionary*, *Strong's Hebrew and Greek Dictionaries*, and *Thayer's Greek Definitions*, *HarperCollins Bible Commentary*, *The Oxford Bible Commentary*, *Adam Clark's Commentary*, *Disciples Study Bible*, *Matthew Henry's Commentary*, and *New Commentary on the Whole Bible*.

As the *International Standard Bible Encyclopedia* politely puts it, "In Gal. 3:16 Paul draws a distinction between 'seeds' and 'seed' that has for its purpose a proof that the promises to Abraham were realized in Christ and not in Israel. The distinction, however, overstresses the language of the Old Testament, which never pluralizes *zera'* when meaning 'descendants.'"

Paul's "proof" is invalid, embarrassingly absurd, and downright dishonest. He isn't dictating truth direct from God, he isn't interpreting truth by the power of the Spirit, he's twisting the truth of scripture to validate his own personal theology, which today we call Christianity, the faith of a chimerical second covenant.

Paul's magical thinking still grips a large portion of humanity. Only truth can loosen the stranglehold.

Chapter 6

Deconstructing Paul

Early in my born-again phase I began to be turned-off by Christians who seemed to revere Paul even more than Jesus. Long before I began to doubt the validity of the Bible as a whole, I began to doubt the validity of Paul.

Fundamentalists say that we must trust his words because they're scripture, which makes them the Word of God: Paul's words are God's words.

But are *all* of Paul's words inspired by God if Paul himself says in his second letter to the Corinthians, "That which I speak, I speak it not after the Lord, but as it were foolishly, in this confidence of boasting" (2 Cor. 11:17)? In 1 Corinthians 7:6 and 7:12 he admits, "But I speak this by permission, and not of commandment . . . But to the rest speak I, not the Lord." Surely, I thought, the words of a self-proclaimed boasting fool were not divinely inspired scripture. At the very least, some sections of his letters were not God's words, per Paul himself; they were certainly not scripture in the sense of being God-breathed.

It's odd that something we already know can suddenly hit us like a revelation. That's how it felt when I realized the obvious fact that Paul's letters were *letters*. Paul's letters were written by Paul, not dictated by God.

Why should I accept Paul's opinion as absolute truth? Why should I believe that Paul's opinions were God's opinions? Wasn't equating Paul's theology with God's absolute truth a form of idolatry forbidden by the First Commandment? Wasn't lifting up the entire Bible as divine the same kind of idolatry that motivated Hezekiah to break in pieces the bronze serpent of Moses to which the people of Israel made offerings (2 Kings 18:4)?

I wondered how seriously I should take Paul's claims when they often contradicted claims found elsewhere in the Bible. For example, according to Paul, " . . . by being the first to rise from the dead, [Jesus] would proclaim light to our people and to the Gentiles" (Acts 26:23). But Jesus was not the first to rise from the dead; other people rose from the dead before him, according to both Old and New Testament accounts. Jesus raised Jairus's daughter (Mark 5:22-42; Luke 8:41-55); Jesus raised the widow of Nain's son (Luke 7:11-15); Jesus raised Lazarus (John 11:43-44); Elijah raised the widow of Zarephath's son (1 Kings 17-22); Elisha raised the Shunammite woman's son (2 Kings 4:35); a dead man rose when his corpse touched Elisha's bones (2 Kings 13:21).

How could Paul, or the Bible as a whole, be infallible when Peter and Paul, both of whom presumably had "the mind of Christ" (1 Cor. 2:16), disagreed on important issues right there on the biblical page?

In Acts 20:22, Paul tells the Ephesian elders, "And now, as a captive to the Spirit, I am on my way to Jerusalem, not knowing what will happen to me there." On his way there, Paul "looked up the disciples and stayed there for seven days. Through the Spirit they told Paul not to go on to Jerusalem" (Acts 21:4). But against the advice of the disciples, Paul says, "When our days there were ended, we left and proceeded on our journey" (Acts 21:5).

In the Spirit, Paul heads for Jerusalem. In the Spirit, the disciples advise him to not go there. Presumably still in the Spirit, against the advice of the disciples who are in the Spirit, Paul continues on. Is the Spirit sending mixed messages?

Furthermore, Luke, the presumed author of Acts, presents this part of his narrative in the voice of Paul, even though these events occurred long before Luke recorded them and even though Luke was not present. Are we to accept these quoted words of Paul's via Luke as God-breathed?

As I studied Paul's letters and Acts, I began to realize that it was Paul himself who asserted that he was one of the chosen few speaking for God.

Yet at the same time, he seemed to doubt himself. For example, in this passage from Acts, after years of preaching his version of the new religion, Paul needed to assert himself as someone validated by Christianity's "acknowledged leaders."

> Then after fourteen years I went up again to Jerusalem with Barnabas, taking Titus along with me. I went up in response to a revelation. Then I laid before them (though only in a private meeting with the acknowledged leaders) the gospel that I proclaim among the Gentiles, in order to make sure that I was not running, or had not run, in vain. But even Titus, who was with me, was not compelled to be circumcised, though he was a Greek. But because of false believers secretly brought in, who slipped in to spy on the freedom we have in Christ Jesus, so that they might enslave us—we did not submit to them even for a moment, so that the truth of the gospel might always remain with you. And from those who were supposed to be acknowledged leaders (what they actually were makes no difference to me; God shows no partiality)—those leaders contributed nothing to me. On the contrary, when they saw that I had been entrusted with the gospel for the uncircumcised, just as Peter had been entrusted with the gospel for the circumcised (for he who worked through Peter making him an apostle to the circumcised also worked through me in sending me to the Gentiles), and when James and Cephas [Peter] and John, who were acknowledged pillars, recognized the grace that had been given to me, they gave to Barnabas and me the right hand of fellowship, agreeing that we should go to the Gentiles and they to the circumcised. They asked only one thing, that we remember the poor, which was actually what I was eager to do.

After fourteen years of preaching the gospel, Paul feels compelled to get a stamp of approval from the "acknowledged pillars" of Christianity. This compulsion is interpreted to be a revelation. His phrase "response to a revelation" left undescribed suggests that it's not a dramatic vision type revelation, but rather something more subtle to which he responds. After fourteen years of preaching, Paul needs to make sure his message is okay with the big guys.

It struck me as odd that Paul would assume that perhaps Titus would want to be circumcised, even though he was a Greek. Paul seemed more than a bit paranoid in assuming that there were "false believers secretly brought in, who slipped in to spy on the freedom we have in Christ Jesus, so that they might enslave us." Though true, there might have been Jews who were suspicious of Paul's views about abolishing the covenant God established with Abraham by demanding that everyone discontinue the circumcision ritual.

Reading this passage with the mystique brushed away, it's easy to see that it's a very human Paul that can't help but show his contempt for the acknowledged leaders he wants to impress. Now they are "those who were *supposed to be* acknowledged leaders." His aside shows his bravado, perhaps in response to having been scrutinized, slighted, and offered no money—"those leaders contributed nothing to me," and in fact they asked Paul to "remember the poor," as if Paul needed reminding. (And perhaps he did. According to Acts 11:27-30, the whole region was afflicted by a severe famine, and "The disciples determined that according to their ability, each would send relief to the believers living in Judea; this they did, sending it to the elders by Barnabas and Saul," Saul, of course, being Paul.)

Paul's bravado adds the parenthetical "what they actually were makes no difference to me." But a few seconds earlier they had made a great deal of difference, and why else would Paul have journeyed to Jerusalem after fourteen years to get their approval? He adds, "God shows no partiality," which means they are not superior to Paul. It's worth mentioning that in Acts 10:34-35, after Peter has a vision that leads to his conversion of Gentiles, he says to them, "I truly understand that God shows no partiality, but in every nation anyone who fears him and does what is right is acceptable to him." Please note that this is not a claim to the power of faith, à la Paul, but to the power of fear (also translated as awe or reverence) and good works.

Mentioning James, Peter, and John by name and noting that they were "acknowledged pillars," even following his comment that God shows no partiality, suggests that Paul was indeed eager for approval and that the leaders' status was important to him. Was it really such a big deal for them to give a preacher of the gospel the right hand of fellowship? Anyone could preach the gospel of Jesus, and many people did. Didn't Paul say that he had the "mind of Christ," was able to "discern all things," and was "subject to no one else's scrutiny"? Here again Paul makes it a point to state that the acknowledged pillars agreed that Paul should go to the Gentiles (where he had been going for the past fourteen years) and that the others, including Peter, should go to the Jews. Yet in Acts 10-11,

Peter had already been designated, via powerful visions, to deliver to the Gentiles the gospel and the Holy Spirit.

I began to wonder if it was somehow irreligious to elevate Paul to the same level as Jesus. Unlike the gospel accounts of Jesus, Paul's letters and Acts reveal a human personality with character flaws. Here Paul appears to be jealous of Peter's leadership role in converting the Gentiles. The purpose of his journey to Jerusalem appears to be to "correct" any credit Peter has been given for converting the Gentiles and to make sure that everyone was on the same page in bestowing all the credit upon him (Paul).

According to Holman's Bible Dictionary,

> Despite Peter's role among the disciples and the promise of his leadership in the early church (see especially Matt. 16:17-19), Peter did not emerge as the leader of either form of primitive Christianity. Though he played an influential role in establishing the Jerusalem church, James, the brother of Jesus, assumed the leadership role of the Jewish community. Though Peter was active in the incipient stages of the Gentile mission, Paul became the "apostle to the Gentiles." Peter probably sacrificed his chances to be the leader of either one of these groups because of his commitment to serve as a *bridge* in the early church, doing more than any other to hold together the diverse strands of primitive Christianity.

In his role of "apostle to the Gentiles," again from *Holman's*,

> Paul's typical procedure was to enter a new town, seek out the synagogue, and share the gospel on the sabbath day. Usually Paul's message caused a division in the synagogue, and Paul and Barnabas would seek a Gentile audience. From Paul's earliest activities, it became evident that the gospel he preached caused tension between believers and the synagogue.

In those early days, even among the "acknowledged pillars" and "leaders," there was no consensus about the meaning or requirements of the Christian religion. But Paul comes across as more than a bit insistent that his way is *the* way.

I heard a trumpeting of human personality rather than divine inspiration when Paul, who had the mind of Christ, severely criticized Peter, who had the mind of Christ, as recorded by Paul in Galatians 2:11-14:

But when Cephas [Peter] came to Antioch, I opposed him to his face, because he stood self-condemned; for until certain people came from James, he used to eat with the Gentiles. But after they came, he drew back and kept himself separate for fear of the circumcision faction. And the other Jews joined him in this hypocrisy, so that even Barnabas was led astray by their hypocrisy. But when I saw that they were not acting consistently with the truth of the gospel, I said to Cephas before them all, "If you, though a Jew, live like a Gentile and not like a Jew, how can you compel the Gentiles to live like Jews?"

When I finally took his words at face value, I found it rather shocking that Paul, who formerly had hunted down Christians for the persecuting Roman authorities, now has the audacity to reprimand Peter, one of the original twelve disciples, about whom Jesus had said, "Upon this rock I will build my church," and who was serving as a bridge between Jewish and Gentile Christians.

I asked myself, how would Paul know that Peter withdrew because of fear of the Jews who came with James, the brother of Christ and leader of the Jewish Christian community? Maybe Peter preferred eating with his old friends for a time. Maybe he was respecting the preferences of Jewish Christians rather than Gentile Christians (Paul's Christians, who had basically thrown *the* symbolic ritual of faith, circumcision, out the window, and had thereby symbolically thrown out the Old Testament and Judaism with it). Maybe Peter was not willing to make eating with Gentiles an issue. Maybe he was building one end of a bridge. According to Paul himself, most Jews and Gentiles were not instantly zapped "perfect" by Paul's standards, or even Christ's. Certainly Peter could argue that Christ did not condemn or dismiss the covenant of circumcision—a covenant of faith even according to Paul himself. Paul had no right to judge the "circumcision faction" when Paul himself claimed that according to his theology of faith, people had freedom "in the Spirit" to make their own decisions about right and wrong.

Rather than discuss his concern privately with Peter, who possessed the mind of Christ that discerns all things, Paul rather arrogantly opposed Peter "to his face . . . before them all." How was eating with whom you choose hypocrisy, I wondered? Paul's complaint as he stated it didn't really make sense. Was Peter living like a Gentile just because he ate with them? Was that simple gesture enough for Paul to claim that Peter was therefore not living like a Jew, or even like a Christian? Presumably, even for Paul there surely must have been more to living like a Jew than eating with Jews and not with Gentiles. How was Peter, who had been converting Jews and Gentiles to Christianity, compelling Gentiles to live like Jews?

Once I accepted Paul's fallibility, it was quite clear to me that Paul was presenting remarkably irrational and exaggerated claims. Perhaps his rivalry with Peter over who should be credited with having taken the gospel to the Gentiles motivated his public attack.

Notice Paul's elitist judgment of Gentiles in his next comment about "Gentile sinners" (Gal. 2:15-21):

> We ourselves are Jews by birth and not Gentile sinners; yet we know that a person is justified not by the works of the law but through faith in Jesus Christ. And we have come to believe in Christ Jesus, so that we might be justified by faith in Christ, and not by doing the works of the law, because no one will be justified by the works of the law. But if, in our effort to be justified in Christ, we ourselves have been found to be sinners, is Christ then a servant of sin? Certainly not! But if I build up again the very things that I once tore down, then I demonstrate that I am a transgressor. For through the law I died to the law, so that I might live to God. I have been crucified with Christ; and it is no longer I who live, but it is Christ who lives in me. And the life I now live in the flesh I live by faith in the Son of God, who loved me and gave himself for me. I do not nullify the grace of God; for if justification comes through the law, then Christ died for nothing.

Nowhere in the Gospels does Jesus say that believers are justified by faith alone and not held accountable for their works. Nowhere in the Old Testament is there a claim that the law is to be abandoned for "faith," that no one will be justified by good works, or that every jot and iota of the law must be followed perfectly in order for a person to be deemed righteous. (Even Jesus transgressed the law when he ate the grains on the Sabbath, in Matthew 12.) Certainly faith was part of Christ's message, but that was because many people didn't believe that he was the Messiah. Nowhere in Christ's message as it has been transmitted to us does it say or imply that faith in Christ alone supersedes good works.

Yes, Christ said that believers must be perfect as God is perfect, meaning that the goal must be nothing less than perfection. But that doesn't mean that less than perfectly good people would go to hell. Christ revised details of the law, or perhaps re-defined their original intent, but his revision was to bring good works closer to a motivation of inward goodness rather than to permit a legalistic gesture for the sake of getting a reward.

How does eating with a group of Jews build up what was torn down? What was torn down? Paul seemed to think it was the law.

Paul's Law of Faith v. God's Law and Abraham's Faith

Ironically, Paul creates his own law—faith—and seems to think that eating with Jews violates his new law. Even granting Paul's own unique version of the Christian religion, how does eating with Jews violate the law of faith? And how is Paul's deeming Peter a hypocrite not itself hypocritical? Paul slams the law, then sets up his own law. Why should we trust the "new" religion of such a seemingly twofaced, irrational legalist?

And why should the Jews trust Paul's demolition of their God-given law?

Should the "circumcision faction" disobey God's charge to Abraham in Genesis 17? "I will establish my covenant between me and you, and your offspring after you throughout their generations, for an everlasting covenant, to be God to you and to your offspring after you." Everlasting. Paul begs to differ with God.

Should the "circumcision faction" disregard God's instructions to Abraham's descendants? "As for you, you shall keep my covenant, you and your offspring after you throughout their generations. This is my covenant, which you shall keep, between me and you and your offspring after you: Every male among you shall be circumcised. You shall circumcise the flesh of your foreskins, and it shall be a sign of the covenant between me and you."

Should the "circumcision faction" disbelieve the consequence of breaking the covenant that God established with Abraham? "So shall my covenant be in your flesh an everlasting covenant. Any uncircumcised male who is not circumcised in the flesh of his foreskin shall be cut off from his people; he has broken my covenant."

Amazingly, Paul calls those who still observe this ritual of faith in the scriptural covenant "transgressors." He is saying that by doing what is right according to the law, one demonstrates that one is a transgressor. That's absurd. Even granting Paul's extremist position of no law and all faith, how does fulfilling a commandment of God, a ritual instituted by Abraham, the "father of faith," make one a transgressor? Ironically, it is this covenant with God that makes Abraham worthy to be, in Paul's judgment, the father of Christian faith.

I thought it ironic that Paul's Old Testament legalism still cropped up so late in his career among the Gentiles, to whom he had preached salvation by grace through faith, that faith and that faith alone having been reckoned as righteousness.

Paul couldn't seem to make up his mind about the law—replace the law with faith, or make faith the law. Once I saw Paul's contradictions and tangled reasoning, I distrusted the legitimacy of his interpretation of the gospel. And he seemed to disparage Judaism as aggressively as he had persecuted Christians.

Not only did Paul's odd anti-Semitism make me doubt the validity of his theology, but his self-righteous stance on circumcision also made me dislike, or at least be suspicious of, Paul as a person. How could such a person be the spokesperson for God? Maybe Jesus was the Jewish Messiah; maybe Paul's Christianity was a perversion of Judaism. (At one point, I seriously considered siding with the Jews by becoming a Jew.) Certainly Paul drove a great and dangerous wedge between Jews and Christians. Yet his stance was, in my view, clearly unclear.

> Listen! I, Paul, am telling you that if you let yourselves be circumcised, Christ will be of no benefit to you. Once again I testify to every man who lets himself be circumcised that he is obliged to obey the entire law. You who want to be justified by the law have cut yourselves off from Christ; you have fallen away from grace. For through the Spirit, by faith, we eagerly wait for the hope of righteousness. For in Christ Jesus neither circumcision nor uncircumcision counts for anything; the only thing that counts is faith working through love (Gal. 5:2-6).

Even now I bristle at Paul's self-righteous pronouncement that "Christ will be of no benefit to you" who are circumcised to fulfill Abraham's covenant with God. Even Jesus (Luke 2:21) and John the Baptist (Luke 1:59) were circumcised. "I, Paul, am telling you"? Who does Paul think he is? Who is Paul to establish a kind of eternal death penalty for anyone unwilling to abandon God's law in order to fulfill Paul's new law of non-circumcision? Again, Paul is telling Jews to abandon God's law, the law of today's Christians' Old Testament.

Again, there was nothing about the ritual of circumcision that suggested it obliged the circumcised to obey the entire law. When the ritual of circumcision was commanded by God, the law of Moses didn't even exist yet. There were no such legalistic strings attached to circumcision that Paul imposes here.

"You . . . have cut yourselves off from Christ." (No pun intended, I'm sure.) Jesus spent his entire career instructing people in the true ways of goodness and fulfillment of the law. The only time he ever even mentions circumcision is in John 7:19-24.

> "Did not Moses give you the law? Yet none of you keeps the law. Why are you looking for an opportunity to kill me?" The crowd answered, "You have a demon! Who is trying to kill you?" Jesus answered them, "I performed one work, and all of you are astonished. Moses gave you circumcision (it is, of course, not from Moses, but from the patriarchs), and you circumcise a man on the sabbath. If a man receives circumcision on the sabbath in order that the law of Moses may not be broken, are you angry with me because I healed a man's whole body on the sabbath? Do not judge by appearances, but judge with right judgment."

Jesus is certainly not condemning circumcision, and it could be argued that he is lifting it up as a righteous, sacred act of such holiness that it could be lawfully performed on the sabbath. It is an act worthy of comparison with the even more righteous and reverent act of healing. Obeying this law in the spirit originally intended would certainly not cut off a believer from Christ. In pronouncing that ultimate judgment, "you have fallen away from grace," even on believers, doesn't Paul demonstrate that extreme lack of humility that constitutes a kind of blasphemy against the Spirit of grace?

Certainly we are taught "through the Spirit" how to be righteous, but Jesus never taught that righteousness was merely a hope that could not be accomplished in the present. In fact, he said that believers had already been cleansed by his message (John 15:3). Which didn't mean you don't occasionally need to have your feet washed (John 13:10, 14).

Isn't Paul just a bit presumptuous to pronounce absolutely Christ's views on circumcision? Paul never even met Christ. Furthermore, if neither circumcision nor uncircumcision counts for anything, as Paul asserts, why is Paul so obsessively judgmental toward those who are circumcised?

If the only thing that counts is faith working through love, why is the act of circumcision—a ritual symbol of faith—so heinous? Paul's oversensitivity to this issue makes his *legalistic* theology of grace through faith self-contradictory.

Paul amps up his judgments in verses 7-12 (Gal. 5):

> You were running well; who prevented you from obeying the truth? Such persuasion does not come from the one who calls you. A little yeast leavens the whole batch of dough. I am confident about you in the Lord that you will not think otherwise. But whoever it is that is confusing you will pay the penalty. But my friends, why am I still being persecuted if I am still preaching circumcision? In that case the offense of the cross has been removed. I wish those who unsettle you would castrate themselves!

Here again Paul judges those who, according to his standards, were running well. Does he really think he is the superior judge of what constitutes "the truth"? Does he really believe he knows all the truth that could come from "the one who calls you," meaning Christ? Instead of presenting a persuasive case to refute the case of "whoever it is that is confusing" them, Paul is more intent on making sure they know that God will make them "pay the penalty." Not persuasion, but judgment and punishment are Paul's tactics of indoctrination.

Paul then implies that someone, such as he himself, preaching circumcision would not be persecuted; only someone preaching against circumcision (Paul) would be persecuted. History records a reality in which both Jews and Christians were persecuted for various reasons, most of them having to do with challenges to Roman rule and worship. If Paul was "persecuted" by the Jewish community, perhaps it was because of his in-your-face, Romanesque/authoritarian preaching style. After all, to reiterate a point made earlier (again quoting from *Holman's Bible Dictionary*), in his role of "apostle to the Gentiles," Paul's "typical procedure was to enter a new town, seek out the synagogue, and share the gospel on the sabbath day. Usually Paul's message caused a division in the synagogue, and Paul and Barnabas would seek a Gentile audience. From Paul's earliest activities, it became evident that the gospel he preached caused tension between believers and the synagogue."

The charge against Paul when he was arrested in Jerusalem was that he was "the man who is teaching everyone everywhere against our people, our law, and this place [the temple]; more than that, he actually brought Greeks into the temple and has defiled this holy place" (Acts 21:27-28). But when Paul was presented to the governor, Felix, he claimed that he had been innocently worshipping in Jerusalem.

Paul must have felt the tension of being both a Roman and a Jew long before he added persecution of Christians and then his new Christian faith to his balancing act. Paul's unsuccessful attempt to integrate these disparate aspects of himself could explain psychologically the contradictory nature of his prose in terms of both its form and its content. His obsession with moral and especially sexual purity and with punishment for slight offenses, combined with his contradictory obsession with salvation as resulting *only* from faith, indicates an inner turmoil that quite possibly stemmed from his guilt complex for having persecuted the early Christians. It would make sense that his bravado in the presence of the "authoritarian leaders" like Peter and James and the leaders of the synagogues would have been compensation for his feeling of psychological and spiritual impotence. It would also make sense that by persecuting the non-Christian Jews (that he had once been among and had served), he was projecting his guilt onto them in a gesture that would serve both as retaliation and self-punishment—yet another layer of self-contradiction.

If Paul could have resolved his inner conflicts, or at least have lightened up and accepted the forgiveness of Christ that he so fervently preached, perhaps his life and letters would not have fomented the kind of intense inter-religious conflicts that still plague the world today.

WAS PAUL HOMOSEXUAL?

Another turn-off for me as I studied Paul's letters was his overkill homophobia, especially since it served as both inspiration and validation for today's hate crimes against gays.

Exploitation of bigotry has always served high priests needing an extra jolt of power-over or looking for a fundraising gimmick. Today, the scapegoat of choice for most Pauline fundamentalists is the homosexual. Homosexuals are so loathed that, as Rev. Fred Phelps puts it, "God doesn't hate you because you're homosexual. You're homosexual because God hates you."

Next to the Genesis story of Sodom and Gomorrah, the opinion of Paul expressed in Romans 1:18-27 is probably the most widely cited biblical "proof" that homosexuality is evil.

> For the wrath of God is revealed from heaven against all ungodliness and wickedness of those who by their wickedness suppress the truth. For what can be known about God is plain to them, because God has shown it to them. Ever since the creation of the world his eternal power and divine nature, invisible though they are, have been understood and seen through the things he has made. So they are without excuse; for though they knew God, they did not honor him as God or give thanks to him, but they became futile in their thinking, and their senseless minds were darkened. Claiming to be wise, they became fools; and they exchanged the glory of the immortal God for images resembling a mortal human being or birds or four-footed animals or reptiles. Therefore God gave them up in the lusts of their hearts to impurity, to the degrading of their bodies among themselves, because they exchanged the truth about God for a lie and worshiped and served the creature rather than the Creator, who is blessed forever! Amen. For this reason God gave them up to degrading passions. Their women exchanged natural intercourse for unnatural, and in the same way also the men, giving up natural intercourse with women, were consumed with passion for one another. Men committed shameless acts with men and received in their own persons the due penalty for their error.
>
> And since they did not see fit to acknowledge God, God gave them up to a debased mind and to things that should not be done. They were filled with every kind of wickedness, evil, covetousness, malice. Full of envy, murder, strife, deceit, craftiness, they are gossips, slanderers, God-haters, insolent, haughty, boastful, inventors of evil, rebellious toward parents, foolish, faithless, heartless, ruthless. They know God's decree, that those who practice such things deserve to die—yet they not only do them but even applaud others who practice them.

In other words, homosexuality is the result of worshipping images of humans or animals, and as a result of that, homosexuals are full of every vice, sin, and evil known to man, and they applaud others like them. By implication, heterosexuals, on the other hand, do not worship images of humans or animals, are not full of every vice, sin, and evil known to man, and do not applaud others like them.

Contrary to Paul's opinion, the truth is that there is absolutely nothing that could substantiate claims that homosexuals are any more likely than heterosexuals to worship images of animals or humans, or that homosexuals are any less loving, good, and spiritual than heterosexuals. The inference that homosexuals are categorically evil God-haters, and by inference that heterosexuals are not, is so absurd that one wonders how this passage could be accepted today as God's word or even as a valid opinion. Stereotyping stems from prejudice, but maligning such as this, with such vile and distorted scorn, betrays a more profound bigotry.

Many apologists try to prove that Paul did not say what he did in fact say: that homosexuality is evil and that homosexuals deserve to die. But the words speak for themselves.

Certainly Paul's assertion contradicts the vision Peter had early in his career, the vision that led to his conversion of the first Gentiles.

> About noon the next day, as they were on their journey and approaching the city, Peter went up on the roof to pray. He became hungry and wanted something to eat; and while it was being prepared, he fell into a trance. He saw the heaven opened and something like a large sheet coming down, being lowered to the ground by its four corners. In it were all kinds of four-footed creatures and reptiles and birds of the air. Then he heard a voice saying, "Get up, Peter; kill and eat." But Peter said, "By no means, Lord; for I have never eaten anything that is profane or unclean." The voice said to him again, a second time, "What God has made clean, you must not call profane." This happened three times, and the thing was suddenly taken up to heaven.

This is not just about eating food considered abominations. In 10:28 he expands his revelation, "and he said to them [the Gentiles], 'You yourselves know that it is unlawful for a Jew to associate with or to visit a Gentile; but God has shown me that I should not call anyone profane or unclean.'"

Yet Pauline fundamentalists would have us believe that profane, unclean homosexuals (as opposed to heterosexuals) are filled with every kind of wickedness, evil, covetousness, malice. Full of envy, murder, strife, deceit, craftiness, they are gossips, slanderers, God-haters, insolent, haughty, boastful, inventors of evil, rebellious toward parents, foolish, faithless, heartless, ruthless. They know God's decree, that those who practice such things deserve to die—yet they not only do them but even applaud others who practice them. If they accept Paul's words as God-breathed truth, they accept Paul's words as God-breathed truth. If they accept these words of Paul's written in the letter to the Romans, they reject Paul's notion of saved by faith (or Luther's saved by grace through faith), and they reject the revelation of Peter's vision.

In Matthew 12:1-8, Jesus demonstrates the principle of love versus legalism:

> At that time Jesus went through the grainfields on the sabbath; his disciples were hungry, and they began to pluck heads of grain and to eat. When the Pharisees saw it, they said to him, "Look, your disciples are doing what is not lawful to do on the sabbath." He said to them, "Have you not read what David did when he and his companions were hungry? He entered the house of God and ate the bread of the Presence, which it was not lawful for him or his companions to eat, but only for the priests. Or have you not read in the law that on the sabbath the priests in the temple break the sabbath and yet are guiltless? I tell you, something greater than the temple is here. But if you had known what this means, 'I desire mercy and not sacrifice,' you would not have condemned the guiltless. For the Son of Man is lord of the sabbath."

The Pharisees' misinterpretation of religion as legalistic sacrifice rather than the compassion of love is the kind of error that Paul makes, the kind of error that leads to the fundamentalist's vicious judgment against two gay people who love each other.

Paul's excessive disgust for homosexuality (physical/moral) and circumcision (moral/spiritual) suggests a problem with his own sexuality that possibly involves a castration complex. Certainly the male genitals represented power. Homosexuality represented the inversion of male dominance and power. Circumcision was a kind of castration-lite. Besides being a powerful ritual representing Jewish faith, circumcision was perhaps the most intimate ritual in being performed directly and permanently on one's own personal self. Once Paul recognized his error in persecuting Christians, he must have felt shame in being one of the circumcised.

On the other hand, Paul's theology was certainly not phallo-centric in the literal physical sense. Paul boasted that he was unmarried and encouraged others to remain single, and he spent an inordinate amount of ink admonishing even trivial "sexual immorality." Many have wondered if the thorn in his flesh (2 Cor. 12:7) might refer to homosexuality or castration. Or might Paul be a *repressed* homosexual? One thing is certain: Paul was uptight about sex, as even a casual reading of his letters makes clear.

In 2 Cor. 11:1-6, Paul's bravado about his status is couched in sexual imagery:

> I wish you would bear with me in a little foolishness. Do bear with me! I feel a divine jealousy for you, for I promised you in marriage to one husband, to present you as a chaste virgin to Christ. But I am afraid that as the serpent deceived Eve by its cunning, your thoughts will be led astray from a sincere and pure devotion to Christ. For if someone comes and proclaims another Jesus than the one we proclaimed, or if you receive a different spirit from the one you received, or a different gospel from the one you accepted, you submit to it readily enough. I think that I am not in the least inferior to these super-apostles. I may be untrained in speech, but not in knowledge; certainly in every way and in all things we have made this evident to you.

The "super-apostles" were possibly Peter and James. Certainly the apostles were some or all of the disciples of Jesus. (It's worth noting that we aren't sure who exactly the disciples were. According to *Easton's Bible Dictionary*, the term apostles was

> generally used as designating the body of disciples to whom he [Jesus] entrusted the organization of his church and the dissemination of his gospel, "the twelve," as they are called (Matt. 10:1-5; Mark 3:14; 6:7; Luke 6:13; 9:1). We have four lists of the apostles, one by each of the synoptic evangelists (Matt. 10:2-4; Mark 3:16; Luke 6:14), and one in the Acts (Acts 1:13). No two of these lists, however, perfectly coincide.

Paul's fixation was on circumcision as a symbol of Jewish refusal to accept his version of Christianity. Or put another way, the Jewish law that forbade homosexuality denied him the freedom to be gay and thus had castrated him. He wanted a new religion that gave him that freedom, but being a Roman and a Jew, he needed the rule of law; he needed a new law, the law of faith, the law of love. But Paul's old God said No.

As if to expose his problem with "circumcision," in a phrase almost extreme enough to be a Freudian slip, Paul hisses in a manner quite unchristian, "I wish those who unsettle you would castrate themselves!" (Gal. 5:12). This sounds less like the "authoritarian leaders" building bridges than a schoolyard bully. Such a comment, directed to an "immature" church, contradicts Paul's absolutist claim to maturity (1 Cor. 2:6).

In the next passage, he projects his own judgmental attitude onto others. "For you were called to freedom, brothers and sisters; only do not use your freedom as an opportunity for self-indulgence, but through love become slaves to one another. For the whole law is summed up in a single commandment, 'You shall love your neighbor as yourself.' If, however, you bite and devour one another, take care that you are not consumed by one another" (Gal. 5:13-15).

Freudian interpretation aside, who is biting and devouring if not Paul?

Paul's self-negating theology continues: "Live by the Spirit, I say, and do not gratify the desires of the flesh. For what the flesh desires is opposed to the Spirit, and what the Spirit desires is opposed to the flesh; for these are opposed to each other, to prevent you from doing what you want. But if you are led by the Spirit, you are not subject to the law."

Doesn't Paul sound a bit like today's ex-gays, who can't do (sexually) what they want and therefore want you, too, to be deprived of doing what you want—and calling that communal deprivation spiritual?

No doubt most of us who are not subject to the law would not want Paul dictating what it means to live by the Spirit. Most of us don't really believe that gratifying the desires of the flesh—things like eating cheesecake, enjoying the weather, petting a kitten, playing baseball, appreciating a gothic cathedral, listening to Bach, dancing, smelling roses, making love, or any other pleasurable, sensuous physical activity—are opposed to the Spirit that created and still creates the blessings of the universe. Surely it's really the dichotomy between freedom and legalism, not between spirit and flesh that has prevented believers throughout the ages from doing what they want—what they have the right to want if they are in the Spirit, love their neighbors, and are not subject to the law.

As Paul himself puts it in Romans 14,

> Welcome those who are weak in faith, but not for the purpose of quarreling over opinions. Some believe in eating anything, while the weak eat only vegetables. Those who eat must not despise those who abstain, and those who abstain must not pass judgment on those who eat; for God has welcomed them. Who are you to pass judgment on servants of another? It is before their own lord that they stand or fall. And they will be upheld, for the Lord is able to make them stand.

Once again Paul is speaking out of both sides of his mouth. Don't pass judgment? Who is Paul to pronounce vegetarians as weak in faith?

> Some judge one day to be better than another, while others judge all days to be alike. Let all be fully convinced in their own minds. Those who observe the day, observe it in honor of the Lord. Also those who eat, eat in honor of the Lord, since they give thanks to God; while those who abstain, abstain in honor of the Lord and give thanks to God.

Likewise those who love someone of the same gender, who want to be married in a church or mosque or synagogue like anyone else who is a free believer that wants to honor the Lord. "We do not live to ourselves, and we do not die to ourselves. If we live, we live to the Lord, and if we die, we die to the Lord; so then, whether we live or whether we die, we are the Lord's. For to this end Christ died and lived again, so that he might be Lord of both the dead and the living."

Circumcised and uncircumcised, Jew and Gentile, heterosexual and homosexual. "Why do you pass judgment on your brother or sister? Or you, why do you despise your brother or sister? For we will all stand before the judgment seat of God. For it is written, 'As I live, says the Lord, every knee shall bow to me, and every tongue shall give praise to God.' So then, each of us will be accountable to God."

Why, Paul, do you pass judgment on your gay brothers and sisters? Why do you despise them? Are gay individuals—let's narrow it even further—are gay Christians accountable to you and your homophobia or to God? You yourself said, "Let us therefore no longer pass judgment on one another, but resolve instead never to put a stumbling block or hindrance in the way of another. I know and am persuaded in the Lord

Jesus that nothing is unclean in itself; but it is unclean for anyone who thinks it unclean."

Did I hear that right? Do not pass judgment? Never put a stumbling block or hindrance in the way of another? Nothing is unclean in itself? Circumcision, and homosexuality, and gratifying the God-given desires of the flesh are only unclean for someone who thinks them unclean—someone, for instance, like Paul? The same Paul who despises circumcision, homosexuality, and eating with Jews, the same Paul who said, "If your brother or sister is being injured by what you eat, you are no longer walking in love. Do not let what you eat cause the ruin of one for whom Christ died. So do not let your good be spoken of as evil. For the kingdom of God is not food and drink but righteousness and peace and joy in the Holy Spirit"?

Is this not the principle Peter followed when he ate with the circumcised, which Paul condemned publicly to his face (Gal. 2:11)? Personally, I don't think that Christians eating with Jews or even those fearless souls on reality TV eating squiggly slugs injure or cause the ruin of one for whom Christ died, or anyone else.

> The one who thus serves Christ is acceptable to God and has human approval. Let us then pursue what makes for peace and for mutual upbuilding. Do not, for the sake of food, destroy the work of God. Everything is indeed clean, but it is wrong for you to make others fall by what you eat; it is good not to eat meat or drink wine or do anything that makes your brother or sister stumble. The faith that you have, have as your own conviction before God. Blessed are those who have no reason to condemn themselves because of what they approve. But those who have doubts are condemned if they eat, because they do not act from faith; for whatever does not proceed from faith is sin.

There is nothing inherently "unclean" about being gay. If gay marriage proceeds through faith, it is clean. If a straight marriage proceeds through doubt or a lack of faith, specifically Christian faith, it is sin, for the Christian. Gay Christians who marry because they have faith do not sin. Straight Muslims, Jews, Buddhists, Hindus, atheists, agnostics, or people who marry for reasons other than faith (love, commitment, companionship, or children, for instance) sin. Thus asserts Paul in the 14th chapter of Romans, the same book that began with Paul's extreme condemnation of homosexuality. Paul's complicated self-contradictions suggest a deep-seated *confusion*.

Just as some Christians today challenge the weight and strength of Paul's letters, so did some of the early Christians, as evidenced by Paul's defensive comment, 2 Cor. 10:8-10:

> Now, even if I boast a little too much of our authority, which the Lord gave for building you up and not for tearing you down, I will not be ashamed of it. I do not want to seem as though I am trying to frighten you with my letters. For they say, "His letters are weighty and strong, but his bodily presence is weak, and his speech contemptible."

The authoritative Paul was overbearing enough to frighten people despite his weak presence and rough, aggressive, and no doubt rude way of speaking. Paul himself was always battling this dichotomy: Circumcision is *the* rejection of faith: Circumcision is *the* covenant of faith. Perhaps this contradiction made the frustrated Paul angry.

I believe that Paul's unresolved attempts to reconcile these two contradictory positions reflect his attempt to forgive ("justify") himself for his persecution of Christians within the context of his moral-based Judeo-Christian religion. I believe that despite Paul's aggressive pushing of salvation by grace through faith, which would let him off the hook, he just couldn't believe his own theology to the extent that he himself could feel truly forgiven. Paul's overzealous moralizing is a projection of his own guilt. Even though he champions a new religion of faith alone, he continues to condemn others because he can't forgive himself.

Circumcision is *the* symbol that locates Paul's attempt to reconcile his own self-contradiction (faith + morality), often by outright denying his guilt (faith alone). Paul's letters, if closely read, reveal the schizophrenic tension that Paul must have experienced throughout his life. Had he lived today, he would have been a perfect candidate for ex-gay ministries.

In the end I decided that Paul was not a man I needed to trust. Any human court of law would throw out such an inconsistent testimony as invalid. How much more should we challenge, and if need be reject, the clearly misleading opinion of a mixed-up, tormented, repressed evangelical who claimed to represent God.

Chapter 7

To Worship God, Not the Bible

Giving up belief in the Bible as God's Word is one of the most difficult steps that some of us ever take. There's a sense of security in believing that we are standing on the same firm truth that others have stood on for centuries. For some, the Bible has its own numinous quality, if only by its being linked to positive experiences, like the initial spiritual high that many call being born-again, or social camaraderie within a church community.

As I discussed in Chapter 3, although I was raised by agnostics, I went through a born-again phase beginning at age nineteen, and at first, I did accept a biblical literalist stance. I call my relinquishment of belief in biblical infallibility a spiritual step, but really it was a process that took place over many years. The initial letting go in my early twenties happened in an instant, when I just had to admit that the Bible was not literally perfect or even close and that all the explanations for its incongruities were just plain absurd. Even realizing that, I continued trying to make some watered-down version of Bible belief fit my relatively new but still firmly established Christian worldview. For years, even decades, I continued to think of myself as a Christian and to acknowledge the Bible as somehow having a direct connection to God.

Eventually I decided to seriously research the origins of the Bible using scholarly rather than specifically Christian sources like those sold in Christian bookstores. That inquiry branched out into investigations into Church history, complete with its Vatican orgies, massacres of Jews and Muslims and other "holy" wars, and of course its famous inquisitions, which led to documented connections between fundamentalism and crime, the exploitation of "God" by pandering politicians, and the outrageous hypocrisy of mega-mammon TV evangelists. Gradually I came to understand that many evils committed in the name of religion occurred because victims trusted the Bible (or other religious text) and those who claimed to represent it.

It's likely that many people reading this book believe that the Bible is from God or are uncomfortable with having abandoned that belief. If you're one of those people, in the following chapters I will try, as gently but directly as possible, to demystify your belief in a divine or divinely dictated book. Rest assured that if I am wrong, your belief can only be strengthened. But if I am right and you are honest, you will need to read-just your stance. If the process makes you uncomfortable, I understand. I'll be taking you down the same path I traveled myself, but with the weeds cleared away. In maybe an hour you'll take a whirlwind tour of ground it took me years to cover.

Let me clarify again that for me, Deism is the worship of one universal God at the exclusion of all other gods; therefore, Bible-worship is, to put it technically, idolatry. If you're thinking to yourself that you don't actually worship the Bible, you merely revere it as God's words, let me ask you a question I finally asked myself: If you had to suddenly worship God without the Bible, could you? And what and who would that God be?

This is a valid question, because although fundamentalism claims to be monotheistic and a monotheist by definition can't worship both Deity and Book, many well-meaning believers have chosen to revere to the point of adoration—i.e., have chosen to worship—the Bible *as* God and therefore *instead of God* without even realizing it.

The moment came when I understood that if I believed deep down that God would not butcher innocent women and children or condone molestation even of the children of infidels, but according to Numbers 31 God ordered Moses to butcher innocent women and male children and the blessed Moses gave the innocent girls to the butchers for their pleasure, only by denying my own God-given conscience could I accept the biblical account as true and righteous, and I certainly couldn't condone upholding it as an acceptable model for the treatment of infidels. If I saw self-contradictions in the biblical accounts, and I saw a multitude, only by denying my God-given reason could I continue to believe in the Bible's divinity or divine origin.

Very early on I began to realize that belief in such seemingly harmless and beneficial concepts as grace often led to passivity and irresponsibility and was often exploited to mask a multitude of sins.

Thomas Paine once commented, "Accustom a people to believe that priests or any other class of men can forgive sins, and you will have sins in abundance."

It didn't take long for me to catch on that many people who believe in forgiveness of sins freely commit sins with a conscience easily cleared by proxy. A theology of blanket forgiveness early on pinched my sense of justice.

I experienced a dramatic lesson on the dangers of "grace" while still an undergraduate. I remember sitting alone inside the front of the campus church one evening a year or so into my born-again phase. I was leaning back against the altar, reading Carl Jung's *Man and His Symbols* in the spotlight bouncing off the cross as I waited to meet a friend who had class in the wing just off the sanctuary. I was deeply absorbed in my book when I realized that I had heard the front door open and someone was now sliding into a pew. I wanted to slip through the side door to the wing of classrooms, but I knew it was only unlocked on the other side. I decided to just stay put, hidden behind the altar. I continued reading.

Suddenly a man's voice wailed to the rafters, "Almighty God, forgive me. Oh God, I know you have the power to forgive me. You always forgive if a person asks, and I stand on that promise, I stand on that promise of forgiveness, oh Lord please, please forgive me." On and on he pleaded. Then it got quiet. I listened hard. Curious, I glanced around to see an ordinary looking man a few pews from the front, head down, kneeling in prayer in the dim light. Then the wailing began again. "Please, Lord, forgive me. I'm so sorry. I'll never do it again. I know if I ask you to forgive me, you have to."

The man's pleas intensified. He confessed that he had raped another girl. I realized immediately that he must be the campus rapist responsible for several assaults over the previous several months. I knew about this only by word of mouth. A woman professor had been fired for being a lesbian, and that was well publicized on this campus that wouldn't teach Virginia Woolf or Gertrude Stein because they were lesbians, but the campus rapes, and there had been several, had been hushed up even when professors and students tried posting fliers and otherwise letting students know. Plenty was done to make students aware that homosexuality was forbidden on our conservative Methodist campus, but nothing had been done to protect women students like me from this rapist, sitting here now, a few pews back from where I sat alone and barely hidden behind the altar.

On and on he cried out to the God he knew would forgive him yet again, would always forgive him, because God had no choice but to fulfill his promises, and anyone who confessed and believed would be saved. I sat perfectly still, barely breathing, my heart pounding as loud as his confessions. At one point I stifled a sneeze. He stopped mid-sentence. After a long, terrifying moment, he was off and running again. The more he prayed, the more I felt a powerful presence of evil.

When the rapist finally felt sufficiently justified and sanctified to leave—I could sense him moving down the aisle—I reported the incident to the police, but I had only a generic description to give them. As far as I know, the rapist was never caught. But I do know he did rape again.

Since that time I have come to understand that rape isn't about sex or any physical drive, desire, or pleasure; it's about sadistic pleasure of torturing and destroying another's being, the very essence of the self. It's about hate, control, power-over—that's spiritual murder. "When I rape, when I kill, only then do I feel alive." How many psychopaths have said something to that effect?

Alive? They are killing life-force itself, and that makes them feel alive? I don't think so.

I began to see that sadistic behavior includes the self-justifying cruelty of judgmental Christians claiming that their cruelty is love. I was puzzled and in time shocked by holier-than-thous hammering their scriptures into lightning bolts to fling through "sinners'" hearts.

I gradually saw, and saw clearly, the link between religion and bigotry: misogyny, racism, homophobia, anti-semitism, anti-humanism, and profound loathing for any religious outsider, no matter how small the religious difference, no matter how complex the ethical disagreement.

I remember getting another lesson on self-righteousness up close and personal one Saturday morning in the mid-80s when I lived in Los Angeles. I and several other NOW members had volunteered to help lower income patients enter a clinic outside L.A. that was being blocked by right-to-lifers, and to explain to the patients, most of whom did not speak English, just what was happening. One right-to-lifer was a young UCLA graduate student—the only black and the only non-member of the right-to-life action group. She was a Christian feminist with whom I had a long conversation that left us both confused yet relieved that our positions were not so far apart. We were both concerned about over-population, poverty, women's rights to make decisions about our own bodies, and adequate birth control that would end all need for abortions. We agreed that what the world desperately needed was rejuvenation of spiritual prerogatives, including the primal values of love, freedom, and human dignity.

High on that encounter, I introduced myself next to a cold, bitter Sunday-school teacher in dress, heels, pearls, and wide-brim hat. My attempts at connection were short-circuited by her non-stop scolding on the perversions of feminism, which was only interrupted by the leader of the pro-life action, a middle-age man wearing shorts, a tee shirt that did not quite cover his large belly, and a ball cap, who carried a Bible with a few wives-be-submissive-to-your-husbands and thou-shalt-not-kill pas-sages marked with ribbons—marked by his pastor, I discovered after a few minutes of discussion, because this man knew nothing about the Bible ("that was the pastor's job"). Yet he claimed, and I think he actually believed, that the Bible was absolutely true and that he was there "in the authority of God the Father."

When I explained to him that the clinic was not "an abortion clinic," but rather a medical clinic visited by mostly poor Hispanic women, he responded by saying that I and all NOW members were sluts and whores and the only reason we were there was because we had all had abortions. I informed him that none of the dozen or so members present had had an abortion and some were lesbians and two were obviously men and that the abortions performed at the clinic were infrequent and necessary. I will never forget his response: "If you girls wouldn't pull down your pants, you wouldn't get pregnant."

His continuing cartoon tirade about sluts and whores and birth con-trol leading us down the path to Armageddon was interrupted when a car that had just pulled into the parking lot was swarmed by other right-to-lifers. One frail pro-life woman, who every ten minutes or so had been falling to her knees wailing, holding up a tiny plastic fetus she called the baby Jesus, had just slammed against the young Hispanic couple's windshield her large, cumbersome placard decorated with pictures of fetuses and gruesome photographs of Nazi concentration camps framed by childish drawings of flaming pregnant devils complete with horns and tails. In bold letters were the captions Abortion, Evil, Abomination, Whores of Babylon, as well as Women Belong In the Home, beneath which was quoted *Kinder, Küchen, Kirche* followed by its translation, Children, Kitchen, Church, which this poor woman surely did not know was the slogan on billboards of smiling young blonde Christian German women in aprons that Hitler plastered all over Germany as part of his Aryan race propaganda. As the young Hispanic man attempted to emerge from his car, which was being rocked by the right-to-lifers, the frail woman shoved, and I do mean shoved, the plastic fetus in his face. When I and a few other members attempted to help his frightened wife from the other side of the car, the frail fetus-shover rushed around and bashed me over the head with her placard, and the organizer spit on me and called me and my friends bitches, witches, whores. All this as the police sat across the street in their cruisers. The young man and woman slid back into their car and drove away.

Inside the haven of the clinic, where I had gone for a drink of water, an angry nurse, checking my head and attending to the deep cut I hadn't noticed on my arm, told me she had asked the woman, who had been recently raped, to come in that morning to see the doctor because the woman's test results just back from the lab indicated not only that she was pregnant; she had cancer. I will carry that poor, anonymous Hispanic woman's look of terror with me to the grave.

I began to realize that all fundamentalist dogma and ostensible behavior was justified by the belief that the Bible was the equivalent of God. But did that explain the utter insensitivity of so many believers? The mean behavior of the right-to-lifers I encountered that day dramatically demonstrated the fallout of misogynist attitudes common among fundamentalist Christians, even women.

That day in L.A., I was amazed at the extent to which those believers were willing to relinquish the rights and responsibilities of their faith—the core of who and what they were, the essence of life's meaning—to a second party whose only credentials were a piece of paper and maybe a collar. I realized that the most intimate and the only ultimately critical engagement between a person and God had been delegated to a committee of so-called experts—preachers, evangelists, "Christian writers." The ignorance, naïveté, and laziness of believers, combined with unreasonable respect for authority, concentrated religious power in a few hands that aggressively distorted their own gospel faith into a mockery of itself.

Although fundamentalists argue that the Bible is God's infallible Word, I've never met two Christians who completely agree about what the Bible actually says, much less what it *means*. One thing I have discovered is that most Christians have never studied, or even read, every single biblical text. Even widely read and studied texts are interpreted differently by different groups and individuals.

By definition, Christian fundamentalists believe that the Bible is God's absolutely infallible Word, perfect in every way. The Bible has become so mystified that believers are unwilling to objectively read what it actually *says*, if only because the Bible contradicts itself and fundamentalists must stay in denial in order to uphold their faith in infallibility. Isn't that dishonest? Aren't those believers engaging in a codependent relationship with a surrogate God? The Bible is so revered that many believers equate it with God. Isn't that idolatry by the Bible's own standards?

The truth is that the Bible is not God; it is a book, or rather a collection of books. The canonical text we call the Bible resulted from editorial decisions by its early publishers. There were many "books" (separate texts written on scrolls) circulating during the first few centuries after the presumed death of Jesus. There were thousands of different pre-printing press versions of the texts that were finally chosen to be included in the Bible. The theological/political elite known as the "church fathers" made those choices, often amid bitter and sometimes violent argument. To this day, agreement is not unanimous. The Roman Catholic Bible contains more books than the Protestant Bible, and the Greek Orthodox text includes all the books of the Roman Catholic Bible plus other books.

It's surprising how easy it is to substantiate that the Bible's long deification process, begun centuries after the death of Jesus, was the result of human, not divine, intervention. Nobody knows for certain who wrote any of the specific books collected as the Bible. I have met Christians who believed that Moses wrote the entire Old Testament, and that the disciples, Matthew, Mark, Luke, and John, wrote the gospels known by their names.

But the Old Testament was written over hundreds of years by anonymous authors. The New Testament gospels were written by anonymous authors many decades after the death of Jesus. Even assuming that the Bible is true, some of the events recorded in *Matthew* occurred before Matthew even knew who Jesus was. John could not have written "his" entire gospel, because near the end of that text, the author explains why John had died contrary to the rumor that Jesus had said he would not die. Luke became a follower late in Jesus's career and would not have witnessed the events he describes. Mark was not one of the original twelve disciples; he was recruited by Barnabas to assist Paul, who originally persecuted the early Christians and became a Christian himself well after Jesus's death. We are fairly certain that Paul wrote four of the books bearing his name, but again, Paul himself never even met Jesus.

The Bible books' original versions—the *autographs*—were not necessarily written by eyewitnesses. They could just as easily have been written accounts of previously received hearsay.

The writer of Luke, for instance, makes no claims to have witnessed what he describes in his gospel. Nor does he make claims to divine revelation. His text opens,

> Since many have undertaken to set down an orderly account of the events that have been fulfilled among us, just as they were handed on to us by those who from the beginning were eyewitnesses and servants of the word, I too decided, after investigating everything carefully from the very first, to write an orderly account for you, most excellent Theophilus, so that you may know the truth concerning the things about which you have been instructed (Luke 1:1-4).

This opening to Luke's gospel is clearly not the utterance of a prophet possessed by divine afflatus. Luke was more like a reporter who interviewed people—who knew people (who knew people) who were eyewitnesses—as part of his investigation. Even the actual eyewitnesses would not have perfectly or in precisely the same way observed, interpreted, and remembered exactly what happened, nor would all or probably any of them have remembered verbatim what anybody said. "Many had undertaken" the task of writing gospel accounts. The writer of Luke attempts to present his version as an "orderly account," with correct chronology presumably being a concern. The person believed to be addressed is

Theophilus, the Bishop of Antioch during the latter half of the second century. That would mean that Luke's gospel was written well after the events narrated by Luke would have occurred.

Dating biblical material is not as objectively historical as many Christians assume. To a large extent, dating surviving biblical texts is pure guesswork. Conservative Christian scholars date the four gospels close to the time of Jesus, while progressives assign later dates and convincingly document their reasons. The assignments of dates to Old Testament texts are even more divergent. Conservatives seem intent to prove that ignorant primitives borrowed from God's truth and perverted it into myths and superstitions, while progressive scholars argue (and largely prove) that the Bible texts are mainly composites of circulating mythic materials often of far more ancient origin. Conservatives assign dates that most present the biblical stories as historical rather than mythical, because if they are mythical just like the stories of the other religions—and those stories bear striking resemblance to the biblical ones—then Judaism and Christianity are no more valid than any other religion. If conservatives admit that, religion as they know it disintegrates.

The truth is that there is no way to know if the events narrated in the Old Testament ever took place; when they took place; the accuracy of the narration; or the date of the writing of the related event. The written version relating the event could have been first committed to writing centuries after the event actually occurred. The written version inscribed a verbal telling that had evolved after repeated telling and retelling by people of varying memory abilities who were capable and willing to embellish to make a point or to entertain. To deny this is to deny that the storytellers were human.

To prove that God created the Bible, apologists refer to the Bible's so-called unity, beginning with the unity of God they claim is present throughout all its pages. But glean all the passages referring to God, His attributes and activities, then separate them into classifications, and it becomes clear that the image of God presented in the Bible is as fractured, inconsistent, and self-contradictory as any pagan god. We don't even know if God is one or "us" (Gen. 3:22).

Apologists try to impose a fictitious linear timeline to prove a divinely inspired unity to the biblical stories, as if they had been structured with a beginning, middle, and end into a unified whole like a Greek tragedy or

Homeric epic. Such a unity only exists in the minds of those whose interpretations now create it. The fabricated unity of the Bible as the God-
directed historical revelation to a chosen elite is a misrepresentation
based on inaccuracies. The Bible's narratives appear unified, revealed,
and perfect only to those indoctrinated to believe that they are. The biblical "gestalt" argues less for inherent unity than for the deeply human
need to find unity and to aesthetically represent our inklings of unity or
to create unity for ourselves out of the given materials.

The supposed unifying themes, such as creation, providence,
redemption, justice, retribution, temptation overcome, and survival in
the wilderness, as well as the unifying personages, such as wise prophets,
shrewd chieftains, and a son of God king, are found in other ancient
religious traditions and are to a great extent the very reason any religion survives. All successful religions claim divine inspiration and all
persuade the credulous.

Scholars point out that biblical law derived from and was essentially the same as the more ancient Sumerian laws of Ur Nammu and
Lipit Ishtar, the Old Babylonian laws of Eshnunna and Hammurabi, the
Middle Assyrian laws from Asshur, and the Hittite law code. All these
collections of cuneiform law are older than the legal collections of the
Old Testament. In fact, the Old Testament law is part of a common law
tradition shared throughout the region of Mesopotamia, Syria, and
Palestine. The only unique feature of the Hebrew laws was its claim to
special divine inspiration. It took a Hebrew genius to realize that obedience would be more efficiently elicited if it were viewed as the human
end of an elitist covenant with the Divine. Obey because you're special
and will be specially blessed was a more successful motivation for obedience than "obey, or be punished."

The Psalms read essentially the same as hymns and psalms of other
Near Eastern cultures, especially Egypt and Mesopotamia. The wisdom
literature, patriarchal stories, prophecies, the Song of Songs, even the
blueprint for construction of the sanctuary have parallels in the litera-
tures of other, more ancient religions.

The HarperCollins *Bible Dictionary* makes this comment under its
entry, "Archaeology, History, and the Bible":

> The Bible creates special problems for interpreters because it is
> a composite corpus of literature. It is not a primary historical

source; in fact, some of its historical sources are quite late. The biblical text is sometimes poorly preserved, ambiguous, or tendentious. The Philistines are a classic example of biased reporting. The biblical writers fail to acknowledge the Philistine contribution to Canaanite technology, art, and architecture.

As a book of faith, the Bible is not always free of prejudice, presenting, as it does, historical events from a theological point of view. The Bible's chief interest in relating an event is not "what happened" but "what it meant" . . . It is imperative that biblical texts be interpreted by literary-critical analysis, including form, tradition, textual, historical, and redaction criticism.

The Bible was written "from faith for faith." But is such a faith really blind faith? Is such a faith authentic and relevant today? Is the conservative presentation of the Bible as divinely inspired dishonest in being inaccurate?

Certainly the nineteenth-century scholars were often more accurate, honest, and courageous than many religious scholars writing in the twentieth century. This makes sense: The later scholars have been battling against the disintegration of Christianity by sidling up to fundamentalism, which sprang up and quickly spread at the turn of the century. They had no choice, and still don't. If the Bible is not a definitive source of historical truth, then it's not a definitive source of spiritual truth. In the case of the gospels, conservatives would rather be dishonest in placing the texts closer to the source: Jesus and his disciples. The Old Testament books need to be "proven" to be more ancient than the myths they so obviously appropriated. Given the immense amount of scholarship available, I'm certain that these conservative scholars must know they're being deceptive. Probably they would rather rewrite history—i.e. lie—than witness the demise of their religion.

Well over a century ago, Nietzsche proclaimed: God is dead: He died laughing. The real God, of course, has always been alive and well creating and sustaining the universe. But "God," the "God" created in our image, the abstract Zeus-esque representation of God propagated by human religion, couldn't stop laughing at our absurd superstitions. By the end of the nineteenth century, that gut-busted God was dead as a doornail.

In other words, religious representations had displaced the actual God so that God no longer lived in the human spirit, at least not the spirit cannibalized by religion. The letter of the law replaced the spirit of the law. Indoctrination supplanted universal communion with God. The hierarchy of mediation had become so vast that God had long disappeared beyond the vanishing point parade of clerics.

In a sense, Nietzsche's critique echoed an ancient understanding. The wisest Greek philosophers and poets, for instance, understood that God, mythically represented as the local chief "Zeus" or collectively as gods, played a minor role among the heroes of art, poetry, and drama, and even lesser roles in actual human life they amplified. Temples of gods magnified human characteristics. Rituals and prayers signified humanity's yearning to transcend itself, usually but not always in a positive sense. Art, like the preconscious art of dreams, moved us to desire self/conscious enlightenment and catharsis, or at least to face our shadow. And what is the shadow if not our desire to be God in order to get what we want, including immortality?

God, the deified representational "God," is dead and in fact was never really living except in the human imagination. The problem with imagination is that the uneducated often mistake representation for the thing represented. But a painting of Socrates is not Socrates himself. God the Father is not a blow-up facsimile of a human father.

Starting at the end of the nineteenth century, fundamentalism erupted into history to rewrite history by revitalizing the dead God of superstition. The impossibility of the story of Jesus as related by the contradictory gospels was transcended with the greater impossibility that all the biblical texts were God-breathed. One superstition supplanted another.

Scholars of the nineteenth century had not been shy about pointing out that none of the writings of the Apostolic Fathers, Clement of Rome, Barnabas, Hermas, Ignatius, and Polycarp, written for the most part early in the second century, contain any mention of the four gospels. Justin Martyr, the most eminent of the early Fathers, wrote about the middle of the second century. In his *First Apology 66* he makes one mention of gospels in the sense of written notes of instructions on the taking of the consecrated bread and wine that had been passed down among written reminiscences of the apostles.

Apostles were not the twelve disciples; they were subsequent adherents to the new religion centered on Jesus. Paul was an apostle, as were later followers such as Barnabas (Acts 14:14), Andronicus, and Junias

(Rom. 16:7). The term, which literally means "one who is sent out," was still being used during the second century and beyond to refer to preachers, teachers, missionaries and priests; many evangelicals today refer to themselves as apostles and disciples.

Justin's mention of reminiscences doesn't prove the existence of the four New Testament gospels. The word "gospel" literally meant "good news," a term used in the Old Testament and among the Romans. The Roman proconsul Paulus Fabius Maximus, for instance, used the word when establishing the birthday of Caesar Augustus as the beginning of the new year, proclaiming the day of Caesar's birth "good news" (the same Greek word for "gospel") for the whole world. In the New Testament, the term designates a message, teaching, or preaching. Paul, for instance, speaks of "my gospel" (Rom. 2:16; 16:25) and "our gospel" (2 Cor. 4:3), claims that his is the only gospel (Gal. 1:7), that his is the revealed gospel direct from God (Gal. 1:16; 1:11-12), that believers should turn from other gospels (2 Cor. 11:4; Gal. 1:6), and that his gospel demands obedience (Rom. 10:16).

Justin's extensive writings arguing proofs of the divinity of Christ used more than three hundred quotations from the books of the Old Testament and nearly one hundred from the Apocryphal books of the New Testament, but none from the four gospels, which would have been the definitive source of his proofs had they existed. He never even mentions the names of Matthew, Mark, Luke, or John in any of his writings. There is no evidence that the four gospels existed prior to the time of Justin. The evidence indicates that Matthew, Mark, and John were written or pieced together like Luke's gospel sometime in the latter half of the second century.

The strikingly different Gospel of John begins with a description of the Logos, or Word, which personified an emanation or essence of divine wisdom. Although a very ancient concept developed by many philosophers and religions, John's version especially echoes Philo, a philosopher living in or near Jerusalem during the time of Jesus. In all his writings, the prolific Philo never mentions Jesus or any of the newsworthy events relating to his life. Yet the writer of John, writing many decades after the death of Jesus, almost quotes Philo verbatim. Philo wrote: "The Logos is the Son of God" (*De Profugis*); "The Logos is considered the same as God" (*De Somniis*); "He [the Logos] was before all things" (*De Leg. Allegor.*); "The Logos is the agent by whom the world was made" (*De Leg. Allegor.*); "The Logos is the light of the world" (*De Somniis*); "The Logos only can see God" (*De Confus. Ling.*).

Christianity is a composite religion; the Bible is its composite text of texts that mixed and evolved over time.

Once the new religion centered on Jesus caught fire, it spread out into a multitude of verbal and written adaptations. The new religion was from the start not a single religion but many interpretations, many religions. Once churches began to form, verbal teachings needed to be given consistency. Committing the teachings to writing conferred authenticity and authority. Texts expressing each church's concrete theology became a necessary means of shaping and maintaining cohesion. Then the various churches needed to be consolidated into a single church. Preachers taught, many of them traveling like pollen in springtime. Most of the teachings were rejected by what established itself as the church hierarchy. Most of the writings were tossed out. It's likely that most early Christian writings were destroyed and their ideas repressed during the first and second centuries, never to be heard of again.

The New Testament texts referred to Old Testament texts that were regarded as sacred to Judaism, yet it wasn't until the end of the first century A.D. that the Old Testament canon was established by the Council of Jamnia, likely in response to the heresy of Christianity and other local religions. Even then, not all collections of Jewish writings contained the same canonical books.

By the time the Bible as we know it was complied in 397, there were thousands of manuscript versions of the various books that would finally be admitted into the Bible. There were over 5,000 versions of New Testament books alone, not counting thousands of additional versions of the Greek translations. No two of those thousands of manuscripts were exactly alike. Some books considered for inclusion were rejected altogether; this rejection was via vote, not divine instruction. Of the books voted to be included, none of the original autograph versions still existed. Each autograph original would have been written on papyrus or parchment, which disintegrated within a few years, making it necessary to recopy each manuscript, and then each copy, over and over and over. Because each had to be copied by hand (the printing press was not invented until 1450), human errors continuously crept in, which were then copied and passed on. Each copyist would pass on his version's errors, while all the other copyists were passing on their own completely different sets of errors, so the discrepancies proliferated exponentially. Scribes glossed their copies with corrections, grammatical clarifications, and interpretive notes; they were free to do so, since the books had not yet been assigned their "divinely inspired" status. Some of the additions were eventually incorporated into the actual text, and sometimes scribes adjusted one version of a text to better align with another.

By 397, there were no autographs. Even autograph versions of the gospels were likely written compilations of accounts circulating via hearsay. Even if the original versions of the gospels and other texts were inspired or God-directed, when the church fathers voted in 397, there were no pure, literally perfect original versions, only error-ridden copies that contained more differences among themselves than there are words in the New Testament, as biblical scholar Bart Ehrman puts it.

Furthermore, the Hebrew and Arabic Old Testament texts were written in consonants only, so each word had to be interpreted in context and vowels inserted during transcription. For instance, to make a comparison in English, b_t might be interpreted as bat, bet, bit, but, beet, beat, bate, abate, abut, and so on. Michelangelo's *Moses* has horns protruding from his head because the Hebrew words that could have been translated *horns* or *rays of light* in the Renaissance Bible became horns.

The consonants JHVH or JHWH, which stood for God in the Masoretic Hebrew text, were erroneously transliterated Jehovah. The letters of a separate word, Adonai (Lord), were inserted to remind the scribes who read the Hebrew text aloud that the word for God was too sacred for expression, according to their interpretations of texts such as Exodus 20:7 and Leviticus 24:11. Some later translators, however, assumed that this was the actual name of God, not a marking to remind the reader not to speak it.

All religious literature, including the Bible texts, were composed by actual persons, each person writing within a specific historical context with its own figures of speech, cultural associations, and pool of knowledge, each person having his or her own discrete attitudes, assumptions, mores, and literary abilities. Vernaculars and figures of speech had to be interpreted. Interpretations could vary. Interpretive mistakes could be made. Jesus once commented that it's harder for a rich man to enter heaven than for a camel to pass through the eye of the needle, but with God all things are possible. If Jesus was referring to the eye of a sewing needle, the text means one thing. But a different, even opposite, interpretation becomes possible once we learn that the "eye of the needle" was the name of a passageway in the Jerusalem Wall so narrow that only very small camels could pass through, and only after their cargo had been unloaded and left outside the gate to be schlepped in later by humans.

All this is fact that has been known for centuries. Even so, some fundamentalists today insist that discrepancies did not appear in the literally perfect "original Bible." The truth is that there never was an original Bible. At no time did all the original autograph versions of the books of our Bible exist side-by-side in one volume, or anywhere else.

Furthermore, God evidently allowed errors to creep in. One could even argue that God "directed" the creation of a *fallible* Bible. Perhaps God wanted to prevent the very idolatry—the worship of a graven image (text)—committed by contemporary fundamentalists. Perhaps God was concerned about the likelihood that Bible worship would replace the worship of God.

It was centuries after the death of Jesus that believers began to think of the Bible as scripture. Even then, "scripture" simply meant literally "something written." Only after the church had organized was *graphe* mystified to mean sacred writings, and only later still were the sacred writings apotheosized as the "God-breathed," literally perfect Word of God.

Fundamentalists argue that because the Bible says that certain behaviors or beliefs are wrong, God says they're wrong. This argument falls apart if the Bible is not God, if the Bible was not directly inspired, or if the Bible is not literally word-for-word perfect. If the Bible is not God's infallible Word, it is not God's infallible Word. Biblical arguments then cease to be valid as anything more than opinion.

Fundamentalists can't help but find themselves in a morally precarious predicament when they must lie to uphold the "truth" of the infallible Bible. Sometimes they don't lie but rather readjust, or purposely maintain their own ignorance as an excuse for inconsistency. For instance, most fundamentalists accept the Old Testament as infallible because it's part of the infallible Bible. But most fundamentalists who accuse others of this or that "abomination" don't know that practically every day they themselves commit abominations that require the death penalty.

Among the abominations most often committed are eating shell-fish (Lev. 11:10); eating unclean or unsanitary food, even if you were a Katrina victim (Lev. 5:2-3; 7:19-21; Lev. 11); eating meat with blood in it, even if it's served medium rare at Sizzler (Gen. 9:4); eating pork, even bacon on Atkins (Lev. 11:7); children who are drunks or gluttons, even if it's McDonalds or Thanksgiving (Deut. 21:18-23); children, including terrible-twos and teenagers, disrespecting, cursing, or striking a parent (Lev. 20:9; Exod. 21:17; 21:15); piercings and tattoos (Lev. 19:28) (with no loophole to wipe away mutilation sins with reconstructive surgery); women wearing men's clothing, such as pants (Deut. 22:5); having contact with a woman for seven full days while she's "in her period of menstrual uncleanliness" (Lev. 15:19-24); adultery, which includes sex before marriage (Exod. 20:14; Lev. 20:10); a woman who marries when she's not a virgin (Deut. 22:13); coitus interruptus or masturbation (Gen. 38:7-10) (had the death penalty prescribed for this abomination been in any generation actually rendered, the population of the planet would have been decimated centuries ago; perhaps it's best to continue the tradition of exemption); defiling a neighbor's wife (Ezek. 18:11), which probably includes window peeping and *Playboy* perusal, according to Jesus (Matt. 5:30); doing yard work or taking the kids to the movies or even just gathering sticks or firewood on the Sabbath (Exod. 31:15 and 35:2; Num. 15:32-36); approaching the altar of God if you have an astigmatism or any other defect or don't have 20/20 vision (Lev. 21:20); males trimming the hair around their temples (Lev. 19:27); touching the skin of a dead pig, like, say, a football (Lev. 11:6-8); planting two different crops in the same field, or wearing garments made of two different kinds of threads, like a cotton/polyester blend (Lev. 19:19); cursing (Lev. 24:10-16); sleeping with in-laws (Lev. 20:14) (which contradicts Deut. 25:6, which stipulates that if a man dies, his brother must marry his sister-in-law); a violent son, a shedder of blood, one who eats upon the mountains (Ezek. 18:10-11) (which includes soldiers and picnickers); a raped girl who did not, or could not, cry for help (Deut. 22:23-27); incense, like that burned during Catholic High Mass (Isa. 1:13); loaning money for profit and accruing interest, like banks do (Ezek. 18:13); pride, including, say, school pride, or pride in America (Prov. 16:18); kidnapping (Exod. 21:16; Deut. 24:7); lying, even white lying (Prov. 11:22; 12:22; Lev. 19:11) (Never mind that Abraham, Isaac, Jacob, and David all told lies: Gen. 12:12, 13;

20:2; Gen. 26:7; Gen. 27:24; 1 Sam. 20:6); obstinately disobeying a relative, even your drug-dealing uncle (Deut. 18:21); sowing discord in your family (Prov. 6:19); preventing foreign worshippers from entering your church (Ezek. 44:7); marriage of a believer and a nonbeliever (Gen. 24:3); race-mixing (Deut. 7:3); cursing or insulting royalty, even the English or Saudis (2 Sam. 16:9 and 2 Kings 6:31-32); touching Mount Sinai, even if while on a Smithsonian tour (Exod. 19:12-13); oppressing/exploiting the poor and needy, even if indirectly (Ezek. 18:12); idolatry and idol worship, even Hollywood idols (Lev. 20:1-5; Deut. 13:2-18; 17:2-7); whoever would not seek the God of Israel (as opposed to the Christian God) (2 Chron. 15:13); and so on and so on.

Even a glance at a list like this one (and it barely scratches the surface of the thou shalts, thou shalt nots) demonstrates that the moral injunctions of the Bible are relative at best. Even biblical literalists can't help being selective in picking and choosing what they want to believe is *really* God's Word, and what is *really* an abomination. Many biblical scholars, who simply cannot let go of their belief in a God-breathed Bible, insist that the Bible doesn't *really* condemn this or that behavior; the Bible's idioms, metaphors, and contexts simply need to be reinterpreted, the seemingly damning texts need to be retranslated. Many "literalists" treat the biblical text as a kind of Divine code still in need of cracking.

Deconstructionists argue that Christianity is fraudulent because it is authorized by a text that is not literally perfect and therefore not a legitimate source of truth or religion. In response, fundamentalists have been forced to maintain that the Bible must be word-for-word perfect to be true at all. Yet I have never met a fundamentalist yet who lived what he said he believed; yet most fundamentalists are quick to judge others, especially those who don't ascribe to their particular version of their particular religion.

If believers could acknowledge fallibility, if people could set aside religious elitism, superstition, egotism, and petty differences, our spiritual focus would shift *away* from the dictatorial constriction of organized religion and *toward* loving, living communion with the one God and with each other. In my view, the world could effect no greater good.

Chapter 8

The Fallible Bible

I wasn't raised fundamentalist and only in college started thinking in Christian terms. Interestingly, at the same time I was accepting the Bible as God's Word, my religion classes were challenging the privileged Christian perspective, especially biblical infallibility.

I studied the Bible on my own, Genesis through Revelations, closely underlining and writing marginal notes in several translations. I got books, concordances, commentaries, and tapes at Christian bookstores, joined Campus Crusaders and other campus Christian groups, attended a missions conference, read Christian magazines, went to churches (plural), engaged in lots of conversation and asked lots of questions. Although I accepted Biblical infallibility for a time, it was inevitable that I would have to let go of that belief for one fundamental reason: The Bible wasn't infallible.

One thing I know from experience is that if your mind is bent toward believing the Bible, it's going to take a little effort on your part to allow reality to seep in. Even though my belief in the Bible was relatively new, I still felt considerable anxiety and depression when I went through the process of relinquishment. Of course that's a natural response to any major life transition, especially one involving a critical paradigm shift. But the negative feeling didn't last long. In time I felt a tremendous sense of relief. One thing I've learned is that in the end, truth always feels better than blind faith in myths, regardless of how many perks come with blind faith.

In a few short years I'd made a major shift into Christian faith and another back out of that faith. Although in both cases there was a definite threshold that marked the start of the shift, the total volte-face in each case took many years. Not until my forties was I able to consider myself entirely a Deist. But at the same time, the truth is that deep down I've always been a Deist. Spiritually, God has always been Number One, and truth has always been the fundamental ground of what I believe and what I am. The question, of course, is: What is truth? Certainly there is truth that transcends mundane fact. But that truth never contradicts mundane fact. Higher truth and "lower" truth are always part of Truth. One never excludes the other.

Ironically, I first saw the Bible's fallacies in a religion class I was taking just before my initial born again experience. The emotion of the born again process and the influence of my many Christian friends and professors turned my head away from criticism and toward exploration and acceptance. But because I studied the Bible so closely for myself, it was inevitable that I would right away start seeing incongruities. Then I started looking for them, seeking them out, checking for outside resources. I found an immensity of proof that the Bible was not infallible, not by any stretch of the imagination.

Not only that, scholars and lay people alike had been noting biblical incongruities for centuries. It would be impossible to cite them all. I think it important to provide ample examples, if only to help the reader, especially a fundamentalist reader, experience to some extend the process of relinquishment.

To keep it simple, in addition to recent scholarly works and popular books and websites, for my primary sources I rely heavily on works that for me were most influential: *The Christ: A Critical Review and Analysis of the Evidence of His Existence* by John E. Remsberg; *The Life of Jesus Critically Examined* by David Friedrich Strauss (1892 edition translated by George Eliot); the writings of Thomas Paine (esp. *The Age of Reason*); and *Understanding the New Testament*, a college textbook by Howard Clark Kee, Franklin W. Young, and Karlfried Froehlich.

Scholars have detailed numerous contradictions between biblical accounts and other, more reliable historical records. I avoid comparisons to outside sources, because the Bible's own histories contain ample incongruities; I'm relying on the reader's innate reason rather than on outside knowledge.

I will concentrate on inter-text inconsistencies, which occur when two different text accounts of the exact same event contain contradictory elements, or when specific facts given in one text are different from those facts given in another text. Some textbooks comparing the New and/or Old Testament lay out the texts in columns, which is especially useful when showing inconsistencies in chronology or detail. Apologists sometimes offer absurd explanations in order to force-fit the discrepancies into a distorted version of "truth." My task here isn't to critique the apologists but rather to present a case via examples appealing to any reader's common sense.

Consider first these inconsistencies: The sons of Eliphaz were Teman, Omar, Zepho, Gatam, and Kenaz (Gen. 36:11) v. The sons of Eliphaz were Teman, Omar, Zepho, Kenaz (Gen. 36:15-16) v. The sons of Eliphaz are Teman, Omar, Zephi, Gatam, Kenaz, Timna, and Amalek (1 Chron. 1:35-36).

And: The fathers of the twelve tribes of Israel were Reuben, Simeon, Levi, Judah, Zebulun, Issachar, Dan, Gad, Asher, Naphtali, Joseph, and Benjamin (Gen. 49:2-28) v. The fathers of the twelve tribes of Israel were Reuben, Simeon, Levi, Judah, Zebulun, Issachar, Manasseh, Gad, Asher, Naphtali, Joseph, and Benjamin (Rev. 7:4-8).

And: Jethro was the father-in-law of Moses (Ex. 3:1) v. Hobab was the father-in-law of Moses (Num. 10:29; Judg. 4:11).

Maybe most Christians don't really care about the genealogy of Eliphaz, don't know why the fathers of the twelve tribes might be significant, and don't have much interest in the wife of Moses, much less her father. But what about the bloodline of Jesus's father, Joseph? Surely that's important. But accounts differ. Joseph's father was Jacob (Matt. 1:16) v. Joseph's father was Heli (Luke 3:23).

One might ask a literalist to explain why Matthew's genealogy of Jesus is so different from Luke's. Matthew 1:17 says, "So all the generations from Abraham to David are fourteen generations; and from David to the deportation to Babylon, fourteen generations; and from the deportation to Babylon to the Messiah, fourteen generations." That's a total of forty-two generations. Luke's list goes all the way back to Adam, the son of God, but from Abraham forward, Luke lists fifty-seven generations, not forty-two. Matthew and Luke are close in their list, starting with Abraham and ending with David, but Luke lists fifteen generations, not fourteen. The first fourteen for each are the same except that from Hezron to Boaz, Matthew lists Aram, Aminadab, Nahshon, and Salmon, but Luke lists Arni, Admin, Amminadab, Nahshon, and Sala. From that point on, the genealogies are completely different.

These discrepancies cast immense doubt not only on the ancestry of Jesus, but also on the accuracy of Old and New Testament genealogies in general and on the literal perfection of the Bible as a whole.

Some "small" discrepancies make a big difference theologically. For instance, "No one has ascended into heaven except the one who descended from heaven, the Son of Man" (John 3:13) v. "Elijah ascended in a whirlwind into heaven" (2 Kings 2:11) and "Enoch walked with God; then he was no more, because God took him" (Gen. 5:24), and "By faith Enoch was taken so that he did not experience death; and 'he was not found, because God had taken him'" (Heb. 11:5). Besides the fact that by being born, Jesus "descended" just like everyone else, accepting the assumption of John while ignoring the other texts casts doubt on the special Assumption of Christ, which casts doubt on his special ability to resurrect from the dead and to resurrect others from death, which casts doubt on his special saving grace. John's assumption could justify an otherwise invalid conclusion that Jesus was the special Son of Man, the Son of God, or God. (And making Jesus one Person of the Triune God introduces polytheism into previously monotheistic Judaism; one might even assert that Christianity *is* the polytheizing of Judaism.)

Sometimes seemingly small discrepancies have more complicated implications. For instance, Jacob was buried in a cave at Machpelah bought from Ephron the Hittite (Gen. 50:13) v. Jacob was buried in the sepulchre at Shechem, bought from the sons of Hamor (Acts 7:15-16). This discrepancy is important. For one thing, the writer of Acts is quoting Stephen, who was filled with the Holy Spirit and who saw the glory of God and Jesus standing at the right hand of God (v. 54-55). Could someone so inspired incorrectly quote the scriptures? It's just plain common sense that God didn't inspire at least one of these key players: the writer (or re-writer) of Genesis, the writer of Acts, or Stephen. (It should be noted with irony that Saul, aka Paul, that quintessential misquoter, witnessed and approved the stoning of Stephen, according to Acts 7:58-8:1).

Can a true believer, speaking in the Spirit, get the facts wrong? Is the Bible simply recording human fallibility infallibly, or is the Bible itself fallible?

We might accept that Stephen was a mere mortal with imperfect recall, but what about Jesus? Shouldn't we be able to trust the Son of God's words as literal truth?

According to Matthew 13:31-32, Jesus said, "The kingdom of heaven is like a mustard seed that someone took and sowed in his field; it is the smallest of all the seeds, but when it has grown it is the greatest of shrubs and becomes a tree." The problems here are that the mustard seed is not the smallest of all seeds (seeds of orchid, poppy, petunia, begonia, millet, amaranth, and tobacco, to name just a few examples, are smaller); the mustard seed does not produce the greatest of shrubs; and shrubs do not grow into trees.

What do these inaccuracies prove? That God is ignorant about his own Creation? Then God is not omnipotent. That God doesn't care about accuracy? Then there could be no claim that any of the Bible is word-for-word perfect. That the text is "accurate" within the context of that biblical time and place? Then that and any other given text need not literally apply to us here and now. That the text is merely symbolic? But symbols only work if they accurately represent something that exists, and besides, the entire content of the Bible, including the resurrection, the histories, and the existence of God, could then be considered merely symbolic. Do these inaccuracies prove that Jesus was ignorant of the facts? Then Jesus is not God or even privy to all that God knows. Or do they prove that the Bible was not written by God but by human beings?

In Luke 4:17-21, Jesus misquotes Isaiah 61:1-2. If Jesus is not infallible, the Bible is not infallible.

Who killed Saul? It matters. Saul killed himself (1 Sam. 31:4) v. A Philistine killed Saul (2 Sam. 21:12) v. An Amalekite killed Saul (2 Sam. 1:9-10) v. God put Saul to death (1 Chron. 10:14). Theologically, there is a huge difference between being killed by an enemy (and which enemy has its own implications), committing suicide, and blaming God.

Those in the "end of the world" camp cite Matthew 24:35, Mark 13:31, Luke 21:33, Psalms 102:25-26, 2 Peter 3:10, and Hebrews 1:10-11 to prove that heaven and earth will pass away. But other passages claim that the earth remains forever—Ecclesiastes 1:4 and Psalms 78:69, for instance.

Sometimes the truth about God would be nice to know because it would give us a sense of security. For instance, God tempts no man (James 1:13); God tempted Abraham (Gen. 22:1); "Lead us not into temptation" (Matt. 6:13).

2 Sam. 24:1 says, "Again the anger of the Lord was kindled against Israel, and he incited David against them, saying, 'Go, count the people of Israel and Judah.'" But in a different version of this same story, recounted in 1 Chronicles 21:1, "Satan stood up against Israel, and incited David to count the people of Israel." Most of us would say that being incited by God is the opposite of being incited by the devil.

Although the census must have been important, given that David had to be incited either by God or Satan, does anyone in this century really care about the census count results, which differ in each account (2 Sam. 24:9 v. 1 Chron. 21:5)?

Does God change his mind? No: (Num. 23:19; Mal. 3:6; James 1:17) v. Yes: (Exod. 32:14; Num. 14:12, 20; 2 Sam. 24:16) v. God changes his mind, then changes his mind again (Amos 7:1-6), in which case, God relents on one curse only to create another.

One of the biggest theological discrepancies in the Bible as a whole is whether or not one reaps what one sows in this life, and whether or not one is justified by works or by faith. Some sow wheat but reap thorns (Jer. 12:13). Some sow but will reap nothing (Mic. 6:15). Some reap without sowing (Matt. 25:26; Luke 19:22). A man reaps what he sows (2 Col. 9:6; Gal. 6:7). We are justified by works, not by faith (Matt. 7:21; Luke 10:36-37; Rom. 2:6; James 2:24). We are justified by faith, not by works (John 3:16; Rom. 3:20-26; Eph. 2:8-9; Gal. 2:16).

Many Christians worry that they might have committed blasphemy against the Holy Spirit, the one unforgivable sin (Matt. 12:31-32; Mark 3:29; Luke 12:10). But how can there be an unforgivable sin if all sins are forgivable (Acts 13:39; Rom. 3:21-26; Col. 2:13; Heb. 10:12; 1 John 1:9)? If blasphemy is truly unforgivable, wouldn't that mean that forgiveness is weaker than sin? Wouldn't that imply that evil is greater than good, that the power of Satan is greater than the power of God?

In Mark 2:26, Abiathar was said to be the high priest when David ate the bread. But Mark has misquoted 1 Samuel 21:1-6, which says that

Ahimelech was high priest when David ate the bread. Since Abiathar was the son of Ahimelech, and both son and father were priests, this error in detail might seem inconsequential.

But each man's role in David's life has a radically different *significance*. Ahimalech was the priest of Nob to whom David fled from the wrath of Saul (1 Sam. 21:1-15). It was he that gave David and his men the holy bread. He also gave David the sword of Goliath. Saul had Ahimelech and most of his family killed for helping David.

Abiathar, on the other hand, escaped the murder of the priests of Nob and joined David's outlaw band, serving as David's personal priest (1 Sam. 23:6). Although Abiathar became chief priest as a reward for his loyalty to David, he was later banished by King Solomon because he had supported Adonijah, Solomon's rival to the throne (1 Kings 2:26-27).

Was Lot Abraham's nephew (Gen. 14:12) or brother (Gen. 14:14,16)? Was Joseph sold into captivity by the Midianites (Gen. 37:36) or by the Ishmaelites (Gen. 39:1)? Did Aaron die on Mt. Hor (Num. 33:38) or in Mosera (Deut. 10:6)? After Aaron's death, did the Israelites journey from Mt. Hor, to Zalmonah, to Punon, etc. (Num. 33:41-42) or from Mosera, to Gudgodah, to Jotbath (Deut. 10:6-7)? Did Joshua himself capture Debir (Josh. 10:38-40), or was Debir captured by Othniel, who thereby obtained the hand of Caleb's daughter, Achsah (Judg. 1:11-15)?

And just for the record, the total of all three tribes is 22,300, not 22,000 (Num. 3:17). The number of cities listed is thirty-six, not twenty-nine, as is summarized in the last verse (Josh. 15:21-32). The cities listed are fifteen, not fourteen (Josh. 15:33-36). The cities listed number fourteen, not thirteen (Josh. 19:2-6).

More inconsistencies: Sisera was sleeping when Jael killed him (Judg. 4:21) v. Sisera was standing when Jael killed him (Judg. 5:25-27). Jesse had seven sons plus David, or eight total (1 Sam. 16:10-11, 17:12) v. Jesse had seven sons total (1 Chron. 2:13-15). Saul knew David well before his encounter with Goliath (1 Sam. 16:19-23) v. Saul did not know David at the time of his encounter with Goliath and had to ask Abner and then David himself who David was (1 Sam. 17:55-58). David killed Goliath with a slingshot (1 Sam. 17:50) v. David killed Goliath (again?) with a sword (1 Sam. 17:51). Saul inquired of the Lord but received no answer (1 Sam. 28:6) v. Saul died for not inquiring of the

Lord (1 Chron. 10:13-14). Michal had no sons and would have no sons (2 Sam. 6:23) v. Michal had five sons with David (2 Sam. 21:8).

David took 700 horsemen (cavalry) from King Hadadezer (2 Sam. 8:4) v. 7,000 cavalry (horsemen) (1 Chron. 18:4). David killed 700 Aramean chariot teams and 40,000 horsemen (2 Sam. 10:18) v. 7,000 Aramean charioteers and 40,000 foot soldiers (1 Chron. 19:18). 800,000 men in Israel and 500,000 men of Judah were able to draw the sword (2 Sam. 24:9) v. 1,100,000 men in Israel and 470,000 men of Judah drew the sword (1 Chron. 21:5). David paid 50 shekels of silver for the purchase of a property (2 Sam. 24:24) v. 600 shekels of gold for the same spread (1 Chron. 21:22-25).

Solomon had forty thousand stalls for his horses (1 Kings 4:26) v. four thousand stalls (2 Chron. 9:25). Solomon had 3,300 supervisors in charge of the stonecutters and laborers (1 Kings 5:16) v. 3,600 overseers in charge (2 Chron. 2:18). Solomon had two thousand baths (1 Kings 7:26) v. three thousand baths (2 Chron. 4:5). Ahaziah began to rule at age twenty-two (2 Kings 8:26) v. age forty-two (2 Chron. 22:2). Solomon had 550 chief officers (1 Kings 9:23) v. 250 chief officers (2 Chron. 8:10). Jehoiachin was eighteen years old when he began to reign in Jerusalem, and he reigned three months (2 Kings 24:8) v. Jehoiachin was eight years old he reigned three months and ten days (2 Chron. 36:9). Nebuzaradan came to rule Jerusalem on the seventh day of the fifth month (2 Kings 25:8) v. the tenth day of the fifth month (Jer. 52:12).

Seven males and one female do not total five (1 Chron. 3:19-20). But the names of five sons of Shecaniah are listed, not six. (1 Chron. 3:22). But the names of five sons of Jeduthun are listed, not six. (1 Chron. 25:3). The total of the gold and silver vessels is 2,499, not 5,400 (Ezra 1:9-11). The whole assembly together is 29,818, not 42,360 (Ezra 2:64). The whole assembly together is 31,089, not 42,360 (Neh. 7:66). Ezra 2 and Neh. 7 list the subclans that returned from the Captivity and the number in each. Out of approx thirty-five subclans listed, over half of the numbers disagree.

Jehoram was thirty-two when he began to reign and he reigned eight years, until his death at age forty (2 Chron. 21:20). His youngest son, Ahaziah, immediately took over the reign at age forty-two (2 Chron. 22:1-2). How could a son, much less the youngest son, be two years older than his father?

The devil took Jesus to the pinnacle of the temple, then to the mountaintop (Matt. 4:5-8) v. The devil took Jesus first to the mountaintop, then to the pinnacle of the temple (Luke 4:5-9). "Again, the devil took him to a very high mountain and showed him all the kingdoms of the world and their splendor" (Matt. 4:8). Even from the tallest mountain, even with 20/20 vision, no one could see our entire spherical world at a glance.

"Now when Jesus heard that John had been arrested, he withdrew to Galilee. He left Nazareth and made his home in Capernaum by the sea, in the territory of Zebulun and Naphtali" (Matt. 4:12-13). Nazareth and Capernaum are both in Galilee. He didn't withdraw to Galilee if he was already there. This is like saying he withdrew to California, leaving San Francisco to make his home in L.A.

"Then he returned from the region of Tyre, and went by way of Sidon towards the Sea of Galilee, in the region of the Decapolis" (Mark 7:31). Sidon is to the north of Tyre on the Mediterranean Sea, and the Decapolis is south of the Sea of Galilee, both of which are south of Sidon and Tyre. It's like saying he returned from Tulsa, and went by way of Chicago towards Atlanta in the region of Florida.

Jesus gave the Sermon of [on] the Mount and later healed Peter's mother-in-law (Matt. 5:3-12; 8:14-15) v. Jesus healed Peter's mother-in-law and later gave the Sermon of [below] the Mount (Luke 4:38-39; 6:20-26). Jesus heals the leper before entering Peter's house (Matt. 8:1-2; 8:14) v. Jesus heals the leper after leaving Peter's house (Mark 1:29; 1:40). Jesus calms the storm and later calls Matthew (Matt. 8:23-27; 9:9) v. Jesus calls Matthew and then calms the storm (Luke 5:27-28; 8:22-25). The cleansing of the temple occurs at the end of Jesus's career (Matt. 21:12-13) v. The temple cleansing occurs near the beginning of Jesus's career (John 2:13-16).

The fig tree withers immediately after being cursed by Jesus; the disciples see it and are amazed (Matt. 21:19-20) v. The disciples first see the withered fig tree the following day (Mark 11:13-14; 20-21). Jesus curses the fig tree and then cleanses the temple (Mark 11:13-15) v. Jesus cleanses the temple and then curses the fig tree (Luke 4:5-9). Jesus was crucified at nine o'clock in the morning (Mark 15:25) v. Jesus was brought to Pilate at about noon (John 19:14-15). Satan enters Judas before the supper (Luke 22:3-23) v. Satan enters Judas during the supper (John 13:27).

Not everyone who calls on the name of the Lord will be saved (Matt. 7:21) v. Whoever calls on the name of the Lord will be saved (Acts 2:21; Rom. 10:13) v. Those God calls to himself will be saved (Acts 2:39).

The Transfiguration occurs six days after Jesus foretells his suffering (Matt. 17:1-2; Mark 9:2) v. The Transfiguration takes place about eight days after Jesus foretells his suffering (Luke 9:28-29).

The presence of Jesus's betrayer is revealed during the Last Supper (Matt. 26:21; Mark 14:18) v. The presence of Jesus's betrayer is revealed after the Last Supper (Luke 22:14-21). Jesus is tempted in the wilderness and later John is arrested (Mark 1:12-13; 6:17-18) v. John is arrested and later Jesus is tempted in the wilderness (Luke 3:19-20; 4:1-13). Jesus begins his ministry after the arrest of John the Baptist (Mark 1:14) v. Jesus begins his ministry before the arrest of John the Baptist (John 3:22-24). After the feeding of the 5000, Jesus and the disciples go to Gennesaret (Mark 6:53) v. they go to Capernaum (John 6:17-25).

Regarding the crucifixion: Was Jesus's robe scarlet (Matt. 27:28) or purple (Mark 15:17; John 19:2)? Was the robe put on Jesus during his trial (John 19:1-5) or after Pilate delivered him to be crucified (Matt. 27:26-28; Mark 15:15-17)? Mark 15:25 says that Jesus was crucified at the third hour, Luke 23:43-44 says it was before the sixth hour, and John 19:14-16 says it was after the sixth hour.

Who first arrived at the empty tomb after the resurrection? Mary Magdalene and the other Mary arrived first (Matthew) v. Mary Magdalene, Mary the mother of James, and Salome (Mark) v. "The women" (Luke) v. Mary Magdalene (John).

When did she/they first arrive at the tomb? When it was still dark (John) v. As day was dawning (Matthew) v. Early dawn (Luke) v. When the sun had already risen (Mark).

Who first sees Jesus? Mary Magdalene and the other Mary (Matthew) v. Mary Magdalene (Mark and John) v. Cleopas and another follower of Jesus; possibly Peter at the same time (Luke).

Given what a pivotal character Judas was in the story of Jesus's betrayal and crucifixion, one would think that Christians would have etched in stone the story of his life's end. But notice how the accounts given in Matthew and Acts differ. In Matthew, Judas returned to the priests the thirty pieces of silver he got for turning Jesus over to the authorities, then hanged himself; the priests used the silver to buy the potter's field as a place to bury foreigners, hence its name Field of Blood (Matt. 27:3-10). According to the Acts account, Judas bought the field with the silver; and falling headlong on the field, he burst open in the middle and all his bowels gushed out, hence the name Field of Blood (Acts 1:16-20).

Contrary to what it claims, the passage quoted in Matthew 27:5-10 is not in Jeremiah. Some argue that it refers to Zechariah 11:12-13. But this passage refers not to Judas, but to the prophet Zechariah, who, "on behalf of the sheep merchants . . . became the shepherd of the flock doomed to slaughter." The thirty shekels of silver were Jeremiah's wages for the good work of a shepherd, money that God instructed him to throw into the treasury. Judas's work was betrayal of a person for blood money, which by God's law could not be given to the treasury. In Zechariah there is no mention of a potter or a field.

Compare the stories of the Capernaum centurion, Matthew 8:5-13, and Luke 7:1-10. The centurion comes to Jesus in person (Matt.) v. The centurion sends Jewish elders to Jesus (Luke). The centurion says, "I am not worthy to have you come under my roof . . ." (Matt.) v. The centurion's friends say, "I am not worthy to have you come under my roof . . ." (Luke). The exact quotes differ in each account. The gist of the two passages is the same, but one is a direct quote of the centurion, the other an indirect quote from the centurion via friends. One claims that the servant will be healed, the other humbly asks that the servant be healed.

Contrary to the claims of Creationists, there are many problems with the Creation story found in the first few chapters of Genesis. What was the source of light on the first day if there was no sun, moon, or stars until the fourth day? How could there be Day and Night on the first day if there was no sun? How could a vegetable kingdom in a stage highly organized and advanced enough to be reproducing fruit bearing trees exist on the third day without photosynthesis from the sun? Planet earth was derived from and could not have existed before the sun and stars that make up our galaxy. It has taken millions of years for the light of many of the stars in our galaxy to reach earth. *Yom* in Hebrew and *hemera* in Greek both mean a twenty-four-hour period from sunset to sunset, not an era or period of millions of years as claimed by some "literalist" fundamentalists. If a day equals an era, Adam, Eve, Cain, Noah, and the other characters of that period would have lived millions of years and the daily events of their lives would have taken vast amounts of time. How could plants and animals survive a million year night with no sunlight?

"And to every beast of the earth, and to every bird of the air, and to everything that creeps on the earth, everything that has the breath of life, I have given every green plant for food." Carnivores are not vegetarians.

"So out of the ground the Lord God formed every animal of the field and every bird of the air, and brought them to the man to see what he would call them; and whatever the man called every living creature, that was its name. The man gave names to all cattle, and to the birds of the air, and to every animal of the field." It would be impossible for a representative of every single of the tens of millions of species of living creatures to be delivered alive at Adam's feet for naming. Many creatures, such as penguins, polar bears, whales, or salmon, could not survive in Adam's Middle East environment. How would Adam even see microorganisms?

Which is correct? Trees were created before man was created (Gen. 1:11-12, 26-27) v. Man was created before trees were created (Gen. 2:4-9). Birds were created before man was created (Gen. 1:20-21, 26-27) v. Man was created before birds were created (Gen. 2:7, 19). Animals were created before man was created (Gen. 1:24-27) v. Man was created before animals were created (Gen. 2:7, 19). Man and woman were created at the same time (Gen. 1:26-27) v. Man was created first, woman sometime later (Gen. 2:7, 21-22).

God warned Adam that he could eat freely of every tree of the garden of Eden except for the tree of the knowledge of good and evil, "for in the day that you eat of it you shall die," yet Adam did not die that day; he lived to be 930 years old (Gen. 5:5).

The Lord God said to the serpent, "Because you have done this [tempted Eve], cursed are you among all animals and among all wild creatures; upon your belly you shall go, and dust you shall eat all the days of your life." How would a serpent "go" in the first place if not on its belly? Do serpents eat dust?

"Then Cain went away from the presence of the Lord, and settled in the land of Nod, east of Eden. Cain knew his wife, and she conceived and bore Enoch; and he built a city, and named it Enoch after his son Enoch. To Enoch was born Irad." Adam and Eve had two sons, Cain and

Abel, and Cain killed Abel. Where did Cain's wife come from? Where did Enoch's wife come from?

Here are some of the problems with the story of Noah's Ark.

First, the ark measures 450 feet by 75 feet by 45 feet, which could not hold two of every animal representing tens of millions of species, not to mention their food.

"I am going to bring a flood of waters on the earth, to destroy from under heaven all flesh in which is the breath of life; everything that is on the earth shall die." How were sea creatures killed, if they thrived in the waters?

Noah was to take seven pairs of all clean animals and birds (Gen. 7:2-3) v. Noah took two of each animal, including clean animals (Gen. 7:8-9). Did all those animals just voluntarily show up right on schedule from all over the world? How did animals from other continents cross the oceans? How did polar bears withstand Middle East climate? How did tiny critters and microorganisms and creatures with very short lifespans travel thousands of miles to reach the ark? What did animals with specialized diets, like pandas and koalas, eat during their trek to the ark and during the flood? How were animals kept from killing their natural prey? How did water creatures like whales and lobsters survive on board?

Noah and his family enter the Ark (Gen. 7:7). Then, a little while later, Noah and his family enter the Ark (Gen. 7:13).

According to Genesis 8:10-11, "He waited another seven days, and again he sent out the dove from the ark; and the dove came back to him in the evening, and there in its beak was a freshly plucked olive leaf; so Noah knew that the waters had subsided from the earth." Couldn't he have just glanced overboard? If all life, including vegetation, had been destroyed after a year underwater, where did the freshly plucked olive leaf come from? If all life had been destroyed, how was the vegetation revived, and what would the herbivores eat in the meantime? What would the carnivores eat if not each other; and given that there were only two of each animal remaining, that would mean instant extinction for many species. Where did all that subsiding water go?

According to Genesis 6:4, there were Nephilim (giants) before the flood. If all creatures were annihilated by the flood, including all humans except for Noah and his clan, how could there still have been Nephilim after the flood (Num. 13:33)?

After the planet had dried out, people started repopulating. Eventually it became necessary to record genealogies to keep the nations of families straight. Genesis 10:5 begins the lists of Noah's descendants: "These are the descendants of Japheth in their lands, with their own language, by their families, in their nations." But one chapter later, Genesis 11:1-6 says: "Now the whole earth had one language and the same words . . . And the Lord said, 'Look, they are one people, and they have all one language.'" Did these nations of families have one language or many?

Terah was 70 years old when his son Abram was born (Gen. 11:26) v. Terah was 205 years old when he died, which makes Abram 135 at the time (Gen. 11:32). Abram was 75 when he left Haran; this was after Terah died; thus, Terah could have been no more than 145 when he died; or Abram was only 75 years old after he had lived 135 years (Gen. 12:4; Acts 7:4).

The accounts of Hezekiah recorded in Isaiah 38:1-8 vary considerably from the same accounts in 2 Kings 20. In addition, the Isaiah account says, "This is the sign to you from the Lord, that the Lord will do this thing that he has promised: See, I will make the shadow cast by the declining sun on the dial of Ahaz turn back ten steps." If the earth stopped rotating at its normal speed or moved backward, the impact would be so catastrophic that the world as we know it would cease to exist.

Joshua 10:12-14 records a similar event: The sun and moon stopped "for about a whole day. There has been no day like it before or since, when the Lord heeded a human voice; for the Lord fought for Israel." No day before or since when the Lord heeded a human voice? Wrong. The Old and New Testaments are full of instances of the Lord heeding human voices, including Hezekiah's. The sun did not stand still as it did for Joshua; it moved backwards.

Habakkuk 3:11 also makes note of the moon standing still in its place. Such an image, even if only meant metaphorically, betrays the OT writer's ignorance about physics. Such ignorance might be forgivable in a work of literature, given the era in which it was written, but when that literature is taken as absolute word-for-word God-breathed perfection in an age that should know better, the consequences can be as catastrophic as our planet standing still.

Matthew 26:47-56 ends, "But all this has taken place, so that the scriptures of the prophets may be fulfilled." The details of "all this" are: The large crowd with weapons; Judas betraying Jesus with a kiss; the arrest of Jesus; one of the disciples cutting off the ear of the high priest's slave with a sword; Jesus telling them that "all who take the sword will perish by the sword"; Jesus not calling legions of angels to save him. But not a single detail of "all this" fulfills any scripture or prophecy.

1 Peter 3:18-22 misinterprets the story of Noah's ark:

> For Christ also suffered for sins once for all, the righteous for the unrighteous, in order to bring you to God. He was put to death in the flesh, but made alive in the spirit, in which also he went and made a proclamation to the spirits in prison, who in former times did not obey, when God waited patiently in the days of Noah, during the building of the ark, in which a few, that is, eight persons, were saved through water. And baptism, which this prefigured, now saves you—not as a removal of dirt from the body, but as an appeal to God for a good conscience, through the resurrection of Jesus Christ, who has gone into heaven and is at the right hand of God, with angels, authorities, and powers made subject to him.

Noah was not saved "through"/by/because of the waters, he was saved *from* the waters. Peter is saying that when Christ died, he "went" in spirit to make a proclamation to all those bad people that God had destroyed with the flood. He doesn't mention whether or not Christ saved those people. How does the flood prefigure baptism, when Noah and his family were the only ones to *not* get wet? Peter implies that the flood was meant to remove dirt from the body, which makes no sense. The analogy between the flood and baptism is not only confused, it means the opposite of what Peter intends. The flood waters destroyed; baptismal waters save.

Similarly, Matthew 12:17-21 misquotes Isaiah 42:1-4.

Matthew 13:35 misquotes Psalms 78:2-3.

John 13:18-19 misinterprets Psalms 41:4-9.

In Acts 1:15-20, Peter misquotes Psalms 109:8 and Psalms 69:25.

In Acts 2:16-17, Peter misquotes Joel 2:28. It probably doesn't matter whether the old men dreamed dreams or saw visions, or if the young men saw visions or dreamed dreams. What matters is that Peter assumed that the Spirit had been poured out because it was the last days, which, 2000 years later, we know was not the case.

What is Peter quoting in Acts 4:26-27? He is probably misquoting Psalms 2:1-2.

Romans 9:33 and 1 Peter 2:6-8 both misquote and misinterpret Isaiah 8:14-15 and Isaiah 28:16.

1 Peter 2:21-22 misquotes Isaiah 53:9.

Besides these textual problems, there are issues of common sense that cast doubt on fundamental Christian assumptions. For example, thinking Christians have realized that if Jesus was born of Mary, then Mary is his mother. If God is One, and if God (the Holy Spirit) is the father, and if Jesus is God, then Mary is his "wife" (concubine, "handmaid"). If Jesus is God and if God is the Father of all mankind, then Mary is Jesus's daughter. If Mary is the daughter of God and if Jesus is the son of God, then Mary is Jesus's sister.

If Jesus is God, then the son is the father and the father is the son, which by definition is impossible, since the father is the source of the son and the son the offspring of the father. The son must be younger than the father, in which case they could not be equal, or equally eternal. If God is One, then God cannot be two. If God cannot die, and if Jesus died, then Jesus cannot be God.

Trinitarians should look up and read these excerpts from the Gospel of John, all of which are spoken by Jesus. Clearly Jesus and God are not the same being. (3:17; 3:34; 3:35; 5:19-20; 5:24; 6:29; 6:38; 6:57; 7:16-18; 7:28-29; 8:18; 8:28-29; 8:42-43; 8:54-55; 8:58; 10:14; 10:17; 10:18; 10:34-36; 10:38; 13:20; 15:1, 5; 16:26-28; 17:20-23).

If you looked them up, you realize that these few verses from John alone make it obvious that Jesus and God are two separate beings. Yet fundamentalist contortionists torque the most embarrassing intellectual and moral explanations to force-fit God into Jesus. Jesus and God are two "persons" of the same God?—Or according to TV evangelist Benny Hinn, nine persons, three each for God, the Spirit, and Jesus?

No. Jesus is clearly not God. Only God is God. If Jesus were a manifestation, aspect, or "person" of God, then God is the supreme egomaniac, giving birth to himself, praying to himself, worshipping himself, glorifying himself, even committing suicide for himself. But as should be obvious to anyone who has actually read the gospels, the Jesus portrayed there is in fact not a psychotic projection or half of a divine split personality; he is a loving child of God, and he is Messiah (whatever that might mean). Of course, in reality he might be a myth or legend deified by the Bible writers.

The doctrine of the Trinity, proclaimed absolute and eternal 350 years after the death of Christ (by the Council of Constantinople in 381, when it ratified the Nicene Creed), is a dramatic instance of belief in an anthropomorphic male God giving rise to idolatry.

Some conceive Jesus as half man, half God. But half God is not God. For some, Jesus is all-God by virtue of his being part of a Trinity that is pure, absolute Deity. That perspective waters down God, elevates the human to the status of Divinity, and slices the God pie into three unequal pieces. Any way you slice it, mystifying the human Jesus diminishes the One God.

Those who quote "the Father and I are one" (John 10:30) should also quote "I ask . . . on behalf of those who will believe in me through their [the disciples'] word, that they may all be one. As you, Father, are in me and I am in you, may they also be in us . . . so that they may be one, as we are one, I in them and you in me, that they may become completely one" (John 17:20-23).

If being in communion with God is being God, then Christians are pantheists, not monotheists.

The biblical Jesus makes our relationship clear when he says that he is the vine, we are the branches, and God is the gardener. Though branches are dependent upon the vine for survival, branches are part of the vine and of the same vine substance. The gardener is of a completely different substance. The dependence of the vine and its branches upon the gardener is categorically different than the dependence of the branches upon the vine.

The Bible writers are branches witnessing to the vine. The gospel writers are branches. Readers of the gospels are branches. We are not God. The gospel writers are not God. Jesus is not God, according to the biblical Jesus himself.

Once I'd worked through all this, it was clear to me that the Bible was not God, was not the Word or words of God, was not an aspect or extension of God, was not the exclusive revelation of God. Only God was God.

Although I didn't yet know it, that was a decidedly Deist position, and I was a Deist. But until I realized that, until I understood that a shift in

God context was not the Nietzschean death of God, my lost faith anxiety could not be relieved.

Chapter 9

Mythic Origins of the Bible

Once I recognized the Bible's fallacies, I couldn't accept biblical infallibility without being dishonest. And really, neither can you. I would even go so far as to say that in this day and age, being ignorant of the Bible's contradictions is being dishonest, or at least irresponsible.

Once I saw the Bible's fallibility, of course I wanted to share this new insight. My fundamentalist comrades tended to be indifferent if not hostile. Because they believed that their religious ideology was absolute, not only religious myths, but also self-contradictions and obvious inaccuracies in objective fact were disregarded, "explained" with fallacious arguments or downright lies, or deflected with mantras of memorized Bible verses.

Never have I met a fundamentalist who has memorized the entire Bible or even more than a handful of select verses stocked to prove his convictions. Verses that disprove those same convictions are not just ignored; the person pointing them out is usually met with hostility. I myself have several times been called a child of the devil and worse just for showing fundamentalists—nicely, I might add—self-contradictory Bible verses.

No doubt most staunch fundamentalists fear every "liberal" challenge to their preordained status quo, even honest soul-searching, because they fear change. Since their assumptions are absolute black-and-white, even a slight shift in perspective could bring their religion crashing down. If their Bible is not literally perfect, then there is no basis for faith, no Christ, no God, no afterlife, no reason to live; life is meaningless if they can't derive ultimate certainty from their pre-expounded God-breathed

Bible. If a new idea or updated fact contradicts their transcending religious ideology, staunch fundamentalists reject it without even considering it. Alternative interpretations of their version of biblical truth are shunned like Satan himself, because considering any variation would be tantamount to doubting the absolute truth, which is equal to unbelief, a one-way ticket to hell.

Pointing out the slippery slope fallacy of their reasoning doesn't always convince. Thinking outside the narrow box they were born (or born-again) into is too scary for some fundamentalists to consider. Reexamining received doctrine for the sake of elucidative re-vision risks profanation and its retribution. Doubt contradicts faith; therefore, tolerance is a threat, pluralism anathema. Thinking itself becomes spiritual quicksand, soul-searching a descent riskier than Dante's. The massive scholarship proving the pagan and ancient religious roots of every major aspect of Judaism and Christianity is the manifestation of Satan himself.

It's a jungle out there, and hacking ones way beyond the beaten path is dangerous. It makes sense that fundamentalists prefer to remain cooped up like a potted plant whose roots wrap around and around until the soil is depleted and the stunted plant shrivels up and dies.

Stephen Jay Gould warned that when a species ceases to evolve, it becomes extinct. For humans, this principle applies to us not just physically, but intellectually, psychologically, spiritually. We are not meant to be automatons on an assembly line, stamping the same little seal over and over. Evolution, progress, just plain growth requires creative adaptation; each life is created in the image of Creation. Even fundamentalists claim that it was the gutsy, innovative love-perspective of Jesus, not the cautious, stagnant absolutism of the Pharisees that generated the revolution we now call "Christianity."

Fundamentalists must agree that love, not legalism, was Jesus's fundamental message: "'You shall love the Lord your God with all your heart, and with all your soul, and with all your mind.' This is the greatest and first commandment. And a second is like it: 'You shall love your neighbor as yourself.' On these two commandments hang all the law and the prophets" (Matt. 22:37-40).

Simple. Who would argue with that? But that overarching, predominating message resulted in Jesus's persecution and murder with the blessing of his own people: *Crucify him!* Words that sound frighteningly familiar in this era Pat Robertson, Fred Phelps, Randall Terry, James Dobson, James Kennedy, and Tom DeLay.

Even when I gave up my faith in a God-breathed Bible, I still believed in Jesus, though I wasn't sure who or what he was. The Jesus I believed in had claimed that the very clear directive of love had come directly from God. And yes, the guy was, after all, "different," as religious trailblazers usually are. By now, I thought, we should have learned the bitter lesson that rejection of difference can be spiritually catastrophic. History, personal experience, even the Bible teaches that. As Martin Luther King, Jr. reminded us, "Salvation lies in the hands of the creatively maladjusted."

Many believers who identify themselves as fundamentalist are retreating because they are uncomfortable with self-righteous, judgmental, fear-fueling fundamentalists, and more importantly, because they have doubts about the literal perfection of the Bible. Many are on a quest for a more enlightened alternative to the fundamentalist versions of their religions.

But society's advance into progressivism is taking centuries, despite the availability of massive biblical scholarship that contradicts the claims of fundamentalism. Looking at Western history of the past two centuries is like watching a paradigm shift in slow motion. I believe that the paradigm can be shifted to warp speed with a good dose of strategic education. Thoughtful Christians, Jews, and Muslims of integrity are already meeting on common ground and adapting to progressive stances toward sacred texts and traditions.

Staunch fundamentalists, of course, will refuse to listen, stubbornly marching along to their "special" antiquated tune, the one repeating over and over from the broken record: "If you're not a born-again Christian, you're a failure as a human being," as Moral Majority founder Jerry Falwell put it. Born-again Christian meaning fundamentalist, according to fundamentalists.

Deconstructing the Bible's supposed revelation doesn't preclude the possibility that some of the texts are true or are based on true events. Biblical fallibility doesn't prove that Jesus didn't exist or even that he didn't perform miracles or rise from the dead. But though it is possible (though unlikely) that he lived, taught, inspired, and died on a cross, it is highly improbable (though not strictly impossible) that he performed miracles or rose from the dead. Religion has a moral responsibility to sift through the data to glean obvious truth from probable fiction. Faith without skepticism is blind faith, which is not faith at all.

Historically, high priests have sometimes manufactured the faithfully blind and stoked their bigotry with fear, especially fear of scapegoats buttressed by fear of a god that enforces his (their) bigotry with retribution. Radical fundamentalists like Jerry Falwell and Pat Robertson continued that tradition by claiming that their authority to promote bigotry (by whatever whitewashed name) was vested in biblical ideology. Their spiritual preference was clearly the image of the law-God who punishes to the exclusion of the grace-God who blesses.

Once the Bible mystique had cleared, I realized that the values decreed by the Bible were nothing extraordinary. It didn't take a divine conscience to "reveal" its rudimentary morality. The Ten Commandments, neither original nor profound, were obvious moral principles necessary to the order and stability of any society. The primitive Old Testament laws and codes seemed crude beside the ancient and sophisticated ethics of Confucius or philosophy and law of the Greeks. The distilled morality of the more recent Jesus stood on its own, without, or perhaps in spite of, all the miraculous bells and whistles. Paul took a giant step back from the simple maxims of Jesus (which evidently Paul never heard since he never refers to them), tangling himself in moral dilemmas he could never resolve.

Many people today have asked what authority has deemed the Bible to be the ultimate authority. We don't know who wrote any of the Old Testament, we don't know who wrote any of the gospels, and we don't know for sure which of the letters were written by Paul. Should we blindly accept as absolute truth an anonymous presentation of God's words, acts, and character just because it is tradition? Once I knew these facts, for me the answer was No.

In the land of the free, blindness isn't imposed; blindness is the refusal to open one's eyes. Even among the well-educated, the Bible is accepted as authentic history without any valid documentation. The Bible's books written in other genres of testimony are considered to be as objectively accurate as the histories. Clearly, to evaluate the authority of any history or other testimony we first need to know who the writer was and whether that writer was trustworthy. Next we need to consider whether the writer's history or testimony contradicts other histories or testimonies. Finally we need to judge whether the testimony rubs against the grain of our inherent conscience and common sense.

If you heard that a friend of a friend of a friend of a friend had been abducted by aliens twenty years ago and had given birth to an alien's child, would you believe it? If you heard tenth-hand that in some perfect garden paradise in Tennessee, someone you've never met said that a talking snake tempted a woman to eat an apple, and that in doing so, she damned the whole world, would you believe it? Would you believe that God allowed or caused the snake to tempt the woman? If by remote rumor you heard that God raped a woman, who was engaged to another, and impregnated her with a "redeemer" to be "sacrificed," murdered for the crime the snake woman committed in eating an apple (which wasn't at all fair, since she was fully innocent and incapable of choosing), wouldn't that raise an eyebrow?

What moral person or court of law would execute an innocent person as a stand-in for a guilty party, even if the innocent person were willing? As Thomas Paine pointed out, surely God is too moral to murder his innocent son, and too smart to be put into a position of needing to.

Rather than display the love of God, as claimed, the Judeo-Christian myth betrays the amateurish ability of its storytellers. There is no actual accomplished redemption in the Bible, but rather a precedent for collecting sacrifices, tithes, pardons, dispensations, indulgences, and all the other holy-gilded spoils of priests. Demanding blind faith in an obvious fable primes even smart believers to believe foolishly.

Who first knew of Mary's impregnation? In one gospel, it was Joseph, who was informed by an angel. In another, it was Mary herself, who was informed by an angel. Did either or both in turn tell other people, who actually believed them? Wouldn't it be more sensible for the hearers of this news to suspect that the couple had committed adultery (which was what sex before marriage was back then, which was an abomination punishable by death), or that Mary had been raped? What kind of people would make up such a tale to cover their sin, we would ask today? If you had lived then, and you heard from a friend of a friend of a friend that someone you had never met supposedly claimed to know that some guy named Jesus was the Son of God (though he never made that claim himself), wouldn't you be a bit suspicious? Or perhaps you would just shrug, given that back then there were dozens of gods who were said to be sons of some god, even sons of the highest god—like say, Zeus, Vishnu, Odin, or Osiris. It's not surprising that the genealogies for Jesus presented in the gospels of Matthew and Luke differ radically from each other. Each author had different resources and was trying to force-fit a different meaning.

Well, you insist, this is different. We're talking about the Bible here, the Word of God. We're talking about the real Son of God.

Says *who*? That *who* is some unknown writer who told these stories about Jesus long after Jesus was dead and gone. That is the first and final authority of your faith. A nameless storyteller. Many nameless storytellers, and not always very good ones at that by literary standards. Such faith is blind faith, which is anything but authentic faith. To attribute amateurish, childish fables to the Almighty not only insults the Almighty, it does so by rejecting our God-given faculties, including reason, conscience, and experience. Rather than dig for the actual facts regarding Jesus, fundamentalists have settled for contradictory interpretations by anonymous writers who were not even around when Jesus was alive and teaching.

Would God make belief in a "Son of God" contingent upon believing the unbelievable—unbelievable in being utterly contrary to God's Creation? That would be confusing and mean. But God makes himself perfectly clear through the sublime eloquence of reality, an intrinsically reliable reality that can be discovered, understood, and depended upon, thanks to the nature of objective Creation and to the reliability of our God-given faculties. God's benevolence in providing us with stable existence, consciousness, and conscience inspires in us benevolent gratitude. Benevolence is natural; faith in unbelievable premises of a manmade religion rooted in barbarism is unnatural and leads to barbarous persecution.

If the resurrection is the center of Christian faith, why are Christians asked to believe that it occurred as reported by unknown writers, and why did the big event occur in secret? Jesus supposedly appeared secretly to a few people in hiding; *which* few people varies from gospel to gospel. Very suspicious, if the point was to *prove* the real existence of such a monumental sign as resurrection. Why not resurrect publicly, so everyone could see and believe? It's not like Jesus could be apprehended and killed again. Making belief a condition of faith in fifth-hand reporting is itself suspiciously typical of primitive priest-craft.

Why would a good, loving "savior" ask anyone to believe a preposterous story told years after the fact by people who were not even there? Or even by people who supposedly were there? Why should we believe them? Should we believe the claims of miracle-working by contemporary faith healers? No miracle has ever been verified. Should we believe in aliens? Not without proof. The highly verified historian Tacitus tells us about a report that Vespasian cured a lame man and a blind man in the same way that the Bible writers later attributed to Jesus. Should we believe that earlier account? According to Josephus, another highly trustworthy historian, rumors circulated that the sea of Pamphilia opened to let Alexander and his army pass, just like the Red Sea parted in Exodus. Did it happen? Christmas and Easter are themselves each a collage of preexistent mythic material relating to equinox and solstice celebrations of this or that son of a god or goddess, some, such as Attis, Osiris, Dionysus, and Orpheus, born of a virgin and later killed and resurrected. Yet fundamentalists who celebrate these appropriated pagan holidays curse the obviously fictional Harry Potter books as satanic witchcraft.

In his book, *The Christ: A Critical Review and Analysis of the Evidence of His Existence*, John E. Remsberg shows the parallel between Jesus and his contemporary Galilean, the Pythagorean teacher, Appolonius of Tyana.

According to his biographers—and they are as worthy of credence as the Evangelists—his career, particularly in the miraculous events attending it, bore a remarkable resemblance to that of Christ. Like Christ, he was a divine incarnation; like Christ his miraculous conception was announced before his birth; like Christ he possessed in childhood the wisdom of a sage; like Christ he is said to have led a blameless life; like Christ his moral teachings were declared to be the best the world had known; like Christ he remained a celibate; like Christ he was averse to riches; like Christ he purified the religious temples; like Christ he predicted future events; like Christ he performed miracles, cast out devils, healed the sick, and restored the dead to life; like Christ he died, rose from the grave, ascended to heaven, and was worshiped as a god. The Christian rejects the miraculous in Apollonius because it is incredible; the Rationalist rejects the miraculous in Christ for the same reason.

Remsberg's writing, addressing the everyday reader, is clear, straightforward, and well-organized. Like other freethinkers writing in the late nineteenth and early twentieth centuries, Remsberg was not afraid to show the parallels between Jesus and pagan gods, to reveal the mythic sources of Judaism and Christianity, or to explicate contradictions within the Bible and in church history. People responded by understanding. In retaliation, fundamentalism was born.

Presenting so many of Remsberg's examples, as I do below, might seem like overkill, but truly, they only scratch the surface. My summaries paraphrase Remsberg; his examples reference numerous scholars.

Mythic Sources, Summarizing Remsberg

Krishna, eighth Avatar or incarnation of the god Vishnu, one of the Hindu Trinity, "appeared in all the fullness of his power and glory" 900 to 1,200 years before Christ, at about the time of Homer (950 B.C.). His birth was similar to the birth of Jesus in these details: miraculously conceived; born of a virgin; divine incarnation; of royal descent; angels (devatas) sang songs of praise at his birth; cradled among cowherds; visited by neighboring shepherds; reigning tyrant, fearing he would be supplanted in his kingdom by the divine child, sought to destroy him; saved by friends who fled with them in the night to distant countries; foiled in his attempt to discover the baby, issued a decree that all infants should be put to death. Interesting intersection: In their flight with the baby Jesus, Mary and Joseph stopped at a place called Maturea. Krishna was born at Mathura. Details of Krishna's adulthood are also similar: mission salvation of mankind; performed miracles; healed the sick, cleansed the leprous, and raised the dead; died for man by man; washed the feet of his disciples (Brahmins); taught his disciples the possibility of moving a mountain; earliest followers from lower classes; many early followers were women; called "the savior of men."

Buddha, ninth Avatar or incarnation of Vishnu, one of the Hindu Trinity, was (like "Christ") known by his title, "Buddha," meaning "the enlightened one." He lived from about 643 B.C. to 563 B.C. The canon of the Tripitaka, the principle "Bible" of the Buddhists, was determined at the Council of Pataliputra, 244 B.C., more that 600 years before the Christian canon was established. Buddha's birth paralleled the birth of Jesus in many details: conception announced by a divine messenger; annunciation hymn resembling that of Mary; born of a virgin; genealogy traced descent from ancestral kings; voluntary incarnation; miracles at his birth; nature altered its course to keep a shadow over his cradle; wise men came from afar offering gifts and worshipped him; presented in the temple; "the child waxed and increased in strength"; prophecies of the aged saint Asita (like Simeon in story of Jesus) at his formal presentation to his father; discoursed before teachers; fasted in the wilderness; was tempted; ministered by angels (devatas); bathed in the Narajana (as Christ was baptized in the Jordan); about thirty years old when he began his ministry; fasted seven times seven nights and days; had a band of disciples; traveled from place to place and preached to large multitudes; his first sermon the "Sermon on the Holy Hill"; the phraseology of the sermons in many instances the same as the sermons of Jesus; at his Renunciation "he forsook father and mother, wife and child"; mission "to establish the kingdom of righteousness"; promised salvation to all; compared himself to sower sowing seed; simile of mustard seed is used; "Perishable is the city built of sand"; speaks of "the rain which falls on the just and on the unjust"; story of prodigal son; similar account of the man born blind; story of righteous man who came by night (like Nicodemus); a converted prostitute, Ambapali, followed Buddha (like Mary Magdalene followed Jesus); commanded his disciples to preach his doctrine in all places and to all men; self-conquest and universal charity his fundamental principles; commanded his followers to conceal their charities; "return good for evil"; "overcome anger with love"; "love your enemies"; commanded of followers: "Not to kill; not to steal; not to lie; not to commit adultery; not to use strong drink"; traitor figures in his story; triumphal entry into Rajagriba (like Jesus into Jerusalem); "my kingdom not of this world"; eternal peace (like eternal life of Jesus). Both religions recognize a trinity. Catholicism's similarities to Northern Buddhism: priests shave their heads; bells and rosaries; images and holy water; popes and bishops; abbots and monks of many grades; processions and feast days; confessional and purgatory; worship of the virgin; devoted missionaries spread the faith all over Asia, and as far as Egypt, Asia Minor, and Palestine, long before the Christian era.

Remsberg points out an interesting parallel. "Three centuries after the time of Buddha, Asoka the Great, emperor of India, became a convert to the Buddhist faith, made it the state religion of the empire, and did more than any other man to secure its supremacy in the East. Three centuries after Christ, Constantine the Great, emperor of Rome, became a convert to the Christian faith, make it the state religion of his empire, and won for it the supremacy of the West."

Confucius, the great Chinese sage, was born 551 B.C. His followers believed him to be divine. His birth was attended by prodigies; magi and angels visited him as celestial music filled the air; his genealogy gave him a princely descent. Confucius gave us the Golden Rule: "What you do not like when done to yourself do not to others." Remsberg points out that because the religions of both Jesus and Confucius enjoin absolute obedience to national rulers, "Confucianism became and has remained the state religion of China, while Christianity became and has remained the state religion of Europe."

Laou-tsze of China was born 604 B.C. His similarities to Jesus are: entry into world and exit attended by miracles; miraculously conceived; ascended bodily into heaven; incarnation of an astral god (like star in Magi story); the "Tao" of his gospel, *Tao Te Ching*, means "the Way"; man both material and spiritual being; by renunciation of riches and worldly enjoyments the soul attains immortality; translated to heaven without suffering death (like Enoch and Elijah); taught men to be righteous and must become "as little children"; cast out evil spirits that caused diseases. His devotees live in monasteries and convents; his followers believe in a triune God.

Bacchus was a Roman modification of the Greek god Dionysos. He was the god of wine who cultivated the vine, made wine, and hosted Bacchanalian feasts. His worship was united with the Eleusinian mystery rites of the goddess Ceres (Demeter). Cakes were eaten in her honor. Rituals included partaking of the bread of Ceres and wine of Baccus. Athenians celebrated the allegorical giving of the flesh to eat of Ceres, the goddess of corn and grain, and the giving of the blood to drink of Bacchus, the god of wine. Like Mithraic worship, which also included communion, worship of Bacchus included use of holy water for purification, purified themselves, and an image of a phallus that looked much like the early Church cross was carried in their processions. The Roman government suppressed the later Bacchanalian and Eleusinian feasts, along with the Christian Agape, which was celebrated exactly the same as the pagan feasts, because of their debaucheries, obscenities, and supposed infant sacrifices. The church became a temple, and the table of the communion an altar. That the Eucharist was a continuation of the

Eleusinian mysteries, complete with the pagan's incense, garlands, and lamps or candles, seems confirmed by St. Paul's use of the word *teleiois*.

Saturn, one of the oldest and most renowned of European gods, was worshipped in Italy more than a thousand years before Christ, centuries before Rome rose to power. One of the planets and one of the days of the week are named in his honor. In honor of Saturn, god of agriculture, most specifically bread, and of recurring fertility, the Saturnalia was celebrated for seven days, concluding on December 25. From the Saturnalia come the Christmas tables laden with bounties, giving of presents, and burning of many candles. The Romans decked their halls with garlands of holly, sacred among sun gods as a symbol of good will and joy, and to Saturn as symbol of health and happiness. Christmas lights and ornaments evolved from the Roman custom of placing decorative candles in live trees and hanging small masks of Bacchus, the god of wine, on pine trees during the Saturnalia festival.

The immensely influential Persian prophet Zoroaster lived and wrote at least 1200 years before the Christian era. Judaism and Christianity derived some of their most fundamental doctrines from his teachings. From Persian theology we got the idea that the universe is ruled by two great powers, Ormuzd (God) and Ahrimanes (Satan), the one represented by light, the other darkness, the one being good, the other evil. Zoroaster placed man at the center of the perpetual war between these two forces, each striving for his soul. God created man with a free will to choose between good and evil. Those who choose good are rewarded with everlasting life in heaven; those who choose the evil are punished with endless misery in hell; those in the middle go to purgatory. God sent a savior, Zoroaster, with a divine revelation, the "Zend Avesta." Zoroaster had these features in common with those of Jesus: was of supernatural origin and endowed with superhuman powers; believed that Satan would be dethroned and cast into hell; believed that the end of the world and the kingdom of God were at hand; taught followers to worship God; was tempted by Satan; performed miracles; was slain by those whom he had come to save; instructed followers to obey the word and commandments of God. Zoroaster taught that those who obey the word of God will be free from all defects and immortal; God exercises his rule in the world through the works prompted by the Divine Spirit, who is working in man and nature; God hears the prayers of the good; all men live solely through the bounty of God; the soul of the pure will hereafter enjoy everlasting life; the wicked will undergo everlasting punishment. Devils and angels, baptism, communion, and confirmation rites are of Persian origin. Jews living under Persian rule in the region of the Euphrates and Tigris absorbed many of Zoroaster's concepts. Remsberg comments, "The writings of Zoroaster were the principle source of the most important theological doctrines ascribed to Christ, as the Buddhistic writings were of his ethical teachings." The "magi" of the birth of Jesus story were Zoroasterian priests who had been instructed to follow an especially bright star to find a spiritual king.

In even more ancient Persia, the god Mithra was the offspring of the Sun, and next to Ormuzd and Ahrimanes, held the highest rank among the gods of ancient Persia. Like Jesus: was one of a trinity; was born of a virgin; was the mediator and the spiritual light contending with spiritual darkness; through his work the kingdom of darkness would be lit with heaven's own light, the Eternal would receive all things back into his favor, the world would be redeemed to God; through him the impure are purified and evil made good. Mithras is the Good; his name is Love. He is the source of grace; life-giver; source of life; redeemer of the souls of the dead into the better world. His ceremonies included baptism to remove sins; anointing; confirmation that gives the power necessary to combat the spirit of evil; a Lord's supper that imparts salvation of body and soul. A consecrated wine, believed to possess wonderful power, played a prominent part. His birthday was December 25. His followers organized a church with a developed hierarchy; held Sunday sacred; preached a categorical system of ethics; regarded asceticism as meritorious and counted among their principal virtues abstinence and continence, renunciation and self-control; believed in Heaven inhabited by beatified ones, situated in the upper regions, and in Hell, peopled by demons, situated in the bowels of the earth; placed a flood at the beginning of history; assigned as the source of their condition a primitive revelation; believed in the immortality of the soul, last judgment, resurrection of the dead, and final conflagration of the universe."

Remsberg tells us, "In the catacombs at Rome was preserved a relic of the old Mithraic worship. It was a picture of the infant Mithra seated in the lap of his virgin mother, while on their knees before him were Persian Magi adoring him and offering gifts."

The Mithraic worship flourished throughout the ancient world into the second century. Manes, one of the Christian Fathers and founder of the heretical sect known as Manicheans, believed that Christ and Mithra were one. "Christ is that glorious intelligence which the Persians called Mithras . . . His residence is in the sun."

Sosiosh, the Messiah of the Persians, is the son of Zoroaster and constitutes part of the Persian Trinity. Zoroaster prophesied that he would be born of a virgin and that a star would indicate the place of his birth. "As soon, therefore, as you shall behold the star, follow it whithersoever it shall lead you and adore that mysterious child, offering your gifts to him with profound humility." The magi of the birth of Jesus story were Zoroastrian priests. Like Jesus, Sosiosh was supernaturally begotten, but unlike Jesus, he exists only in a spiritual form. When he comes again he will bring with him a new revelation, and he will awaken the dead and preside at the last judgment.

One of the most ancient of the sons of gods, Adonis, Tammouz, Tamzi, or Du-zi, as he was variously called, the god of light, life, and love, was a Babylonian deity whose worship gradually spread over Syria, Phoenicia, and Greece. In Phoenicia he was associated with the worship of Istar, and in Greece with that of Venus. The Jews worshipped Adonis by the name of Tammouz (Ezek. 8:14). Biblically he is "the only son." The Hebrews named one of the months after him. According to some scholars, that the Jews considered eating or handling pork an abomination had its origin in the legend that Adonis was killed by a wild boar. Until recently, Catholics ate fish on Friday; Friday was consecrated to Venus by her Asiatic worshipers and fish was eaten in her honor.

Most Old Testment stories derive from similar but far more ancient Babylonian and Persian stories such as those recorded in the Babylonian epic, the "Assyrian poem," which cannot be later than the seventeenth century B.C. It antedates the oldest books of the Bible by at least 1,000 years, according to Remsberg's dating. From the first pages of the Bible we find the sacred tree of Babylonia, with its guardian cherubs and flaming sword with seven heads. The flood account of Genesis not only agrees in details, "but even in phraseology with that which forms the eleventh lay of the great Babylonian epic." As in Genesis, the Babylonian flood expresses deity's chastisement of man's corruption. The Assyrian poem details the building of the ark, into which are introduced the various pairs of male and female animals, the shutting of the doors of the ark, the duration, increase, and decrease of the flood, the sending out of a dove, a swallow, and a raven, and so on. The Noah figure is Tam-zi or Tammuz, "the sun of life," who sails upon his ark behind clouds of winter to reappear when the rainy season is past. He is called Sisuthrus of Berosus, that is, Susru "the founder," a synonym of Na, "the sky." His ark rested on a mountain in Nisir; on its peak the first altar was built after the flood. From the Babylonian stories came those of the tower of Babel or Babylon, of the Creation, of the fall, and of the sacrifice of Isaac—the latter forming the first lay of the great epic, which further describes the descent of Istar into Hades in pursuit of her dead husband Du-zi, "the offspring," the Babylonian Adonis.

Osiris, the son of Seb (earth) and Nu (heaven), appears in hieroglyphics of Egypt as early as 3427 B.C. The Savior of Egypt, his worship, universal in Egypt, spread over much of Asia and Europe, including Greece and Rome. Parallels between the Osiris myth and Jesus stories include: slain by Typhon (Satan), but rose again and became the ruler of the dead; presides at the judgment; good are rewarded with everlasting life, wicked are destroyed; immortality and bodily resurrection; worship of a divine mother and child; doctrine of atonement; vision of a last judgment; resurrection of the body; sanctions of morality; lake of fire; torturing demons; eternal life in the presence of God; personification of moral good. Isis, the sister and wife of Osiris (as Mary was technically the sister and wife of Jesus, if Jesus is God), was the greatest of female divinities. Her worship, like Mary worship of Catholicism, was coexistent and coextensive with that of her divine brother and husband. Remsberg points to the following picture of Isis in the Apocalypse: "And there appeared a great wonder in heaven; a woman clothed with the sun, and the moon under her feet, and upon her head a crown of twelve stars" (Revelation xii, 1). Isis was the ruling deity of the land to which the parents of Jesus fled when warned that Herod would try to kill them. Isis worship continued in Rome and Alexandria and commingled with early Christianity.

The son of Osiris and Isis, the god Horus completed the Egyptian trinity. Horus, the rising sun, existed even before the incarnation of his father, Osiris, the setting sun. Although the doctrine of the trinity existed elsewhere—Brahma, Vishnu, and Siva of India, for instance—the doctrine of the trinity in unity, which was accepted eight centuries before

Christ, was an Egyptian one. As an infant, Horus was carried out of Egypt to escape the wrath of Typhon (Satan) (Jesus fled *to* Egypt to escape the wrath of Herod). He was carried out of Egypt, like Moses, who led his people out to escape Pharaoh. Like Moses, the baby Horus was hidden among the reeds by his mother. The story of his mother, Isis, stopping the sun and moon is echoed in the story of Joshua doing the same.

Zeus, also called Jove and Jupiter, was the greatest of the sons of gods worshipped by Greece and Rome. His parents were the god Kronos (Time) and the goddess Rhea (Earth); one might say that Zeus was the child of space-time. Like Christ, Zeus assumed the form of man; his life was imperiled during infancy; he was secreted away and saved. As ruler of heaven and earth, he was, like the God of Genesis, dissatisfied with the human race, and with the aid of Pandora, who brought death into the world, he tried to destroy it that he might create a new race. Persophone, or Life (Eve also means Life), was the daughter of Zeus and Demeter, the Earth, goddess of earth and her bounty (like the Garden of Eden). Hades (later personified as Satan), the god of hell, seized Persephone and carried her to the lower world where she was forced to become his wife. At his urging, Persephone ate some of the enchanted pomegranate (the Garden of Eden apple is now considered to be more accurately translated as pomegranate). Although Demeter appealed to Zeus to return her daughter to earth, Persephone had to return to the underworld one month for every seed she had eaten. Her exit and entrance back to Hades causes the seasonal changes; Demeter's joy and grief result in her engagement and disengagement in earth's birthing and fruiting.

Apollo, one of the principal solar deities, was the son of the virgin Leto, who was ravished by Zeus, who came to her in the form of a swan (like an angel) in light (as the Spirit came to Mary in the form of a dove in light). Leto gave birth on the barren isle of Delos, which was illuminated by a flood of light (like Jesus's manger while sacred swans (like the angels) made joyous gyrations in the air above them. Apollo grew to become one of the most beloved gods of Greece. One of the most perfect types of manly beauty, he lived a lowly life as a herdsman; came to reveal the will of his father; was endowed with miraculous powers; was the Savior who rescued the people from the deadly python (like the Edenic snake).

Because it had long ago been prophesied that the virgin Danae would give birth to the god Perseus, the Herod-like ruler Acisius confined Danae in a tower, where Zeus "overshadowed" her in a shower of gold. Acisius placed the newborn Perseus and his mother in a chest and cast them upon the waters (much like Moses). They drifted to an island and the child was saved, grew to manhood, performed many wonderful works, vanquished his enemy, and ascended the throne.

The solar god Hercules was the son of Zeus and the virgin Alcmeni. Like Herod, Hera tried to destroy him. Like Jesus, Hercules died a death of agony; his pyre was surrounded by dark cloud amid thunder and lightning; he ascended to heaven; he descend into Hades. His twelve labors, like the twelve apostles of Christ and the twelve tribes of Israel, correspond to the twelve signs of the Zodiac. Hercules's festivals, Lenaea and the Greater Dionysia, correspond to Christmas and Easter, the last day of the festival being a sort of All Souls' Day devoted to the gods of the underworld and the spirits of the dead.

Dionysos, or Zagreus, son of Zeus, was slain by Titans, was buried at foot of Mt. Parnassus, and rose from the dead as Dionysos. He was the god of fruit and wine, the beloved son who occupied a throne at the right hand of his father. His empty tomb at Delphi was long preserved as proof of his death and resurrection. Resurrection stories like those of Adonis in Phoenicia, Osiris in Egypt, and Dionysos in Greece were ancient when Jesus was born.

When Zeus became enraged at mankind, the Titan god Prometheus, like Christ, came to earth to intercede and suffer for the race. In his book, *Evolution of Israel's God*, A. L. Rawson notes in his consideration of the great Greek tragedy, *Prometheus Bound*, "Its hero was their friend, bene-factor, creator, and savior, whose wrongs were incurred in their behalf, and whose sorrows were endured for their salvation. He was wounded for their transgressions, and bruised for their iniquities; the chastise-ment of their peace was upon him, and by his stripes they were healed." R. B. Westbrook writes regarding the death of Prometheus, "The New Testament description of the crucifixion and the attending circum-stances, even to the earthquake and darkness, were thus anticipated by five centuries."

Esculapius, illegitimate son of the nymph Coronis by Apollo, was spared death at the hand of Diana, although his mother was killed. Esculapius was called "The Good Physician" for his wonderful curative powers that could heal all diseases, could make whole the lame, the paralytic, and those born blind, and could restore the dead to life. He was struck by a thunderbold and ascended to heaven.

The vestal virgin, Rhea Silvia, bore twins by the god Mars. Because the twins were heirs to the crown, the evil ruler Amulius attempted to protect his usurped throne by drowning them, but they were miraculously preserved and rescued by a shepherd. Romulus became the founder and king of Rome. After his reign of thirty-seven years, he was translated by his father and eventually became the tutelary god of the Romans, named Quirinus; the sun was eclipsed, and he was gone. Mars carried him up to heaven (like Elijah) in a chariot of fire. He reappeared in a glorified form to Proculus Juilus, who prophesied the future greatness of the Roman people, and told him he would watch over them as their guardian god. Next to the Saturnalia, the most important religious festival of pagan Rome was the Quirinalia, which celebrated the Ascension of Quirinus.

Odin, the All-Father, held the highest rank in the Northern pantheon and was worshipped by the Scandinavians, Goths, Saxons, other ancient German tribes, a thousand years or more before the Christian era. They believed in two worlds, one the warm South, the other the ice North. Like Eden, the entrance to the South was guarded by flaming sword. Out of two trees Odin made man and woman, breathed into them the breath of life, and for their abode, planted a fruitful garden in the center of the earth. Beneath the earth dwells Hel, the goddess of the dead. Like the Satan of Revelations, Loki, the god of evil, will be chained for a time and then released; a bloody war will ensue between Lodi and the hosts of Hell, and Odin and his followers. Loki will triumph, mankind will be destroyed, and heaven and earth will be consumed by fire. But Odin will create a new heaven and a new earth, and dwelling in heaven, will be the ruler of all things.

Thor, the son of the virgin Earth and Odin, was the first born son of God and the "Christ" of the Scandinavian Trinity. Like Christ, Thor died for man and was worshiped as a Savior. The evil Midgard had a serpent that threatened to destroy the human race. Thor attacked and slew the monster but was killed by the venom.

The good and noble Baldur, one of the purest, gentlest, and best beloved of all gods, the beautiful son of Odin and Freya, was like many gods born on December 25. Loki (Satan) shot arrows, but it was the blind god Hoder that pierced his body with an arrow of mistletoe so that he passed into the power of Hel and descended into hell. In another and better world, where envy and hatred and war are unknown, Baldur will rise again. The ancient Germanic Yuletide festival celebrating the return of the sun god (and the sun) centered around the Yule log, cut from the heart of a tree trunk and dragged to a large fireplace, where it burned for twelve days, which later became the twelve days of Christmas. Apples were hung as ornaments from evergreen trees, sacred to Baldor, as a reminder that spring and summer would come again. In many ancient religious traditions, the evergreen was sacred to sun gods and to gods resurrected at the spring equinox or summer solstice. Candles were burned and good-luck gifts called Stenae (lucky fruits) were exchanged. The Druids contributed the tradition of kissing under the mistletoe, a divine plant symbolic of love and peace.

Most of us never think of the Greek philosopher Plato as a god, but the legend of his immaculate conception via the god Apollo can be traced back to his nephew, Spensipus. Immaculate conceptions were among the most frequently recurring incidents in the myths and legends of ancient Greece. When Perictione, a pure virgin (like Mary), was impregnated by Apollo, the god declared the parentage of the child to her betrothed, Ariston (like Joseph). Many of Plato's views were ascribed to Jesus: there is but one God, and we ought to love and serve him; the Word formed the world and rendered it visible; knowledge of the Word will make us happy; the soul is immortal, and the dead will rise again; death is "the separation of the soul from the body"; here will be a final judgment; the righteous will be rewarded, and the wicked punished. Plato's design argument is the chief argument relied upon by Christians to prove the divine origin of the universe.

The ancient philosopher Pythagoras taught in the sixth century B.C. at about the time of Buddha, Laou-Tsze, and Confucius. Greece was his native country, but he lived most of his life in Italy and traveled extensively in Egypt and India, where his ideas took hold. Like Plato, Pythagoras was the son of Apollo, performed miracles, and was endowed with the gift of prophecy. The Essenes, a Jewish sect to which Jesus was believed to have belonged, adopted much of the teachings of Pythagoras.

Numerous other examples could be cited, but the point is that like all mythmakers, the Bible writers borrowed familiar material. And much material about a particular god could well have originated with an actual person who was magnified into a legend and then deified as a myth. It's possible that Jesus was a philosopher or spiritual teacher so revered that eventually he was deified.

Some scholars point out that the claim that the Bible is God-breathed is contradicted by the amateurish writing style of so many of its books; none is even close to the quality of Tacitus or Josephus, or any of the great poets and philosophers of distant antiquity; certainly God could have done better. And the texts of those great geniuses have been better authenticated than any of the Bible books, with the possible exception of some of the letters of Paul.

As one proof that the Christ of Christianity is a myth and not a historical character, scholars point to the profound silence of the writers who lived during and immediately following the time he is said to have existed. None even of the great historical biographers living where Jesus lived during his lifetime wrote so much as a word of his biography.

Among the prolific writers who lived and wrote during the time of Christ or within a century after the time but who wrote nothing about Jesus were: Josephus, Philo-Judaeus, Seneca, Pliny the Elder, Suetonius, Juvenal, Martial, Arrian, Petronius, Dion Pruseus, Paterculus, Appian, Theon of Smyrna, Phlegon, Persius, Plutarch, Justus of Tiberius, Apollonius, Pliny the Younger, Tacitus, Quintilian, Lucanus, Epictetus, Silius Italicus, Statius, Ptolemy, Hermogones, Valerius Maximus, Pompon Mela, Quintius Curtius, Lucian, Pausanias, Valerius Flaccus, Florus Lucius, Favorinus, Phaedrus, Damis, Aulus Gellius, Columella, Dio Chrysostom, Lysias, Appion of Alexandria.

Enough remains of the writings of these authors to form a library. Many of those writings are about the very region and time within which Jesus supposedly lived, openly taught, and riled up religious and political leaders. But Jesus Christ is mentioned only in two proven forged passages in the works of a Jewish author, and two disputed small passages in the works of Roman writers—hardly probable if Jesus performed miracles and caused a revolution, given that many of these writers wrote many chapters and even entire books about every noteworthy person and event. The Dead Sea Scrolls, written up through the early part of the first century A.D. and by far our earliest surviving scrolls from the gospel period, make no mention of Jesus, John the Baptist, or early Christians.

Jesus is simply absent from history until decades after he died (if he lived), and to pretend otherwise is patently dishonest.

People of the Bible era lived in an age when myths and legends abounded, so a miracle-worker who rose from the dead was no harder to believe than any other ghost story. Julius Caesar was said to have done the same, and many believed it. I am not asserting that it is fact that neither rose from the dead. I am arguing the need for skepticism. Even widespread rumors were recorded by the historians; shouldn't we have heard something about an amazing miracle worker who inspired multitudes with his preaching, for whom a multitude turned out in praise at his Triumphal Entry? Yet no legal or historical record survives from the age of meticulous Roman documentation.

In times past, as today, it was not uncommon for martyrs to be glorified into exaggerated versions of themselves. If a real-life hero was unjustly or cruelly murdered, it was human nature to try to make that good person look even better as a kind of compensation for his having been cheated of life and good report. Sometimes the mythologizing was a kind of collective wish-fulfillment that the almost-supernatural hero could still serve and protect at an even higher supernatural level. Sometimes the hero story was just good entertainment. Sometimes the superman served as an exemplum. To boost its claims to religious superiority, the early Christians glorified their martyrs as supernatural heroes, and their powers were "documented" by the Church in the official legends and lives of the saints, complete with dragons, unicorns, and of course miracles.

In this day and age, even believers understand the mythmaking tendencies of human nature; know that the biblical stories originated in the age of myths and legends among peoples of unbounded credulity; acknowledge that myths and legends can spread like wildfire, accumulating embellishments along the way; and cannot doubt that those stories were passed down by unknown witnesses that do not even agree among themselves.

BORN-AGAIN, WITHOUT JESUS?

Even if Jesus was largely a myth, something about him or the myth of him has gripped humanity. At the same time, even if Jesus was a real man of extraordinarily inspiring wisdom, the Jesus of the Bible and Christianity is largely a myth.

Given that, what explanation is there for Christians for whom being born-again involves what they call a personal relationship with Jesus Christ, meaning they have had a spiritual encounter with an actual spiritual entity? I say "they," but I include myself in this category.

There are millions of such people. We're not all liars or crazy. I know I'm not. If the born-again sense of Presence was not a Jesus revelation or encounter, what, then, was it?

It's important to acknowledge that people of other religious traditions have similar born-again experiences, though they call them by other terms and attribute them to other sources. The spiritual dimension does exist, and quite a few people in this life do enter into that realm (for lack of better description). The high that accompanies that entry is something anyone can experience, regardless of one's religious persuasion.

I've often observed that the spiritual high comes with at least two different states of consciousness: the epiphany high and the encounter high.

Many people have felt the exhilaration of suddenly understanding something sublime. It's mostly an intellectual high, though it could involve other faculties, such as emotions or aesthetic sensibility. That's an epiphany high. Many people have felt the exhilaration of falling in love, or connecting with a person or group that is so rewarding that one's response is a high. That's an encounter high.

In my experience, the spiritual, "born-again" high is the fusion of an epiphany high and an encounter high. If we experience the high in a Christian context, say of being "saved" or drawn into the fold, we assume that the high is the direct result of the context itself or of some embedded principle.

But I think the high derives from something that transcends the context but that uses the context as a representation or a conduit, like an idea expressed in words, and the words presented through a medium like the human voice or pen and paper and an understanding mind. Jesus, or the myth of Jesus (it doesn't matter which), is a representation of deeply human wisdom, which includes a deeply human urge for transcendence, that needed, and still needs, articulation—or further articulation; it's not that most of this wisdom had not been expressed before. Carl Jung might view Jesus as a primitive archetypal overcoming of our shadow.

We sometimes think we are experiencing the spiritual directly, but in fact our experience is always mediated by our own human qualities as they "live" in relationship with some aspect of the world itself. Existence is always dynamic. It's as if the Creator God speaks to us not through an anthropomorphic, authoritarian voice booming through the clouds but through the Creation process itself, which for us means our living experience of, really our engagement with, something or someone else, be it nature, art, a religion, philosophy, love—whatever. My assumption is that God is real, that God does communicate to the receptive in a variety of ways, and that all this interconnected communication is dynamic wisdom expressing the immanent love and friendliness of a personal—but *not* human—God.

Because people experience God in different ways, we need to stop judging one another and throwing lightning bolts at anyone whose context of spiritual experience differs from our own. We each find a context or contexts that we feel comfortable with, usually because they're familiar. My pillow isn't your pillow, but we all lie back and dream a human Paradise, which is merely a representation of a transcendental reality we can only vaguely glimpse.

But something about that glimpse strikes us to the core as being ultimately real. No wonder people get so intense about protecting their vision. We just have to remember that what we think we see is different from what others think they see, but what we actually are looking at is the same thing: God, by whatever name; and we are all seeing that God "through a glass darkly" and are all hoping to see God more directly in an afterlife.

Acknowledging that God is One could save the world. Given the arrogance of our ideologies and the magnitude of our weapons, denying it could well destroy us.

When I went through my fundamentalist period, I was about as defensive as a person can get. I was a passionate believer. Passion can be a good thing, and it's easy to understand someone passionate about what is perceived to be ultimate truth wanting to defend that truth to the death.

But there's a difference between wise and foolish passion. It's not just the object, or "truth," of the passion that makes it wise or foolish, but the way one expresses the passion. Now I understand that damning the passionate truths of others is foolish, though of course one must deconstruct with common sense blind truths and lies. Passionately wanting to destroy those whose truths differ from our own is perhaps the most perverse and dangerous evil perpetrated by humanity.

Chapter 10

The Witches' Hammer in the Twenty-First Century

History bears witness to colossal evils that persons or groups employ to enforce religious ideology. The Christian Satan isn't just a myth created by humans. The devil in any tradition is the representational projection of human evil. And how much more charged is that shadow when manifested through the very religion that professes to oppose it. It's hard to imagine a devil-worshipping cult more satanic than the Church of the Inquisition.

The urgency of our Founding Fathers' demand for freedom of religion, still resounding today, addressed five centuries of religious tyranny that had murdered millions of heretics since its inception in the thirteenth century, when Pope Gregory IX wrote his *Excommunicamus* (1231) and Pope Innocent IV officially sanctioned torture as a means to extract truth from suspects (1252). The pope approved the establishment of a Spanish Inquisition at the request of King Ferdinand V and Queen Isabella I in 1478, shortly before the king and queen financed Christopher Columbus's search for a shorter route to India that led him to "discover" America in 1492.

Witch-hunt hysteria commenced in earnest in 1484, when Pope Innocent VII issued the papal bull *Summis Desiderantes*, which became the preface of *Malleus Maleficarum*, a kind of Inquisition textbook published in 1486 by Dominican inquisitors Heinrich Krammer and James Sprenger.

In 1542, Pope Paul III responded to the Protestant insurgency by establishing the Congregation of the Inquisition in Rome, also called the Roman Inquisition of the Holy Office. In its attempt to suppress heretical ideas, the first Index of Forbidden Books was issued in 1559. The witch craze began to decline during the Enlightenment, although a late outbreak occurred in Salem, Massachusetts, in 1692. The Inquisition was finally suppressed in Spain in 1834, fifty-eight years *after* the signing of our Declaration of Independence in 1776, and forty-six years *after* our Constitution was ratified in 1788.

For most of us raised in the U.S. during the twentieth and twenty-first centuries, the Inquisition is an abstraction tucked away in a dusty history book. Viewing the Inquisition more concretely helped me to understand our Founders' concern to guarantee our religious and civil freedoms and to recognize the continued inquisitional spirit of fundamentalism. The fictional statistics and studies of Paul Cameron, the embarrassing "exegesis" of Fred Phelps, the absurd prophesies and judgments of Benny Hinn, Pat Robertson, Paul Crouch, Jerry Falwell, and all the other hysterical misrepresentations spewed by American evangelicals who wanted not-fundamentalists destroyed, betrayed an inquisitional spirit held in check only by humanist mores and laws founded on principles established by our Founders.

The pope decreed the *Malleus Maleficarum* to be the Church's official guidebook for the prosecution, punishment, and execution of witches because, as the *Malleus* put it, "after the sin of Lucifer, the works of witches exceed all other sins." It was incontestable that the heresy of witches was "the most heinous of the three degrees of infidelity; and this fact is proved both by reason and authority." The "reason and authority" exemplified in the *Malleus* was a complete mockery of its model, the advanced reason and authority achieved centuries earlier by Greco-Roman civilization.

Witches caused natural disasters like storms, hail, and floods. They were seen transporting themselves through the air on animals, furniture, and broomsticks. They cast spells of love, hate, and madness, caused miscarriage and drying of the milk in animals and women, and were responsible for demonic possession, sickness, and death.

When I first read the *Malleus*, I was surprised that the authors were so particularly preoccupied with the witch-inspired evils of sex. Dozens of pages graphically described sexual problems among men, complete with fantastical "scientific" explanations of witch's spells, including demonic possession. Impotence, rape, incest, weak erection, lust for a married woman, demonic attack on sleeping nuns, rape or molestation by priests, lack of attraction to women, masturbation, adultery, sterility, disappearance of a man's "members," a man's members falling off, and the detailed, almost pornographic information concerning witches who copulate with devils—all this was quaintly, yet viciously, substantiated with quotes from philosophers, the Church Fathers, ancient literature, "the poets," legal discourse, and of course, the Bible.

"And what, then, is to be thought of those witches who in this way sometimes collect male organs in great numbers, as many as twenty or thirty members together, and put them in a bird's nest, or shut them up in a box, where they move themselves like living members, and eat oats and corn, as has been seen by many and is a matter of common report?" Indeed, what can be said about them, I've asked myself? More to the point, what can be said about the inquisitors? Perhaps the fear of witches, like the fear of feminists, gays, blacks, and Muslims, is the shadow expression of a castration complex.

More than fifteen centuries after the height of advanced Greek civilization, official representatives of Catholic superstition asserted,

> A certain man tells that, when he had lost his member, he approached a known witch to ask her to restore it to him. She told the afflicted man to climb a certain tree, and that he might take which he liked out of the nest in which there were several members. And when he tried to take a big one, the witch said: You must not take that one; adding, because it belongs to a parish priest.

It doesn't take a Freudian scholar to decipher the subtext. When a society is sexually repressed, and represses fear of castration, all kinds of shadow delusions serve to compensate, rationalize, and project blame. The *Malleus* is steeped with stories of demonic witchcraft that unwittingly demonstrate that repression often manifests as a shadow.

Once a witch was accused, a confession was sought. Many accused witches, unsure of the rules of the inquisitional game, truly believed that to confess to the grave sins of witchcraft, even if innocent of such sins, would jeopardize the eternal salvation of their souls. To confess to acts of witchcraft was often considered by both the accused and the accuser to be equivalent to committing the act, much like a child (or an inquisitor) might believe that saying it was going to rain made it rain. Or like childish beliefs can become the magical truths of myth, folklore, legend, religion, and the *Malleus*. Because the accused was questioned in the torture chamber, usually following "light" torture (like being suspended a few feet from the ground by her thumbs), she could easily assume that to confess guilt would result in even more torturous punishment and execution, usually by burning if not by the chamber torture itself.

Because "Theologians and Canonists" differed on whether evil for the sake of good should be done to witches, the *Malleus* allowed judges to decide for themselves whether or not to lie to witches in order to obtain a confession. To enhance its effectiveness, the lie was generally told in the torture chamber, accompanied by leading questions spelling out the accusations, which the accused need simply affirm. A suspected witch could be promised that she would not be tortured, that she would not be tortured further, that she would not be burned, and even that she would be set free. At all costs, a confession must be obtained. Even in the Dark Ages, confession validated the superior role of the priest or other Church official. If a woman was accused of witchcraft, or if any "abnormal" circumstance required an explanation—a devastating hailstorm, for instance—, someone had to burn. Pick a witch, any witch. Then get that confession.

No wonder so many were "bound to deny true and sacramental confession," which the *Malleus* authors called "the evil gift of silence which is the constant bane of judges." Many witches refused to confess because they would rather endure torture than risk eternal damnation. Some refused to confess because they saw through the inquisitor's evil game. If the witch would not confess, however, she was often tortured into confession. It was a catch-22; damned if you do, damned if you don't. Others preferred to confess because once "being" guilty, they could be forgiven, or so they were told. Most believers prior to the Reformation and most Catholics after believed that the pope literally held the keys to heaven and hell, and that a decision by him or any of his designates, even if he himself was evil, could decide the person's eternal fate. Better to confess and be pardoned via sanctifying torture and death than to go to hell.

Once extracted, a witch's "confession" became proof of the prevalence of witches. The inquisitors, who were lawyers and/or clerics under the jurisdiction of the Church, were eager to promote witch-scares to produce witches to prosecute, because all the witch's possessions and all the possessions of her extended family, including descendents, and sometimes even friends, servants, or anyone who might be even remotely suspect as an accessory to the crime—all that wealth, minus execution expenses, went into the pockets of the inquisitor and those who assisted him. Even dead heretics could be dug up and burned and their property confiscated. It's not difficult to see why so many witches were brought to trial. The *Malleus* authors Krammer and Sprenger were themselves indicted for various crimes like forging notarized documents to embezzle fees for indulgences. The Bishop of Brixen expelled the infamous Krammer from his territory because he disapproved of the inquisitor's fraudulent means of framing women as witches and overseeing their torture.

The inquisitors themselves were protected from the spells of witches by spells authorized by Catholicism, such as traditional and holy rites of the Church, exorcisms furnished in the aspersion of Holy Water, taking consecrated salt, carrying the blessed candles on the Day of the Purification of Our Lady and palm leaves on Palm Sunday.

Today, in addition to rosaries, candles, and crosses, prayer helps, especially if you rub the talisman you received in your donation request envelope and then call or mail in your prayer request accompanied by a substantial donation to the soliciting evangelist's "ministry."

Although not "afflicted" by devils, inquisitors were "pestered" day and night, "now in the form of apes, now of dogs or goats, disturbing us with their cries and insults; fetching us from our beds at their blasphemous prayers, so that we have stood outside the window of their prison, which was so high that no one could reach it without the longest of ladders; and then they have seemed to stick the pins with which their head-cloth was fastened violently into their heads." Could the woman's "blasphemous" prayers have been genuine appeals for salvation? Were the inquisitors fetched by witches, or were they jolted awake by the shadow erupting from their own nightmares? Luckily, God took pity, and "preserved us as unworthy public servants of the justice of the Faith."

The inquisitors naturally had legal Catholic reasons why women, i.e. witches, were evil and needed the severest punishment. And not only witches, but "their followers, protectors, patrons and defenders incur the heaviest penalties," and even "their children to the second generation on the father's side, and to the first degree on the mother's side, are admitted to no benefit or office of the Church." No benefit or office of the Church meant they were excommunicated, which meant they would not go to heaven. And of course the children were deprived of their paternal inheritance. The inquisitors not only cast everyone into hell, they got all that *male* controlled money and property, hence the second-generation penalties on children on the *father's* side, but only first-generation penalties on the mother's (witch's) side.

"But to punish witches in these ways does not seem sufficient, since they are not simple Heretics, but Apostates." Witches deserved the severest punishment "Because of the temporal injury which they do to men and beasts in various ways." That injury, however, is pure myth, as is their supposed insider knowledge of Heaven: "Just as the degrees of blessedness in Heaven are measured in accordance with the degrees of charity and grace in life, so the degrees of punishment in hell are measured according to the degree of crime in this life." Of course, there is biblical documentation. "See *Deuteronomy* xxv: The measure of punishment will be according to the measure of sin. And this is so with all other sins, but applies especially to witches. See *Hebrews* x."

The means to torture witches to extract confessions and then to punish exceed the imaginations of most of us today. In order to appreciate the perversity of the Church sanctioned Inquisition, it's important to avoid abstraction and to face the concrete facts. The truth is that cults, dictators, and totalitarian governments throughout the world still use Inquisition torture devices. Exhibits of torture devices, like the exhibit I viewed some years ago in San Francisco, have been touring worldwide. Permanent exhibits are on view at museums such as the Torture Museum in Ruesdesheim, Rhine, Germany. Photographs of the torture devices can be viewed online. It's important to be vividly aware of the ever-present possibility of perverse brutality by the self-righteous claiming to be doing us a favor.

Before being interrogated, witches were stripped naked and shaved to reveal birthmarks or moles—"devil's marks," which proved guilt. Larger moles, warts, or other skin growths, which most of us today would simply ignore or treat with over-the-counter ointments or with a quick trip to the dermatologist, were considered to be extra breasts, further proof of demonic congress. After being tortured, a witch was often thrown in a filthy, rat-infested dungeon, sometimes for a year or more, where she could (naked, of course) mull things over until she died or was further tortured and eventually burned. Of course, incarcerated witches would be routinely available for rape by inquisitors and their staff, including those employed as torturers.

Here are descriptions of some of the more common torture devices:

- Simply designed of two metal plates that screwed together with the suspect's thumbs between them, thumbscrews were small enough to slip in a large pocket, affording busy inquisitors convenient, efficient portability.
- Often the tongue was cut out of a victim that talked too much or too little. Commonly, the accused was whipped with scourges, often with sharpened barbs dipped in boiling salt-sulfur water at the tips of the flails, until the ribs poked through and the internal organs protruded.
- The breast ripper, an iron tong with four hooked claws, often fired red-hot, shredded the breasts of suspected witches during the judicial interrogation process and was used to punish witches and unwed mothers.
- A similar device, the cat's paw, or Spanish tickler, an iron claw attached to a handle, shredded the flesh off the bones of a naked victim suspended dangling by chains or ropes against a plank.
- The Branks, or Scold's Bridle, was a locked metal cage headpiece with protruding metal tongue-piece, often fitted with spikes or a rowel (small spiked wheel), that gagged and silenced scolding housewives. Chains decked with bells served to humiliate the nag escorted through town and secured to the hook attached to her family's fireplace. More elaborate versions served as torture devices for witches.
- Engraved with "I recant," the heretic's fork was a sharp-pointed fork, reminiscent of a classic devil's pitchfork, attached to a collar. With its bottom two prongs stuck deep in the sternum, and the top two prongs stuck into the chin's underside, the heretic's fork propped up the head, immovable and barely able to murmur "I recant."
- Pressing was accomplished by crushing the victim under weighted boards (aka, "the turtle"), sometimes as she lay on top of a wooden or metal wedge.
- Racking took many ingenious forms, but the principle was the same—stretch the limbs until the joints were dislocated. Sources document cases of victims being painfully slow-racked until their

bodies were elongated by twelve inches. Some variations included stretching out the victim on a rack of spiked rollers, or incorporating other forms of torture, like branding the flesh with red-hot iron crosses, ripping off genitals, nipples, noses, or ears with red-hot pinchers, or forcing the victim to watch as her intestines were slowly wound onto pulleys.

- Quartering was a kind of ultimate racking, usually accomplished by tying each limb to one of four horses, then sending each horse racing simultaneously in a different direction.

- According to A. Hyatt Verrill's *The Inquisition*, in 1497, Girolamo Savonarola, fiery critic of Vatican corruption, became perhaps the most famous person put to the *tratti di fune or strappado*, which consisted of tying the prisoner's hands behind his back, hoisting him by the wrists, letting him drop for several feet and stopping him with a jerk before he reached the ground. This proving ineffectual, weights were attached to Savonarola's feet and he was dropped fourteen times. Weeks later, he was burned at the stake in the Plaza della Signoria.

- Perhaps the most painful torture device was the wheel, aka the "Catherine Wheel" after St. Catherine of Alexandria, a historically dubious martyr of the early fourth century. The naked victim, staked spread-eagle to the spokes, had her bones smashed by clubbers as the wheel turned, until she was transformed, according to a seventeenth-century chronicler, "into a sort of huge screaming puppet writhing in rivulets of blood, a puppet with four tentacles, like a sea monster, of raw, slimy and shapeless flesh mixed up with splinters of smashed bones," who, still alive, was then "braided" through the wheel and hoisted on a pole for crows and vultures to feast on. Several women wheeled together provided one of the throngs' most common forms of public entertainment. In some versions, the shattered rag dolls were hung up in cages for better viewing.

- The pear, shaped like the fruit or like hands folded in a rounded prayer position, and often engraved with the face of Satan, was inserted into the vagina, anus, or mouth, opened with the twist of its screw-action handle, then closed, extracting gutsy confessions from those chosen few who survived.

- The Judas cradle was a tall, pyramidal stool topped with a wood or metal pyramid seat onto which the harnessed naked victim, hoisted with chains, was lowered, the weight of her vagina, anus, or coccyx positioned on the point. Whether the adjusted pressure was just barely touching or total body weight, the victim could be rocked, or hoisted and dropped onto the point. The French called the Judas cradle "the wake" or "nightwatch."
- The headcrusher was a metal helmet attached to a metal grid topped with a large screw used to exert the helmet's pressure down on the head. On some devices, the screw lowered the helmet, torturing or executing the victim; on other versions, the pointed tip screwed through the helmet and into the skull.
- A victim's neck was attached to the garroting chair with a metal collar equipped with a pointed screw that protruded through a hole in the chair and drilled into the back of the neck.
- The rapidly spun whirligig simply caused the caged victim to vomit. Repeatedly.
- Shaped much like a baby's highchair, the chair of spikes was just that. As if being strapped in was not enough, weights could be added and blows with mallets could enhance the spikes' piercing power. Survivors of this form of torture, imprisoned in dungeons, often died of ensuing infection and tetanus.
- To quote historian William Manchester's book, *A World Lit Only By Fire*, the iron maiden "embraced the condemned with metal arms, crushed him in a spiked hug, and then opened, letting him fall, a mass of gore, bleeding from a hundred stab wounds, all bones broken, to die slowly in an underground hole of revolving knives and sharp spears."

Sometimes impatient inquisitors resorted to more expedient means to prove a witch's guilt. For example, a common method was to tie heavy stones or iron weights to the accused and then throw her into a lake or river. If she drowned, she was guilty, or innocent, depending on the inquisitor's preference.

Not all bishops and magistrates, not even all inquisitors, resorted to the fallacious rhetoric and zealous sadism characteristic of witch-hunts. Many priests and their flocks piously faded into the woodwork of the Black Forests of the world, and even some of the more outspoken rebels, humanists and horrified Christians alike, managed to avoid excommunication and the heretic's stake.

Nonetheless, millions of "witches" and other heretics were tortured and murdered. Those who challenged the assumption that witches were real—and there were many such skeptics—were themselves deemed heretics by the *Malleus*.

Just like today, the medieval inquisitors had biblical reasons for their misogyny. "There was a defect in the formation of the first woman, since she was formed from a bent rib, that is, a rib of the breast, which is bent as it were in a contrary direction to a man. And since through this defect she is an imperfect animal, she always deceives." The reference is to the Genesis Garden of Eden myth, which does mention that Eve was formed from the rib of Adam, but doesn't mention "bent," "contrary direction to a man," "defect," "imperfect animal," and "always deceives." The *Malleus* asserts that a woman is more carnal "as is clear from her many carnal abominations." Even "the word woman is used to mean the lust of the flesh. As it is said: I have found a woman more bitter than death, and good woman subject to carnal lust."

> All wickedness is but little to the wickedness of a woman. Wherefore St. John Chrysostom says on the text, It is not good to marry (St. Matthew xix): What else is woman but a foe to friendship, an inescapable punishment, a necessary evil, a natural temptation, a desirable calamity, a domestic danger, a delectable detriment, an evil of nature, painted with fair colors! Therefore if it be a sin to divorce her when she ought to be kept, it is indeed a necessary torture; for either we commit adultery by divorcing her, or we must endure daily strife.

According to the male authors of the *Malleus*, men were not likely to become witches. Naturally, "women voluntarily prostitute themselves to Incubus devils." But "when men have connection with Succubus devils, yet it does not appear that men thus devilishly fornicate with the same full degree of culpability; for men, being by nature intellectually stronger than women, are more apt to abhor such practices." Of course logically, if men were smarter and knew better, they should have been *more* culpable.

Women are more superstitious, more credulous, more impressionable, "more ready to receive the influence of a disembodied spirit." Women have "slippery tongues," are weak, "find an easy and secret manner of vindicating themselves by witchcraft." They are feebler both in mind and body, are intellectually like children, which is why "No woman understood philosophy except Temeste," and of course a fair woman without discretion is "a jewel of gold in a swine's snout." Women have little faith, like Eve, who "when the serpent asked why they did not eat of every tree in Paradise, she answered: Of every tree, etc.—lest perchance we die. Thereby she showed that she doubted, and had little in the word of God." All this "is indicated by the etymology of the word; for *Femina* comes from *Fe* and *Minus*, since she is ever weaker to hold and preserve the faith."

Witches are sneaky, too. "They try as far as possible to conform with divine rites and ceremonies." Why? "They can more easily deceive men under the mask of an outwardly seeming pious action." It never occurs to the *Malleus* authors that these women might be genuinely pious. "For in the same way they entice young virgins and boys into their power; for though they might solicit such by means of evil and corrupt men, yet they rather deceive them by magic mirrors and reflections seen in witches' finger-nails, and lure them on in the belief that they love chastity, whereas they hate it. For the devil hates above all the Blessed Virgin, because she bruised his head." Biblically speaking, it was actually Eve that bruised the serpent's head.

Men are victims, according to the *Malleus*. Although women are witches, far more men are bewitched. "And the reason for this lies in the fact that God allows the devil more power over the venereal act, by which the original sin is handed down, than over other human actions. In the same way He allows more witchcraft to be performed by means of serpents, which are more subject to incantations than other animals, because that was the first instrument of the devil. And the venereal act can be more readily and easily bewitched in a man than in a woman, as has been clearly shown."

Why do these men think Eve's original sin was sex? There was no sex involved, unless eating a piece of fruit is considered a sex act. Clearly the serpent is a phallic symbol. But wouldn't Eve, then, be the victim of the phallus—a kind of victim of spiritual rape, perhaps? A victim of a Satanic Inquisition?

Hatred of sex is fear of sex. Fear of sex is fear of death at the most primal, animal level: fear of non-propagation. It could be argued that male fear of non-propagation has given "rise" to all organized religion, even though religion is supposed to be about the spirit, not the flesh. Women are the most heinous of all heretics. If a man can't control the means of reproduction, his line might be cut off—meaning, his penis might be cut off, his life might be cut off. For this he blames the woman herself. Boys can be macho boys for sexual display, because they need to sow their seed, even if by force. Women are sluts when out of a man's grip, because the man doesn't really know whose seed produced "his" children. Add to that some men's propensity for sadism, and you get an inquisitor, or a punishing fundamentalist.

And it's not just Christian fundamentalists. Absolute control of women is inherent in all forms of fundamentalism. Women are only good if so controlled. Mohammed's law for removing part or all of a girl's clitoris to rid her of sexual desire—a common practice in many parts of the world—is still "a noble practice which does honor to women," in the opinion of Sheik Gad Al Haq Ali Gad Al Haq.

Or in the opinion of thoroughly modern American Rev. Jerry Falwell,

> I listen to feminists and all these radical gals—most of them are failures. They've blown it. Some of them have been married, but they married some Casper Milquetoast who asked permission to go to the bathroom. These women just need a man in the house. That's all they need. Most of the feminists need a man to tell them what time of day it is and to lead them home. And they blew it and they're mad at all men. Feminists hate men. They're sexist. They hate men—that's their problem.

Satan symbolizes male fear turned sadistic; cursed with slithering, he personifies the de-mobilized shadow ever at a man's feet, ready to strike Achilles' heel, rendering him motionless, impotent, dead. He blames Eve, unfairly—she was innocent when she ate the fruit. Adam alone chose freely to eat of the tree of the knowledge of good and evil. They both had their eyes opened, and to this day they stand face to face glaring at each other. The male/female dichotomy is supposed to be transcended through love. Unfortunately, the inquisitional misogynist spirit destroys love.

Serpents, classic devil images, were associated with witchcraft in the Dark Ages. Witches cast the spell of hatred by means of the serpent, "for the serpent was the first instrument of the devil, and by reason of its curse inherits a hatred of women; therefore they cause such spells by placing the skin or head of a serpent under the threshold of a room or house. For this reason all the nooks and corners of the house where such a woman lives are to be closely examined and reconstructed as far as possible." Find a snake under the house or front porch, and the wife is burned for witchcraft. And not only snakes. Any object, "such as a stone or a piece of wood or a mouse or some serpent," can be the devil's visible instrument of witchcraft, especially if it is found in a hole.

Ever been in love? During the Dark Ages, this was *Philocaption*, or inordinate love of one person for another. "He who loves his wife to excess is an adulterer." Being "bewitched by love" a la Hollywood would have consummated in a hot date with the stake.

Sexual control is always the subtext, if not the text, of inquisitors. Agendas of the unholy trinity (selfishness, greed, and pride) climax as sexual control, because sex represents the free expression of love and the uncontrollable propagation of life-force, and love and life-force represent ultimate power. This explains why rightwing Dominionists and other cult leaders today are obsessed with homosexuality, abortion, the inferior status of women, and domination of others. Aristocratic money-grubbing arrogance is a form of sexual perversion.

Suppose you marry and want children but the man is impotent. "Extrinsically they [witches] cause it at times by means of images, or by the eating of herbs, sometimes by other external means, such as cocks' testicles. But it must not be thought that it is by the virtue of these things that a man is made impotent, but by the occult power of devils' illusions witches by this means procure such impotence, namely, that they cause man to be unable to copulate, or a woman to conceive."

Sometimes impotence isn't the problem, it's miscarriage, or rape. "Sometimes persons only think they are molested by an Incubus when they are not so actually." Actually they are molested by human men projecting the blame onto subhuman women.

"At times also women think they have been made pregnant by an Incubus, and their bellies grow to an enormous size; but when the time of parturition comes, their swelling is relieved by no more than the expulsion of a great quantity of wind." Luckily for accused witches, the *Malleus* authors presume that women don't know the difference between pregnancy and indigestion.

Suppose you marry and are lucky enough to avoid the spell of miscarriage. What Catholic witches do to infants is the stuff of legends and fairy tales. They offer them up to the devil and then eat each succulent limb and organ. Or they take the woman's child and devils replace it with one of three varieties of changeling. "Some are always ailing and crying, and yet the milk of four women is not enough to satisfy them. Some are generated by the operation of Incubus devils, of whom, however, they are not the sons, but of that man from whom the devil has received the semen as a Succubus, or whose semen he has collected from some nocturnal pollution in sleep." Today we call this adultery. Or rape.

"And there is a third kind, when the devils at times appear in the form of young children and attach themselves to the nurses. But all three kinds have this in common, that though they are very heavy, they are always ailing and do not grow, and cannot receive enough milk to satisfy them, and are often reported to have vanished away." Missing children were blamed on witches.

Clever witches can transform themselves. Today, male witches transforming themselves are called gay; women are of course feminazis. The *Malleus* authors cite the case of Staufer of Berne, who "could change himself into a mouse in the sight of his rivals and slip through the hands of his deadly enemies." Eventually, "when the Divine justice wished to put an end to his wickedness, some of his enemies lay in wait for him cautiously and saw him sitting in a basket near a window, and suddenly pierced him through with swords and spears, so that he miserably died for his crimes." Talk about overkill. Superstition evolves into a story passed on as fact.

The details of witchcraft are not only actual; they are also symbolic representations of fears. Superstitions of inquisitors, now as in the Dark Ages, drip with male sexual anxieties.

Witches drying up the milk in women and in cows were treated by the inquisitors with equal concern, because women and cows were essentially equal. That the drying of milk in women is due to witchcraft is substantiated with reference to Blessed Albert's *Book on Animals*, "Milk is naturally menstrual in any animal; and, like another flux in women, when it is not stopped by some natural infirmity, it is due to witchcraft that it is stopped." Nursing and menstruation are aspects of female, i.e. animal, sexuality that men have no control over. Hence, even to this day, nursing and menstruation are "dirty," or at least embarrassing.

The more important drying of milk in cows, a far more direct loss for men, was a bit more complicated. "For on the more holy nights according to the instructions of the devil and for the greater offence to the Divine Majesty of God, a witch will sit down in a corner of her house with a pail between her legs, stick a knife or some instrument in the wall or a post, and make as if to milk it with her hands." The gesture itself is aggressively sexual, but the description is made more so by its relationship to milk, pregnancy (via sex), and breasts/udders. "Then she summons her familiar who always works with her in everything, and tells him that she wishes to milk a certain cow from a certain house, which is healthy and abounding in milk. And suddenly the devil takes the milk from the udder of that cow, and brings it to where the witch is sitting, as if it were flowing from the knife." The subtext insinuates a woman's violent masturbatory congress with the devil, which implies that aggressive sexuality in a woman is evil.

If you're lucky enough to get milk, an important ingredient in delicious foods available to men, then you should be able to have butter, which makes sensuous culinary experiences even more scrumptious. Women who delete men from sexual experience are even more evil when they also deprive men of their milk and butter. The inquisitors further control women by dictating the proper means of executing superstitious rituals that control the outcome of their churning and therefore the success of their role as churners.

> There are women who, when they have been churning for a long while to no purpose, and if they suspect that this is due to some witch, procure if possible a little butter from the house of that witch. Then they make that butter into three pieces and throw them into the churn, invoking the Holy Trinity, the Father, the Son, and the Holy Ghost; and so all witchcraft is put to flight. Here again it is a case of opposing vanity to vanity, for the simple reason that the butter must be borrowed from the suspected witch. But if it were done without this, if with the invocation of the Holy Trinity and the Lord's Prayer the woman were to commit the effect of the Divine Will, she would remain beyond reproach. Nevertheless it is not a commendable practice to throw in the three pieces of butter; for it would be better to banish the witchcraft by means of sprinkling Holy Water or putting in some exorcised salt, always with the prayers we have mentioned.

In such cases, it was not "superstitious to carry out Holy Relics or the Eucharist as a protection against the plagues of the devil." Since cows are often destroyed by witchcraft, and milk and butter come from cows, people should "remove the soil under the threshold of the stable or stall, and where the cattle go to water, and replace it with fresh soil sprinkled with Holy Water" purchased from the local priest.

Love your neighbor and do unto others has been smothered under centuries of superstitious tricks meant to force God to aid and forgive—and, of course, to punish. Rituals, rites, benedictions, prayers, indeed all religious beliefs and practices have replaced God with idolatrous human gestures of spiritual control.

For the inquisitors, rites and rituals expressed fear, not faith, gratitude, or sacred connection. In many ways, their version of religion was the antithesis of true spirituality. Their focus was the devil, not God. In a very real sense, the devil was the God of the Inquisition.

Any herbal or other medical remedies were considered deluded if not demonic. Many alchemists were burned at the stake during the Inquisition, just like believers, especially women, who happened to be folk doctors and pharmacists (chemists), were burned as witches, in part because the church-supported guilds, like drug companies of today, did not want their competition. Some contemporary preachers call New Age herbalists and practitioners of alternative medicine "the heirs of witchcraft." But Catholicism did sanction the use of certain herbs and stones, especially in exorcisms.

Sickness and disease were also assumed to be the direct result of witchcraft. "For we have often found that certain people have been visited with epilepsy or the falling sickness by means of eggs which have been buried with dead bodies, especially the dead bodies of witches, together with other ceremonies of which we cannot speak, particularly when these eggs have been given to a person either in food or drink."

The famous Salem witch trials in 1692 took place when some young girls began to suffer from hallucinations and convulsions, the natural symptoms of ergot poisoning. Ergot is a fungus that grows on rye, barley, and other cereal grasses during specific weather conditions, such as those present in districts where those grains were ground into bread and witch-hunts ensued, including the district of Salem. Ergot, the source of LSD, has been found in the guts of bog people, including the famous

Gramella Man. In 1951, in Pont-Saint-Esprit, France, exorcisms were performed on victims of ergot poisoning until one doctor's research finally produced the scientific facts. In the early 1970s, psychologist Linnda Caporael made the connection between ergot and witch-hunts by showing correlations between rainy seasons in grain growing districts and outbreaks of witch-hunts. Of course the early Puritans had not been schooled in the medical symptoms of ergot poisoning, but had they not been predisposed to judge and condemn as evil what they didn't understand, they could have erred on the side of natural science and compassion for the sick, as would have, say, the ancient Greeks.

Many of us associate witches with the traditional black cats of Halloween. According to the *Malleus*, black cats could be witches' familiars or actual witches. In one instance, a man accused of beating women got off the hook by countering that he actually beat some large cats that had attacked him.

Battering was a charge easy to deflect. Notice how the *Malleus* authors exonerated this battering husband lurking in the subtext: "When a cow's supply of milk has been diminished by witchcraft, they [witches] hang a pail of milk over the fire, and uttering certain superstitious words, beat the pail with a stick. And though it is the pail that the women beat, yet the devil carries all those blows to the back of the witch; and in this way both the witch and the devil are made weary. But the devil does this in order that he may lead on the woman who beats the pail to worse practices." Instead of prosecuting the batterer, the Inquisition sent battered women to the stake.

Although dark and stormy nights were just as spooky in the Dark Ages as they are today, back then it was a witch rather than a boogieman that sent shivers down the spine. Luckily, today we don't burn people at the stake for causing storms. Even so, the superstitious witchcraft-storm cause-and-effect is no more ridiculous than Pat Robertson's assertions, "If the widespread practice of homosexuality will bring about the destruction of your nation, if it will bring about terrorist bombs, if it'll bring about earthquakes, tornadoes, and possibly a meteor, it isn't necessarily something we ought to open our arms to," and "When you see the rise of blatant open homosexuality and lesbianism, what you also know is God has given a society up . . . and we're at the mercy of the elements, the mercy of war, the mercy of economic disaster."

It's no more ridiculous than fundamentalists warning parents that Harry Potter books are demonic instruments that teach their children witchcraft.

The *Malleus* agrees that natural "acts of God" are demonic in origin. However, witches themselves can be the agents and can cast spells that the devils honor. "Blessed Albertus Magnus in his work *De passionibus aeris* says that rotten sage, if used as he explains, and thrown into running water, will arouse most fearful tempests and storms."

To ward off hailstorms and tempests, "Three of the hailstones are thrown into the fire with an invocation of the Most Holy Trinity, and the Lord's Prayer and the Angelic Salutation are repeated twice or three times, together with the Gospel of St. John, *In the beginning was the Word*. And the sign of the Cross is made in every direction towards each quarter of the world. Finally, *The Word was made Flesh* is repeated three times, and three times, 'By the words of this Gospel may this tempest be dispersed.'" One needed to be meticulous, though, for "if the hailstones were thrown into the fire without the invocation of the Divine Name, then it would be considered superstitious." And the person should throw them "into the fire rather than into water, because the more quickly they are dissolved the sooner is the devil's work destroyed."

This sounds to me like fighting witchcraft with witchcraft.

TV evangelists tap into the same archetypal superstition with its ritual religious obedience, for instance when Marilyn Hickey and Oral Roberts make up special instructions to activate the fruit-bearing blessings guaranteed to every Seed Faith donation made to them.

Perhaps faith-based Republicans who pooh-pooh global warming would agree that to still a tempest raised by witchcraft, you need to say this: "I adjure you, hailstorms and winds, by the five wounds of Christ, and by the three nails which pierced His hands and feet, and by the four Holy Evangelists, Matthew, Mark, Luke and John, that you be dissolved and fall as rain."

The *Malleus* relates a quaint story told in the *Formicarius*, which it cites as an authority, about a man who could raise hailstorms and tempests but was prevented from doing as much harm as he wished "because of the guardianship of good Angels . . . We can only injure those who are deprived of God's help; but we cannot hurt those who make the sign of the Cross." Many people today still make the sign of the cross to ward off impending disaster. The man told how using certain words in the fields conjured the chief of devils to attack their target. "Then, when the devil has come, we sacrifice to him a black cock at two cross-roads, throwing it up into the air; and when the devil has received this, he performs our wish and stirs up the air, but not always in the places which we have named, and, according to the permission of the living God, sends down hailstorms and lightnings." This is the exact same method used by the homosexuals, feminazis, and Muslim terrorists who conjured Katrina and all those Florida hurricanes, according to religious radicals like Pat Robertson.

When you think witchcraft is in the air, remember, "It is lawful in any decent habitation of men or beasts to sprinkle Holy Water for the safety and securing of men and beasts, with the invocation of the Most Holy Trinity and a Paternoster. For it is said in the Office of Exorcism, that wherever it is sprinkled, all uncleanness is purified, all harm is repelled, and no pestilent spirit can abide there." Keep in mind that "in the case of a Blessed Candle, although it is more appropriate to light it, the wax of it may with advantage be sprinkled about dwelling-houses."

Is this sacred ritual, or just plain old superstition: "But the surest protection for places, men, or animals are the words of the triumphal title of our Savior, if they be written in four places in the form of a cross: IESUS † NAZARENUS † REX † IUDAEORUM †. There may also be added the name of MARY and of the Evangelists, or the words of St. John: The Word was made Flesh."

Today it might just be easier to purchase the magical trinkets sold by TV evangelists.

Chapter 11

The Reformation Myth

During the Dark Ages, Inquisition popes and their subordinate keepers of the keys to the kingdom became infamous not only for overwhelming psychological oppression but also for their murderous brutality, wild orgies, libraries of pornography, parade of mistresses and illegitimate children (some via incest), recreational gang-rape, and obscene wealth and the means of procuring it, all of which were well documented by clerical and secular contemporaries and by official records.

Hatred of priests, which had been seething for centuries, came to a boil when Pope Innocent VIII institutionalized simony by establishing an official board to oversee the marketing of favors, absolution, and papal bulls. Medieval and Renaissance churchmen sold indulgences to erase transgressions in much the same way that TV evangelists peddle salvation today.

Church abuses kindled the Reformation revolution. In 1517, Luther tacked (he did not "nail") his ninety-five theses to the Castle Church door. As was customary in many university towns, the church door was used as a bulletin board to post issues for further discussion, often formally at the university. Luther's position, which he titled *Disputation for the Clarification of the Power of Indulgences*, appeared along with other postings. An innocent spark of academic inquiry exploded into a thousand heretical fires.

Luther's scholarly defiance of the pope inspired instant mayhem throughout Germany. In *A World Lit Only By Fire*, historian William Manchester describes protesting (Protestant) students who tore crucifixes and pictures from the walls of local churches and were joined by mobs as they ravaged the countryside, destroying homes and libraries, gutting churches, hewing with axes Catholic icons, altars, and paintings hacked to kindling to stoke the flames; priests were scattered, and women were stoned as they knelt before images of the Madonna.

Inquiry backfired into inquisitions. Retaliation swelled into violent spiritual chaos. Executions became a new spectator sport. Within four years of "Luther's" revolt, the number of Germans killed approached a quarter-million.

God's battle wasn't just between Lutherans and Catholics. Protestantism immediately split into the Lutheran Church and the Reformed. Huldrych Zwingli, John Calvin, and John Knox formed their own sects. Splinter groups erupted—Anabaptists, Mennonites, Bohemians, and the forerunners of Baptists, Congregationalists, Presbyterians, and Unitarians—each as repressive and intolerant as Catholicism.

Perhaps the clearest example of the intolerance of that era was the repressive "Reich" of John Calvin. His city-state of Geneva, known as the Protestant Rome, became a virtual police state of strictly enforced doctrinal regulations managed by a consistory of five pastors and twelve lay elders.

Manchester's description of "the bloodless figure of the dictator" strikes a startling similarity to Hitler.

> Frail, thin, short, and lightly bearded, with ruthless, penetrating eyes, he was humorless and short-tempered. The slightest criticism enraged him. Those who questioned his theology he called "pigs," "asses," "riffraff," "dogs," "idiots," and "stinking beasts." One morning he found a poster on his pulpit accusing him of "Gross Hypocrisy." A suspect was arrested. No evidence was produced, but he was tortured day and night for a month till he confessed. Screaming with pain, he was lashed to a wooden stake. Penultimately, his feet were nailed to the wood; ultimately he was decapitated.

Calvin's theocracy, established in 1542, instituted an oppression that today's authoritarians can only dream of. He preached longwinded sermons three or four times a week, and attendance was mandatory; slackers were burned at the stake. Like Hitler's Nazis, Calvin's Consistory could enter homes, summon anyone, do its own investigations, create its own charges, and punish at will, all in the name of their God.

Our Founders defended against this kind of invasiveness by guaranteeing our constitutional right to privacy and freedom of conscience, and all our other amendment rights. Calvin was a perfect exemplum of religious control our Deist Founders feared and rejected. His institution of biblical austerity, rivaled by the tyranny of Hitler, exemplifies the coveted dominion of today's Christian Reconstructionists.

Calvin respected no rights except his right to control—by the authority of God, of course. His legislation determined the number of dishes to be served at each meal; the color of garments worn; the kind of garments allowed, which were determined by one's class. Declining to take the Eucharist was a crime. "Feasting" was proscribed. According to Manchester, so were "dancing, singing, pictures, statues, relics, church bells, organs, altar candles; 'indecent or irreligious' songs, staging or attending theatrical plays; wearing rouge, jewelry, lace, or 'immodest' dress; speaking disrespectfully of your betters; extravagant entertainment; swearing, gambling, playing cards, hunting, drunkenness; naming children after anyone but figures in the Old Testament; reading 'immoral or irreligious' books; and sexual intercourse, except between partners of different genders who were married to one another."

A father spent four days in jail for naming his newborn Claude, as did a woman who had worn her hair at an immoral height. A child was beheaded for striking his parents. Pregnant single women were drowned, along with their impregnators. Calvin executed his own relatives for committing adultery. The plague afflicting Geneva was blamed on fourteen witches, who were burned alive.

As I read Manchester's book, I could see the Christian tradition where today's inquisitors, who actually believe that infidels bring about natural disasters, terrorism, and national decay, and deserve to die, might get their oppressive notions. Certainly Calvin's inquisition provided models of judgment and punishment for contemporary fundamentalists like Randall Terry, Fred Phelps, Benny Hinn, Paul Crouch, James Dobson, and Pat Robertson, to name but a few. Calvin and the other Protestant theocrats, like fundamentalists today, condemned those who held religious beliefs that differed from their own.

Hitler, a student of Luther and Calvin, inspires contemporary fundamentalist cults like the Neo-Nazis. Hitler's Reich imposed puritanical ideals meant to cleanse the world by his standards, to include purging the

world of Jews. First, condemn and control normal, healthy appetites—
itself a kind of perverting of nature.

> Parallel to the training of the body a struggle against the poison-
> ing of the soul must begin. Our whole public life today is like a
> hothouse for sexual ideas and simulations. Just look at the bill of
> fare served up in our movies, vaudeville and theaters, and you will
> hardly be able to deny that this is not the right kind of food, par-
> ticularly for the youth . . .
>
> Theater, art, literature, cinema, press, posters, and window dis-
> plays must be cleansed of all manifestations of our rotting world
> and placed in the service of a moral, political, and cultural idea.

Had he lived today in America, Hitler might have chosen a lucrative
career in TV evangelism. Certainly today's evangelists are Calvinist in
their rhetoric, if not in their lives.

Bob Jones, for instance, echoed Calvin's condemnation of heretical
Catholicism when he commented, "I would rather see a saloon on every
corner than a Catholic in the White House. I would rather see a nigger
as president." (Like other fundamentalist schools, Bob Jones University
forbids interracial marriage or dating.)

Calvin's accusations spread like wildfire that still burns today.

Medieval Catholics were not to be surpassed by the Protestants in the
righteous cause of punishment. Thomas de Torquemada, the Dominican
monk who presided over the Spanish Inquisition, devised many of that
era's more grizzly devices of Christian brotherly chastisement. Perhaps
the most famous instrument ever devised to teach a lesson was the old
iron maiden. To use Manchester's description, "The Jungfer embraced
the condemned with metal arms, crushed him in a spiked hug, and
then opened, letting him fall, a mass of gore, bleeding from a hundred
stab wounds, all bones broken, to die slowly in an underground hole of
revolving knives and sharp spears."

Terror and pain—effective forms of instruction—insured obedience
and punished anyone straying from the Christian status quo, especially
women (aka "witches"), but even the handicapped and mentally ill, who
were regularly tormented and tortured to death, and of course Jews,
blacks, homosexuals, and other minorities were closely scrutinized and
found wanting. Scholars (except for scholars employed by the Catholic
Church) estimate that as many as four million people, mostly women,

were killed during the Inquisition for various forms of heresy and other sins. Eventually bloodlust became an end in itself, and the Inquisition developed into a demonic frenzy in which not only "the different" were removed, but whole communities of unauthorized Christians were exterminated, and even animals, birds, and insects were tried, tortured, and publicly executed as witches and heretics. Even corpses were dug up, tried, and burned.

Bigotry has always served the high priest in his battle to secure power and control. Priests construct a sacred hierarchy with themselves on top. The segment discriminated against is on the bottom. The large segment in the middle, the gullible masses, can be persuaded that the scapegoat on the bottom is inferior, bad, evil. The scapegoat is demonized as the real perpetrator of abomination. With a little indoctrination and a splash of fear, the masses can be riled up into zealots of hate.

In order to be at the top—in the case of the high priest, the absolute top—others have to be beneath. The priest on his pedestal peers down on the lowly servants bowed to him in supplication. Sometimes the priest is a priest-king, like Moses or David; Charlemagne established a Holy Roman Empire. Sometimes the divine-right king elevates himself to the status of divinity, like some of the Pharaohs or Caesars, and sometimes others elevate him, as in the case of Jesus or Buddha. Sometimes priests wanting to rule challenge the authority of divine-right kings. The Holy Roman Empire, for instance, split roughly into two ruling factions, kings and priests. Once Luther challenged the pope, smoldering power struggles erupted into the Reformation, an unholy slaughter with royalty and priests battling against each other, and even, often most brutally, against themselves. John Calvin split from both the church and state to create his own religious dictatorship in Geneva, complete with his own witch-hunts, tortures, and burnings.

Religious wars are secular wars wrapped in priestly robes; the battles are battles for power-over, and power-over requires displays of control over a hierarchy. The power structure is always essentially the same. The entitled priest and/or divine-right king rules from on high. Beneath the ruler are the elite aristocrats. The royal court of aristocrats sometimes includes other elites such as chief warriors or politicians, but no matter how much power they wield, elites, aristocratic or otherwise, are always inferior to, always subjects of, the ruler. Subjects help the ruler govern the more inferior servants, and servants help subjects manage slaves. Subjects, servants, and slaves are all necessarily faithful followers of the ruler (or in some cases, his stand-in shadow ruler). Except in true democracies, the agenda of the ruler is always necessarily subjugation of inferiors.

Bigotry serves to establish a threatening "other" that only the high priest and/or divine-right king on top, with the help of his obedient followers, can conquer, often via punishing extermination. The Christian Crusades massacred Muslims, along with Jews. Muslims retaliated by slaughtering Christians. The Inquisition sadistically tortured and burned or otherwise dispatched millions of innocent souls called heretics, especially those supreme heretics, witches.

The Nazis continued a long history of punishment, ostracism, and extermination of Christ-killing, host-nailing "pigs," also known as Jews. Historian Dagobert Runes estimated that 3.5 million Jews died at the hands of Christians from the 1100s through the 1500s alone. Add to that another six million executed by Hitler and you have a sampling of the many millions of Jews murdered by numerous religious holocausts that span two millennia. And that doesn't include Jews forced to convert to Christianity, Jews "relocated," Jews robbed, raped, tormented, and denied basic human rights, Jews forced by various popes to wear armbands signifying inferiority tantamount to damnation. A few Roman tyrants had responded similarly toward some early Christians.

In a speech delivered on April 12, 1922, Adolf Hitler expressed the traditional Christian viewpoint:

> My feelings as a Christian points me to my Lord and Savior as a fighter. It points me to the man who once in loneliness, surrounded only by a few followers, recognized these Jews for what they were and summoned men to fight against them and who, God's truth! was greatest not as a sufferer but as a fighter. In boundless love as a Christian and as a man I read through the passage which tells us how the Lord at last rose in His might and seized the scourge to drive out of the Temple the brood of vipers and adders. How terrific was His fight for the world against the Jewish poison. Today, after two thousand years, with deepest emotion I recognize more profoundly than ever before in the fact that it was for this that He had to shed His blood upon the Cross. As a Christian I have no duty to allow myself to be cheated, but I have the duty to be

a fighter for truth and justice . . . And if there is anything which could demonstrate that we are acting rightly it is the distress that daily grows. For as a Christian I have also a duty to my own people . . . When I go out in the morning and see these men standing in their queues and look into their pinched faces, then I believe I would be no Christian, but a very devil if I felt no pity for them, if I did not, as did our Lord two thousand years ago, turn against those by whom today this poor people is plundered and exploited.

Hitler's cleverly sanctified bigotry is classic Orwellian "newspeak." Substitute Muslim for Jewish and you have the sentiment of many Americans after 9/11.

It wasn't until 1961 that the World Council of Churches condemned anti-Semitism, and only in 1962 did the Vatican delete the words "perfidious Jews" from Good Friday worship services. In 1965, the Vatican finally decided to stop assigning collective Jewish guilt for the death of Jesus.

In 1994, the Evangelical Lutheran Church pledged "to oppose the deadly workings of anti-Semitism in church and society," repudiating the anti-Semitic writings of Martin Luther and acknowledging their use by the Nazis. In question were texts like this one, penned by Luther:

What then shall we Christians do with this damned, rejected race of Jews? First, their synagogues or churches should be set on fire . . . Secondly, their homes should likewise be broken down and destroyed . . . They ought to be put under one roof or in a stable, like gypsies. Thirdly, they should be deprived of their prayer-books and Talmuds in which such idolatry, lies, cursing, and blasphemy are taught. Fourthly, their rabbis must be forbidden under threat of death to teach any more . . . Fifthly, passport and traveling privileges should be absolutely forbidden to the Jews . . . Sixthly, they ought to be stopped from usury. All their cash and valuables of silver and gold ought to be taken from them and put aside for safe keeping . . . Seventhly, let the young and strong Jews and Jewesses be given the flail, the axe, the hoe, the spade, the distaff, and spindle, and let them earn their bread by the sweat of their noses as is enjoined upon Adam's children . . . To sum up, dear princes and nobles who have Jews in your domains, if this advice of mind does not suit you, then find a better one so that you and we may all be free of this unsufferable devilish burden—the Jews.

Even Luther, the instigator of the Reformation, the father of Protestantism, the great emissary of "salvation by grace through faith," could not protest his own dis-grace or reform his bigot's faith in sacrifice. One wonders why Luther revered the Jew-written Bible or the Jew Jesus and his Jewish disciples, or why the critics of Luther continue to be Lutherans.

The rift decisively effected by Luther—the schism between Catholics and Protestants—continues today, even in America. Globally, religious rifts threaten the survival of our species. And all religious rifts rest on claims of religious infallibility proven by each religion's infallible religious texts.

It's tepid comfort, perhaps, that the Catholic Church can at times admit its errors, if not its fallibility. In 1992, for instance, three centuries after the Inquisition sentenced Galileo to life in prison for supporting scientific theories, especially Copernican, that supposedly contradicted Aristotle, the Vatican admitted its error by declaring Galileo "rehabilitated," the less than perfectly spherical earth continued revolving around the sun, and even the pope became subject to the laws of gravity.

How did this "rehabilitation" come about? "Clarifications furnished by recent historical studies enable us to state that this sad misunderstanding now belongs to the past," announced Pope John Paul II. By 1992, Galileo's case had become "the symbol of the church's supposed rejection of scientific progress."

Supposed? Sad misunderstanding? Estimates of the number of people murdered by the supposed sad misunderstanding of the Church's Inquisition range to four million, many of them killed for heresies of the kind for which Galileo was prosecuted. (The modern Vatican made no mention of rehabilitating or forgiving those other untold millions imprisoned or burned at the stake as heretics.)

Ironically, Galileo had always been a devout Catholic who saw no conflict between his religious and scientific beliefs. Along with many others then and before him, Galileo believed that Scripture revealed spiritual, not scientific, knowledge.

Like other mathematics professors, Galileo was required to teach an astronomy course that assumed the theory that the sun and planets revolved around the Earth. This scientific "proof" in turn validated biblical "fact." Although Copernicus himself taught heliocentrism as theory rather than as his own belief in order to avoid censure by the church (which would likely take the form of excommunication or death), Galileo was more out with his views. In 1613, he wrote a letter arguing the consistency of Copernican theory and Catholic doctrine. He further argued, this time before the Roman inquisitors, that Scripture had always been interpreted allegorically by the Church, and that his interpretation simply differed from the Church's. Galileo's was a light punishment this time. The inquisitors ordered that he not "hold or defend" the Copernican theory.

But in 1632, Galileo boldly defied the church gag by publishing *Dialogue Concerning the Two Chief World Systems*, a discussion among three characters, the Ptolemaic-Aristotelian theory, the superior Copernican theory, and the church, represented by Simplicio, meaning "fool." This time Galileo was tried on "vehement suspicion of heresy." Forced to swear that he "abjured, cursed, and detested" the work's errors, he was sentenced to life imprisonment, which he was permitted to serve under house arrest due to his old age, blindness, and ill health. Undaunted, and faithful to his understanding of truth, Galileo completed his *Discourse on Two New Sciences*, published in 1638.

"The sun also ariseth, and the sun goeth down, and hastenth to his place where he arose," Melanchthon pressed, quoting Ecclesiastes 1:4-5. "The eyes are witnesses that the heavens revolve in the space of twenty-four hours . . . It is the part of a good mind to accept the truth as revealed by God, and to acquiesce in it . . . The earth can be nowhere if not in the centre of the universe." This university professor, who at age twelve had changed his surname, Philipp Schwarzert, to its Greek equivalent, Melanchthon, meaning "black earth," was the theologian most responsible for popularizing the teachings of his Wittenberg colleague, Martin Luther. Never mind that because of his attempts to create harmony between Protestantism and Catholicism and thus avert civil war—he was the author of the twenty-one articles of faith known as the Augsburg Confession, presented at the Diet of Augsburg in 1530—the Lutherans branded him a heretic. Like Luther, Melanchthon wanted all those who agreed with Copernicus silenced. And many were, by an Inquisition manned by Catholics and Protestants alike. The Dark Ages grew darker.

More than three hundred years before the birth of Christ, Aristotle had determined that the planet was a sphere, and four centuries later,

Ptolemy almost perfectly calculated the earth's circumference and accurately partitioned the earth into climatic zones. Centuries later, the medieval Church rejected such facts, rediscovered via Muslims by humanist scholars, claiming that the facts did not coincide with its literal interpretation of the Scriptures. Instead the Church sided with the monk Cosmas, whose *Topographia Christiana*, based on his literal reading of the Bible, concluded that the world was a flat, rectangular plane, above which was sky, and above that, heaven. At the rectangle's center was Jerusalem, edged by the Garden of Eden, which was watered by the four rivers of Paradise.

Copernicus was attacked not only by the Catholic Inquisition, but also by the new Inquisition faction of Reformation heretics. Luther wrote, "People give ear to an upstart astrologer who strove to show that the earth revolves, not the heavens or the firmament, the sun and the moon . . . This fool wishes to reverse the entire scheme of astrology; but sacred Scripture tells us that Joshua commanded the sun to stand still, not the earth." John Calvin quoted the Ninety-third Psalm, "The world also is stabilized, that it cannot be moved," and asked, "Who will venture to place the authority of Copernicus above that of the Holy Spirit?"

Countless thousands were burned at the stake for proclaiming the truth of Copernicus. James J. Walsh, K.C. St. G., M.D., Ph.D., Litt.D., L.L.D., Dean, Fordham University School of Medicine, Professor of Physiological Psychology, Cathedral College, pointed out that the Roman Inquisition that prosecuted Galileo "endeavored to make a Church tribunal the judge of scientific truth, a function . . . which it was not competent to exercise."

Copernicus simply would not go away. In his Italian dialogues, philosopher Giordano Bruno declared that a rotating, orbiting earth was an unassailable fact. Because Bruno also believed that God was immanent in Creation, the Roman Inquisition burned him at the stake for the heresy of pantheism.

Certainly the proprietors of absolutist salvation feared the superior intellectual powers of innovative geniuses like Leonardo da Vinci. According to Manchester,

> Leonardo, *sui generic*, questioned everything . . . So mighty was his intellect and so broad the spectrum of his gifts—he was, among other things, a master of engineering, biology, sculpture,

linguistics, botany, music, philosophy, architecture, and science—that presenting an adequate summary of his feats is impossible. However, it is worth noting that at a time when Europe was mired in ignorance, shackled by superstition, and lacking solid precedents in every scholarly discipline, this uneducated, illegitimate son of an Anchiano country girl anticipated Galileo, Newton, and the Wright brothers. He did this by flouting absolute taboos.

Leonardo was a formidable threat to Catholic society but was spared execution for heresy due to the corruption of the Borgia popes, especially Cesare, who (among more heinous vices) exploited artists to enhance his rule with an aura of aesthetic grandeur. As Manchester eloquently points out, "Da Vinci, like Copernicus, threatened the certitude that knowledge had been forever fixed by God, the rigid mind-set which left no role for curiosity or innovation. Leonardo's cosmology, based on what he called *saper vedere* (knowing how to see) was, in effect, a blunt instrument assaulting the fatuity which had, among other things, permitted a mafia of profane popes to desecrate Christianity."

Still today, sound science is sacrificed on the altar of biblical literalism. Though creationist science might strike most of us as an oxymoron, Henry Morris, the father of the creation science movement, defended it to the day of his death in 2006: "When science and the Bible differ, science has obviously misinterpreted its data." Is it ignorance or arrogance that allowed Morris to claim in 1974, "The only way we can determine the true age of the earth is for God to tell us what it is. And since He has told us, very plainly, in the Holy Scriptures that it is several thousand years in age, and no more, that ought to settle all basic questions of terrestrial chronology."

Morris's statement is similar to that made by Cardinal Bellarmino in 1615, during the trial of Galileo: "To assert that the earth revolves around the sun is as erroneous as to claim that Jesus was not born of a virgin."

"The earth is flat, and anyone who disputes this claim is an atheist who deserves to be punished." This was the view not of a Christian judge presiding over a medieval inquisition; this was a 1993 Muslim edict of Sheik Abdel-Aziz Ibn Baaz, supreme religious authority of Saudi Arabia. Both fundamentalists, the Muslim Sheik and Christian Morris could have shaken hands instead of upholding the tradition of mutual hostility.

Martin Luther's claim, "Reason is the greatest enemy that faith has," echoes through modern religious pronouncements: "You cannot in academic honesty say that 'I am a Christian,' and that 'I am a believer in God' and 'I accept evolution,'" asserted anti-academic, modestly educated fundamentalist guru, Jerry Falwell. According to sex-scandal scathed Jimmy Swaggart, also modestly educated, "Evolution is a bankrupt speculative philosophy, not a scientific fact. Only a spiritually bankrupt society could ever believe it . . . Only atheists could accept this Satanic theory."

James Kennedy added, "Every new advance and every step taken by science confirm not evolution but the Genesis account of creation. Yet evolution still continues to be taught as fact . . . Thus, the honorable place that had been given to human beings by God is surreptitiously aborted, and they are dragged down into the slime." Kennedy's first statement is patently untrue. I have already shown many of the incongruities in the Genesis story, which Kennedy, supposedly being well-educated, must surely have noticed. Given that, isn't Kennedy being dishonest?

I can't help but notice that many fundamentalists exploit a perverse brand of creationism to make big bucks. Should we trust, for instance, Kent Hovind's famous young Earth creationist seminars, given that in 2006 he was convicted of fifty-eight federal tax offenses and relate charges?

Certainly part of the conservative agenda is to keep the wool fastened securely over the sheep's eyes. Updating the science of ancient beliefs might raise questions that couldn't be honestly answered in Christian terms.

As Adolph Hitler put it,

> For how shall we fill people with blind faith in the correctness of a doctrine, if we ourselves spread uncertainty and doubt by constant changes in its outward structure . . . Here, too, we can learn by the example of the Catholic Church. Though its doctrinal edifice, and in part quite superfluously, comes into collision with exact science and research, it is nonetheless unwilling to sacrifice so much as one little syllable of its dogmas . . . it is only such dogmas which lend to the whole body the character of a faith.

"We were convinced that the people need and require this faith," Hitler understood, like today's rightwing Republicans and TV evangelists. "We have therefore undertaken the fight against the atheistic movement, and that not merely with a few theoretical declarations: we have stamped it out."

Hitler's stamping out "atheism," meaning opposition to biblical literalism, is what dominionists like James Kennedy work to accomplish.

Judge Braswell Dean, quoted in *Time Magazine*, March 1981, concurs with fundamentalist creationists: "This monkey mythology of Darwin is the cause of permissiveness, promiscuity, prophylactics, perversions, pregnancies, abortions, pornotherapy, pollution, poisoning and proliferation of crimes of all types." Alliteration aside, this playful prose poetically proves a paucity of common sense. It is disconcerting that in 1981, the monkey mind was as ignorant of slippery slope and basic biology as it was during the Scopes Trial of 1925.

When Clarence Darrow defended John Scopes, who had broken the law by violating the Butler Act, a Tennessee law that forbade the teaching of the theory of evolution in public schools because it contradicted the biblical account of Creation, at issue was not just the scientific validity of evolution and the constitutionality of the Butler Act; what was at stake was the accuracy of biblical literalism and the absolutist claims of religious tradition.

Contrary to fundamentalist assertions, Charles Darwin was not an atheist. In his *Autobiography*, published in 1876, Darwin describes his decision, at his father's suggestion, to consider training for the church rather than qualifying in medicine:

> I asked for some time to consider, as from what little I had heard and thought on the subject I had scruples about declaring my belief in all the dogmas of the Church of England, though otherwise I liked the thought of becoming a country clergyman. Accordingly I read with great care Pearson on the Creeds and a few other books on divinity; and as I did not then in the least doubt the strict and literal truth of every word in the Bible, I soon persuaded myself that our Creed must be fully accepted.

Darwin received the preparatory ordination degree from Christ's College Cambridge but immediately upon graduation was diverted away from ordination by an offer to join the scientific crew of the now famous HMS Beagle. In a chapter of his autobiography titled "Religious Beliefs," Darwin describes his years on board:

During these two years (March 1837 to January 1839) I was led to think much about religion. Whilst on board the Beagle I was quite orthodox, and I remember being heartily laughed at by several officers (though themselves orthodox) for quoting the Bible as an unanswerable authority on some point of morality. I suppose it was the novelty of the argument that amused them. But I had gradually come by this time (i.e. 1836 to 1839) to see the Old Testament, from its manifestly false history of the world, with the Tower of Babel, the rain-bow as a sign, &c., &c., and from its attributing to God the feelings of a revengeful tyrant, was no more to be trusted than the sacred books of the Hindoos, or the beliefs of any barbarian.

Thus disbelief crept over me at a very slow rate, but was at last complete. The rate was so slow that I felt no distress, and have never since doubted for a single second that my conclusion was correct. I can indeed hardly see how anyone ought to wish Christianity to be true; for if so, the plain language of the text seems to show that the men who do not believe, and this would include my Father, Brother, and almost all my best friends, will be everlastingly punished. And this is a damnable doctrine.

Darwin clearly grappled with the accepted tenets of the organized church. His honest, anti-elitist vision of truth could not discount the beliefs of more than half the world's population.

At present the most usual argument for the existence of an intelligent God is drawn from deep inward conviction and feelings which are experienced by most persons. But it cannot be doubted that Hindoos, Mahomedans and others might argue in the same manner and with equal force in favour of the existence of one God, or of many Gods, or as with the Buddhists of no God.

This argument would be a valid one, if all men of all races had the same inward conviction of the existence of one God; but we know this is very far from being the case. Therefore I cannot see that such inward convictions and feelings are of any weight as evidence of what really exists.

Later, Darwin realized that evolutionary adaptations giving rise to life forms do not contradict the existence of a Creator. In the face of horrendous suffering in the world, he said, we express a kind of existential faith in an omnipotent and omniscient God because "It revolts our understanding that his benevolence is not unbounded."

It revolts our understanding that his benevolence is not unbounded.

Religious rifts revolt our understanding of unbounded benevolence.

Deism, however, does not revolt one's understanding in asserting the unbounded benevolence of God.

Like Darwin, many Deists have scoured the Bible only to discover a disjointed book of incongruous myths and superstitions that contradict anyone's understanding that God's benevolence is unbounded. We have faced the Bible's fallibility and lack of historical authority.

Thanks to Deism, out of the cauldron of perpetual religious wars, inquisitions, and power-mongering emerged the distilled wisdom codified as America's Bill of Rights. But even today, our fundamental rights of religious freedom have been compromised by rightwing authoritarians perverting the truth of America into a Calvin-esque notion of a "Christian nation."

In a world of religious fanaticism armed with nuclear weapons and an end-of-the-world death-wish, we would be wise to advance a healthier, more honest Reformation of universal, truly democratic Deism.

Chapter 12

Freedom of Conscience v. Theocracy: The Rise of Deist Democracy

Far too many Americans take for granted the extraordinary experiment in freedom that our country has undertaken. Our remarkable republic could not have been possible had the powers of church and state not been, in principle at least, thoroughly separated. When church and state fused, as they had for centuries, authoritarian elitists always suppressed the masses into servitude to divine-right masters—themselves.

The Greeks gave the world the democratic ideal more than two thousand years ago, but the long road to equality remains rocky because the powerful refuse to relinquish their power-over, and because many of the not-powerful don't realize they're being exploited.

Early democratic ideals were quickly quashed when Rome overtook Greece and its high culture and ideals. Divine Caesars gave way to popes with their keys of Saint Peter to help them battle Mohammad's Turks. Only after centuries of Roman elitism and Dark Age oppression was the dust blown off the annals of ancient Greece, inspiring humanist intellectuals, who inspired everyman to the hope of truly recovering the democratic spirit bequeathed by the greatest civilization the world had ever known.

During the Renaissance and Reformation, monarchs made a comeback, challenging papal power and establishing their own national churches—the Church of England, for instance—which became more and more independent of the Vatican. By the end of the Thirty Years' War (1618-1648), the secular, centralized state began to dethrone the

Church as the overlord of people's fates. Military and civil bureaucracies expanded to such an extent that by the time of Louis XIV, monarchs were at last rightfully becoming the servants of their own countries. The scientific revolution of the seventeenth century further demystified divine-right worldviews. Philosophy split from Church regulated theology and sided with scientific humanism based on natural law. But as the Greek ideal rose like the Phoenix shaking off its ashes, Deism was born—really reborn like a returning Messiah.

The Enlightenment of our Founders emerged against an immense backdrop of monarchial despotism and ecclesiastical tyranny. The ruled were scratching the itch for self-rule, freedom, and equal rights that wars and insurrections couldn't fully quell. By the end of the eighteenth century, various revolutions, including the American Revolution, struggled to dissolve all forms of dictatorial power-over. Out of it emerged the fundamental assertion that every human being has an innate, God-given, equal right to power over his or her own life.

Revolutions failed and recommenced as intellectuals and common people alike broke the chains of bondage—physical, intellectual, and spiritual. Once their revolts had gained the people their hard-earned freedom, they meant to keep it intact through governments and constitutions of, by, and for the people.

Very different from today's politically conservative Right that tends to vote Republican, Colonial Americans were tax resister Sons of Liberty who rioted like good liberals and abhorred imperialism, civil or clerical. America's Revolution got a tremendous boost from Thomas Paine's immensely popular book, *Common Sense*, which appealed for a manifesto that soon after became our Declaration of Independence.

In France, Jean Jacques Rousseau's doctrine of popular sovereignty inspired the third estate (the common people) to assert its Declaration of the Rights of Man and Citizen in 1789, establishing a constitutional monarchy. America's Declaration of Independence of 1776, a humanist statement of principle asserting the rights of man and the legitimacy of revolution, rejected the sovereign rule of King George III. America completed its Constitution without yielding to the temptation to appoint its own king (which was seriously discussed on the floor) in favor of establishing a permanent republic of elected representatives who would run the state machine that ensured liberty and equality.

Our Founders also saw to it that God was left out of the Constitution, not because they didn't believe in God, but because they wanted to prevent religious groups that thought they controlled God from thinking they controlled the country and its people.

The Declaration of Independence

When the call for independence was made by Richard Henry Lee on June 7, 1776, the colonists had failed to gain rights from King George and had created a Congress to make formal demands, all of which were denied or ignored. Congress appointed a committee of five—Thomas Jefferson, John Adams, Benjamin Franklin, Robert Livingston, and Roger Sherman—to draft a declaration of independence. All were erudite, but the young Jefferson was recruited to write the declaration due to "the Elegance of his pen," as Adams put it.

According to historian John P. Kaminski,

> The genius of Thomas Jefferson is that he infused the Declaration with "the proper tone and spirit called for." Jefferson took a huge body of political literature—twenty-two thousand pamphlets published in Britain in the seventeenth century and several thousand more published during the eighteenth in Britain and America—and distilled it into five sentences—fewer than two hundred words—the introduction to the Declaration of Independence. Those five sentences constitute arguably what is the greatest statement in political literature.

The Declaration asserts:

> We hold these truths to be self-evident, that all men are created equal, that they are endowed by their Creator with certain unalienable Rights, that among these are Life, Liberty, and the pursuit of Happiness,—That to secure these rights, Governments are instituted among Men, deriving their just powers from the consent of the governed.

Jefferson was influenced by Enlightenment thinkers who believed that the natural world was organized by God in a logical and reasonable "self-evident" pattern accessible to God-given human reason.

For Enlightenment thinkers, all men, being part of God's natural Creation, are created equal in being equally human, and each person possesses certain unalienable rights. Jefferson upheld John Locke's "social contract" by which government exists by consent of the governed, who should rebel if their natural rights are violated, as the American Revolutionaries who established the United States rebelled against British rule, both the monarchy and the Church of England. Like many early Americans influenced by the Enlightenment, Jefferson embraced the principle of "freedom of conscience." That fundamental freedom ensured that corruption would not jeopardize our other freedoms.

In *Age of Reason*, Thomas Paine stressed the importance of codifying the Declaration's ideal of religious freedom in writing in a formal constitution.

> The circumstance [French Revolution] that has now taken place in France of the total abolition of the whole national order of priesthood, and of everything appertaining to compulsive systems of religion, and compulsive articles of faith, has not only precipitated my intention, but rendered a work of this kind [Constitution] exceedingly necessary, lest in the general wreck of superstition, of false systems of government, and false theology, we lose sight of morality, of humanity, and of the theology that is true.

Our Founders agreed with Locke that

> the magistrate ought not to forbid the preaching or professing of any speculative opinions in any Church because they have no manner of relation to the civil rights of the subjects. If a Roman Catholic believes that to be really the body of Christ which another man calls bread, he does no injury thereby to his neighbor. If a Jew does not believe the New Testament to be the Word of God, he does not thereby alter anything in man's civil rights. If a heathen doubt of both Testaments, he is not therefore to be punished as a pernicious citizen. The power of the magistrate and the estates of the people may be equally secure whether any man believes these things or no.

THE CONSTITUTION OF THE UNITED STATES

In words that rank among the most momentous of all time, our Constitution begins with a succinct summation of our motivations and the overall structure of our intended government:

> We the People of the United States, in Order to form a more perfect Union, establish Justice, insure domestic Tranquility, provide for the common defense, promote the general Welfare, and secure the Blessings of Liberty to ourselves and our Posterity, do ordain and establish this Constitution for the United States of America.

Like many of their contemporaries, the authors of our Constitution believed in the Enlightenment ideal of the perfectibility of humanity and government, which could only occur when individuals were allowed the freedom to develop their truest nature. The only purpose of government and law was to protect each individual's freedom and security, which, by extension, protected society's freedom and security.

Laws could not be passed to impose the moral code of any person or group, religious or otherwise. The Founders did stress the importance of ethics in maintaining freedom and security, but the standards they established were not religious in the sense of being the province of one religion or sect, but were rather the Creator-given, *necessary* principles of conscience inherent in human *nature*. Those principles are summed up in the word *freedom*, one's own freedom and respect for the freedom of others. *Security* means the preservation of any and all freedom, except what thwarts, damages, or destroys the freedom of others. Making love is a freedom; rape is not. We make laws to provide *security* from the rapist's violation of another's *freedom*.

Liberating our natural freedom to pursue happiness has allowed us to coexist as a peaceful, productive society. Truly happy people don't threaten the freedom and security of others. Denying freedom and security destroys peace and productivity, and it chains our chances for the happiness our Declaration of Independence sanctified in the phrase, "pursuit of happiness," a fundamental right often reiterated by Thomas Jefferson. "The care of human life and happiness and not their destruction is the first and only legitimate object of good government," he told the Maryland Republicans in 1809. The following year he wrote to Thaddeus Kosciuski, "The freedom and happiness of man . . . [are] the sole objects of all legitimate government." And a year later, "The happiness and prosperity of our citizens . . . is the only legitimate object of government and the first duty of governors." In 1812, he wrote to M. van der Kemp, "The only orthodox object of the institution of government is to secure the greatest degree of happiness possible to the general mass of those associated under it."

THE FIRST AMENDMENT

Even though the Constitution was itself a declaration of our rights, some of our Founders—the Anti-Federalists—refused to sign the Constitution until it was agreed that our basic rights would be explicitly spelled out in a Bill of Rights, which became the Constitution's first ten amendments. The First Amendment was first for a reason: Those basic rights were absolutely paramount, non-negotiable, and irrevocable for the survival of a radically new kind of Union based on equality, freedom, and justice.

The First Amendment states this, in its entirety: "Congress shall make no law respecting an establishment of religion, or prohibiting the free exercise thereof; or abridging the freedom of speech, or of the press, or the right of the people peaceably to assemble, and to petition the Government for a redress of grievances."

The phrase "establishment of religion" is called the Establishment Clause; "free exercise thereof" is known as the Free Exercise Clause. The Establishment Clause forbids not only practices that "aid one religion" or "prefer one religion over another," but also those that "aid all religions."

"Separation of church and state" refers to a phrase used by Thomas Jefferson in his letter dated January 1, 1802, addressed to the Danbury (Connecticut) Baptist Association to assure them of their religious freedom:

> Believing with you that religion is a matter which lies solely between man and his God, that he owes account to none other for his faith or his worship, that the legislative powers of government reach actions only, and not opinions, I contemplate with sovereign reverence that act of the whole American people which declared that their legislature should "make no law respecting an establishment of religion, or prohibiting the free exercise thereof," thus building a wall of separation between church and State. Adhering to this expression of the supreme will of the nation in behalf of the rights of conscience, I shall see with sincere satisfaction the progress of those sentiments which tend to restore to man all his natural rights, convinced he has no natural right in opposition to his social duties.

The "wall of separation" was intended to protect religion from the meddling of government, and government from the meddling of religion. Separation of church and state was so important that it was worded as the very first phrase of the first amendment in our Bill of Rights.

Our Revolution and Constitution insured separation of church and state to preserve freedom against the challenges of civil despotism and religious tyranny that included not only mighty kings but also the monolithic Catholic Church of the Inquisitions, Crusades against Muslims, and Jewish pogroms; the Puritans with their dictatorial "City Upon a Hill"; Lutheranist-Calvinist theocraticism; and the domineering Church of England.

Our Founders eloquently pledged their intellectual and moral allegiance to the principle of separation of church and state, ensuring our freedom of religion, an imperative component of freedom of conscience. The operative word here is *freedom*. All citizens have the exact same freedom. Being forced against our will and conscience to abide by someone else's religious mores is not freedom of religion.

CONSTITUTIONAL RIGHTS AND PROTECTIONS

The Fourteenth Amendment, ratified in 1868, states, "No State shall make or enforce any law which shall abridge the privileges or immunities of citizens of the United States, nor shall any State deprive any person of life, liberty, or property, without due process of law; nor deny to any person within its jurisdiction the equal protection of the laws." Two clauses, Due Process and Equal Protection, both protect, for instance, the right to gay marriage and all other gay rights; the right to worship freely as a Deist, Christian, Jew, Muslim, Buddhist, agnostic, or any other faith, or to not worship at all; the right to own a house without auxiliary economic restraints imposed by the state, insurance companies, banks, and other institutions; the right to not be exploited by filthy rich capitalists destroying equal individual freedoms and property/economic rights and creating mandatory serfdom under the guise of "free" enterprise.

What the Supreme Court calls "Substantive Due Process" extends constitutional protection to cover personal rights like the right to privacy and the personal rights to marry, have children, and raise children according to parental preference. In the 1965 case *Griswold v. Connecticut*, the Supreme Court struck down a Connecticut state law prohibiting married couples from using contraceptives, because the law interfered with the basic intimacy of marriage. In 1973, the *Roe v. Wade* decision concluded that states cannot bar a woman from having an abortion, thereby upholding a woman's constitutional right to privacy and her constitutional right to control her own body.

In 1954, the Equal Protection Clause came to the fore in the landmark case, *Brown v. Board of Education*, which ruled that "separate-but-equal" is "inherently unequal." Because racially segregated black schools can never be equal to white schools, desegregation was mandated.

Segregating a segment of the population on the basis of sexual preference is also inherently unequal. Bias against gay marriage is analogous to bias against interracial marriage. Even though the Court ruled in the 1967 *Loving v. Virginia* decision that the States (specifically the State of Virginia) could not make it illegal for black and white persons to marry, many fundamentalists still believe the Old Testament law that race-mixing is an abomination. Some fundamentalist cults, like Christian Identity and the KKK, are even more extreme in their bigotry toward non-Christian non-whites and toward all gays.

"Integration and equality are myths; they disguise a new segregation and a new equality," argues R.J. Rushdoony, founder of Reconstructionism, which advocates reinstituting slavery and the death penalty for homosexuality and other abominations. "Every social order institutes its own program of separation or segregation. A particular faith and morality is given privileged status and all else is separated for progressive elimination."

Rushdoony is a man who would be king of nazi discrimination and extermination, American style. He dishonestly distorts the concept of equality, implying with a kind of whining bravado that fundamentalists are the ones being discriminated against. He pits his actual elitist agenda of segregation and inequality against a fictional anti-fundamentalist agenda of democracy. Ironically, it's fundamentalist anti-Darwinists, not progressives, who maintain an obsolete, survival-of-the-fittest worldview. Bigotry, including the religious bigotry of reconstructionism, betrays ingratitude for everything America represents, and it thwarts fulfillment of the American ideal.

Presently, the denial of gay marriage rights is probably the most blatant violation of the Constitution. The myth of "traditional family values" stands at the center of most anti-gay arguments.

Many Americans don't know that in the U.S., marriage is simply a legal contract—specifically, the civil marriage license—between the couple and the government. The actual document can be signed in the vestibule of a church, synagogue, temple, or mosque—or at a court, city hall, clerk's office, park, house, or rented back room in a Vegas hotel. The place of ceremony is of no legal consequence; what matters is that the witness officiating the signing is designated by the government to do so.

Even a high mass wedding is technically only a civil marriage. The sacramental aspect of the wedding ceremony performed within a religious institution is not a requirement of marriage and stands apart from the legal definition of marriage. In fact, the wedding ceremony is optional, and when performed, it is auxiliary. Over forty percent of marriages performed in the U.S. today are purely civil ceremonies that include no ritualistic or religious aspects whatsoever, and that percentage is rising.

Many Americans don't know that the sacrament of marriage is not an institution thousands of years old, as the sanctity of marriage coalition would have us believe. For more than its first thousand years, the Church was not involved with marriage at all; marriage was not an official sacrament, weddings were not then performed in churches, and based on strict biblical interpretation (which anticipated the imminent coming of Christ), celibacy and even abandonment of one's family were considered spiritually superior to marriage (Luke 20:34-35; Matt. 19:10-12; Matt. 22:30-32; Luke 14:26; Mark 13:12; Matt. 10:35-36; Mark 3:31, 33-35; Matt. 8:21-22; Matt. 4:21-22; 1 Cor. 7).

Many Americans don't know that the traditional family of one man, one woman, and children was not the norm or even necessarily an option prior to modern times, contrary to what the traditional family values coalition would have us believe. Throughout the ages, marriage represented dynastic or property arrangements. Arranged marriages were common, sometimes even between infants of different countries whose families had never met. In ancient times, the "basic family unit" might include a child bride, harem, concubines, or eunuchs. Quite a few "basic family units" came into existence via pillage and rape. Families were male-dominated *households* consisting of extended families and their servants and slaves, and by some definitions, their animals. In many cultures, households extended to encompass clans, villages, and nations. These antiquated structures are still upheld in some area of the world.

The status of marriage for women in America before the twentieth century was based on the concept of coverture, a common law doctrine under which a wife, like a slave, was "civilly dead." Women were wives, and wives were slaves in having no independent legal existence apart from her master, her husband. Only men could request divorces. Women could not write wills, sign contracts, or obtain loans. Their property rights were very limited. Women had almost no access to education. They had basically no legal rights over their children. Nearly everywhere, no laws existed to prevent their being brutally raped or beaten by their husbands. Very limited types of work were open to them, even though many women were expected to contribute to the family income. Equal pay for equal work was not even a concept.

The oppression of womanly men and manly women is another chapter in the history of oppression of women: Fundamentalists want gay men and all women to get back into their proper, assigned roles. Blacks, other racial minorities, and people of other religious traditions have also been relegated to the inferior, secondary, "womanly" position by white men who want power-over.

Limitations that create inequality define the woman's role that fundamentalists today are reclaiming as part of their biblical package of traditional family values. It's likely that deep down, even staunch fundamentalist women dread relinquishing to inferior values their natural right to equality.

Blacks experienced limitations similar to those endured by women prior to the first wave of feminism. Progress accelerated when the common causes of blacks and women fused into a single revolution for equality. Today, gay is being called "the new black" due to the many levels of discrimination, hatred, and judgment the gay community is currently enduring.

And of course family values Americans are still squeamish about sexuality. But the times are changing. Interracial marriage is acceptable in progressive circles; although it's always been a constitutional right, for most of America's history it has been illegal. Sodomy became legal in July 2003 with the landmark *Lawrence v. Texas* Supreme Court decision, which ruled state sodomy laws unconstitutional. The Supreme Court not only overturned its prior decision in the 1986 case, *Bowers v. Hardwick*, which had upheld the right of states (specifically Georgia) to enact sodomy laws (married couples could spend years in prison for having non-missionary-position sex in their own homes), but also for the first time ever, the U.S. Supreme Court openly critiqued itself. It had been a mistake to rule that the government had any business voyeuristically policing the sexual behavior of two consenting adults in the privacy of their own bedroom.

Perhaps the exceedingly loud cry for family values is merely a cover-up for sexual license. The news is full of the sexual improprieties of prominent evangelists and family values politicians, though the media has largely failed to highlight the blatant hypocrisy of those adulteries, molestations, domestic violence, homosexual trysts and other sexual escapades, not to mention other "sins" and crimes.

The Myth of Traditional Family Values

What does traditional marriage mean today in our egalitarian society when over sixty percent of marriages end in divorce? (And that percentage is rising.) "The American family must be kept together at all costs, says Mr. Gingrich, Bob Dole and Phil Gramm—all of whom are on their second marriages and looking the other way at Bob Packwood's sexual escapades," to quote a 1994 *New York Times* article. And that was back in the good old days of budding "family values." The collective sins of all-powerful Gingrich, for instance, currently on his third marriage (and busted for various adulteries), led to a far more heinous fall from political grace.

What does traditional marriage mean when a substantial majority of families are headed by a single parent, usually mothers who receive little or no support from the father, who as a rule earns substantially more than she does? Is traditional marriage an institution worth continuing, given the high rate of spousal abuse, child abuse, and familial molestation within traditional families? Is there something wrong with this picture of happy traditional families when by some expert estimates, over half of all women will be raped at some point in their lifetimes, mostly by men married to other women?

Even the Christian-based marketing research company, Barna Research Group, Ltd., reported in an article, "Christians Are More Likely to Experience Divorce Than Are Non-Christians," that according to their large-scale study, conservative born-again Christians had a higher divorce rate than less conservative Protestants and non-Christians.

Liberal blue states are in fact more classically conservative than the "conservative" fundamentalist red states. In his book, *Crimes Against Nature*, Robert F. Kennedy, Jr. points out that divorce rates and unmarried pregnancy rates tend to be far lower in blue states than red ones. Massachusetts has the most durable marriages in America. Divorce and teen birth rates in Texas are nearly double those of the Bay State's.

> Every single one of the nine states with the highest divorce rates went for Bush. The nine states with the lowest divorce rates went for Kerry. Marriage itself is less popular in Texas than in Massachusetts. In Texas, the percentage of unmarried people is 32.4 percent; in Massachusetts, it's 26.8 percent. Red state residents are more likely to watch salacious shows like *Desperate Housewives*, buy pornography, commit murder and other violent crimes, and impregnate your teenage daughter than blue state citizens.

Numerous studies on domestic violence have concluded that violence against wives results from patriarchal customs and laws that historically have perpetuated stereotyped masculine gender roles, which have always given men an incontestable status of domination and control over women. As sociologists Richard J. Gelles and Ann Levine explain in their textbook, *Sociology: An Introduction*, "The Bible was interpreted as teaching that woman was created from Adam's rib, as an afterthought, to serve man's needs; that she was weak by nature and easily lured into temptation; and that as punishment for Eve's transgression, she must live a life of subjugation." In their book, *Battered into Submission: The Tragedy of Wife Abuse in the Christian Home*, James and Phyllis Alsdurf show that as the rigidity of the church's teachings about gender roles and hierarchy increases, so does the probability of wife abuse.

The expectation of absolute obedience required by fundamentalism is one explanation why women can't grasp the self-deprecating, self-destructive incongruity of a stance held by women that opposes basic rights for women. In her book, *Cults In Our Midst: The Continuing Fight Against Their Hidden Menace*, cult expert Margaret Thaler Singer explains that within oppressive groups, enforcement of obedience depends on punishment patterns that include ridicule and name-calling. If you doubt or question, the group uses its own disparaging terms to make you feel like a renegade, a spy, an agent, a nonbeliever, or Satan—or abortionist, feminist, Marxist, humanist, or Christian-hater. The closed logic of the cult is reinforced by peer pressure, and the internal language meant to ridicule and denigrate is always present. The simple choice is to stop doubting and questioning, to adapt, conform, go with the flow. It's easier to conform and to learn to be a good believer, a good follower, rather than resist the dictates of the group.

This is the kind of cult coercion that keeps religious women in their timid, inferior, subservient role, the same kind of coercion that enforces gays' futile attempts at becoming ex-gay, the same kind of coercion used by wealthy politicians to push down anyone who challenges their economic superiority. America is not a straight "Christian nation" in the sense that the fundamentalists mean it. Oppressive coercion is what revolutionaries like our Founders have always fought against.

Ironically, a 1989 survey of Christian women found that only three percent looked to their ministers for moral guidance. Yet fundamentalist women at the top of anti-feminist organizations who are ordering women to submit to hierarchical marriage are apparently looked up to for advice. And these women at the top are being made rich by that advice. It's not unreasonable to speculate that these rich manly women at the top could well be repressed lesbians who remain repressed because of their faith in an infallible Bible. Guilt and the shame of stigma keep repressed lesbians lying even to themselves about their natural sexual orientation. Women raised in authoritarian homes could easily misconstrue male control as love, so they content themselves with being submissive, i.e. heterosexual.

Sociologists Charles W. Peek, George D. Lowe, and L. Susan Williams conducted a study in 1991 that revealed that although conservative Christian men and women are equally sexist, fundamentalist men derive their sexism via affiliation with fundamentalist groups, but women's sexist attitudes stem from their biblical literalism. In their article, "Gender and God's Word: Another Look at Religious Fundamentalism and Sexism," they noted that "Women who take the word of God with a grain of salt are less sexist."

The superior male is validated by association with other superior males. Each male plays out the same God-ordained role, which "proves" collective superiority. Fundamentalist men collectively play out the myth of themselves. It could be argued that the internal self eventually smothers behind the mask, so that only the mythic external self remains. At that point, the fundamentalist man *is* the myth of himself.

Because it is biblical literalism, especially as pontificated by male evangelicals, that coerces fundamentalist women to accept their inferior position, demystifying the Bible is critical to effecting equality for women, and by extension, for gays.

For women, the destructiveness of sexism is internalized. For men, it is projected outward. Both tendencies are consistent with the tendencies of violent criminals: women internalize and become self-destructive, but men externalize their violence.

The correlation between sex role socialization and rape of women and gay men has been firmly established. Rape is one means misogynist men subordinate, degrade, humiliate, and punish women and gays. Numerous studies and statistics have demonstrated the correlation between fundamentalism and violence against women. Opposition to equality and reinforcement of sex roles make rape more likely.

In her article, "The Worst Sexual Sin: Sexual Violence and the Church," Christine Gudorf, Professor of Theology at Xavier University in Cincinnati, points out that the Church's interpretation of the crucifixion is used to rationalize sexual violence when it tells victims that it's God's will, that it's "good to suffer," that victims "earn God's special favor." Catholic researchers report that nearly thirty percent of nuns have experienced sexual violence from within the church. 14.1 percent of Southern Baptist clergy have sexually abused members. The actual incident rates could well be much higher. Because these victims often fail to report being raped, perpetrators know there will be no repercussion for their acts, so their rapes continue and incidents increase.

Domestic violence worldwide is the leading cause of death of women between the ages of fourteen and forty-four. In the U.S., a woman is beaten every fifteen seconds, and one-third of women murdered are victims of husbands, boyfriends, or former partners. One in four women will be raped at some point during her lifetime (some experts say the rate is closer to one in two, or half of all women).

Two decades of research have indicated that in an average twelve-month period, at least two million women in the U.S. would be victims of severe assaults by their male partners. Most assaults against women are committed by current or former male partners. "At least twenty-one percent of all women are physically assaulted by an intimate male at least once during adulthood. More than half of all women (fifty-two percent) murdered in the United States in the first half of the 1980s were killed by their partners," as Dr. Lisa Goodman summed it up during her testimony before a congressional hearing on domestic violence.

Is it any wonder that a 1999 study by the University of Chicago found that nearly half of all women have sexual dysfunction? But it's not just those disgusted with male violence that are turned-off. Masters and Johnson found that many sexually dysfunctional women were religious conservatives who had internalized negative views about sexuality for the sake of pleasure. Hypoactive sexual desire disorder and sexual aversion disorder are commonly the result of fundamentalist upbringing, and are also common among those "trying to have sex with a partner of the non preferred sex."

Among animals, only humans have sex purely for pleasure, and only humans have sex whenever they choose, not just when fertile females are "in season." Ironically, the fundamentalist bias is *against* normal human sexuality and *for* the base animal preoccupation with strictly procreative sex. Pleasure is one of the most powerful expressions of love—an experience that is uniquely human. Shouldn't Christians be less concerned about sex and love and more concerned about their absence?

Do women, even fundamentalist women, really want to be relegated to the inferior, passive position dictated by the apostle Paul (Eph. 5:22-27)?

> Wives, be subject to your husbands as you are to the Lord. For the husband is the head of the wife just as Christ is the head of the church, the body of which he is the Savior. Just as the church is subject to Christ, so also wives ought to be, in everything, to their husbands. Husbands, love your wives, just as Christ loved the church and gave himself up for her, in order to make her holy by cleansing her with the washing of water by the word, so as to present the church to himself in splendor, without a spot or wrinkle or anything of the kind—yes, so that she may be holy and without blemish.

According to Paul's reasoning, women are to men as men are to Christ. Given that according to conservative Christianity, Christ is God, Paul is saying that women are to men as men are to God—which (given how much lower even male humans are from God) locates women a few planes lower than amoebas. (In Romans 1, Paul pushes gays and lesbians down further from divinity, down through the cusp into hell.) Women are saved and made holy and pure not by Christ, certainly not by her own works or faith, but via her husband serving the middleman role of Christ in his priestly, savior role. Even most conservative women today laugh at such traditional machismo fanning its sanctified peacock feathers.

Which is not to say that their conservative husbands are laughing. Take Pat Robertson, for instance: "I know this is painful for the ladies to hear, but if you get married, you have accepted the headship of a man, your husband. Christ is the head of the household and the husband is the head of the wife, and that's the way it is, period."

Men aren't superior because the Bible says so; the Bible says so because men are superior. Of course it was men in superior positions who wrote the texts that other superior men chose to be part of what we call the Bible. That choice codified patriarchal power as the incontestable, absolute tradition. The "superior" male must maintain the myth of his moral superiority, even at the expense of reason, honesty, and fairness, not to mention the larger half of humanity.

Anti-feminist women would be enlightened if they checked out the stats available online via resources such as the National Sexuality Resource Center, San Francisco State University; the professional website of Karen Franklin, one of the top experts in forensic psychology; or the professional website of G.M. Herek, Psychology Professor at the University of California at Davis, whose team has done extensive research on gay violence; or Kimberly Blaker's *The Fundamentals of Extremism: The Christian Right in America*.

Even given that many rapes are committed by repeat offenders, probably at least 10% of men have committed rape. 25% of men surveyed in recent studies admitted "sexual aggression," and 35% or so admitted "sexual coercion," both of which could be defensive admittance of rape. 35% of male college students admitted that they might rape a woman if they could be assured of not getting caught. That's more than one in three of our all-American guys.

Assaults against gays fulfill the same motivations as assaults against women, according to most experts. Karen Franklin's study of high school and community college students in the very liberal San Francisco Bay Area revealed surprisingly high levels of expressed homophobia. Studies of community colleges in Northern California and elsewhere have shown even higher levels. 10% of college students admitted to having threatened or physically assaulted a gay man or lesbian; 24% of college students, 32%

of community college men, and 50% of male college students, and 70% of San Francisco Bay Area college males admitted to name-calling (this could be because of the larger, more visible gay population); 35% said they would harass or assault a gay man or lesbian if flirted with or propositioned; 18% had physically assaulted a gay man or lesbian.

In her published articles (available online), Franklin cites statistics from a 1992 overview complied by Berrill summarizing two dozen national, regional, and local victimization surveys. Franklin considers these to be perhaps the most comprehensive. Berrill's overview revealed the extent of experiences we call collectively "gay bashing": 80% verbal harassment; 44% threats of violence; 33% chased or followed; 25% pelted with objects; 17% physically assaulted; 13% spat upon; 09% assaulted with objects or weapons.

Also included in Franklin's articles are statistics derived from the 2001 national survey by the Gay Lesbian & Straight Education Network. These stats are important, because most rape victims and most gays who have been assaulted don't report the crime to police. Women don't want to re-experience the trauma through repeated examination and cross-examination, which is what the legal process demands.

That gays don't report makes sense, given that in 2002-2003, for instance, in 15%-20% of assaults on gays reported to police, the officers refused to accept a report. The gay violence stats also exclude closeted gays and heterosexuals who were mistakenly thought to be gay, an estimated 10% of victims. Furthermore, police often don't classify incidents as antigay hate crimes or report them to the FBI under the voluntary guidelines of the Crimes Statistics Act of 1990. Though the guidelines are being updated, attitudes within law enforcement still need to be adjusted through education and sensitivity training.

According to the Gay Lesbian & Straight Education Network national survey of 2001, 91% of homosexuals heard frequent antigay comments at school; 14% had been punched or kicked; 28% had been shoved, pushed, or otherwise physically harassed.

Interestingly, according to Franklin, "Many of these assailants were not vehement in their antigay attitudes, instead citing negative societal stereotypes about homosexuality as justifications for their assaults. Key stereotypes cited were that gay people violate gender norms and that they are sexually predatory."

Gay people are sexually predatory? How ironic, coming from predatory men—I mean the large segment of the male population that have
admitted having committed coercion, sexual aggression, or rape. It's
unlikely that gay men are any more predatory than straight men. In
fact, if a gay man hits up on another man, isn't he doing what a straight
man does? Isn't it the male's role to "hit up"? Doesn't our culture endorse
male sexual assertiveness? In effect, straight men are condemning gay
men for doing what men are supposed to do, by the straight men's own
standards.

Gay people violate gender norms? A gender norm is a fad. Not that
long ago, women couldn't wear pants, couldn't cut their hair short,
couldn't have rights equal to a man's. Men couldn't stay home with the
kids, couldn't grow their hair long (remember the Crosby, Stills, Nash,
and Young lyric, "letting my freak flag fly"?), couldn't share rights
equally with a woman. There's a new gender norm now. It's called
diversity.

Legal Queries Regarding Gay Marriage

Can the government justly deny any consenting persons the right to
have sexual relations of any kind within the privacy of their own homes?
To do so would codify discrimination; it would deprive citizens of the
freedom and security it was appointed to protect.

On what basis can the legislature or the Supreme Court dictate the
legally sanctioned rules for or against marriage between consenting
adults? Is it the government's right to support denial of marriage rights—
which could equally be called rites—to gays and lesbians in committed,
monogamous relationships while supporting those rights—and rites—
for straight couples?

What right does the government have in the first place to require
a state document confirming a private, often sacred, act of marriage?
Doesn't that violate separation of church and state? What justification is
there to demand an act of marriage to legitimize a relationship between
consenting domestic partners? Why require civil marriage at all?

The practical answer is that legal marriage grants to each person protections from and responsibilities to each other, their families, and society—protections and responsibilities that the courts and legislatures are
denying segregated citizens.

The Constitution first and foremost honors the fundamental principles articulated in the Declaration of Independence, the self-evident truths that all human beings are created equal and that all are endowed by their Creator with certain unalienable rights, including life, liberty, and the pursuit of happiness. In addition, government derives its just powers from the consent of the governed, not from the commands of dictators, religious or otherwise.

Rather than uphold fundamental constitutional purposes, contemporary society, government, and the judicial system have permitted ostracism of gays and lesbians; have admitted laws that abet persecution through prosecution of obsolete, sexually restrictive offenses (most of which apply equally to straight couples, though prosecution is far more often against gays); and have refused to validate the rights of gays and lesbians as full and equal citizens.

This nation's government has fomented disorder and thwarted perfect union by denying gays and lesbians equal rights and protections guaranteed by the Constitution, including the right to religious freedom, as well as the right to privacy as it has evolved through court interpretation; has institutionalized injustice by upholding certain tenets of a conservative, fundamentalist minority and thereby unjustly validated them as the norm of society; has undermined the domestic tranquility of gays and lesbians wishing to marry, raise children, and generally participate in society without meddling, harassment, and legal prosecution; has deprived gays and lesbians of full legal protection from persecution, discrimination, and violence; has not promoted the general welfare, especially given that a large segment of the population is gay, lesbian, or bisexual, or friendly toward those groups; has denied gays and lesbians the blessings of liberty by forbidding certain activities that are not the province of government to dictate or forbid.

Denying gays and lesbians the right to marry relegates a substantial segment of the country's population to a position of second-class citizens—a position that is not supposed to exist under the equality ethic of democratic America.

The government has shirked its responsibility, according to the definition of its role in protecting the gay person's right to happiness; denying gays and lesbians the right to equal marriage deprives them, their children, and their friends and relatives of happiness in many contexts.

192 • *Born-Again Deist*

VIOLATIONS OF CHURCH/STATE SEPARATION

The Establishment Clause prohibits fundamentalist or any other version of Christianity from imposing its definition of marriage on American citizens. The Free Exercise Clause prevents government intrusion in the rite of marriage.

Yet gays and lesbians are denied equal protection against discrimination and refused the full privileges granted to straight couples. Gays and lesbians married in Massachusetts are being denied equal protection within other states. Lawmakers try to legislate inferior substitutes for marriage, such as civil unions and domestic partnerships. But separate but equal is as inherently unequal for gays and lesbians of this nation as it has been for blacks and women.

Marriage is still forbidden to gays—which is clearly unconstitutional—because fundamentalists have succeeded in persuading a sizable segment of the public and several lawmakers that somehow gays are not entitled to the same status as every other American. Jews can marry. Muslims can marry. Native Americans can marry. Buddhists can marry. A hundred-year-old woman can marry an eighteen-year-old boy. But gays, even gay Christians, cannot marry—only because fundamentalists have incited enough public sentiment against gay rights to promote their own unconstitutional religious bigotry.

In denying homosexuals the exact same equal right to marriage that it offers to heterosexuals, in denying even progressive Christian homosexuals the exact same equal right to marriage that it offers to fundamentalists, the state acquiesces to fundamentalist demands to enact laws, promote mores, thwart freedom, obstruct rights, disallow equality, and foment oppression, all in preference to one religion—or rather, one version of one religion. This nullifies the intent of our nation's Founders, who institutionalized freedom of religion as a sacred right. Separation of church and state was codified to prevent both ecclesiastical and governmental despotism at the very least through a kind of balance of separate powers. The union of church bigotry and state subjugation was the marriage our Founders committed to extinction.

All of the First Amendment rights protect our freedom; they protect us from governmental intrusion, even on the seemingly small scale of legal restraints. Yet today, when gays are denied the civil right to marry, the government illegally forces restraints that express antiquated, conservative religious biases, thus colluding with religion, in direct opposition to our Constitution.

Despite the claims of Jefferson's letter and of the First Amendment, which both stipulate that religion is not the business of government or politics, legislatures in several states are instituting laws respecting fundamentalist beliefs about the sin of homosexuality.

According to Jefferson and the Constitution, legislature cannot dictate faith and worship, and for that reason, it cannot define or even acknowledge sin. Yet today, several state legislatures are passing laws making it illegal for gays to enjoy the full rights granted to those who partake of the sacrament of marriage within churches that do not identify homosexuality as a sin.

Legislature cannot make a law that prefers—establishes—one religion's views over another's. Yet again, state legislatures are passing laws that dictate fundamentalist Christian perspectives to the exclusion of other beliefs, including progressive Christian. Denying gay marriage is a specifically fundamentalist agenda, because homosexuality is a sin according to literalists who assume biblical infallibility. But of course even literalists are selective about which infallible abominations they choose to admonish and which they choose to practice themselves. Homosexuality is a selective sin and homophobia is selective bigotry.

Legislature can never pass a law that prohibits the free exercise of any religion or belief. Yet state legislatures are passing laws prohibiting the free exercise of secular, religious non-Christian, and even progressive Christian beliefs that allow for the free exercise of gay marriage.

The Constitution has built a wall of separation between church and state. Yet in denying gay rights, the state is tearing down that hard-earned wall by passing laws that dictate one particular, narrow, conservative Christian religious stance toward gay marriage.

Chapter 13

Interlude: A Word From Our Founders and Distinguished Guests

For most of the Founders most instrumental in creating and upholding our Constitution, freedom of religion and separation of church and state were considered absolutely fundamental to the survival and integrity of our nation.

Those Founders would have supported equal rights, including today's hotly-debated gay rights, gay marriage, and gay adoption, because they supported absolutely each citizen's right to freedom of conscience.

America is not a Christian nation. We are, and have always been, a religious melting pot. Many of our most distinguished and influential Founders understood the danger of succumbing to the demands of authoritarian superstition.

The Enlightenment replaced the dictates of blind faith with the scientific method and ideals grounded in common sense. Scholars debated the validity of sacred texts as a source of historical fact or spiritual truth.

Thomas Jefferson even revised the Bible, omitting from his *Jefferson Bible*, or *The Life and Morals of Jesus of Nazareth*, as it is formally titled, the supernatural elements, which he believed were padded onto the actual events after the fact to legitimize the deification of Jesus. As Jefferson explained in a letter to Joseph Priestley, his version of the Bible would admit only the remaining "principles of pure deism" (his words) taught by Jesus.

As he undertook his task of distillation, he wrote to John Adams,

In extracting the pure principles which he taught, we should have to strip off the artificial vestments in which they have been muffled by priests, who have travestied them into various forms, as instruments of riches and power to themselves. We must dismiss the Platonists and Plotinists, the Stagyrites and Gamalielites, the Eclectics, the Gonstics and Scholastics, their essences and emanations, their logos and demiurges, aeons and daemons, male and female, with a long train of . . . or, shall I say at once, of nonsense. We must reduce our volume to the simple evangelists, select, even from them, the very words only of Jesus, paring off the amphibologisms into which they have been led, by forgetting often, or not understanding, what had fallen from him, by giving their own misconceptions of his dicta, and expressing unintelligibly for others what they had not understood themselves. There will be found remaining the most sublime and benevolent code of morals which has ever been offered to man. I have performed this operation for my own use, by cutting verse by verse out of the printed book, and arranging the matter which is evidently his, and which is as easily distinguishable as diamonds in a dunghill. The result is an octavo of forty-six pages, of pure and unsophisticated doctrines.

Not only was the United States of America not founded as a Christian nation, it was founded specifically to prevent the domination of any religion, Christian or otherwise. Freedom of conscience was and is the cornerstone of our nation.

To illustrate my point, in the spirit of Jeffersonian cut-and-paste I have called here as witnesses a few of our most famous and influential Founders. In each author's case, numerous quotes have been collaged together into a discourse that argues for freedom of conscience.

We will hear first from French philosopher John Locke, who perhaps more than any other philosopher of the time inspired their democratic ideals. Then we will hear from Thomas Paine, Thomas Jefferson, Benjamin Franklin, James Madison, John Adams, and Samuel Adams.

JOHN LOCKE (from *A Letter Concerning Toleration* and *Second Treatise of Government*)

The toleration of those that differ from others in matters of religion is so agreeable to the Gospel of Jesus Christ, and to the genuine reason of mankind, that it seems monstrous for men to be so blind as not to perceive the necessity and advantage of it in so clear a light.

No private person has any right in any manner to prejudice another person in his civil enjoyments because he is of another church or religion. All the rights and franchises that belong to him as a man, or as a denizen, are inviolably to be preserved to him. These are not the business of religion.

Those whose doctrine is peaceable and whose manners are pure and blameless ought to be upon equal terms with their fellow-subjects. Thus if solemn assemblies, observations of festivals, and public worship be permitted to any one sort of professors, all these things ought to be permitted to the Presbyterians, Independents, Anabaptists, Arminians, Quakers, and others, with the same liberty. Nay . . . neither Pagan, nor Mohammedan, nor Jew ought to be excluded from the civil rights of the commonwealth because of his religion.

The care of souls is not committed to the civil magistrate, any more than to other men. It is not committed unto him, I say, by God; because it appears not that God has ever given any such authority to one man over another as to compel anyone to his religion. For no man can, if he would, conform his faith to the dictates of another.

The care of souls cannot belong to the civil magistrate, because his power consists only in outward force; but true and saving religion consists in the inward persuasion of the mind, without which nothing can be acceptable to God.

A church, then, I take to be a voluntary society of men, joining themselves together of their own accord in order to the public worshipping of God in such manner as they judge acceptable to Him and effectual to the salvation of their souls. I say it is a free and voluntary society.

But, after all, the principal consideration, and which absolutely determines this controversy, is this: Although the magistrate's opinion in religion be sound, and the way that he appoints be truly Evangelical, yet, if I be not thoroughly persuaded thereof in my own mind, there will be no safety for me in following it. No way whatsoever that I shall walk in against the dictates of my conscience will ever bring me to the mansions of the blessed. It is in vain for an unbeliever to take up the outward show of another man's profession. Faith only and inward sincerity are the things that procure acceptance with God. In a word, whatsoever may be doubtful in religion, yet this at least is certain, that no religion which I believe not to be true can be either true or profitable unto me. In vain, therefore, do princes compel their subjects to come into their Church communion under pretence of saving their souls. If they believe, they will come of their own accord, if they believe not, their coming will nothing avail them. And therefore, when all is done, they must be left to their own consciences.

It is not the diversity of opinions (which cannot be avoided), but the refusal of toleration to those that are of different opinions (which might have been granted), that has produced all the bustles and wars that have been in the Christian world upon account of religion. The heads and leaders of the Church, moved by avarice and insatiable desire of dominion, making use of the immoderate ambition of magistrates and the credulous superstition of the giddy multitude, have incensed and animated them against those that dissent from themselves, by preaching unto them, contrary to the laws of the Gospel and to the precepts of charity, that schismatics and heretics are to be outed of their possessions and destroyed. And thus have they mixed together and confounded two things that are in themselves most different, the Church and the commonwealth.

This is the unhappy agreement that we see between the Church and State. Whereas if each of them would contain itself within its own bounds—the one attending to the worldly welfare of the commonwealth, the other to the salvation of souls—it is impossible that any discord should ever have happened between them.

THOMAS PAINE (from *Age of Reason* and *Common Sense*)

The intellectual part of religion is a private affair between every man and his Maker and in which no third party has any right to interfere. The practical part consists in our doing good to each other. But since religion has been made into a trade, the practical part has been made to consist of ceremonies performed by men called priests, and the people have been amused with ceremonial shows, processions, and bells. By devices of this kind, true religion has been banished; and such means have been found out to extract money even from the pockets of the poor, instead of contributing to their relief.

No man ought to make a living by religion. It is dishonest so to do. Religion is not an act that can be performed by proxy. One person cannot act religion for another. Every person must perform it for himself; and all that a priest can do is to take from him; he wants nothing but his money and then to riot in the spoil and laugh at his credulity.

As to religion, I hold it to be the indispensable duty of all government to protect all conscientious professors thereof, and I know of no other business which government hath to do therewith. Let a man throw aside that narrowness of soul, that selfishness of principle, which the niggards of all professions are so unwilling to part with, and he will be at once delivered of his fears on that head. Suspicion is the companion of mean souls and the bane of all good society.

For myself, I fully and conscientiously believe that it is the will of the Almighty that there should be diversity of religious opinions among us: It affords a larger field for our Christian kindness. Were we all of one way of thinking, our religious dispositions would want matter for probation; and on this liberal principle, I look on the various denominations among us to be like children of the same family differing only in what is called their Christian names.

I believe in one God, and no more; and I hope for happiness beyond this life. I believe in the equality of man; and I believe that religious duties consist in doing justice, loving mercy, and endeavoring to make our fellow-creatures happy.

All national institutions of churches, whether Jewish, Christian or Turkish, appear to me no other than human inventions, set up to terrify and enslave mankind and monopolize power and profit. I do not mean by this declaration to condemn those who believe otherwise; they have the same right to their belief as I have to mine. But it is necessary to the happiness of man that he be mentally faithful to himself. Infidelity does not consist in believing, or in disbelieving; it consists in professing to believe what he does not believe.

To God, and not to man, are all men accountable on the score of religion.

Be ye sure that ye mistake not the cause and ground of your testimony. Call not coldness of soul religion; nor put the *Bigot* in the place of the *Christian*. O ye partial ministers of your own acknowledged principles.

THOMAS JEFFERSON (from *The Writings of Thomas Jefferson*, America Series)

We have solved, by fair experiment, the great and interesting question whether freedom of religion is compatible with order in government and obedience to the laws. And we have experienced the quiet as well as the comfort which results from leaving every one to profess freely and openly those principles of religion which are the inductions of his own reason and the serious convictions of his own inquiries. I have no fear, but that the result of our experiment will be that men may be trusted to govern themselves without a master. Could the contrary of this be proved, I should conclude either that there is no God, or that He is a malevolent being.

There are certain fences which experience has proved peculiarly efficacious against wrong, and rarely obstructive of right, which yet the governing powers have ever shown a disposition to weaken and remove. Of the first kind is freedom of religion. Our Constitution . . . has not left the religion of its citizens under the power of its public functionaries. To suffer the civil magistrate to intrude his powers into the field of opinion and to restrain the profession or propagation of principles on supposition of their ill tendency is a dangerous fallacy which at once destroys all religious liberty, because he being of course judge of that tendency will make his opinions the rule of judgment and approve or condemn the sentiments of others only as they shall square with or differ from his own.

I consider the government of the U S. as interdicted by the Constitution from intermeddling with religious institutions, their doctrines, discipline, or exercises. This results not only from the provision that no law shall be made respecting the establishment, or free exercise, of religion, but from that also which reserves to the states the powers not delegated to the U.S. Certainly no power to prescribe any religious exercise, or to assume authority in religious discipline, has been delegated to the general government.

This blessed country of free inquiry and belief has surrendered its creed and conscience to neither kings nor priests. All religions are equally independent here, our laws knowing no distinction of country, of classes among individuals, and with nations, our [creed] is justice and reciprocity. The manners of every nation are the standard of orthodoxy within itself. But these standards being arbitrary, reasonable people in all allow free toleration for the manners as for the religion of others. This country, which has given to the world the example of physical liberty, owes to it that of moral emancipation also.

That differences of opinion should arise among men on politics, on religion, and on every other topic of human inquiry, and that these should be freely expressed in a country where all our faculties are free, is to be expected. But these valuable privileges are much perverted when permitted to disturb the harmony of social intercourse and to lessen the tolerance of opinion. The inquisition of public opinion overwhelms in practice the freedom asserted by the laws in theory.

It is inconsistent with the spirit of our laws and Constitution to force tender consciences. Single acts of tyranny may be ascribed to the accidental opinion of a day; but a series of oppressions, begun at a distinguished period and pursued unalterably through every change of ministers, too plainly prove a deliberate, systematic plan of reducing to slavery.

I suppose belief to be the assent of the mind to an intelligible proposition. Our opinions are not voluntary. The opinions and belief of men depend not on their own will but follow involuntarily the evidence proposed to their minds. Our particular principles of religion are a subject of accountability to God alone.

Ignorance and bigotry, like other insanities, are incapable of self-government. With such persons, gullibility, which they call faith, takes the helm from the hand of reason, and the mind becomes a wreck. Bigotry is the disease of ignorance, of morbid minds; enthusiasm of the free and buoyant. Education and free discussion are the antidotes of both. We are destined to be a barrier against the return of ignorance and barbarism.

What an effort . . . of bigotry in politics and religion have we gone through! The barbarians really flattered themselves they should be able to bring back the times of Vandalism, when ignorance put everything into the hands of power and priestcraft. The clergy, who have missed their union with the State . . . and the political adventurers, who have lost the chance of swindling and plunder in the waste of public money, will never cease to bawl on the breaking up of their sanctuary.

In every country and in every age, the priest has been hostile to liberty. He is always in alliance with the despot, abetting his abuses in return for protection to his own. The law for religious freedom . . . [has] put down the aristocracy of the clergy and restored to the citizen the freedom of the mind.

The advance of liberalism . . . [encourages] the hope that the human mind will some day get back to the freedom it enjoyed two thousand years ago. But a short time elapsed after the death of the great reformer of the Jewish religion before his principles were departed from by those who professed to be his special servants, and perverted into an engine for enslaving mankind and aggrandizing their oppressors in Church and State. The clergy, by getting themselves established by law and engrafted into the machine of government, have been a very formidable engine against the civil and religious rights of man.

Millions of innocent men, women, and children since the introduction of Christianity have been burnt, tortured, fined, and imprisoned, yet we have not advanced one inch toward uniformity. As the Creator has made no two faces alike, so no two minds, and probably no two creeds. The Christian religion, when divested of the rags in which they [the clergy] have enveloped it, and brought to the original purity and simplicity of its benevolent institutor, is a religion of all others most friendly to liberty, science, and the freest expansion of the human mind.

I have ever thought religion a concern purely between our God and our consciences, for which we were accountable to Him and not to the priests. But it does me no injury for my neighbor to say there are twenty gods, or no God. It neither picks my pocket nor breaks my leg. I am for freedom of religion, and against all maneuvers to bring about a legal ascendancy of one sect over another.

We ought with one heart and one hand to hew down the daring and dangerous efforts of those who would seduce the public opinion to substitute itself into that tyranny over religious faith which the laws have so justly abdicated. It would seem impossible that an intelligent people with the faculty of reading and right of thinking should continue much longer to slumber under the pupilage of an interested aristocracy of priests and lawyers, persuading them to distrust themselves and to let them think for them. Awaken them from this voluntary degradation of mind!

No provision in our Constitution ought to be dearer to man than that which protects the rights of conscience against the enterprises of the civil authority. Our civil rights have no dependence upon our religious opinions more than our opinions in physics or geometry. The purpose of government is to maintain a society which secures to every member the inherent and inalienable rights of man, and promotes the safety and happiness of its people. Protecting these rights from violation, therefore, is its primary obligation.

The principles of government . . . [are] founded in the rights of man. It is to secure our rights that we resort to government at all. The most sacred of the duties of a government [is] to do equal and impartial justice to all its citizens. The general insurrection of the world against its tyrants will ultimately prevail by pointing the object of government to the happiness of the people, and not merely to that of their self-constituted governors.

Every man, and every body of men on earth, possesses the right of self-government. The republican is the only form of government which is not eternally at open or secret war with the rights of mankind. The God who gave us life gave us liberty at the same time; the hand of force may destroy, but cannot disjoin them. A free people [claim] their rights as derived from the laws of nature, and not as the gift of their chief magistrate. Natural rights [are] the objects for the protection of which society is formed and municipal laws established.

Under the law of nature, all men are born free, every one comes into the world with a right to his own person, which includes the liberty of moving and using it at his own will. This is what is called personal liberty, and is given him by the Author of nature, because necessary for his own sustenance. The constitutional freedom of religion [is] the most inalienable and sacred of all human rights.

The equal rights of man, and the happiness of every individual, are now acknowledged to be the only legitimate objects of government. It issued finally in that inestimable state of freedom which alone can ensure to man the enjoyment of his equal rights. God . . . has formed us moral agents . . . that we may promote the happiness of those with whom He has placed us in society, by acting honestly towards all, benevolently to those who fall within our way, respecting sacredly their rights, bodily and mental, and cherishing especially their freedom of conscience, as we value our own.

The Giver of life gave it for happiness and not for wretchedness. The only orthodox object of the institution of government is to secure the greatest degree of happiness possible to the general mass of those associated under it.

Bear in mind this sacred principle, that though the will of the majority is in all cases to prevail, that will, to be rightful, must be reasonable; that the minority possess their equal rights, which equal laws must protect, and to violate would be oppression.

Rebellion to tyrants is obedience to God. If ever there was a holy war, it was that which saved our liberties and gave us independence. We are bound, you, I, and every one to make common cause, even with error itself, to maintain the common right of freedom of conscience.

BEN FRANKLIN (from *A Dissertation on Liberty and Necessity, Pleasure and Pain*; *Benjamin Franklin On the Federal Constitution, Speaking before the Convention in Philadelphia, 1787,* and his letter to Ezra Stiles, March 9, 1790)

There is said to be a First Mover, who is called GOD, Maker of the Universe. He is said to be all-wise, all-good, all powerful. These two propositions being allowed and asserted by people of almost every sect and opinion, I have here supposed them granted, and laid them down as the foundation of my argument; what follows then, being a chain of consequences truly drawn from them, will stand or fall as they are true or false.

Most men, indeed, as well as most sects in religion, think themselves in possession of all truth, and that wherever others differ from them, it is so far error. Steele, a Protestant, in a dedication, tells the pope that the only difference between our two churches in their opinions of the certainty of their doctrine is, the Romish Church is infallible, and the Church of England is never in the wrong. But, though many private persons think almost as highly of their own infallibility as of that of their sect, few express it so naturally as a certain French lady, who, in a little dispute with her sister said: "But I meet with nobody but myself that is always in the right."

I believe in one God, creator of the universe. That he governs it by his Providence. That he ought to be worshiped. That the most acceptable service we render to him is doing good to his other children. That the soul of man is immortal, and will be treated with justice in another life respecting its conduct in this. These I take to be the fundamental principles of all sound religion, and I regard them as you do in whatever sect I meet with them.

As to Jesus of Nazareth, my opinion of whom you particularly desire, I think the system of morals, and his religion, as he left them to us, the best the world ever saw, or is likely to see; but I apprehend it has received various corrupting changes, and I have, with most of the present dissenters in England, some doubts as to his divinity; though it is a question I do not dogmatize upon, having never studied it, and think it needless to busy myself with it now, when I expect soon an opportunity of knowing the truth with less trouble. I see no harm, however, in its being believed, if that belief has the good consequence, as it probably has, of making his doctrines more respected and better observed, especially as I do not perceive that the Supreme takes it amiss, by distinguishing the unbelievers in his government of the world with any particular marks of his displeasure.

I shall only add, respecting myself, that, having experienced the goodness of that being in conducting me prosperously through a long life, I have no doubt of its continuance in the next, though without the smallest conceit of meriting such goodness.

I have ever let others enjoy their religious sentiments, without reflecting on them for those that appeared to me unsupportable and even absurd. All sects here, and we have a great variety, have experienced my good will in assisting them with subscriptions for building their new places of worship; and as I have never opposed any of their doctrines, I hope to go out of the world in peace with them all.

JAMES MADISON (from *Letters and Other Writings of Madison*, Published by Order of Congress)

The experience of the United States is a happy disproof of the error so long rooted in the unenlightened minds of well-meaning Christians, as well as in the corrupt hearts of persecuting usurpers, that without a legal incorporation of religious and civil polity, neither could be supported. A mutual independence is found most friendly to practical religion, to social harmony, and to political prosperity.

Union of religious sentiments begets a surprising confidence, and ecclesiastical establishments tend to great ignorance and corruption, all of which facilitate the execution of mischievous projects.

Poverty and luxury prevail among all sorts. Pride, ignorance, and knavery among the priesthood, and vice and wickedness among the laity. This is bad enough. But it is not the worst. I have to tell you that diabolical hell-conceived principle of persecution rages among some, and to their eternal infamy, the clergy can furnish their quota of imps for such business. This vexes me the most of anything whatever. There are at this in the adjacent county [Virginia] not less than five or six well meaning men in close goal for publishing their religious sentiments, which in the main are very orthodox . . . So I leave you to pity me and pray for liberty of conscience to revive among us.

That liberal catholic and equitable way of thinking as to the rights of conscience, which is one of the characteristics of a free people . . . is but little known among the zealous adherents to our hierarchy.

That religion or the duty we owe to our Creator, and the manner of discharging it, being under the direction of reason and conviction only, not of violence or compulsion, all men are equally entitled to the full and free exercise of it according to the dictates of conscience; and therefore, no man or class of men ought on account of religion to be invested with peculiar emoluments or privileges, nor subjected to any penalties or disabilities. Religious bondage shackles and debilitates the mind and unfits it for every noble enterprise, every expanded prospect.

We hold it for a fundamental and undeniable truth "that religion or the duty which we owe to our Creator and the manner of discharging it can be directed only by reason and conviction, not by force or violence." The religion, then, of every man must be left to the conviction and conscience of every man; and it is the right of every man to exercise it as these may dictate. This right is in its nature an unalienable right. It is unalienable because the opinions of men, depending only on the evidence contemplated by their own minds, cannot follow the dictates of other men. It is unalienable also because what is here a right towards men is a duty towards the Creator. It is the duty of every man to render to the Creator such homage and such only as he believes to be acceptable to him. This duty is precedent, both in order of time and in degree of obligation, to the claims of civil society. Before any man can be considered as a member of civil society, he must be considered as a subject of the Governor of the Universe.

We maintain, therefore, that in matters of religion, no man's right is abridged by the institution of civil society and that religion is wholly exempt from its cognizance. If religion be exempt from the authority of the society at large, still less can it be subject to that of the legislative body. Who does not see that the same authority which can establish Christianity, in exclusion of all other religions, may establish with the same ease any particular sect of Christians, in exclusion of all other sects?

If "all men are by nature equally free and independent," all men are to be considered as entering into society on equal conditions; as relinquishing no more, and therefore retaining no less, one than another, of their natural rights. Above all are they to be considered as retaining an "*equal* title to the free exercise of religion according to the dictates of conscience." While we assert for ourselves a freedom to embrace, to profess, and to observe the religion which we believe to be of divine origin, we cannot deny an equal freedom to those whose minds have not yet yielded to the evidence which has convinced us. If this freedom be abused, it is an offence against God, not against man: To God, therefore, not to man, must an account of it be rendered.

Experience witnesses that ecclesiastical establishments, instead of maintaining the purity and efficacy of religion, have had a contrary operation. During almost fifteen centuries has the legal establishment of Christianity been on trial. What have been its fruits? More or less in all places, pride and indolence in the clergy, ignorance and servility in the laity, in both, superstition, bigotry, and persecution. Enquire of the teachers of Christianity for the ages in which it appeared in its greatest lustre; those of every sect point to the ages prior to its incorporation with civil policy.

If religion be not within the cognizance of civil government, how can its legal establishment be necessary to civil government? What influence, in fact, have ecclesiastical establishments had on civil society? In some instances they have been seen to erect a spiritual tyranny on the ruins of the civil authority; in many instances they have been seen upholding the thrones of political tyranny; in no instance have they been seen the guardians of the liberties of the people. Rulers who wished to subvert the public liberty may have found an established clergy convenient auxiliaries. A just government instituted to secure and perpetuate it needs them not. Such a government will be best supported by protecting every citizen in the enjoyment of his religion with the same equal hand which protects his person and his property, by neither invading the equal rights of any sect, nor suffering any sect to invade those of another.

Are the U. S. duly awake to the tendency of the precedents they are establishing in the multiplied incorporations of Religious Congregations with the faculty of acquiring and holding property real as well as personal!

JOHN ADAMS ("Thoughts on Government, 1776")

Upon this point all speculative politicians will agree, that the happiness of society is the end of government, as all divines and moral philosophers will agree that the happiness of the individual is the end of man. From this principle it will follow that the form of government which communicates ease, comfort, security, or, in one word, happiness, to the greatest number of persons, and in the greatest degree, is the best.

All sober inquirers after truth, ancient and modern, pagan and Christian, have declared that the happiness of man, as well as his dignity, consists in virtue.

If there is a form of government, then, whose principle and foundation is virtue, will not every sober man acknowledge it better calculated to promote the general happiness than any other form?

Fear is the foundation of most governments; but it is so sordid and brutal a passion, and renders men in whose breasts it predominates so stupid and miserable, that Americans will not be likely to approve of any political institution which is founded on it.

SAMUEL ADAMS (*The Rights of the Colonists*, "The Report of the Committee of Correspondence to the Boston Town Meeting," November 20, 1772)

Every natural right not expressly given up, or, from the nature of a social compact, necessarily ceded, remains. All positive and civil laws should conform, as far as possible, to the law of natural reason and equity.

As neither reason requires nor religion permits the contrary, every man living in or out of a state of civil society has a right peaceably and quietly to worship God according to the dictates of his conscience.

"Just and true liberty, equal and impartial liberty," in matters spiritual and temporal, is a thing that all men are clearly entitled to by the eternal and immutable laws of God and nature, as well as by the law of nations and all well-grounded municipal laws, which must have their foundation in the former.

In regard to religion, mutual toleration in the different professions thereof is what all good and candid minds in all ages have ever practiced, and, both by precept and example, inculcated on mankind. And it is now generally agreed among Christians that this spirit of toleration, in the fullest extent consistent with the being of civil society, is the chief characteristic mark of the Church. Insomuch that Mr. Locke has asserted and proved, beyond the possibility of contradiction on any solid ground, that such toleration ought to be extended to all whose doctrines are not subversive of society.

In the state of nature every man is, under God, judge and sole judge of his own rights and of the injuries done him. By entering into society he agrees to an arbiter or indifferent judge between him and his neighbors; but he no more renounces his original right than by taking a cause out of the ordinary course of law, and leaving the decision to referees or indifferent arbitrators.

The natural liberty of man is to be free from any superior power on earth, and not to be under the will or legislative authority of man, but only to have the law of nature for his rule.

In short, it is the greatest absurdity to suppose it in the power of one, or any number of men, at the entering into society, to renounce their essential natural rights or the means of preserving those rights, when the grand end of civil government, from the very nature of its institution, is for the support, protection, and defense of those very rights, the principal of which, as is before observed, are life, liberty, and property. If men, through fear, fraud, or mistake, should in terms renounce or give up any essential natural right, the eternal law of reason and the grand end of society would absolutely vacate such renunciation. The right to freedom being the gift of God Almighty, it is not in the power of man to alienate this gift and voluntarily become a slave.

Amen, and thank you.

Fundamentalists can argue that the opinions of these men are unchristian, according to their definition of that religion. We are all entitled to our opinions. My opinion is that these men and their principles speak more directly to the values of Jesus than does the elitist propaganda of domineering Christians. The Dominionists' contention that our Founders intended to establish a Christian nation, however, is not opinion; it is a false assertion of fact based on ignorance and/or deception. Dominionists distort the theology of Jesus and the ideals of our Founders. That makes them hypocritical on the first count, un-American on the second.

We Deists rest our case.

Chapter 14

The Exploitation of Magical Thinking

Sometimes it seems as if humanity has barely reached puberty. We're like a kid processing the news that Santa isn't real, trying to decide if giving up the myth will stop the flow of gifts.

While it seems that collectively we humans aren't yet mature enough to alleviate the world's evils, what's not so clear is whether we're smart enough to instigate those evils on such a grand scale. And if we aren't that smart, who or what, then, is instigating them?

Evil exists in humanity, that's clear enough. But how and why does evil originate in us? Is evil behavior a reaction to some threat to our survival? Are selfishness, greed, arrogance, and violence survival traits of the strong, or symptoms of neurosis in the weak? Do we judge the sadism of a psychopath devoid of conscience as evil because such a person threatens us? Or do good and evil transcend the brute evolutionary processes of this world?

Evolution isn't the brute process that many seem to think it is. The universe as a whole is not a machine but is more like an organism. Everything is alive in some way. One could consider the changes of the world and of the universe as a process of growing up.

But is it or does it contain some inherent evil?

Is our nature evil? Is it half evil? A quarter evil? A matter of individual nature or personal choice? Is evil the result of immaturity, or stunted maturity the consequence of evil?

Does evil or just a lack of personal development prompt one to victimize scapegoats to assert the superiority of oneself or one's own group? Are we humans irresponsible or just naïve to willingly bow down before authorities that obviously harm us, as a species and as individuals? Is gullibility a kind of masochism?

Are we to blame if the wool has been pulled over our eyes? What can we do to protect ourselves when victimization is conducted most successfully via those who most convincingly claim to be helping us?

Certainly it's dangerous to lift up "childlike" as a sacred virtue, especially when *childlike* usually means *childish*. Humanity is more often than not like a lot of little kids with really big guns. Bullies, brats, or just clueless five-year-olds, it doesn't really matter if you're the one that's been shot.

Today we've reached *the* critical moment of decision: Grow up, or blow up.

Murder is no longer concrete. Instead of looking our human enemy in the eye, we push a button and blow up a point on a map. "The enemy" is an abstraction, their civilization a mere concept. The deaths of few or few thousand or few million innocent men, women, and children who are no different than our own innocent men, women, and children are inconsequential if we've knocked off a couple gang members or terrorists, or flexed our muscles for a few politicians and their corporate bosses.

Why have people throughout the ages destroyed each other? Among primitives, means of survival and religious ideology; among moderns, mammon and religious ideology; among individuals, greed and pride, fused as power, which is playing God, a religious ideology. Whether an individual or group is in charge of the destruction, it needs the willing support of the masses to launch its attacks; it needs to control religious ideology.

Simple conformity and obedience, prized virtues exploited by leaders eager to maintain superiority, can lead to Inquisition witch burnings, racist lynchings, anti-Semitic holocausts, terrorism, and war, all executed in the name of God. In America, gay bashing, execution of blacks and Jews, and murder of uppity women are biblically sanctioned acts of obedience according to radical fundamentalist cults like Neo-Nazis, Reconstructionists, and the KKK, and if we add those who commit these hate crimes in their hearts, we can include a cult of ordinary good Christians.

Religious people throughout the world are not simply being discriminated against in the name of God. For the sake of differences of religious superstitions, people are still tortured and sacrificed on a large scale—Islamic jihads, brutal religious horrors in Iran, Lebanon, Sudan, and India, atrocious oppression at the hands of religious leaders in Saudia Arabia, Egypt, Syria, Kuwait, Afghanistan, Nigeria, and elsewhere throughout the Middle East and Africa, and indeed the whole world. Even in civilized "Christian" nations, Christians are at war even with themselves. Irish Protestants and Catholics are still battling it out. American gay Christians and gay people of other God-worshipping faiths are denigrated, ostracized, and denied basic human rights with unchristian vehemence in contradiction to the fundamental constitutional laws of our "Christian" nation. All over the modern civilized world, gays, blacks, Jews, and Muslims are murdered for being just that in the name of somebody's version of "righteous."

Yes, in some of its incarnations, religion is downright evil. And it's not just pagan religions like, say, the Aztecs, who sacrificed 20,000 victims each year to a sun god who might not shine on them if they didn't provide him with a daily meal of ripped-out hearts and blood. Flesh from victims' arms was ritualistically eaten in a more literal version of "this is my body, this is my blood." As many as 10,000 skulls were displayed at a time on special skull racks designed to impress. The sun god was not the only divinity needing appeasement. Dancing virgins were decapitated and skinned, and their skins worn by priests who continued the dancing to please the maize goddess. Tears of children sacrificed weeping were offered to the rain god.

In the humble view of the Deist, God is not the god of sacrifice created in the image of high priests.

If those Aztec priests were not blood-brothers of Ed Gein, Edmund Kemper, and Jeffrey Dahmer—or Hitler, or the bombers of Hiroshima and Nagasaki, or the Christian Church of Bosnia, or the Christian president who dropped weapons of mass destruction on Iraq for oil "to make the world safe from terrorists"—then perhaps they serve as examples of con artists commanding power by generating fear of extinction among the lowly masses and instituting major sacrifices—over which they preside, of course—to appease the gods and thereby alleviate the fear. The sun had never *not* shone on the Aztecs; it was utterly, documentably steadfast. Perhaps they wanted the sun to back off. Maize harvests and rainfall might have been less predictable—their civilization probably disappeared due to drought—, but what devil decided that a divinity needed tens of thousands of butchered female virgins or children for lunch to alleviate the problem?

The fearful faithful were not really kneeling before the gods; they were bowing down to blood-thirsty, dangerous high priests, lofty in the power and prestige afforded those who can influence the gods. Control the gods and you rule the people.

As long as the sun shines and there's bread on the table, no one complains. Priests are lifted up to the heavens. The gods are brought down to the level of humans. Then the anthropomorphic gods are *controlled* by humans. One god is easier to control. Humans become God and God the servant of humans. God becomes an angry, vengeful, violent servant of the priest sanctified by his priest-written "inspired" Text.

The bloodlust of "God" starts with a simple myth created by power-hungry priests for the sake of exploiting gullible sheep, materially and spiritually—or by terrified priests who believe that other human beings are the cause of the problem and are expendable. Bloodlust culminates in a sadistic sacrificial frenzy for God in the name of God, like the Christian Inquisition or the Crusades.

Witches were the primary recipients of medieval torture. Today spiritual misogynists are usually restrained by humanist laws from such extreme physical abuse. Instead, contemporary inquisitors typically resort to verbal judgment: "The feminist agenda is not about equal rights for women. It is about a socialist, anti-family political movement that encourages women to leave their husbands, kill their children, practice witchcraft, destroy capitalism and become lesbians." When Pat Robertson uses the terms *feminist, agenda, equal rights, women, socialist, anti-family, leave husbands, kill children, witchcraft, destroy capitalism (implying humanism), and lesbians,* he's tapping into antiquated fears associated with the superstitions of the Dark Ages.

Like Robertson, Church of England vicar Rev. Anthony Kennedy seems to miss the good old days, illustrated in his comment about those supporting ordination of female priests, according to a *London Times* article, March 9, 1994:

> I would shoot the bastards if I was allowed, because a woman can't represent Christ. Men and women are totally different, that's not my fault, and Jesus chose men for his disciples. Priestesses should be burnt at the stake because they are assuming powers they have

no right to. In the medieval world that was called sorcery. The way of dealing with sorcerers was to burn them at the stake. It's illegal now but if I had my way that is what would happen to them. In medieval times, I would burn the bloody bitches.

The justification for misogyny and the use of torture devices is, of course, biblical. "Even the devil can cite scripture for his purpose," Shakespeare reminded us. As his friend John Selden put it, "*Scrutamini scriptura* [search the scriptures]. These two words have undone the world."

During his trial for war crimes, Nazi death camp administrator Adolf Eichmann justified his murder of thousands by stating that he was merely following the orders of his superiors. Spiritual terrorists claim that they are merely following the directives of the Bible.

Because of their conformity and obedience, even decent people will commit atrocities commanded by charismatic leaders. Hitler understood that to dominate the world, he would need to spiritually motivate good people to commit acts that they would otherwise consider abhorrent: "Only in the steady and constant application of force lies the very first prerequisite for success. This persistence, however, can always and only arise from a definite spiritual conviction. Any violence which does not spring from a firm spiritual base will be wavering and uncertain."

It could be argued that the Church has survived because of its leaders' successful manipulation of its spiritual base. But although fear and intimidation have always been useful tactics of high priests, at times the laymen revolt and the Church "reconsiders," as in the sainting of Joan of Arc.

Even some Catholic laymen thought the Church made a mistake in canonizing her. Surely not even Dark Age angels in the middle of the Hundred Years War would literally speak to an illiterate teenage peasant girl, much less instruct her at length about her divine mission to reunite France. Others argued that just because the rest of us have never heard angelic voices doesn't prove that Joan of Arc was equally uninspired.

According to Vida Sackville-West's definitive history of the saint, Joan was a mere twelve years old when she began hearing the angelic voices that commissioned her to reunite France. Would an uneducated peasant girl in the thirteenth century have understood enough current affairs to imagine such a sophisticated plot? Perhaps, given her father's active engagement in politics. But then again, maybe she really was divinely inspired.

Whatever the source, by the time she was sixteen, Joan's commission had become urgent. The dauphin, Charles VII, was in exile, and enemy English and Burgundian troops blocked his path to Reims, where kings of France were crowned. Joan's mission was to clear the way for his crowning. Good and faithful disciple that she was, she set about bringing to fruition the angels' prophecy about herself.

Psychologists point out that people with psychological disorders associated with dissociation, including children who have been molested or have suffered other traumas, sometimes hear voices of accusation or comfort. Joan might have been abused. Yet the massive published testimony about her family and childhood indicates otherwise. Perhaps she was a repressed lesbian asserting her spiritual right to name herself *la Pucelle*, the virgin, not by passively withdrawing to a nunnery but by engaging in literal battle to legitimize the illegitimate "neutered" king of France. Charles's illegitimate birth could only be redeemed by his being crowned a legitimate king; Joan could only redeem her illegitimate birth gender by fulfilling his redemption. That makes sense symbolically/psychologically.

Theologians assure us that while psychological explanations might be true, they don't prove that mystics don't communicate directly with the supernatural. The supernatural does indeed exist, and mystics sensitive to its presence are often labeled "crazy." If super-intelligent higher beings such as angels exist, they could be capable of communicating with humans. There is no proof that Saint Joan was not divinely directed.

Historians remind us that most medieval people were uneducated, gullible, and superstitious. Nearly everyone but the most educated humanists believed in fantastical beings, both Christian and pagan: trolls, succubi, witches, fauns, devils, griffins, ancestors, goddesses, and the ever-popular angels, to name but a few. They also had a tendency to inflate their heroes into mythic superheroes.

Theologians counter that trolls and fauns are mythical, but angels and devils are biblical fact. Why shouldn't angels talk to Joan of Arc? Why couldn't she have accomplished ostensibly miraculous feats? History, in fact, proves that she did.

As steeped in legendary detail as Joan of Arc might have been, and as much as we might want to believe that hers was a self-fulfilling prophecy, it is a fact that this petite teenage girl did accomplish the seemingly impossible. Historians find it inexplicable how in less than seven months,

Joan convinced the governor of Vaucouleurs to permit her to travel, disguised in men's clothes as divinely directed, with two of his friends to Charles's court; how she convinced Charles to give her a royal army; how within days of her arrival in Orleans, her troops destroyed the powerful besieging English forces there, a turning point in the war. Although seriously wounded, Joan continued to lead the army. It's worth noting that according to her trial records, she herself never killed anyone or even drew blood. Still, by the sheer power of her presence, this valiant warrior recaptured numerous towns as she cleared the path to Reims, where Charles was crowned with the short teenage girl standing at his side, in armor, her standard in her hand. Everyone present and throughout the country knew all this had come to pass via angelic instruction.

Joan had always been severely devout, and all who knew her well, personally and professionally, attested to her purity and intense devotion to God and her angelic guides. Joan went so far as to endanger herself and her army by halting her troops to listen to church bells, by insisting on her need to attend Mass in dangerous enemy territory, and by refusing to launch critical attacks on Sunday. Ironically, her forced devotions to the higher powers that insured her success led to her downfall.

After being wounded several times in her continued campaigns to recapture French towns, in 1430, Joan herself was captured, sold to the English, and transported in stages to Rouen, where she was tried for various forms of heresy.

Inquisitors interrogated her about her voices, her sense of mission, and the male clothes she refused to give up because she had received no instruction from her voices to do so. Her several guards tormented and mocked her day and night, and she was spied on during her confessions. She was spared the horrors of the torture chamber only because of the shrewd intercession of a sympathizer among her prosecutors. After attempting escape by jumping from the tower of Philip Augustus where she was incarcerated, the country's hero was secured upright in an iron cage, tied by the throat and hands, and bound by her feet to a chain attached to a beam.

Unlike most heretics, who were tried by one or two inquisitors, Joan's case required a whole team of expert prosecutors to flaunt Church authority as a warning to all Christendom, including the warring political powers. Although she could easily have been executed like any other captured soldier—the English were hovering like vultures over her tribunal—, Joan's trial, itself a sham to justify her preordained burning at the stake, required the services of one cardinal, six bishops, thirty-two doctors of theology, sixteen bachelors of theology, seven doctors of medicine, and one hundred and three other associates because she was a woman who had both heard angelic voices and worn men's clothing, without apology, for all the world to see. She was a mystic transvestite superstar, or in their words, a witch. Her heinous offense was adhering "steadfastly to the principle of private judgment which was in conflict with the attitude of simple obedience exacted by the Church." She was granted no advocate; no witnesses were called on her behalf; no one was permitted to assist or direct her (the many who took her side were afraid to voice that opinion for the record); no formal indictment was read to her until her very last days; her team of judges bombarded her with subtle questions meant to confuse and trap her while her other prosecutors watched and scribbled notes.

Officially her judges charged, among other things:

> The woman commonly named Jeanne la Pucelle . . . shall be denounced and declared as a sorceress, diviner, pseudo-prophetess, invoker of evil spirits, conspiratrix, superstitious, implicated in and given to the practice of magic, wrongheaded as to our Catholic faith, schismatic as to the article *Unam Sanctam*, etc., and in several articles of our faith skeptical and astray, sacrilegious, idolatrous, apostate, accursed and mischievous, blasphemous towards God and His saints, scandalous, seditious, disturber of peace, inciter of war, cruelly avid of human blood, inciting to bloodshed, having completely and shamelessly abandoned the decencies proper to her sex, and having immodestly adopted the dress and status of a man-at-arms; for that, and for other things abominable to God and men, a traitor to laws divine and natural and to the discipline of the Church, seductress of princes and the populace, having in contempt and disdain of God permitted herself to be venerated and adored, by giving her hands and her garments to be kissed, heretical, or at any rate vehemently suspected of heresy, for that she shall be punished and corrected according to divine and canonical laws.

Then followed the first of the seventy articles comprising the Act of Accusation. The judges stressed, "If the prelates of the Church do not see to it, subversion of the whole authority of the Church may ensue; men and women may arise on every side, pretending to revelations from God or His angels."

After the judges had presented their case against Joan, it was referred to the University of Paris. Their decision was that "the woman commonly called *la Pucelle* had so disseminated her poison that it had infected the very Christian flock of almost the whole western world." They charged her with being a heretic, sorceress, schismatic, and apostate.

After months of resistance, ill and exhausted, Joan was dragged into the courtyard of the St. Ouen church and forced to sign a statement of abjuration in which she denied that her voices were divine. She was sentenced to life imprisonment and her head was shaved to rid her of her boyish cut. She put on a woman's dress as directed—her voices had given her permission—and on that basis her judges told her she would not be excommunicated. But some English soldiers of the guard forced her to put back on her former clothes, and she was raped by a nobleman. Three days after her abjuration, she retracted. Joan of Arc was excommunicated and sentenced to be executed on May 30, 1431.

Multitudes turned out for the event. In front of the stage erected for the spectacle, her captors erected a board painted with the words: "Jehanne who called herself la Pucelle, liar, pernicious, deceiver of the people, sorceress, superstitious, blasphemer of God, presumptuous, disbeliever in the faith of Jesus Christ, boastful, idolatrous, cruel, dissolute, invoker of devils, apostate, schismatic, and heretic." Many strange signs and wonders were reportedly witnessed by shaken and terrified onlookers, and some of their accounts were officially noted and added to the court record. Many onlookers wept as they brought out the heretic, who continued praying even as her tormentors placed on her head not a crown of thorns but a tall paper cap like a mitre, which bore the words, "Heretic, relapsed, apostate, idolatress."

For the heresy of resolute faithfulness to her mystical guidance, at age 19, Joan of Arc was burned at the stake.

As the flames leapt and crackled, she cried out loudly and repeatedly to Jesus. Even some of her prosecutors wept and turned away in horror. John Tressart, secretary to the King of England, exclaimed, "We are lost; we have burnt a saint." The executioner, frightened and contrite, sought out the priests who had attended Joan, telling them that he was damned and that God would never forgive him for burning the saint. He said that despite all the oil, sulfur, and fuel he had used, Joan's entrails and heart could not be reduced to ashes, so he had thrown all that remained of her into the Seine.

The dramatic example of Joan of Arc still inspires heretics throughout the world. As in the past, heretics today challenge the Church's authority to decide matters of truth, knowledge, belief, and behavior. If you beg to differ on points of dogma or claim to have had a spiritual experience outside the rituals orchestrated by the Church, you position yourself beyond ecclesiastical control. Nothing is more anathema, nothing more blasphemous than challenging the divine right of the high priests to dictate the definition and very essence of your soul.

Twenty-five years after Joan of Arc's public execution, Charles VII and Joan's mother petitioned the pope to restore her to the Church. Among Dark Age Christians, excommunication was a one-way ticket to hell—unless, of course, the pope intervened.

The transcripts survive of the interviews with numerous people who corroborated the truth of Joan's incredible life. Who really was this pious mystic who rallied royalty, nobles, and soldiers to the cause of fulfilling her supernatural mission, this intuitive kid with a gift for debunking false prophets, who defied the highest authorities of the Church with exactly their claim of divine authority? *What* was this non-conformist transvestite and transgressor of conventional mores that centuries after her death forced her persecutors to redefine holiness on her behalf?

Joan wasn't just another heretic. Although Pope Calixtus III revoked her sentence in 1456, the protest over her excommunication continued for over five centuries. Joan of Arc was an actual person whose life transfigured into a legend representing higher spiritual and political meanings that resonated with believers and nonbelievers alike. Both the faithful and the secular weren't content that she be restored to the Church; they wanted their martyred hero canonized. They wanted justice.

Perhaps the infallible Church was just brushing off tedious generations of complainers when in 1920 it reversed her heretic status to sainthood. What harm could come from adding yet another legend to their long roster of saints? The infallible Church, it should be noted, conferred her sainthood matter-of-factly, without admission of error or mention of bonfire.

Or perhaps the Church was shoring-up its crumbling bastion. Modernism challenged not just the Church's claims to divine inspiration, but also the reality of divine inspiration itself.

If talking to angels posed a threat to the Church of the Dark Ages, the impossibility of talking to angels posed an even more serious threat to the Church of the early twentieth century. By the end of the nineteenth century, the Bible had been deconstructed, angels and devils demystified, and the elitist Church hierarchy all but dismembered.

Deeming the historical Joan a saint would be one way to reinvigorate belief in angels, saints, and the Church's power to confer sainthood, the same power that qualified any believer's admittance into heaven. Like other religions, Christianity argued most forcefully through its appeals to superstition. Protestant fundamentalism was spreading like wildfire. Catholicism needed another super-saint to grip the flock's attention. Joan of Arc was the Catholic Church's answer to its rivals, agnosticism and Protestant fundamentalism.

Humanity is addicted to its superstitions. Our habit of answering hard questions superstitiously seems to be hardwired in our DNA, our collective unconscious, perhaps even our spirits. We worship not our gods but our idols, representations, myths, superstitions. We experience God not directly, spirit to spirit, but as in a cracked, dusty funhouse mirror of reflected shapes and light.

Perhaps Joan of Arc personified her own remarkable intuitive gifts as guardian angels. The Greeks believed in guardian spirits they called *daemons*. Even the rational Socrates thanked his guardian daemon for his intuitive military skills that saved his life when he fought with Athens during its war with Sparta. The Romans called these ingenious daemons *genii*, plural for *genius*. Deifying our own strengths gives us hope that there's something "out there" that can supplement those strengths. Our greatest strength is ingenuity. We call upon the gods of ingenuity to make us heroes. We create heroes as our protectors and as models of our potential strength. Our gods and our heroes inspire us to become better than ourselves.

Throughout history it has been common practice to mythologize heroes into legends that greatly inflate and embellish their actual feats. Chieftains and their high priests establish themselves as the official keepers of the mythic legacies, which gives them a mystique of authority and

222 • Born-Again Deist

power by intimate association. The Catholic Church's officially documented lives and legends of the saints, complete with miracles, dragons, and unicorns, provide numerous cases in point. The pope's hypocritical "high drag" and the pomp and ceremony of public appearances, rituals, sacraments, and official pronouncements are props validating his authority to represent the unassuming Jesus. Rich and famous fundamentalist evangelists lift themselves up as representatives of their humble, poor, self-sacrificing Lord. No more false representation of the biblical person Jesus has ever existed than the Christian Church itself.

People long to believe in super-human versions of themselves. People "worship" movie stars, rock stars, and sports heroes. Many adults continue refining the childhood arts of gossip, exaggeration, and make-believe to magnify their humdrum world. Even today educated Americans believe urban legends, like the hook-arm caught on the car door handle at lovers lane, or the drying-off poodle exploded in the microwave. How much easier to persuade gullible believers indoctrinated in mystified Christian tradition that Joan of Arc, the notorious heretic burned at the stake, was now a saint.

Whatever its agenda, the Vatican was surely intent to reinvent itself as the only authority defining one's standing as a soul before God. It was engaged in a public relations campaign to upgrade its image, which upgraded the image of the God housed in the Vatican's privileged Holiest of Holies.

If Joan of Arc had been a man, would he have been tortured and burned? Probably not; more likely he would have been promptly executed by an English firing squad. Joan had committed no act of treason against the Church. She showed all the signs of being a true warrior-prophet of God in the tradition of Moses, Joshua, and David. The problem with Joan was that she was a woman, and according to the Dark Age Church, most women were "bad," the worst were heretics, and the worst heretics were witches. All heroic deeds, political accomplishments, and spiritual anointings were irrelevant for a woman who wore men's clothes.

The sadistic tyranny of the Inquisition murdered millions of heretics, most of them witches. According to the *Malleus Maleficarum* (*The Witches' Hammer*), the Church's official guidebook for the prosecution, punishment, and execution of witches, "after the sin of Lucifer, the works of witches exceed all other sins." The heresy committed by witches was "the most heinous of the three degrees of infidelity; and this fact is proved both by reason and authority."

Heresy is nothing more than any challenge to some ultimate authority. In contemporary America, heresy often represents disrespect for the false authority of the Religious Right. Almost everyone who challenges authority does so on the basis of some other authority. In America, most of us believe in everyone else's right to an opinion. But if my opinion, experience, or religion differs from the fundamentalist's, he will disrespect my authority with the assumption that I am either wrong or lying. It is one person's claim to authority versus another's, but the fundamentalist arrogantly asserts that his claim is the only one that's valid and true.

Are Dominionists today truly interested in instituting a "Christian nation," or is "Christian nation" persistently chanted to ignite a definite spiritual conviction exploited by Dominionist leaders needing violent backing to force their own domination? When spiritual authorities direct Christians to judge, reject, and or hate Muslims or Russians or gays or humanists, many comply even when it makes them uncomfortable doing what deep down they think is wrong. The only way to prevent compliance is to demystify the authority of the Bible and its priests and to remystify conscience and common sense. In America today, that translates as civil disobedience toward the Right and spiritual disobedience toward organized religion.

Is disobedience so much to ask for the sake of truth? Maybe so. For decades scientists have documented just how far people will go to be obedient. In the early 1950's, psychologist Solomon Asch created an experiment in which a subject, along with six researchers posing as fellow subjects, sat at a table and were asked to view several sets of lines, each set consisting of one standard line and three comparison lines. Each subject was then asked in turn to decide which comparison line equaled the length of the standard line. On certain sets, all the researchers posing as subjects purposely selected the wrong line even though the correct line was quite obvious. The actual subject, who knew the right answer but wanted to avoid appearing different, went along with the incorrect majority 37 percent of the time.

Numerous studies have demonstrated that people adjust their behavior to conform to the group even if the adjustment involves lying. Conformity exerts the most pressure when the group is unanimous (say, within a congregation), when the choice is difficult, and in cultures that value inter-dependence, conformity, and social harmony over individual goals. It's easy to see how fundamentalists can be coerced by their churches into damning even good Christians whose views differ from their own.

During the 1960's, psychologist Stanley Milgram conducted a famous series of controversial experiments to demonstrate the extent to which people behave in obedience to authority. 1,000 subjects were asked to act as teachers in a study of the effects of punishment on learning. Each time the learner made a mistake on a memory test, an experimenter would order the subject, the "teacher," to administer painful electric shocks. The intensity of the shocks would increase in increments of 15 volts up to 450 volts.

The learner was actually another experimenter who only pretended to receive the shocks. Usually the "teachers" could not see the learner but could hear audiotaped responses that increased from grunts of pain to shouting to complaints of heart trouble to agonized screams. When the teacher's punishment reached the 330 volt level, the learner became silent. Yet the experimenter continued to order the teacher to raise the intensity of the shock. Though many of the teachers experienced anguish over the pain they thought they were administering, and exhibited signs of distress such as sweating, trembling, lip-biting, and fits of nervous laughter, 65 percent of the teacher subjects delivered the sizzling 450 volt punishment rather than disobey authority.

The shocking truth is that the majority of "average people" will pas-sively, willfully obey authority even if it is obviously abusive—because they have been taught to be obedient. Conformity and obedience are "virtues" drilled by fundamentalists promoting the doctrine of infallibil-ity. How can these "virtues" keep even well-educated believers in denial when they know that for centuries, well-meaning scholars have exposed hundreds of incongruities in the Bible texts that thoroughly disprove biblical infallibility?

Psychologists call the preference to maintain contradictory beliefs rather than amend them *cognitive dissonance*, an aspect of *magical think-ing*. People who lack critical thinking skills and educated information, as well as those who have a vested interest in preserving the contradictory elements, resort to magical thinking to justify their pre-existing beliefs and to avoid the effort of re-vision.

People who make use of magical thinking are often unable or unwilling to distinguish between perceived and actual patterns; they see or fabricate relationships between things that don't exist. Consider this comment by Pat Robertson: "If the widespread practice of homosexuality will bring about the destruction of your nation, if it will bring about terrorist bombs, if it'll bring about earthquakes, tornadoes, and possibly a meteor, it isn't necessarily something we ought to open our arms to."

A Yale educated lawyer and self-proclaimed genius, Robertson presumably would understand the fundamental rules of rhetoric. But here he freely employs several logical fallacies. His argument centers around an "if . . . then" construction, but the "if" begs the question in that Robertson implies as given the source of the disasters (homosexuality) he needs to prove for his "if" clauses to be valid. His circular reasoning supports his assertion with the assertion itself.

Robertson concludes with a *non sequitur* ("it does not follow"); "we ought not open our arms" follows an irrelevant argument. Robertson implies that homosexuality brings about the disasters he has listed, and if homosexuality brings about these disasters, he says, then we ought not be sympathetic to homosexuality. It doesn't take a lot of critical thinking or education to know that earthquakes, tornadoes, meteors, and the destruction of a nation like America are not caused by homosexuality. But faithful Robertson followers trust that they are. Jacked up about the "homosexual menace," they send him money because he tells them to.

Although science explains *how*, it can't answer *why*. Magical thinking provides a "why" answer. Any answer to "why" is always a guess, but if the guess seems plausible and provides a sense (even false) of assurance and security, that guess can become a "fact" in the believer's mind. Robertson's explanation for disasters is so absurd that it's surely a ploy rather than a sincere guess. What matters is that people believe him (and send him money).

As more people are persuaded of the truth of the false "fact," that "fact" accumulates validity. The bandwagon appeal does not prove the validity of the "fact," it simply seduces with the irrelevant argument that "millions of viewers just like you" are already on board. If everybody else in Robertson's "Club" believes it, it must be true. (If everyone else is sending him money, it must be the right thing to do.)

Humans are incorrigibly superstitious, even when their superstitions are self-contradictory. Those who believe that Pat Robertson is a prophet seem unconcerned with the ambiguities of his prophecies. Are his believers simply immature?

In *Witchcraft, Magic, and Oracles Among the Azande*, E. E. Evans-Pritchard relates an incident of a roof falling on a person, which the Azande attributed to a magic spell cast by another person. Although the Azande did "scientifically" understand that the roof collapsed because termites had eaten through the supporting posts, they needed an explanation for why the roof collapsed at that precise moment on that particular man. Coincidences, or contingencies, are explained magically by the superstitious. Robertson's claim that homosexuality causes disasters is equivalent to the claim that magical spells caused the roof to collapse.

How many times have victims of catastrophes shrugged and mumbled that it must have been God's will, they must have needed it, they must have deserved it? Hundreds of tornadoes have ripped through Oklahoma City in the last fifty years, but people keep building and rebuilding flimsy houses above ground in the target zone because a tornado would not shred their homes or kill them if it were not the will of God. Yet they never make the connection to the warning of Jesus to not build their houses on the sand—an analogy that only makes sense if the example makes literal sense.

Magical thinking seeks to verify its beliefs. When one of Robertson's listed disasters occurs, the gullible say, "Aha! That proves it. Robertson was right." Of course, it proves no such thing. This tendency to seek and find substantiation (even false) for an illogical conclusion, which is an aspect of what psychologists call *confirmation bias*, is similar to a baseball player doing his lucky ritual of choking up and tapping his shoe a certain number of times, or a golfer always wearing his lucky shirt. Even though both the ball player and golfer have good and bad games, each will chalk up his victories to his lucky ritual, his lucky shirt. "Luck" is an irrational mental construct designed to verify a fiction.

It's bad luck to think bad thoughts because they will come true and you will thereby be punished. "Instant karma," as many of us have said, only half jokingly. Even mentioning the devil will conjure his appearance, especially if you're alone late at night. Better keep your thoughts on the Virgin Mary, better rub that lucky St. Christopher medal. Light a candle. Burn incense. Cleanse the room with sage. Think positive: If you pray hard enough, if you stand on God's promise to answer the prayers on your list posted on the fridge, if you rub your special Bible like a magic lamp, God will pop up to grant your every wish. But don't step on cracks or you'll break your mother's back. Don't leave church without signing a cross. And of course, if you're wearing holey underwear, you'll be in a car crash.

It's one thing for a child to be superstitious. But adults need to use their brains. Pat Robertson is a master of pontificating the ridiculous because he is unafraid to lie and because his lies appeal to those who refuse to think for themselves. What American adult could believe this, for instance: "The courts are merely a ruse, if you will, for humanist, atheistic educators to beat up on Christians."

Does Robertson, who holds a law degree, truly believe that the purpose of the courts is to serve as a ruse for educators; that all educators are atheist; that all humanists are atheists; or that educators have the time or inclination to "beat up on" Christians? Does Robertson honestly think that there are no Christian employees of the courts, no Christian educators, and no Christian humanists? Does he know the function of the courts? Does he even know the definition of "ruse"?

It's not hard to understand a liar when lying has made him rich. The mystery is that even educated adults believe him and pay him for the honor.

Chapter 15

Snake Oil and Sanctimony

I'm the type that likes clarity. I like standing with my feet balanced firmly on solid ground. I feel most comfortable when good and evil assemble at opposite ends of the playing field. Though I squint at the thin line between naïveté and stupidity—or are they the same thing?—I do understand a naïve Christian, having been one myself.

Perhaps because I prefer the cut-and-dry, and want to rescue the hoodwinked naïve, during my transition from progressive Christian to disillusioned agnostic I became intrigued by the fuzzy blur between the seemingly genuine faith and huckster histrionics of TV evangelists. I was not as uncomfortable with the suckers, having been one myself, as I was with the evangelists themselves, who seemed to actually believe the outrageous lies they told to get filthy rich. Were they schizophrenic?

I was so amazed by the success of their religious infomercials that I started watching their shows just to analyze their games. Word of Faith, or "Seed Faith," was the biggest game in town. Its strategies competed with Send Me Money Because I Said So and Send Me Money To Support My Mission.

It's no coincidence that the rise of mega-rich evangelists coincided with the forging of the Dominionist alliance, which included evangelists along with rightwing politicians, major corporations, and the neocon. Each quarter had its own agenda, but the bottom line was always money and the power that comes with it. Evangelists enjoyed their federal handouts, tax-exempt status, and upper-class lifestyle along with their comrades while providing them with a righteous veneer.

No longer the root of all evil, money had trans-figured into divine usary via the lucrative postmodern doctrine of Seed Faith: You send me money, and God will reward you—with interest. Why? The Prayer of Agreement clause. Jesus promised that where two or more agree on anything in his name, he would grant it to them. I have come to bring you joy, Jesus said. Well, it was clearly money that put the fun in fundamentalism, so there you had joy. And the Bible (but not Jesus himself) said that God wants to prosper you in spirit, and what better prospers the spirit than monetary prosperity? That's what God *really* meant by prosper.

Jesus promised anything. Seed Faith evangelist John Avanzini publically disagreed with Christians who argued that Jesus was addressing his disciples, not the rest of us, and that he certainly wasn't writing a blank check to be filled in by greedy hypocrites. The disciples lived in luxury, Avanzini contended, and God wanted the rest of us to as well. Even Jesus took advantage of the Prayer Clause. Although Jesus seemed to live humbly, he actually was well off, which was proven by the purple robe his tormentors wrapped him in before the Crucifixion. "John 19 tells us that Jesus wore designer clothes. I mean, you didn't get the stuff he wore off the rack. No, this was custom stuff. It was the kind of garment that kings and rich merchants wore."

Religion was Avanzini's life, or at least his chosen livelihood. What bothered me was that to make a buck, Avanzini misrepresented a detail out of context to prove the direct opposite of the context and the gospel as a whole. And viewers bought it. Shouldn't they know that the purple cloak of John 19 didn't belong to Jesus any more than did the crown of thorns? Both were provided by the soldiers for the sake of mocking Jesus. Avanzini would know this, as would the deluded had they checked the passage for themselves.

I watched amazed at how skillfully the hucksters persuaded the desperate and the gullible that God set himself up to be legalistically conned into keeping his word to give anyone, even the most evil psychopath, whatever he or she asked, because *whoops*, God blurted that he would.

How could anyone be gullible enough to believe that? How could I, a decade earlier, have been that gullible? Granted, Seed Faith evangelists are good at their pitch. God doesn't want you to suffer, they argue. God has everything at his disposal; making you rich is no big deal to God.

God doesn't want you to be uncomfortable. God wants you to have nice things, and nice things are expensive.

But I never accepted that all those children in Africa were starving because they weren't Christians, they hadn't prayed to the right God, or hadn't prayed hard enough or with the right intent, they had fallen short, when really they had just been born at the wrong place at the wrong time. Oh but wait, that was predestined. I couldn't wrap my mind or conscience around that explanation. Nor could I drop my hard-earned coins in the collection envelope because if I gave to their relief, God would bless me.

Once I stepped outside the Christian box—epiphany! God's insider tip to the evangelists themselves was that "free" enterprise was the freedom to rip off your neighbor tax free and to call that a "church."

Even though the media had repeatedly busted Seed Faith evangelists for downright fraud, people still sent them their hard-earned money, hoping for a return with heavenly interest. Just get out of the way and let God make you a millionaire. The millionaire evangelists themselves served as advertisement that their program worked. You would be blessed and that was a fact.

Greed—aka "blessing"—was sanctified and glorified in the name of Jesus, Kenneth Copeland assured us all, because God was subject to the laws of faith and words. In other words, God was at our mercy. If you asked for a million dollars in faith, preferably by demanding that God keep his promises, you'd get the million. Never mind that everything Jesus was, did, and taught contradicted any doctrine of greed and any form of spiritual manipulation.

Word of Faith evangelists guaranteed: Agree, pray in faith, use the right abracadabra, and poof, prosperity was yours. Or as Kenneth Hagin put it, in the exact words he received in a vision from Jesus, "Say it. Do it. Receive it. Tell it." Hagen furthered his disbursements through sales of prosperity books such as *Godliness Is Profitable* and *How to Write Your Own Ticket with God.*

The seductive Word of Faith prosperity movement got its start during the early twentieth century, when fundamentalism, which promoted biblical literalism, was coming into existence. Fundamentalism made it easy to mystify the validity of prosperity via the Bible. E.W. Kenyon popularized his idea that the "power of faith" to bring health and wealth was God's idea. He wanted to give gifts, but people needed to ask. Kenyon coined phrases like "What I confess, I possess" to get his Word of Faith message across. Greedy, get-rich-quick Americans *loved* this theology.

Oral Roberts was the great propagator of the Seed Faith tradition. You had to send his ministry seed money to activate the promise. Once you gave, your money would be multiplied many times over, as per the Bible. If you didn't get the payback, you were doing something to "block God's blessing." Most likely, you didn't have enough faith, or you'd held back and were not giving God (i.e. the Roberts ministry) a fair share of the money he had already given you.

The "health and wealth" gospel, aka "name it and claim it" (and "blab and grab"), took no pity on the poor viewer. No matter what your circumstance, you were required to give to the evangelist's "ministry." On his show *Take It By Force*, Clarence McClendon told viewers that God instructed him to tell the financially strapped that they should use their credit cards to "sow a seed."

"Get Jesus on that credit card!" he ordered listeners. In return, God would make sure that their debt would be paid off within thirty days.

Broke or in debt? Send a check today, because God was especially generous to those who gave when they could least afford it. Jesus himself said so regarding the poor widow. Paul Crouch told viewers on one of his telethons, "He'll give you thousands, hundreds of thousands. He'll give millions and billions of dollars."

TV evangelists were just as dependent on direct-mail solicitations as they were on pitches via satellite. The person credited with developing mail solicitation "ministries" was Rev. James Eugene Ewing. Ewing had no ministry, and no church other than a Tulsa post office box by the name of Saint Matthew's Churches (formerly St. Matthew Publishing, Inc.), which took in the millions of dollars generated by direct-mailings sent out to mostly poor, uneducated sheep via operations at Ewing's mansion in Los Angeles. The "church" had two listed phone numbers in Tulsa, both answered by recorded religious messages.

Ewing's seed faith ministry-by-letter often included free gifts like prayer cloths, Jesus eyes handkerchiefs, fake gold coins, communion wafers, and sackcloth billfolds to inspire recipients to a sense of obligation, if the lure of magical reward for seed-cash sewn in faith didn't convince us to send him money. Unlike most seed-faith evangelists, who wanted you to spread the word for them, Ewing often warned recipients to open their special letters in private and to keep the magic secret from less gullible friends or relatives.

When it incorporated in Tulsa in 1997, St. Matthew Publishing Inc. filed IRS forms reporting $15.6 million in revenue. In 1999, the last year it made its tax records public, according to online media, Saint Matthew's raked in $26 million, tax-free, of course, for an abstract "church" that didn't actually exist except as a mail machine generating the millions lining Ewing's pocket.

Not abstract, however, were the millions of fleeced sheep who believed in the Seed Faith prophet's perverted gospel of Jesus.

Ewing's mass-mailing enterprise early on reaped him a crop of seed-faith gigs writing and mailing letters for big evangelists like Robert Tilton, Rex Humbard, and Rev. Ike. Usually the letters were identical except for the signatures. Ole Anthony, head of the Christian watchdog organization Trinity Foundation, christened Ewing "God's Ghostwriter." One of Ewing's letters brought evangelist Rex Humbard $64 per mailing. In 1968, Ewing doubled Oral Robert's cash flow almost overnight. In gratitude, Roberts gave Ewing an airplane, according to Wayne Robinson, a former Roberts aide.

It could be argued that fundamentalism was saved from modernism by the grace of Ewing mass-mailings "signed" by con artists posing as disciples of Christ.

Mega-million dollar evangelist Oral Roberts, the granddaddy of contemporary direct-access TV evangelists, originated the concept "Seed Faith," aka "Giving and Receiving,"—emphasis on *receiving* by giving money to Roberts. Seed Faith claimed the biblical promise that God must return a believer's investment with interest, accrued as a set rate of multiplication, a doctrine Roberts disseminated through his TV programs, books, and Oral Roberts University. God wanted believers to be wealthy, healthy, and happy, Roberts preached, and He wanted them to receive those blessings as reward for generously giving—to Roberts.

As Oral's son Richard put it in a 2004 email newsletter,

> The story of Jesus feeding 5,000 tired, hungry people with two loaves of bread and two fish in John 6:1-14 is a much bigger scene than meets the eye. It's a story about you and me when we're hurting—when we're down to our last few dollars and the bills are piling up. This miracle tells us that when we come to the end of

234 • *Born-Again Deist*

ourselves, we're in position to cross over to the miraculous. If Jesus could stretch the little boy's seed-lunch into miracle proportions to feed a crowd of 5,000, He can multiply our seeds of faith into a miracle supply.

Of course, the kid's lunch wasn't brought as "seed-lunch"; it wasn't brought in faith, it was brought as his lunch. The boy had no clue what Jesus would do with the bread, nor was he motivated by or even aware of the possibility of a miracle "stretching" of the bread to feed the crowd. Jesus didn't perform the miracle because somebody had magical faith and said the abracadabra words to make it happen. Roberts's pitch mixed in sentimentality and trigger words to transmute the passage's "message" from faith in Jesus to faith in one's own faith.

What disturbed me most was that the evangelists themselves seemed to actually believe their own lies. The polar opposites, truth and false-hood, seemed to have risen "beyond good and evil"—a Nietzschean anti-religion concept I had never accepted. I began to reconsider the idea in a new light. Those evangelists weren't psychopathic liars, I thought. Something darker was at play when they could lie even to themselves.

As with the other charismatics, Oral Roberts spent his life perpetually performing the high drama of binding the devil with a binding that pre-sumable didn't work very well, given how often he had to repeat it. And none of Roberts's claims to healings over five decades was ever substanti-ated. Oh, there were plenty of people claiming to have been healed of this or that. But none of those people's ailments were ever medically validated. People with obvious problems—the blind, the lame in wheelchairs, the terminally ill, or folks with missing body parts—never experienced any kind of healing. Doctors couldn't save Roberts's own grandchild, who died two days after birth, even when Roberts was assisted in his faith healing with the prayers and laying on of hands by mega-healer Kenneth Hagin and his wife, other ministers, and Lindsay, the child's mother, who was wheeled to the baby's side.

Shouldn't a faith-healer prophet who lived by the creed of guaran-teed wealth, health, and happiness expect God to heal him? But in 1999 Roberts had an angioplasty procedure following a heart attack. In 2006, The Associated Press reported that Roberts had fallen and broken his hip and that surgery was expected.

Should a faith healer seek the help of modern medicine? Should a *faith* healer build a medical center? Roberts did. And frankly, from what I read in the papers, it was nothing but an outrageous money-making scam. Of course, that's just my opinion. Below are some facts I've based it on, arranged chronologically.

In 1977, Roberts received a vision in which God instructed him (the faith healer) to build the City of Faith Medical Center. A 900 foot Jesus, also present in the vision, added that the City of Faith would be a success.

In 1981, City of Faith opened, still under construction. The same year, the *Associated Press* published Roberts's $178,000 personal income for 1978. In addition he enjoyed generous expense accounts and use of his company-owned jet. And of course he controlled the ministry's millions.

In 1982, Oral Roberts University endowment funds were used to purchase one of Roberts's two California homes, a $2,400,000 house in Beverly Hills to be used as Roberts's West Coast residence and office.

In 1983, Jesus appeared to Roberts in person, not in a vision, to tell him to find a cure for cancer.

In 1986, God told Roberts, "I want you to use the Oral Roberts University medical school to put my medical presence in the earth. I want you to get this going in one year or I will call you home. It will cost $8 million and I want you to believe you can raise it." God said, Fork over $8 million or you're a dead man! Roberts issued a plea to his loyal fans. He got the money.

In 1987, God told Roberts that City of Faith had not sent out medical missionaries. God told him that he would take Roberts's home if he didn't raise $8 million by March to use as scholarships for medical missionaries. Roberts issued a plea to his loyal fans. In April 1987, Roberts announced that he had received $9.1 million.

In September 1988, *Christianity and Crisis* reported that Oral and Richard Roberts were sued by Ruth Creech of Cincinnati for $11.5 million. Roberts's promise of healing had led to $55,000 of unnecessary, crippling operations, which Roberts blamed on Creech's lack of faith.

In November 1988, Roberts announced that City of Faith was closing down. In January 1989, Roberts discontinued the medical scholarships. In March, the scholarship fund went bankrupt, and students were required to repay their scholarships at 18 percent interest. In September, City of Faith, never fully completed, officially closed. Not only Roberts, but God and the 900 foot Jesus had failed the ousted students and unemployed staff and faculty. Of course, being a man of Seed Faith, Roberts himself had made a killing.

In the months and years following, Roberts received numerous revelations from God explaining why his earlier revelation had failed. His trusting, naïve, logically challenged fans continued to send Roberts the donations that made him even richer.

Meanwhile, just as the Jim and Tammy Faye Bakker scandal hit the newsstands, Oral Roberts had a revelation from God telling him that Jim Bakker was innocent and Jimmy Swaggart and the *Charlotte Observer*, the paper that broke the story, were guilty of evildoing.

In a live broadcast in March 1987, Roberts proclaimed, in false prophet rhetoric typical of evangelists,

> And the Word of the Lord in my mouth is to you, my brother [Swaggart], whom we all love, you're sowing discord. And the Lord said, "Discord will come back to you." Free my brother, the Lord is saying to those people in the headquarters of that denomination [Assemblies of God], where Jim out of graciousness turned in his ordination papers because they wanted him to, and you've not accepted it. You've said, "No we're gonna strip him. We're gonna crush him . . ." The Word of the Lord is coming to you from Oral Roberts's mouth today, if you strip Jim Bakker, you've touched God's anointed, you've harmed God's prophet. And the Word of the Lord says, "Touch not my anointed, do no harm to my prophets . . ."
>
> I beg you, headquarters of a great denomination, one that we respect and love, desist, move back, and treat Jim Bakker as what he is, an anointed man, a prophet of God. And the hand of the Lord will not fall upon you. But the Lord will bless you.
>
> And to the great newspaper [*Charlotte Observer*]: You seem so immune to what our God can do. You've come into an unholy alliance with these others in the name of religion and morality. You've set yourself up to be a standard of morality, when you're not. The Word of the Lord comes unto you from my mouth. And the Lord says that He'll create a great dissension in your ranks. You'll have such dissension in your ranks. You'll have such dissension that it'll spread across the news media of America and you will not know what you're doing. There'll be much falling out and falling apart, anger among yourselves. And you'll wonder why this has happened.

Contrary to Roberts's prophesy, Swaggart and Bakker were both disgraced, and so was Roberts. And the media thrived to hang out even more dirty laundry.

Oral Roberts University was $40 million in debt when son Richard Roberts took over the presidency. So much for Seed Faith. But not to worry. Son Richard was also a prophet, just like his dad. Part of his stage act was to interrupt himself in front of millions, saying "Yes, Lord, I'll do that." Only he knew what God just said, because it was uttered only to him, directly via revelation, because only he was that special. Be sure, though, that it had something to do with instructing those millions to send him money.

TV evangelists in action started looking to me a lot like a Wizard of Oz hiding behind his tacky little curtain, pulling levers and pushing buttons to produce awe-inspiring special effects—flashing lights and smoke and a voice booming like God's, plus, of course, that all-important promise of a way back to Kansas. But nope, it was your simple love of home and family that woke you from your dream of magical enchantment and landed you where you always truly wanted to be: right there in your own skin in the real world.

The performances of TV evangelists remind me of a story that Joseph Campbell told Bill Moyers about

> the Australian tribe that used the bullroarer to keep people in awe of the gods. The bullroarer is a long flat board with notches, or slits, at one end, and a rope at the other. When you swing it around your head, the action produces a musical humming. The sound struck the primitive tribes as other-worldly, causing them to tremble in fear that the gods were angry. So the elders would go into the forest and come back with word of what it would take to placate the gods. And the people would oblige.
>
> Now when a young boy in the tribe was ready to become a man, a ritual took place. Wearing masks, the elders would kidnap him and take him into the woods, tie him down, and with a flint knife slice the underside of his penis. It was painful, but the medicine man said this is how you became a man.
>
> It meant shedding one's innocence. At the end of the ritual one of the masked men dipped the bullroarer in the boy's blood and thrust it in his face, simultaneously removing his mask so the boy could see it's not a god at all—it's just one of the old guys. And the medicine man would whisper, "We make the noises."

Ah, yes—it's not the gods after all. It's just the old guys—Uncle George, Uncle Dick, Uncle Don. The "noise" in the woods is the work of the old guys playing gods, wanting you to live in fear and trembling so that you will look to them to protect you against the wrath to come. It takes courage to put their truth-claims to the test of reality, to call their bluff.

These days I wonder what Richard Roberts's God is advising him to do, now that he's been forced to resign as president of Oral Roberts University, having been named in 2007 as defendant in a lawsuit alleging misuse—his personal use—of university funds and resources, which he had attempted to hide, even instructing his accountant to, in the accountant's words, "cook the books."

The Robertses aren't the only crooks. In 2007, Senator Chuck Grassley opened a probe into the finances of other TV evangelists preaching the "prosperity gospel," including Kenneth and Gloria Copeland, Creflo Dollar, Benny Hinn, Eddie L. Long, Joyce Meyer, and Paula White. But they're still on TV, raking in millions.

Why do so many fundamentalist Christians lack the courage to test the truth-claims of big name evangelists? Are they so ignorant, so immature? Or are they just greedy enough to hope against hope that God will make them rich, too?

Personally, I have nothing against wealth. I nod in agreement with Ben Franklin's advice to be healthy, wealthy, and wise. But what if wealth could only be acquired at another's expense? What if religion conspired with the rich against the poor? Certainly a "blessed are the poor" theology keeps the poor satisfied with their poverty and reduces the risk that they'll revolt against the rich.

From a moral standpoint, the problem is the unequal distribution of wealth. It's often been said that if the world's wealth were dispersed equally, every person on earth would be a millionaire. The problem isn't wealth, it's greed and its attendant exploitation and general absence of compassion. Honest labor that results in wealth is one thing, but most of us would agree that to lie, cheat, steal, fraud, coerce, or swindle to get rich is slimy if not downright evil.

What could be slimier than swindling to get rich in the name of God? And by rich we're talking *rich*! Several prominent newspapers and watchdog organizations have reported recently that the roughly 2,000 electronic preachers, including eighty nationally syndicated TV evange-lists, generate billions of dollars per year exploiting the superstitions of their gullible sheep, especially the poor and uneducated. The big evan-gelists are mega-millionaires with multiple million-dollar mansions and all the accouterments.

In 2003, Paul and Jan Crouch's Trinity Broadcasting Network (TBN)—the granddaddy of TV evangelism—claimed it took in more than $184.3 million from its viewer TV ministry, with $71.1 million unspent after expenses, on top of at least $311.6 million invested in securities. In 2002, TBN listed assets of $583 million, including $238 million in Treasury bonds and other government securities and $31 million in cash.

Besides Paul and Jan and the big evangelists who bought expensive air time, TBN depended on several guest "prophets" to help spread the too-good news of quick-fix prosperity and/or healing. Prominent guests included John Avanzini, Kim Clement, Kenneth Copeland, Creflo Dollar, Jesse Duplantis, John Hagee, Kenneth Hagin, Marilyn Hickey, Benny Hinn, T.D. Jakes, Joyce Meyer, Rod Parsley, Frederick K.C. Price, Oral Roberts, Richard Roberts, and R.W. Schambach.

For years Benny Hinn's scandalous rich-and-famous lifestyle compli-ments of the poor was criticized by watchdog groups. TV programs like CNN's "Impact" aired exposés of some of his con games. By 2000, Hinn's ministry brought in $60 million a year in donations. His parsonage was a $3 million, 7,200 square-foot oceanfront house in Dana Point, California, his office a 58,000 square-feet office building that he built and owned. Hinn traveled first class to his "healing" performances. Even several years earlier, members of Trinity Foundation pulled from a dumpster an itin-erary for Hinn's trip from New York to London that included tickets at $8,850 each and hotel suites at $2,200 a night. Hinn's toys include very expensive cars, clothes, jewelry, bodyguards—you get the picture.

In 1989, as part of his pitch Hinn prophesied that in the 1990s, Fidel Castro would die and God would destroy the homosexual community. On the October 19, 1999, TBN program *Praise the Lord*, Hinn prophesied,

> If some dead person be put in front of this TV screen, they will be raised from the dead and they will be by the thousands. I see rows of caskets lining up in front of this TV set and I see them bring-ing them closer to the TV set and as people are coming closer I see loved ones picking up the hands of the dead and letting them

touch the screen and people are getting raised as their hands are touching that screen.

Trinity Foundation provided property records and videos that prompted CNN and the *Dallas Morning News* to question Hinn's "fundraising" for a $30 million "World Healing Center" in Dallas that was never built even though Hinn had raised over $30 million for the project. Hinn also solicited donations to build an orphanage in Mexico City. It, too, was never built. *NBC News* reported on December 27, 2002, that an empty house on the property, owned by the ministry, had a sign, "temporary orphanage," attached, and the local official in charge of construction in the town said the ministry had never been issued a building permit.

Money, money, money, the love of which is the root of all . . .

Evangelist Mike Murdock described himself as just another "Wal-Mart guy." But IRS records from 1993 to 2000 showed his ministry's average yearly earnings at $21,040,299.

Last time I checked, Joel Osteen's Lakewood Church brought in over $50 million in contributions per year.

Creflo Dollar's ministry paid $18 million in cash for his World Changers Church International outside of Atlanta.

Evangelist Juanita Bynum indulged her traditional family values by spending over a million dollars on her wedding, which included an eighty member wedding party, twelve-piece orchestra, flowers flown in from around the world, Swarovski crystals hand-sewn on the gown, headpiece of hand-designed sterling silver, and 7.76 carat diamond ring.

Robert Schuller's "Tower of Power" TV ministry brought in over $50 million a year.

T.D. Jakes of Dallas drove a new Mercedes, wore expensive tailored suits, sported flashy jewelry, and resided in a luxury $2.6 million, seven-bedroom home located next door to oil tycoon H.L Hunt. "I do think we need some Christians who are in first class as well as coach." The locals at his hometown of Charleston, West Virginia, didn't approve of his second million dollar residence, located in town, the "single" residence being two homes side by side that included an indoor swimming pool and a bowling alley. A local columnist called Jakes "a huckster."

Evangelists Paula and Randy White's purchase of a $2.1 million home was no problem. As of 2003, their church was bringing in $10 million yearly.

Joyce Meyer built her 158,000 square-feet ministry headquarters for $20 million, not including the $5.7 million worth of items such as art objects and furniture, and not counting her fleet of vehicles worth approximately $440,000 and a Canadair CL-600 Challenger jet worth $10 million, not including two full-time pilots. Etc.

Evangelicals were coming up with creative new gags and gimics to make big bucks compliments of Jesus. Take Rodney Howard-Browne, whose Tampa area church brought in over $16 million the last time I checked. Witnesses reported that at a camp meeting at the University of South Florida in Tampa, Howard-Browne taught pastors that "sheep needed to be fleeced or they would have too much hair and could not see where they were going. It was the pastor's job to fleece the sheep." Howard-Browne was known among media critics as "a world-class hypnotist. A manipulator leading followers into a cult. A circus ringleader making a good living." He characterized himself as "the Holy Ghost bartender" who served the new wine of Christ until service attendees got "drunk with joy," often breaking out in uncontrollable "holy laughter," shaking like Shakers, dancing and prancing in the aisles, falling to the ground, "slain in the Spirit."

In his book, *Counterfeit Revival*, Hank Hanegraaffe called evangelists like Howard-Browne "false prophets." As president of the nonprofit countercult ministry, Christian Research Institute, and host of *Bible Answer Man*, which airs on 100 Christian radio stations, Hanegraaffe warned that Howard-Browne was "nothing but a good stage hypnotist . . . What he is doing is not harmless. [He] is using sociopsychological manipulation tactics to make people think they've encountered God . . . So many people who come through the front door of these 'revivals' end up falling out the back door into the kingdom of the cult. He's not leading us into a great awakening . . . but a great apostasy."

(Hanegraaffe represents a new money-making angle among evangelists: They sell books that attack each other. But can we trust them? After all, Hanegraaffe, like other evangelists, markets books he claims he wrote that were actually written by ghostwriters. To deny that is called lying, and that's what these evangelists do. Reporters and activists have located ghostwriters of books written by such blockbuster "liars" as Hal Lindsay, Chuck Colson, Jim Bakker, Billy Graham, Oral Roberts, Pat

Robertson, David Wilkerson, Norman Vincent Peale, John Ankerberg, David Jeremiah, and Jerry Falwell.

Sometimes if the money's good, evangelists bash not each other but themselves. But even that can be a lie. In the 90s, for instance, Mike Warnke was just another popular evangelist and comedian with run-of-the-mill multiple marriages, affairs, and divorces. Then critics of his blockbuster *Satan Seller* proved the impossibility of the details of his former career as a satanic priest and drug dealer.)

Not all fundamentalists are deceitful. Thus far trustworthy is Trinity Foundation's Ole Anthony, who said that Howard-Browne's revivals produced "a phony euphoria. He's telling people what they want to hear . . . What happens to these converted people when the crusade packs up and leaves town? They get depressed. They get confused. So all they can do is wait for the next one so they can go back and get another fix."

Joe Davis, general manager of two New York Christian radio stations with a half-million listeners, called a Howard-Browne meeting he attended in Long Island one of the "most bizarre" events he had ever witnessed; he was shocked, he said, by how many people were out of control. But those kinds of charismatic revivals would not succeed at large venues like Madison Square Gardens. In Davis's view, "We're too religiously jaded here in New York to put up with sideshows like that."

And so they should be. It's our responsibility to be clearheaded, responsible, and wary. I'm reminded of an excerpt from Dr. Robert Hare's book *Without Conscience*:

> Psychopaths are often witty and articulate. They can be amusing and entertaining conversationalists, ready with a quick and clever comeback, and can tell unlikely but convincing stories that cast themselves in a good light. They can be very effective in presenting themselves well and are often very likable and charming. To some people, however, they seem too slick and smooth, too obviously insincere and superficial. Astute observers often get the impression that psychopaths are play-acting, mechanically "reading their lines."

Gag lines, Bible verses, prophesies, anecdotes of personal encounters with God, any pitch that reaps money.

When they're not passing the hat, evangelists often become embroiled in outside projects, like Howard-Browne's involvement with Carpenter's

Home Church pastored by his close friend, Dan Strader, who in 1995 was sentenced to forty-five years in prison for 238 felony counts for fleecing $2.5 million from the elderly.

Howard-Browne's resume said that he earned his bachelors, masters, and doctorate degrees from the School of Bible Theology in San Jacinto, California. When the *Tampa Tribune* could find no accreditation, Howard-Browne admitted that it was a correspondence school. The school was a diploma mill, like other diploma mills created to confer bogus degrees on high-roller evangelists. Howard-Browne also received a Doctor of Divinity and Doctor of Theology from another diploma mill, Life Christian University of Tampa. That school advertised that it gave "advanced standing" for published works, presumably including the books by famous evangelists written by ghostwriters. It boasted that "our illustrious alumni include such internationally-prominent ministers as . . ." Besides Howard-Browne, the list included, Joyce Meyer, Kenneth Copeland, Norvel Hayes, Mike Francen, Dick Mills, Benny Hinn, and Kevin McNulty—the usual rich, sanctimonious anti-scholars anointed with the snake oil of moral deception.

TV evangelism thrives because gullible people believe these prophets' claims of divine inspiration and accomplished healing. Are fleeced sheep that expect million dollar miracles but get nothing but ripped off getting what they deserve?

If they could actually have healed, a big contribution might have been worth it. But the truth is that there has never been a documented actual healing in the entire history of faith healing. Faith healing is a con game of mind manipulation. Occasionally a person claims to have been healed. I've seen in person some of those supposedly "healed." Some of them were no doubt hypochondriacs; some were probably narcissists wanting to be on TV; some (I'm guessing most) had no doubt been paid off on the side; and some likely exaggerated or misdiagnosed ailments that would have cleared up on their own anyway. Faith healers are notorious for "healing" only internal conditions that no one can see. The healed are notorious for not producing evidence that they have ever been sick. Gullible sheep believe the faith healer's claim of healing, even though the miracle is something that can't be seen or verified. Sometimes the faith-healer pretends to have the sick person's ailment "revealed" by God. It's hot air. As far back as 1987, evangelist

Peter Popoff's prophetic gifts were debunked when it was proven that he received the divine information about audience members via an in-ear receiver. Benny Hinn, Pat Robertson, Jimmy Swaggart, Richard Roberts and other faith-healing false prophets continue to be outed year after year after year. But people continue to tune in and believe.

Many viewers are not motivated by a need for healing. "All you little people" and "all the little grandmas," as TBN's Jan Crouch has condescendingly called them, often just want answers to little prayers. Many of those little prayers are requests for a little necessary financial help.

"The people on TBN are living the lifestyle of fabulous wealth on the backs of the poorest and most desperate people in our society," according to Ole Anthony. "People have lost their faith in God because they believe they weren't worthy after not receiving their financial blessing."

"It is difficult to fathom how anyone familiar with the abundance of biblical teaching about the 'deceitfulness of riches' could have devised the prosperity gospel," commented William Martin, a Rice University sociology professor and author of a biography of the enormously prosperous Billy Graham.

The prosperity con artists manipulate their victims into colluding with their selfishness. The gullible not only turn over their hard-earned cash to the con artists, they actually believe that in doing so they can righteously con God. Rub that Bible hard enough and the Big Magic Genii will pop out to grant your every wish. He *has* to.

But of course you can't just rub that Bible; you also have to send TBN (or sibling evangelist) money to tap into the "powerhouse of heaven" and receive God's gifts. And then you must spread the news. Get your friends to tune in, send money, allow TBN to expand its outreach to the trusting and the gullible.

Needless to say, the prosperity doctrine has its critics within the Christian community. Many condemn not only the false prophesies and false healings, but also TBN business practices and TBN Seed Faith family's luxurious lifestyles. As owner of TBN, Paul Crouch has occasionally felt obligated to respond to critics, as he did, for instance, on his *Praise the Lord* TV show in November 1997:

> God, we proclaim death to anything or anyone that will lift a hand against this network and this ministry that belongs to You, God. It is Your work, it is Your idea, it is Your property, it is Your

airwaves, it is Your world, and we proclaim death to anything that would stand in the way of God's great voice of proclamation to the whole world. In the Name of Jesus, and all the people said Amen!

For years Crouch literally shook his finger at the camera, angered by those who criticized his self-righteous comments. He blew off his critics with comments like these, from a Praise-a-Thon, April 2, 1991: "I think they're damned and on their way to hell; and I don't think there's any redemption for them." And, "To hell with you! Get out of my life! Get out of the way! I say get out of God's way! Quit blocking God's bridges or God's going to shoot you if I don't. I don't even want to even talk to you or hear you! I don't want to see your ugly face!"

Some viewers of Word of Faith TV shows need a bit more than appeals to greed to get fired up enough to send seed money. Intimidating prophesies often do the trick.

As Paul Crouch once put it, "God spoke to me clearly and said, 'Did I give my son Jesus on the cross expecting nothing in return?' God bankrupted heaven and gave the best gift he could give. You can bring God a gift fully expecting something in return. Get to the phone!" Rod Parsley agreed. "God gave his best at Calvary. He told me, 'Don't you dare come before me if you don't give your best.'"

Both Crouch and Parsley implied that they were prophets with direct access to God and that not getting to the pledge phone was a demonstration of profound ingratitude for all that Jesus and God had done for you. Evidently there were quite a few Christians ignorant enough to believe that heaven was ever bankrupt.

"Have you got something that you have been praying about ten, fifteen, twenty years?" Crouch asked. "You have been praying for it and haven't gotten it? It could be that you haven't gotten it because you're a tightwad and you haven't given your ten percent." Yes, fork over ten percent of your yearly wages to Paul Crouch and you'll get that special something God hasn't yet given you. It's in the Bible.

"You're on the brink of a miracle," cried Parsley. "Go to the phone and give $1,000, $10,000, and $1 million. Go to the phone . . . God has a miracle waiting on your response." And, "To reap a perpetual harvest, you need to sow a perpetual seed." Meaning, don't just give once, give continuously. He added a jingle, "I got a need for seed."

"Get up! Get up! Get up! Go to the phone . . . The spirit of God promised me that he would bless your seed! Go to the phone right now! If you're sowing $1,000, do it now! If you're sowing $100, do it now!" ordered Clarence McClendon, who slyly connected money with the biblical "blessed seed"—literally offspring—of Abraham's faith. Abraham offered up his son Isaac as a sacrifice; all you have to do is send in a few measly bucks.

All the TBN Word of Faith evangelists anointed themselves as special prophets able to impart miracles, blessings, and healings. Marilyn Hickey's special anointing allowed her ministry to "release the power of the prayer agreement" by "bringing our faith into agreement with yours" when viewers sent in prayer sheets. Of course, if they sent in the request, they'd likely feel obligated to include a donation.

Hickey claimed to have special powers to break the spell of generational curses like cancer, poverty, child abuse, alcoholism, bad temper, and depression. The magic abracadabra was spelled out in her book, *Breaking Generational Curses*. "I will sow this book into your life . . . as you sow a gift of $20 or more into the ministry. It's our way of saying 'Thank you' for your support at this crucial time . . . and a way for me to build your faith for miracle results. *I really want you to receive a copy of this book*!" I.e., she wants your money. All the seed swapping was beginning to sound like spiritual adultery.

And then there was the special Miracle Point of Contact Prayer Cloth, the special Blue Christmas Candle Letter, the specially prepared and blended anointing oil, "Outpouring, Special Edition 2001" (and subsequent repeats), available in a gold-colored metal locket, and all the other magical talismans Hickey would like you to have.

Marilyn Hickey was perhaps unique in promising an especially lucrative payback, called a Miracle Overflow Next Generation Anointing, for her paid-up Faith Covenant Partner members and viewers who sent Your Best Seed, the largest offering possible, to be given exclusively to her ministry. A Proxy Seed Faith Offering was also available for those wanting to bribe God on behalf of others.

Hers was the kind of bargain indulgence (*feste dies*) offered as a "jubilee" special by Pope Sixtus IV via Johann Tetzel in 1476. Like Hickey's proxy seed faith offerings, the medieval proxy indulgences could spring from hell even sadistic serial killers who raped nuns. They could even buy forgiveness for future sins. Luther challenged those preposterous propositions by offering theses of concern and correction that got him in heretical hot water and prompted the already brewing Reformation.

We just don't learn. Greed fuels wishful thinking fuels faith in superstition. Our most potent hopes and fears and their miraculous antidotes are all listed in big bold letters on every label slapped on a vial of snake oil.

Chapter 16

The Emperor's No Clothes

Near the U.S. Capitol in Washington, D.C., at 133 C Street SE, sits a building known as C Street Center. Registered in tax records as a religious and commercial building, it houses prominent fundamentalist lawmakers, some of whom counsel each other through their extramarital affairs.

For instance, in July 2009, the media reported that C Street resident Chip Pickering, former conservative Christian congressman from Mississippi, who was known as a defender of decency and who had urged President Bush to declare 2008 The National Year of the Bible, had had an affair that, according to his wife's lawsuit claims, ruined their marriage and derailed his political career.

A month earlier, the front page headlined C Street resident Senator John Ensign of Nevada, a conservative Promise Keeper and member of the Pentecostal International Church of the Foursquare Gospel who had called on President Clinton to resign, had been having an affair with Cynthia Hampton, wife of his best friend and co-chief of staff, Doug Hampton. Ensign resigned as chairman of the Republican Senate Policy Committee in the wake of revelations that his parents had given his mistress and her husband and child $96,000.

Also in June, C Street's pro-life, anti-gay Mark Sanford, South Carolina's conservative governor and former congressman, confessed that he was having an affair with a woman in Argentina. A moment later, the vocal advocate against excess government spending was busted for squandering hundreds of thousands of state taxpayer dollars on private jet trips to Argentina, and other improprieties were being investigated.

The C Street Center, also known as The Family and The Fellowship, a secretive international organization that believes that the elite win power by the will of God, is guided by a mission intent on convincing politicians across the globe that they were chosen by God to help fulfill his divine plan.

Was it part of God's divine plan when Paul Stanley, a forty-seven-year-old married family-values, pro-life, anti-gay Tennessee state senator who loudly opposed sex outside marriage, found himself the victim of extortion by the boyfriend of his mistress, twenty-two-year-old legislative assistant McKensie Morrison, who had been charged with cocaine possession and whose husband was in a Florida prison? Perhaps God should have warned Stanley not to make that disk copy of nude photos, including some of his mistress taken at his apartment.

What you do in the privacy of your own home is one thing. But what must God think of Louisiana senator David Vittner's "serious sin," as he called it, after his phone number appeared on the infamous D.C. Madam's list.

Maybe God was busy thinking about other offenders, like Coy Privette, the Baptist preacher and conservative activist and politician prominent in North Carolina moral battles, who was president of the Christian Action League and sat on the board of directors of the Baptist State Convention, and who in 2007 was charged with six counts of aiding and abetting prostitution.

(And of course in 2008, New York Governor Eliot Spitzer resigned admitting "private failings" that included his involvement in a high-priced prostitution ring.)

No doubt far more prurient peccadilloes lurk undetected in the shadows of whorehouses and noble houses in respectable neighborhoods. Ultra-right Strom Thurmond, for instance, a perennial senator from South Carolina and staunch segregationist, asserted that "All the bayonets of the Army cannot force the Negro into our homes, into our schools, our churches and our places of recreation and amusement." But in his own home, for his own recreation and amusement, he fathered a child by his sixteen-year-old family Negro maid, paid for his mixed-race daughter's university education, and gave her money before she married and after she was widowed. Only after the elderly Thurmond died did seventy-eight-year-old Essie Mae Washington-Williams reveal her father's dark secret. Despite his seeming generosity toward his own DNA, Thurmond's exploitation of a black girl remained classic bigotry. Democratic Christians have also slipped into sins of the flesh. Right after candidate John Edwards told America about his Baptist leanings during a presidential debate, and right after he had won America's heart by pledging his undying love and support for his wife, who was fighting terminal cancer, Americans learned about Edwards's long-term affair with a staff member.

Although it's certainly accurate to cry "hypocrisy," it's only fair to acknowledge the extensive precedent for mixing a little illicit sex in with one's fundamentalism.

Decades ago the believing public was scandalized by the extramarital affair and faked death of angelic evangelist Aimee Sample McPherson. Although for the most part sexual improprieties have been successfully hushed up, more than a few evangelists recently have blessed the public with the titillating details of this or that scandal.

In 2007, the Chapel Hill Harvester Church in Georgia discovered that over the many years, their pastor, Bishop Earl Paulk, had had sexual relations with numerous members of the congregation, including his sister-in-law, who had borne him a son.

In 2008, Joe Barron, minister at Prestonwood Baptist Church—at 26,000 members, one of the largest churches in the U.S.—was arrested for meeting for sex with a minor he had met online.

In 2008, the Christian community gasped when they learned that Todd Bentley, a leader of the Lakeland revival in Florida, had had an affair with a member of his staff.

Also in 2008, Tony Alamo's Christian Ministries headquarters in Arkansas was raided by the FBI as part of a child pornography investigation that included allegations of physical abuse, sexual abuse, polygamy, and underage marriage.

Antigay rhetoric is starting to sound like a mere smokescreen thrown up by prominent conservatives like Idaho's Republican senator Larry Craig, who pled guilty to misdemeanor disorderly conduct for soliciting gay sex in a Minneapolis airport restroom.

We might expect hypocrisy of politicians, but the list of antigay gay ministers might explain why good Christian politicians feel justified in their behavior.

For decades a closeted gay Pentecostal evangelist and a major figure in the Jesus Movement, Lonnie Frisbee died of AIDS in 1993.

When he was photographed in a gay bar in 2000, ex-gay John Paulk, leader of Focus on the Family's ex-gay Love Won Out and chairman of the board for ex-gay Exodus International, claimed he wasn't there. Then he admitted that he often lied about gay matters.

Among the many others busted for the sin of homosexuality in 2006 were Paul Barnes, senior member of the evangelical church, Grace Chapel, and senior pastor of South Tulsa Baptist Church and member of the Southern Baptist Convention, Lonnie Latham, who was arrested for propositioning a male undercover officer.

Some offenders are more diverse. Big-name radio evangelist and author Billy James Hargis founded American Christian College to promote fundamentalist principles but found himself in hot legal water for sexual misconduct with both male and female students, as well as kids in the youth choir, All American Kids.

In the Clinton era, famous family values politicians busted for sexual improprieties could deflect attention by pointing the finger at another politician—Clinton, for instance.

Before running for the nation's highest office, Gary Bauer headed the Family Research Council, one of many multimillion dollar family values organizations created to exploit the "gay agenda" for profit by supporting, among other things, deceptive ex-gay ministries.

A hard-right homophobic, misogynist moralist with a track record dating back to the Reagan White House, presidential hopeful Bauer reminded America, "Adultery is a big deal. Harry Truman knew this, 'How can I trust a man if his wife cannot?' the plainspoken man from Independence said."

Nine members of Bauer's own presidential campaign staff quit because of his big deal adultery. Bauer's campaign manager, Charles Jarvis, and former chief of advance operations, Tim McDonald, publicly protested Bauer's "inappropriate" behavior, emphasizing that they had repeatedly warned Bauer about "the appearance of impropriety" he was creating by traveling alone and spending "hours and hours and hours behind closed doors with a young single woman," twenty-six-year-old deputy campaign manager Melissa McClard. Bauer's secretary of fifteen years, Betty Barrett, and his media consultant, Tom Edwards, also quit. Other inside sources told the media that Bauer traveled with McClard on a daily basis in a "husband-wife relationship." Bauer called a press conference to lie about the "devastating" rumors. He argued that he met privately with every member of his campaign staff. He denied being warned by staff.

Another presidential hopeful, House Speaker Newt Gingrich, the original family values poster boy, "would have won in 1974 if we could have kept him out of the office, screwing her [a young volunteer] on the desk," according to Dot Crews, Gingrich's campaign scheduler throughout the 70s. "It was common knowledge that Newt was involved with other women during his marriage to Jackie . . . he had girlfriends, some serious, some trivial."

One of those girlfriends, Anne Manning, confirmed that he was involved with her during the 1976 campaign. "We had oral sex. He prefers that modus operandi because then he can say, 'I never slept with her.'" Well, at least he's honest. Gingrich's former campaign treasurer, Kip Carter, recounted walking Gingrich's daughters back from a football game and seeing a car with "Newt in the passenger seat and one of the guys' wives with her head in his lap going up and down. Newt kind of turned and gave me this little-boy smile. Fortunately, Jackie Sue and Kathy were a lot younger and shorter then." Even Christian boys will be boys.

"She isn't young enough or pretty enough to be the president's wife," Gingrich said of his first wife, Jackie. "He walked out in the spring of 1980," Jackie recounts. "By September, I went into the hospital for my third surgery [for cancer]. The two girls came to see me, and said, 'Daddy is downstairs. Could he come up?' When he got there, he wanted to discuss the terms of the divorce while I was recovering from my surgery." Left nearly destitute, Jackie ended up taking Gingrich to court to get him to contribute to basic utility bills. Even one of his ex-lovers was appalled by Gingrich's insensitivity. "He's morally dishonest. He has gone too far believing that 'I'm beyond the law.' He should be stopped before it's too late."

By 1995 the press was reporting on Gingrich's latest relationship with Callista Bisek, a "willowy blonde congressional aide twenty-three years his junior," who was spending the night and had her own key to his apartment even as Gingrich was lynching President Clinton for his adultery with Monica Lewinsky. At least Gingrich was still a good Christian. MSNBC reported that Bisek sang in the National Shrine Choir of the

254 • Born-Again Deist

Shrine of the Immaculate Conception, and Gingrich would wait for her at the Shrine, listening to her sing while he read the Bible.

Finally, in August 1999, Gingrich filed for divorce from his second wife, Marianne, perhaps as part of his climb toward the presidency.

Besides womanizing, Gingrich was embroiled in illegal lobbying, creation of non-profits and PACs to fund his own partisan projects, and bouncing a mind-boggling twenty-two rubber checks written on government money. His various scandals led to hundreds of thousands of dollars in fines, criticism from his Republican allies, resignation of the administrator of his congressional offices, IRS investigations, and his eventual resignation as Speaker of the House. He got off easy only because as speaker, he appointed the ethics committee that should have prompted further action against him.

Another big name family values ultra-right Christian Republican, Robert Dornan, was found guilty of a "violent attack" on his wife in 1966. Though he was ordered to go to jail, there is no record of his having served time. His wife Sallie left him a few times and tried to divorce him because he had been beating her for years. In a 1961 divorce suit, she stated that he dragged her "about the house . . . by the hair and . . . exhibited a revolver." Sally recanted when Dornan's opponent in the 1992 election exposed the charges. But should we believe her? After all, Dornan even punched Democrat congressman Tom Downey on the floor of the House of Representatives. Should we believe Dornan, who bounced a rubber check during the House banking scandal and told his heavily Catholic district it was to pay for a grotto of the Virgin Mary in his back yard?

And then there's ultraconservative Oregon state legislator Drew Davis, who led police on a fifteen-mile car chase, and with good reason. In his possession were pornographic magazines, a MAC 11 assault pistol, telephone bugging equipment, a police scanner, and the narcotic Vicodin. A few years later Davis made headlines when the Moonies filed a lien on his mansion and business because he had failed to repay a loan.

And then there's ultraconservative Christian county commissioner Gordon Shadburne of Portland, who sent local fundamentalist churches a letter on county stationery proclaiming that homosexuality was "the stronghold of Satan." This struck the press as odd, because one of Shadburnes top aides, a former county commissioner, was openly gay and wrote the gay rights law that Shadburne opposed. Shadburne fired him, bribing him with four week's severance pay if he wouldn't talk, which prompted another aide to quit. Then Shadburne's ex-wife testified during mediation proceedings that Shadburne himself was homosexual. The County Auditor reported that Shadburne's "friend" and former roommate was being paid $29,000 for nine months of questionable, poorly documented work from home as an independent contractor, which made him one of the highest paid public officials in the county. To top it off, Shadburne was convicted twice for using county money for personal business and was accused of cocaine use and orgies during a business trip billed to the county.

The Shadburne case raises an interesting question: How many family values right-wingers are actually gay? How many gays are outspokenly homophobic fundamentalists as a cover-up? Certainly pretending to be straight can be a kind of "drag" and a form of fleecing donors. Which extremist homophobes are lying and which are repressed?

When Republican senatorial candidate Jane Griffin was invited by Equality Tennessee to attend (not to "address," as she mistakenly assumed) the fifth congressional district candidate forum in 2002, along with all other candidates running statewide, Griffin responded in writing, "It is with deep regret . . . I cannot address your conclave of leeches. It would have been a delight to condemn roundly the most worthless and no-count populace of women in Tennessee. You are too lazy to get yourself out of your filthy practices and who would want to marry a pervert? Certainly no decent man in Tennessee. Womanhood has fallen to a low degree indeed but you are the worst. It is my suspicion that you have a tax-exempt foundation so your perverted donors and fake benefactors can get their April 15 kickback. By the Grace of the God of our Fathers, I will redeem the name of America and Tennessee Volunteer."

One can't help but wonder if Griffin's over-the-top response isn't the knee-jerk overreaction of a repressed lesbian. Could she be hiding something?

Certainly these days, when busted by the media for sexual improprieties, family values violators exploit the gay issue as a red herring. "Who me? Look over there at those *queers*! At least I'm not as bad as those *perverts!*"

In 2006, National Association of Evangelicals president Rev. Ted Haggard, whose clout extended to Congress and the White House, resigned amid accusations from male Denver prostitute Mike Jones that he and Haggard, who called himself Art, had had drug-enhanced sexual encounters nearly every month for three years. Haggard admitted buying meth from the prostitute but said he never used it, and claimed he never had sex with Jones, only a massage after being referred to him by a Denver hotel.

Jones pointed out, "No concierge in Denver would have referred me," because he openly advertised his escort services only in gay publications and on gay websites. He had no idea who "Art" really was until he saw Ted Haggard on TV publicly condemning gay sex and supporting the ballot measure that would amend the state constitution to ban gay marriage.

Eventually Haggard admitted to another gay relationship, with Brant Hass, a male member of his church.

Not long ago, Art—I mean Ted—Haggard proclaimed himself cured and claimed that his ordeal had strengthened his marriage and relationships with his children and his church.

Often conservatives blame others for their sins. Take Republican Florida congressman Mark Foley, who resigned in 2006 after revelations that he had propositioned male pages—alas, minors—sometimes emailing them from the House floor. His excuse? He'd been molested by a priest. Foley did admit being gay, but he just couldn't do it without pointing the finger of blame, continuing the ancient conservative tradition. Though he'd never married, Foley was an avid family values supporter and opponent of same-sex marriage. That's how it works. The party people and lobbyists who give you money to run your campaigns, who offer you political support, who line up as your allies and who tell you what to do, the whole rightwing machine requires that you prove your allegiance to its antigay agenda.

Another fallen angel, Paul Crouch, owner of Trinity Broadcasting Network (TBN)—the world's largest televangelist organization, which pulls in a couple hundred million dollars a year in donations from fundamentalist viewers—was outed back in 1996 by gay TBN employee Lonnie Ford, a convicted felon with whom Paul had sexual relations. In a 1998 settlement, Ford was paid $425,000 to keep quiet. But when TBN breached its end of their confidentiality agreement, Ford offered to sell his memoir about Crouch's forceful seduction and tryst with him.

Although originally hired to work TBN's phone bank, Ford had been reassigned by Crouch to do special projects with him, even though Ford had no knowledge or experience. Having wined and dined his employee for a few days at the expensive Regent Beverly Wilshire Hotel in Beverly Hills, Crouch then had Ford drive them to the TBN-owned cabin at Lake Arrowhead to have sex there.

It wasn't consensual. Ford, an openly gay man and thirty years Crouch's junior, felt compelled because he feared that Crouch would throw him "straight out of that cabin" and fire him. He was sickened by being coerced into sex by his boss, "But at the same time, I still looked up to him. He's a very powerful man, [head] of the largest Christian network in the world. I just put my blinders on." The next morning, Crouch read Ford a Bible passage, Proverbs 6:16-19, and explained that because homosexuality wasn't one of the seven "detestable" behaviors listed, what they had done wasn't a problem for God. But because there were people who "wouldn't understand," Ford should keep quiet. Crouch promised that his ministry would pay Ford's debt of about $17,000 and offered him a rent-free apartment.

Ford offered to sell his memoir of those events to Crouch for $10 million. Crouch's counteroffer was reportedly $1 million.

Even more disconcerting than hypocritical homophobes are overkill homophobes like the Rev. Fred Phelps, whose church exists solely to bash gays. His church websites, God Hates Fags (.com) and God Hates America (.com), proudly proclaim perhaps the most famous homophobic claim of all time: "God does not hate them because they are homosexuals; they are homosexuals because God hates them." (On second thought, he's rehashing St. Paul.)

The in-your-face hate antics of master picketer Phelps includes pickets even of events having only the remotest connection to gays, like the funeral of Bill Clinton's mother and funerals of soldiers, gay or straight, killed in active duty—according to Phelps, the entire army is "fag-infested." Phelps and his relatives—he has thirteen children and fifty-two grandchildren at the time of this writing—shove nasty-gram placards in people's faces and shout through megaphones slogans like "God hates fags," "fags are nature freaks," "AIDS cures fags," "thank God for AIDS," "fags burn in hell," "fags doom nations," "no special laws for fags," and "God is not mocked." God-mocking is reserved for holier-than-thou

Phelps, who *ridicules* God by *mimicking* a barbarian god obsessed with divine retribution.

In the judgment of Rev. Phelps, who dismisses science along with biblical scholarship and common sense, the Asian tsunami was caused not by natural phenomena such as an earthquake but by homosexuality. My question for Phelps is whether homosexuals or God committed all that mass murder.

> Filthy fags and pedophiles have been going to Asia for many, many years to have sex with little children—and suddenly you're worried about children? Shame on you. It is God's prerogative to kill children to punish their evil, Godless, vile, filthy parents and others who were raising them for the devil anyway; they are most certainly better off now than they were in the hands of such evil people. He always has done that, and He always will. Deal with it.
>
> Thank God for the tsunamis—& we hope for 20,000 dead Swedes!!! Let us pray that God will send a massive Tsunami to totally devastate the North American continent with 1000-foot walls of water doing 500 mph—even as islands in southern Asia have recently been laid waste, with but a small remnant surviving. God Hates Fag America! Thank God for Tsunami. Thank God for 3,000 dead Americans.

Politically biblical, Rev. Phelps blames 9/11 not on terrorists but on homosexuals. On his website, he explains his contempt for the New York City "fag fire department."

Phelps's God Hates America website "proves" biblically that the Gulf and Iraq wars were the direct result of homosexuality. "When you fill the army with fags and dykes and spit in the face of God, you have sown the wind, and shall reap the whirlwind," he proclaims like a reincarnate Isaiah. "Pray for more American bodies blown to smithereens by cheap home made Iraqi IEDs—like the IED America bombed WBC [Phelps's Westboro Baptist Church] with August 20, 1995, hoping thereby to terrorize us into silence about America's fag sins."

Sexual impropriety among prominent fundamentalists isn't adultery or homosexuality.

In 1999, Ned Graham, youngest of Billy Graham's five children, admitted to *Christianity Today* his problem with alcohol abuse and "inappropriate" relationships with female staff members. Graham's wife of nineteen years, Carol Graham, had divorced Ned a few months earlier, and not just for alcoholism and adultery. Ned's sins ranged from wife abuse—a judge had issued a restraining order against him—to pornography and drug use. Graham's Southern Baptist church, Grace Community Church of Auburn, Washington, revoked Graham's ministerial credentials. Most of the staff and board members of Ned Graham's East Gates Ministries International resigned amid his ongoing indiscretions.

TV evangelism has always thrived as a circus of sensationalized sins, with lion-tamers leaping through fiery hoops for money.

In March 1987, the *Charlotte Observer* busted the infamous North Carolina TV evangelists, Jim and Tammy Faye Bakker, owners of PTL (Praise The Lord) network, for what back then was considered sexual scandal. For years the *Charlotte Observer* had noted the hypocrisy of the fundamentalist couple's aggressive solicitation of money even from people who couldn't afford it so they themselves could live in unchristian luxury in their oceanfront condo (with its infamous $22,000 floor-to-ceiling mirrors in the bedroom). Besides begging on camera, the Bakkers had fattened their bank accounts with cash taken in from their tacky Christian theme park, Heritage USA, and the illegal pyramid business scheme that landed Jim in prison.

In March 1987, the *Observer* ran its story that in 1980, Jim Bakker had drugged and seduced Jessica Hahn, a church secretary and former *Playboy* playmate from Long Island, and had paid her $250,000 to keep quiet. In the meantime (as you'll recall from a previous chapter), Tammy Faye, famous for her massive makeup, big hair, and tacky, attention-getting attire, had become so obsessively in lust with country singer Gary Paxton that she had broken up his marriage. Both Bakkers admitted their guilt, but Jim nonetheless attacked Jimmy Swaggart, who had publicized the scandal, in Bakker's view so he could take over PTL.

The contrite Bakkers resigned from PTL, leaving it temporarily in the hands of Jerry Falwell, whose Moral Majority and Old Fashioned Gospel Hour were making him even more famous than Swaggart.

Shortly after, Bakker attacked Falwell, accusing him of trying to gain control of PTL. Taking this advantage to appear righteous, Falwell called a press conference to share with the public sworn affidavits by men who had had homosexual relationships with Bakker. Falwell also included Tammy Faye's list of demands she would exchange for disappearing quietly: $300,000 a year for Jim; $100,000 for herself; royalties on all PTL records and books; their mansion, cars, security staff, legal fees, and accountant fees, which would be hefty given the Bakkers' financial irregularities. (Jim Bakker, who was convicted of wire fraud and served five years in prison, has since started a new TV ministry with a new wife in Branson, Missouri, joining the hosts of evangelists peddling religious stuff, plugging money-grubber Christian writers and entrepreneurs, and interpreting Revelations for sadistic fun and mega-mammon.)

Shortly after he denounced the Jim and Tammy Bakker PTL scandal as "a cancer on the body of Christ," Swaggart himself was outed by Rev. Marvin Gorman for openly frequenting a prostitute. Rev. Gorman, one of the many evangelists viciously attacked on Swaggart's TV program, decided to get revenge by hiring a private investigator to document and film a series of Swaggart's visits with a prostitute to the Travel Inn on Airline Highway in Metairie, Louisiana. Gorman requested that Swaggart confess his sin, and Swaggart agreed. Or rather, lied. After four months of waiting, Gorman reported the incidents to Assemblies of God. The story hit the newsstands on February 10, 1988, and the next day Swaggart tearfully confessed to an unspecified sin, comparing himself to King David.

Assemblies of God imposed the mandatory two-year rehabilitation required of all its ministers who fall into sexual sin. When Swaggart refused to cooperate, his ordination was revoked. Swaggart retaliated by trashing Assemblies of God from the pulpit for their "unforgiving" position. When his audience began to turn away, Swaggart claimed that the devil made him do it and that evangelist Oral Roberts had cast out the demons over the phone, cleansing him of any moral defect.

In 1989, Swaggart was outed for having a ten-year affair, and on October 11, 1991, police in Indio, California, stopped the evangelist for driving on the wrong side of the road and found him to be accompanied by prostitute Rosemary Garcia. In 2002, the heirs of Pentecostal Bible teacher Finis Jennings Dake filed a plagiarism lawsuit against Swaggart.

In 2004, the exorcised family values advocate said in a sermon taped at his New Orleans ministry that he would kill gay men. "I'm trying to find the correct name for it . . . this utter absolute, asinine, idiotic stupidity of men marrying men . . . I've never seen a man in my life I wanted to marry. And I'm gonna be blunt and plain; if one ever looks at me like that, I'm gonna kill him and tell God he died." Though his comment implied that he would murder and would lie about it to God, it was met with enthusiastic applause from an audience that included big-name evangelists James Dobson and "ex-gay" Tony Perkins.

Omni 1, a Toronto television station that carries Swaggart's program, apologized publicly to viewers for the "serious breach" of Canadian broadcast regulations after Swaggart's gay threats prompted an investigation by the Canadian Radio Television Commission. Because hate speech is a criminal offense under Canadian law, lawyers contended that both Omni 1 and Swaggart could incur additional charges in addition to penalties imposed by CRTR.

Sometimes fundamentalist big guys exploit their brethren's fall, and sometimes they cover.

Online watchdog activist John Davies complains that *Christianity Today*, founded by Billy Graham, failed to report the alleged rape committed by Ollin Collins, pastor of Harvest Baptist Church in Fort Worth and board chairman at Southwestern Baptist Theological Seminary, the world's largest evangelical seminary. Following the rape of two unsuspecting, trusting women who had sought counseling, Rev. Collins was suspended from his church with pay, and he resigned from his board position the day after the *Fort Worth Star-Telegram* reported the women's allegations and their intent to sue.

On the other hand, Davies points out, *Christianity Today* did report the consensual adulterous relationship committed by Henry Lyons, president of the National Baptist Convention and senior pastor of Bethel Metropolitan Baptist Church in Clearwater, Florida. Davies interprets this as favoritism for a white Southern Baptist over a black National Baptist.

Although there might be some truth to that, Rev. Lyons is no innocent victim. In 1999 he was sentenced to four years and three months in prison and ordered to pay $5.2 million in restitution for federal charges that included tax evasion, bank fraud, and making false statements to a bank officer and the federal government, not including his state sentence for racketeering and grand theft. As part of a plea bargain, federal prosecutors dropped forty-nine of fifty-four charges, which included money laundering, wire fraud, and extortion. His co-defendant, Bernice Edwards, the convention employee with whom he committed adultery, was acquitted.

Nicknamed "the Black Pope," Lyons lived in a posh $700,000 waterfront home and enjoyed a luxurious lifestyle paid for in part by the $4 million swindled via a secret bank account from corporate donations to his organization. Lyons also misused $250,000 the Anti-Defamation League contributed to rebuild Southern black churches destroyed by fires.

Lyons, who declined to testify, continued to profess his innocence outside of court and proclaimed that God would reveal the truth. His wife Deborah and his congregation naïvely continued to believe him. Despite the massive incriminating evidence, supporters like Rev. E.V. Hill of Los Angeles, who testified on Lyons's behalf, claimed that the all-white jury had not given Lyons a fair trial. One witness, Lacy Curry, stated that National Baptist Convention presidents were free to reap rewards from deals made with corporations that wanted to profit from the convention's congregation.

With a classic Baptist flourish, Lyons contended that the devil made him do it. "When the devil came to Jesus Christ, he tempted him with fame, power and wealth, and I've fallen far short of the standards set by our Lord. I'm just a man. I have made mistakes." Yes, rather big "mistakes" committed by a trusted "high priest."

Cover-ups of molestations by Catholic priests are common knowledge; cover-ups of sexual crimes are just as common among fundamentalist organizations.

In 2001, the *Fort Worth Star-Telegram* reported that Dallas Theological Seminary had allowed Dallas-area pastor, Jon Gerrit Warnshuis, to graduate with a master's degree in theology in 1992, even though he had been charged with sexual assault and sexual indecency and had previously been expelled from the seminary for other sexual allegations. Furthermore, the seminary officials didn't disclose information about the charges to prospective employers calling for references for the minister, and the school broke Texas law by failing to alert authorities about Warnshuis's previous incidents.

Also in 2001, the *Houston Chronicle* reported the arrest of Evangel Christian Academy football coach and former principal, Dennis Dunn, for sexually assaulting a fifteen-year-old student. The Shreveport, Louisiana, Assemblies of God school was not only infamous for its staunchly self-righteous Christian approach to education but also for breaking the rules by improperly recruiting players for its top-notch football team (the national high school football champion in 1999).

Extreme right fundamentalist Randall Terry made a name for himself by founding the anti-abortion organization Operation Rescue in the late '80s. Getting himself arrested for his version of the cause has kept him in the news. In 1992, Terry was arrested and sentenced to five months in prison for having a fetus in a jar delivered to Bill Clinton at the Democratic National Convention. Between 1987 and 1994, his organization's activities resulted in over 70,000 arrests.

Terry was co-defendant in the 1994 Supreme Court case *NOW v. Scheidler*. NOW's claim was that the anti-abortion Pro Life Action Network (PLAN) used threat of or actual force, violence, and fear against abortion clinics in order to prevent patients from using clinic services, activities that involved racketeering forbidden by the Racketeer Influenced and Corrupt Organizations Act (RICO). The court did rule that RICO allows anti-abortion activists to be convicted, but they made no decision about NOW's allegations. In a 1998 lawsuit, NOW sought to force anti-abortion leaders to pay damages for attacking clinics. Terry settled out of court, then filed bankruptcy.

In 1998, Terry ran for Congress as a member of the New York State Right to Life Party on a platform of "no property taxes, no IRS, no social security, no abortion, and no homosexuals" and lost by a landslide. In 2002, this prominent family values advocate divorced his wife of nineteen years and remarried. Terry's church of fifteen years censured him for his "pattern of repeated and sinful relationships and conversations with both single and married women." Flip Benham, who inherited Terry's Operation Rescue (renamed Operation Save America) in 1993, further chastised Terry for his lack of "Godly sorrow . . . It's very difficult for him to speak out with any kind of Christian authority with his kind of character flaws."

Soon after, Terry purchased a $432,000 home in Florida, presumably with some of the non-tax-deductible donations he solicited on his website. He bragged that he needed a nice place to entertain "people of stature, people of importance. I have a lot of important people that come through my home. And I will have more important people come through my home." The same month he paid his down payment in Florida, Terry submitted an affidavit in New York stating that he was three months behind on his rent and was selling personal belongings to survive; later that month a New York court found Terry negligent in paying his ex-wife a "fair share of child support."

In 2003, Terry called for the impeachment of the Supreme Court justices ruling in *Lawrence v. Texas,* which decided that Texas law against sodomy violated constitutionally protected rights.

Terry often lies about homosexuality and exploits the fabricated "gay agenda" as a fundraising gimmick. So when his adopted son Jamiel came out in *Out Magazine* in 2004, Terry disowned his son and claimed that he was gay because he was abused before Terry "rescued" him at age eight (according to Jamiel, he was living with the Terrys at age four but wasn't adopted until age fourteen). Randall Terry is part of the fundamentalist Reconstructionist sect that favors the Old Testament death penalty for homosexuals, which presumably includes Jamiel and his partner.

Does Terry's son deserve death? By all accounts, Jamiel was a model church-going child. Terry knew his son's exemplary character so well that he asked Jamiel, still a kid living at home, to work with him on his campaigns. When Terry jilted his wife, he told Jamiel to talk to reporters and to "Christian leaders to keep the story quiet. The story didn't break for eight months because I kept it at bay," Jamiel said. "All I had done since he separated from my mother is protect him and defend him and do everything in my power to make sure that he maintains his reputation."

Jamiel revealed that he had been struggling with "this sin thing . . . I was hating myself" until "I was literally on the verge of suicide, and constantly talking to him about the fact that I was on the verge of suicide" during a period from September 2002 to May 2003. His father wasn't there for him when he needed him. Like many fundamentalist parents of gay kids, Terry dealt with the problem with condemnation rather than comfort.

When his parents divorced, Jamiel did some soul-searching. The divorce "made me question everything I had been raised with. It made me question truth, it made me question morality. Before that, I would have said . . . that the Bible is the infallible word of God. Now I'm like, it's kind of good sayings and I'm sure that God had something to do with it, but it was written by men, so it can be fallible. As for the divorce, in my eyes, he was doing something wrong." Jamiel confesses that he would never choose to be gay, but he is not ashamed of being gay now.

Jamiel naively nailed the contradiction of "Christian" authoritarianism when he commented, "My father has to understand the intense, almost idolatry we kids have for him. When he's talking, he just convinces you to do something, even when you don't want to do it." Here's the crux of Jamiel's conflict. Veneration. Adoration. Obedience. And Randall Terry begs to be lifted up onto the God pedestal. Even members of Mother Teresa's order have denounced Terry as a dangerous extremist, although Terry claims to have received a letter of praise from Mother Teresa herself (many believe it to be a forgery). Terry rejected both his adopted daughters when they became pregnant outside of marriage; one later became a Muslim. Now Terry has forbidden Jamiel to step foot in his house, he says because Jamiel gave CNN pictures of the family, which Terry called "an unbelievable lack of honesty." Perhaps Jamiel will come to see his father's unbelievable lack of honesty.

Republican fundamentalist Alan Keyes is another intolerant parent of a gay child whose personal morality is questionable. Keyes has made a career of running for office; he has run for the senate three times and the presidency twice with minimal credentials—his best is Ambassador to the UN Economic and Social Council under Reagan, a low-power job consisting of no diplomacy and lots of speechmaking. He alienated himself from other Republicans in 1992 when the press revealed that he was paying himself a salary of over $100,000 per year out of campaign funds—unheard of in a presidential race. According to Maryland Republican Party Chair Joyce Lyons Terhes, "When he decided to use campaign funds for his salary, that discouraged a lot of Republicans, and even Maryland voters." Keyes's staff urged him to stop to no avail. When reporters asked his 1992 campaign staffers if they supported his run in 1996, all responded negatively.

But Keyes benefits even from losing. Just running assures a lucrative career as public speaker and radio personality. *Time Magazine* reported that his 1996 campaign doubled his speaking fee from $7,500 to $15,000 per speech.

Given how much money Keyes takes in, it's odd that he has such problems paying his bills. After taking the $100,000 a year from his 1992 Senate campaign, he claimed, "I personally do not owe the debt that was owed by the campaign," which according to the FEC was substantial even not including the additional $20,000 in bad checks written in 1995.

Keyes's strategy is to run, raise campaign money, pay himself an exorbitant salary, take out loans to pay the campaign debt (which he claims is not his debt,) then run again.

Keyes's monetary success depends upon his ultraconservative stump speeches. On a radio interview, he blasted Mary Cheney, the lesbian daughter of Vice President Cheney, calling her a "selfish hedonist." Then added, "If my daughter were a lesbian, I'd look at her and say, 'That is a relationship that is based on selfish hedonism.' I would also tell my daughter that it's a sin and she needs to pray to the Lord God to help her deal with that sin." According to Keyes's lesbian daughter Maya, Keyes had already confronted her about being gay when she was in high school, constantly reminding her that sexuality was wrong and sinful. At the time of her father's public comment, Maya was a college student at Brown and had taken a year off to teach in India. She wrote online, "Most parents would be thrilled to have a child who doesn't smoke, have sex, do drugs, hardly drinks . . . , does well in school, gets good grades, gets into the Ivy League . . . , goes regularly to church, spends free time mentoring kids . . . I'm all about working for global justice. THEY don't care about that. THEY only care that I am an evil dyke." Her parents not only kicked Maya out of the house for coming out, they refused to even talk to her.

Of course there's nothing new about sex-scandal hypocrisy among ultraconservative Christians.

Once in a great while I read a book that absolutely floors me. One such eye-opener was historian William Manchester's *A World Lit Only By Fire: The Medieval Mind and the Renaissance: Portrait of an Age.*

Talk about a paradigm shift!

I already knew from my narrow experience that the Church was less than perfect. But I was not prepared to be jolted awake by Manchester's juicy chronicle of a Church dripping with sordid sins, outrageous blasphemies, and appalling crimes, the details of which survived despite the Church's concerted efforts to rewrite its history. Priests, nuns, bishops, cardinals, popes—no sacred post had gone untainted.

From Manchester I learned shocking details about the infamous members of the Borgia family, one of the most colorful of the papal families. Previously I had only recognized them as subjects of numerous paintings from the Baroque to the present.

In 1456, Rodrigo Lanzol y Borgia (later renamed Alexander) was elevated to the College of Cardinals by his uncle, Pope Calixtus III. In 1460, the now reigning Pope Pius II happened to run into the twenty-nine-year-old Cardinal Borgia at a wild party in Siena, where, Pius noted, "none of the allurements of love was lacking." The party's guest list had included Siena's most beautiful young women, but contrary to customary decorum, their husbands, fathers, and brothers had been excluded "in order that lust be unrestrained" without the protection of any male relatives, according to Pope Pius.

Pius knew lechery when he saw it. As Bishop Aeneas Sylvius Piccolomini, he had fathered several children by various mistresses—but when elected pontiff, he shrugged it off, telling his court, "Forget Aeneas; look at Pius."

From his many illicit affairs, Cardinal Borgia was known to have produced a son and two daughters, and later, in his forties, another daughter and three sons with Rosa Vannozza dei Catanei. As priest, Alexander had married Rosa to two men during the time that she was his lover. Although he had other lovers, Rosa was his "regular." At age fifty-nine, he decided it was time they parted. To soften the blow, he made her brother a cardinal.

Alexander was seeking younger flesh to entice him. One of the young women that excited Cardinal Borgia was nineteen-year-old Giulia Farnese. After her arranged marriage, her husband, Signor Orsini, "was told his presence was required elsewhere," as Manchester put it. Still wearing her bridal gown, Signora Orsini "was led to the sparkling gilt-and-sky-blue bedchamber of the cardinal, her senior by forty years. A maid removed the gown and, for some obscure reason, carefully put it away. She cannot have thought that Giulia would want to keep it for sentimental reasons, for thenceforth Borgia's new bedmate was known throughout Italy as *sposa di Cristo*, the bride of Christ."

In 1483, the lusty Cardinal Borgia became Pope Alexander VI, and his cardinal sins were multiplied. According to Manchester, under Pope Alexander VI,

> Vatican parties, already wild, grew wilder. They were costly, but he could afford the lifestyle of a Renaissance prince; as vice chancellor of the Roman Church, he had amassed enormous wealth. As guests approached the papal palace, they were excited by the

spectacle of living statues: naked, gilded young men and women in erotic poses. Flags bore the Borgia arms, which, appropriately, portrayed a red bull rampant on a field of gold. Every fete had a theme. One, known to the Romans as the Ballet of the Chestnuts, was held on October 30, 1501. The indefatigable Burchard [papal *magister ceremoniarum* from 1483 to 1506] describes it in his *Diarium*. After the banquet dishes had been cleared away, the city's fifty most beautiful whores danced with guests, "first clothed, then naked." The dancing over, the "ballet" began, with the pope and two of his children in the best seats.

Candelabra were set up on the floor; scattered among them were chestnuts, "which," Burchard writes, "the courtesans had to pick up, crawling between the candles." Then the serious sex started. Guests stripped and ran out on the floor, where they mounted, or were mounted by, the prostitutes. "The coupling took place," according to Burchard, "in front of everyone present." Servants kept score of each man's orgasms, for the pope greatly admired virility and measured a man's machismo by his ejaculative capacity. After everyone was exhausted, His Holiness distributed prizes—cloaks, boots, caps, and fine silken tunics. The winners, the diarist wrote, were those "who made love with those courtesans the greatest number of times."

Alexander's daughter with Rosa, Lucrezia Borgia, is perhaps the most famous offspring of any pope. Used as a sexual pawn in her father's political negotiations, at thirteen she was first married to Giovanni Sforza, a powerful Milanese and Lord of Pesaro, who would benefit him in his scheme against the Aragonese dynasty of Naples. He annulled that marriage and the others following, when her charms were needed to help him form yet another important alliance.

In 1497, when Lucrezia was seventeen, Alexander divorced her from her husband, whom he publicly called impotent. Lucrezia's husband, Sforza, retaliated by accusing the pope of an incestuous relationship with his daughter. This was no shock to Rome; her incestuous entanglement with both her brothers was well known and her relationship with her father suspected.

One of Lucrezia's brothers, Cesare Borgia (1475-1507), who as a prince of the Church had committed multiple murders, was the model for Niccolò Machiavelli's *Il principe*. On June 15, 1497, the corpse of her other brother, Juan, who had been stabbed nine times, was found floating in the Tiber. Cesare was assumed to be guilty.

Between marriages, the seventeen-year-old Lucrezia conceived her illegitimate son Giovanni either by her father or by Cesare. Even pregnant, Lucrezia seems to have inspired a re-vision of holiness everywhere she went. The nuns of the Convent of San Sisto on the Via Appia learned a few things from Lucrezia, who had withdrawn there to pass the time to term with one of her lovers, a young Spanish chamberlain. By the time she left, an Italian historian wrote, the nuns had abandoned "the old austerity of their regime" to such an extent that "sweeping reforms were necessary to bring them back to the sublime joys of self-mortification and to exorcise the atmosphere . . . which had grown up inside those pious walls."

In spite of the internal scandal, her secret could have remained cloistered. But her father was impatient to arrange another politically advantageous marriage for her. "Later it would end tragically when Cesare murdered the groom."

A few years after Lucrezia gave birth, Alexander legitimized her child, the *Infans Romanus*, by issuing two papal bulls, one public and the other secret, on September 1, 1501. The public bull identified the child as the offspring of Cesare and an unmarried woman ("*coniugato genitus et soluta*"). According to the second bull, the child was the son of the same woman and Alexander himself (" . . . *non de praefato duce, sed de nobis et de dicta muliere*"). Pope Alexander VI named the boy a duke and awarded him the duchy of Nepi and Camerino (he was, after all, either the pope's son or grandson).

Alexander was not the first pope, and certainly not the last, to decline celibacy. From the 1470s on, pontiffs sleeping with mistresses and granting titles and dowries to their offspring became common practice.

Nepotism was far more damaging to the structural integrity of the Church than the pope's sexual indiscretions at home, though of course the two vices issue from the same gene pool if not the same loins. The legitimacy of the practice of nepotism, like that of lust, trickled down from on high. Sixtus IV (r. 1471-1484) appointed first two of his dissolute nephews to the sacred College of Cardinals, to be followed by three more nephews and a grandnephew. Among his other appointees were two young children, an eight-year-old boy as archbishop of Lisbon and an eleven-year-old boy as archbishop of Milan.

Sixtus's successor, Innocent VII, spoiled his son by a nameless courtesan. Besides gang-raping young women, including nuns, until they were unconscious with serious injuries, Franceschetto Ciboo indulged a lifestyle that forced his pope father to escalate simony and to "mortgage the papal tiara and treasury to pay for [his] wedding." His new bride's fourteen-year-old brother was made a cardinal, who eventually became Pope Leo X.

Even these very few examples from Manchester's book serve my point: A few centuries here, a few millennium there—In spite of all our modern gizmos and sophisticated scientific insights, have we really advanced at all?

Chapter 17

Pat Robertson's Mug Shot

Although the photo's date stamp reads 8/1/1994, according to a Christian Broadcasting Network (CBN) spokesperson the photo of Pat Robertson leg pressing 2,000 pounds was actually taken on February 1, 2003, when Robertson was 73. The elderly evangelist attributes his superhuman strength to regular training with his doctor, who leg presses 2,700 pounds, and to his "age-defying energy shake." Experts say the shake contains essentially the same ingredients as other energy shakes, minus the divinity. (GNC recently stopped carrying it.) So much for the shake. But what about those leg presses?

Robertson's 2000-pound leg press shattered the world record set by mega-buffed Dan Kendra, a Florida State quarterback who later played for the NFL. A special leg press machine had to be modified to fit Kendra's record 1,335 pounds of weights, and the strain during his phenomenal lift was so intense that the capillaries in his eyes burst. But there in the CBN-authenticated photo, a thin, clear-eyed, seventy-something—kicked back, looking relaxed, even casual—tops Kendra's record by 665 pounds.

That's Pat Robertson, Christian Coalition chieftain and owner of CBN, and perhaps the most famous and powerful fundamentalist in America. Certainly among the prophets of profits, he's the superstar people believe in enough to have made him a billionaire. From atop his huge Virginia mountain mansion, complete with private airstrip, Robertson surveys his kingdom, the kind of kingdom that Satan offered Jesus, the kind of kingdom that's built on that grand old-fashioned principle, "There's a sucker born every day," or as Robertson calls it, "God's marvelous system of money management."

It's worth noting that according to his autobiography, *Shout It from the Housetops*, Satan told him early in his Christian life, "Jesus is just playing you for a sucker, Robertson," and then assured Robertson that when he died, he would wind up in hell for having blasphemed the Holy Spirit. It's hard to argue with that. According to Robertson's Bible, Jesus rebuked demonic spirits for disclosing the *truth* about who he was, and Ananais and Sapphira were struck dead for blasphemy when they lied about withholding money from the church (they were allowed to withhold, they just weren't allowed to lie about it).

What does it profit a person if he gains the whole world but forfeits his soul? Jesus asks Pat Robertson at least as much as the rest of us. You have turned my Father's house into a den of thieves, blessed are the poor, etc. Most of us know at least this much Bible to know that Jesus condemned riches.

But unlike Jesus, Robertson plows forward through a fame-and-fortune underworld with the slippery skill of Old Scratch himself, fearlessly tweaking the facts, brazenly rewriting his history, like he did on the resume he distributed during his presidential bid in 1988.

For instance, according to the *Dallas Morning News*, Robertson, who has variously ranked his genius IQ between 137 and 159 (it doesn't take a genius to notice the spread), stated on his resume and in his book, *America's Dates with Destiny*, that he was a "Yale-educated tax lawyer," although he never passed the bar. What Robertson described on his resume as graduate study done at the University of London was only an introductory summer arts course for visiting Americans. Robertson claimed to be a member of the board of directors of the United Virginia Bank, but the *Washington Post* reported that in fact he only served on a community advisory board.

When the *Wall Street Journal* busted Robertson for adjusting his wedding date so people wouldn't know that his wife was seven months pregnant when they wed, Robertson scolded reporters in Philadelphia, "It is outrageous to pry into a man's past and try to do damage to a man's wife and children under the guise of journalism."

Although Robertson claimed to be a combat veteran of the Korean War, he never served at the front or saw combat, thanks to his father, a well-to-do congressman and senator. When Congressman Pete McCloskey, who served in the same unit as Robertson, stated that Robertson had boasted of his father using his influence to "get him out of combat duty,"

Robertson sued for $35 million. But during depositions, Paul Brosman, a retired university professor who had also served with Robertson, confirmed McCloskey's story, and added that Robertson had "consorted with prostitutes and had sexually harassed a Korean cleaning girl who worked in the barracks." Robertson dropped the suit and was ordered to pay part of McCloskey's court costs.

Robertson created the Freedom Council, a political group for born-again Christians, to help fund his presidential campaign. Millions were illegally raised and spent. The Federal Elections Commission audit detailed numerous violations of federal campaign guidelines. "We're talking about very, very substantial amounts of money . . . I'm not aware of any publicly funded presidential candidate exceeding limits by that amount," according to Commissioner John Warren McGarry.

During his trying campaign days, God's marvelous system worked for Robertson in ways that outperformed mere money management. Even during the hectic days of presidential campaigning, Robertson was busy with God's business in other arenas, healing, diverting a hurricane, inadvertently creating international crises when he announced that the Soviets had placed nuclear missiles in Cuba and that he knew the location of American hostages being held in Lebanon.

Closer to home and more recently, he proclaimed that Congress and the president don't have to obey Supreme Court rulings if they don't want to, that only Christians and Jews are fit to hold public office, and that women must obey men, and he concurred with Jerry Falwell in announcing that 9/11 was caused by "the pagans, and the abortionists, and the feminists, and the gays and lesbians who are actively trying to make that an alternative lifestyle, the ACLU, People for the American Way—all of them who have tried to secularize America."

Pat Robertson is a man obsessed with redefining brotherly love as self-righteous loathing. "How can there be peace when drunkards, drug dealers, communists, atheists, New Age worshipers of Satan, secular humanists, oppressive dictators, greedy money changers, revolutionary assassins, adulterers, and homosexuals are on top?" he complains. A notoriously bad Samaritan, he demonizes even other Christians. "You say you're supposed to be nice to the Episcopalians and the Presbyterians and the Methodists and this, that, and the other thing. Nonsense. I don't have to be nice to the spirit of the Antichrist."

Although God let him down on the campaign trail, he never stopped helping Robertson build a mammoth media, educational, and legal kingdom with a current estimated value of over a billion dollars. God's marvelous system of money management kicked in when Robertson founded the CBN in 1960. In addition to fundraising via its 700 Club, CBN's slick marketing targeted millions through direct mail and telephone "counseling centers." A large percent of CBN's airtime was spent selling programs, books, trips, etc. He suckered in thousands of viewers, many of them retirees, to sell coupon books for his new American Benefits Plus program, a Bible-backed multi-level marketing scheme like Amway that promised earnings of $15,000-20,000 a month. When that failed, he changed the name to Kalo Vita and started selling vitamins. Though he couldn't come up with money to help faithful participants recoup their losses on his investment schemes, he did have enough cash to gamble on investments in race horses, including $520,000 for Mr. Pat and a $125,000 stud fee for a horse he bred with one of his mares.

Over the years Robertson's shady business practices got him into plenty of legal hot water, but like a modern-day Faust he flaunted his squeaky clean image and billionaire status. Lying didn't hurt. For instance, in 1997, Robertson sold his International Family Entertainment and its Family Channel for $1.9 billion. Although his website claimed that he sold it to Fox Kids Worldwide, Inc., he actually sold it to Fox owner Rupert Murdock, publisher of the British tabloid *The Sun*, famous for its pin-up nudes, and owner of DirectTV, which was the world's top provider of satellite porn.

CBN viewers never heard of Robertson's high-stakes investments or his legal tangles because they got their news whitewashed on CBN. Among his viewers he was a hero, famous for his political prattle, social sophisms, and unabashed pleas for money to help finance his divinely profit-inspired propaganda. His ongoing back-and-forth on separation of church and state—saying he was against it, then saying he never said that—provided a spiritual sparring of specious and spurious both entertaining and enlightening. Demonization of gays, abortion doctors, ACLU, any liberal cause, hyped to a pitch of Hollywood sensationalism, facilitated God's marvelous system of money management.

Robertson's blasphemies included blatant lying, swindling, and fraud, all well documented, and some instances so outrageous they were downright comical. But Robertson's addiction to business gambles led him to cast his bread upon very dark waters.

Perhaps his most heinous indiscretion was to form business partnerships with Zaire's brutal dictator, President Mobutu Sese Seko, and Liberia's equally brutal dictator, President Charles Taylor.

In 1964, Joseph Désiré Mobutu successfully staged a coup with the help of the CIA and installed himself as president of the Republic of Congo. Cancelling future elections, Mobutu refused to implement democratic reforms, and instead, turned his country, still ravaged by its civil war, into a base of operations for repulsing invasions by successionists backed by communist forces in neighboring Angola. He changed the country's name to Zaire, compelled Zairians to change their non-African names, and renamed himself Mobutu Sese Seko Kuku wa za Banga, "the all-powerful warrior who, because of his enduring and inflexible will to win, will go from conquest to conquest leaving fire in his wake."

During his thirty-year reign, organizations around the world protested Mobutu's ruthless violations of human rights, which included religious persecution, censorship, torture, and the murders of tens of thousands of citizens. Due to Mobutu's atrocities, by 1993, European nations and the U.S. had withdrawn economic assistance, and in 1994, the U.S. Department of State officially charged Mobutu with human rights violations and refused to grant him a visa.

By this time, Mobutu had systematically transferred to his personal accounts in Switzerland and Belgium billions of dollars of Zaire's money and revenues from natural resources, and according to U.S. intelligence agencies, had embezzled billions of dollars in aid given to Zaire during the Cold War. The World Bank reported that in one year alone, $400 million, a quarter of the nation's entire export revenues, disappeared from the books of the government's mining conglomerate. Although the nation's forty-three million people continued living in extreme poverty, Mobutu was one of the world's richest men by the time he partnered with Pat Robertson in 1992.

On February 16, 1992, Mobutu's troops opened fire on demonstrating Zairian Protestants and Catholics asking for reform. On the 700 Club, Robertson criticized the U.S. State Department's criticism of Mobutu's bloody massacre, defending the all-powerful warrior leaving fire in his wake as a loyal U.S. ally in the war against communism.

In June 1992, Robertson chartered the African Development Company to take advantage of the vast lumber and mineral concessions Mobutu granted him along the upper Zaire River and the 50,000 acre farm he would operate outside Kinshasa, the nation's capital. Although African Development Company was a private venture, with Robertson as president and sole stockholder, Robertson used his CBN's non-profit missionary money and equipment, along with Mobutu's personal fleet of planes and yachts and a crew of Zairians that amounted to slave labor, to facilitate his diamond mining operations.

Mobutu continued trying to gain international acceptance by establishing ties to the U.S., and Robertson continued to lobby for him. In the February 27, 1995, issue of *Time*, Dr. Makau Mutua, Projects Director of the Human Rights Program at Harvard Law School, called Robertson "Mobutu's biggest catch." When Laurent Kabila and his rebels closed in on Mobutu's last strongholds in 1996, Robertson sent a personal representative "offering his assistance and cooperation."

Robertson solicited his CBN viewers for donations to fund a "Flying Hospital" to support his Operation Blessing missionary outreach to Africa. But the pilots told the *Virginia-Pilot* and the Virginia Office of Consumer Affairs that the planes and equipment were used almost exclusively by Robertson's African Development Company's private diamond mining operations, which included the Zairian slave laborers. The pilots' testimonies were sealed by the Attorney General's office, perhaps because Attorney General Mark Earley received $35,000 in political contributions from Robertson, and because Robertson gave Governor Jim Gilmore $50,000 in contributions and was a member of Gilmore's transition advisory team.

In legal hot water over Zambia, Robertson shifted his attention to Liberia.

In 1998, Robertson negotiated a business partnership with Liberia's president, Charles Taylor, a U.S. prison escapee turned brutal dictator, who, when Robertson met him, was under UN economic sanctions and indictments for war crimes. Robertson brought his own special CBN program to the Liberia airwaves for eight consecutive nights, after which, at a national three-day prayer and fast rally compliments of Robertson, Charles Taylor declared Jesus president and ordered the 65,000 attending the rally to prostrate themselves and join in song. This might seem miraculous, given Taylor's greed at the expense of his poverty-stricken nation, given Taylor's support for rebel insurgents whose weapons of war included rape, torture, and mutilation of civilians, and given that the U.S. strongly suspected that Taylor was linked to Al-Qaeda terrorist cells.

On the 700 Club, Robertson blasted the U.S. president for adopting a policy of regime change that included implementation via American troops. "We're undermining a Christian, Baptist president [Taylor] to bring in Muslim rebels to take over the country. And how dare the president of the United States say to the duly elected president of another country, 'You've got to step down'. The State Department has tried as hard as it can to destabilize Liberia and to bring about the very outcome we're seeing now. They had no endgame, they have no plan of what to do, they only wanted to destroy the sitting president and his government, and as a result, the place is being plunged into chaos. And it breaks my heart."

Robertson's, of course, was a heart of gold. The 1998 business partnership with Taylor gave Robertson, in exchange for a ten percent kickback, gold mining rights to a plot of land reported to hold five million ounces of pure gold valued at about $1.5 billion. In the tax evading Cayman Islands, Robertson created his new company, Freedom Gold, which was subsequently manned by a crew of thirty-five Liberian slave "miners."

Meanwhile, back home, Robertson said in interviews that the explosion of a nuclear weapon at the State Department headquarters would be good for the country, and on his 700 Club he reiterated, "What we need is for somebody to place a small nuke at Foggy Bottom," Foggy Bottom being the location of the State Department headquarters.

Undaunted by his legal setbacks, Robertson never quit testing the limits of God's marvelous system of money management. On August 22, 2005, Robertson announced that the United States should assassinate Venezuelan president Hugo Chavez. Many speculated that Chavez was standing in the way of some new Robertson enterprise in the works there. Robertson put it, "You know, I don't know about this doctrine of assassination, but if he thinks we're trying to assassinate him, I think that we really ought to go ahead and do it. It's a whole lot cheaper than starting a war . . . We have the ability to take him out, and I think the time has come that we exercise that ability. We don't need another $200 billion war to get rid of one, you know, strong-arm dictator. It's a whole lot easier to have some of the covert operatives do the job and then get it over with."

Two days later, Robertson backpedaled: "Wait a minute, I didn't say 'assassination.' I said our special forces should 'take him out,' and 'take him out' can be a number of things, including kidnapping." Later that day he issued a written statement: "Is it right to call for assassination? No, and I apologize for that statement. I spoke in frustration that we should accommodate the man who thinks the U.S. is out to kill him."

I'm sorry, but put on the dunce hat and go sit in the corner with your global village idiot award.

Chapter 18

Criminal Faith

Charged with at least twenty counts of felony drug tampering for diluting over a hundred doses of chemotherapy drugs, Robert R. Courtney claimed he needed the bucks to pay off his $600,000 federal income tax bill and his $330,000 pledge to his Assembly of God church, where he was a deacon and where his father had ministered. Courtney's minister father, who worked as Courtney's bookkeeper during the time of the fraud, called Courtney "an ideal son in every sense of the word."

Worldcom CEO Bernard Ebbers, once worth $1.4 billion and one of the world's richest men, was busted for receiving huge undisclosed perks from Solomon Smith Barney, including over $11 million in illegal IPO profits while small shareholders were left holding Worldcom's bankruptcy due to $3.8 billion in creative accounting and other offenses. According to the *Wall Street Journal*, when news of the scandal reached Brookhaven, Mississippi, Ebbers told his brethren at Easthaven Baptist Church, where he taught Sunday school, "I just want you to know you aren't going to church with a crook."

Thank God for that. Though Brother Ebbers owed Worldcom $400 million to repay shady loans and was out of work, he would still get his severance pay of $15 million per year. Easthaven's collection plate would not be empty.

Empty, however, is relative. When the media revealed that former Secretary of Education and Drug Czar William Bennett had lost more than $8 million due to his addiction to casino gambling, Bennett filled the tank with tens of thousands in speaking fees earned by rallying audiences to the cause of conservative moral values. The double-dealing author of *The Book of Virtues* reprimanded President Clinton's "moral failure" while arguing that his own moral failure didn't make him a hypocrite because he had never claimed to be a moral authority.

The broadcast "moral failures" of right-wingers became so commonplace that even drug-basher Rush Limbaugh's drug addiction drew little more than a yawn.

Understanding that the Bible was not God-breathed nudged me from born-again to progressive Christianity. Coming to grips with Christianity as "the Christian myth" pushed me into my disillusioned agnostic phase. But it was researching what I called Christian crooks that led to my reconversion back into Deism.

I was already upset by the blatant perversion of Christianity perpetrated by TV evangelists and rightwing Republicans when Al Gore "lost" to George Bush. Within one Bush-Cheney year it was clear to me that the sick, sinister version of Christianity spun by the rich and powerful and their passive sheep was so dangerous that the essence of America was truly in jeopardy. When I checked my emails one day only to witness the first Twin Tower billowing smoke, I thought it had to be a movie trailer. Within a couple seconds I read the caption. It's a pathetic testament to the state of our Union that my first thought was "Dick Cheney."

I wanted to prove to myself just how dark the smokescreen had gotten. Although I viewed Christianity as mythic, I really hadn't fully shaken my faith in the Christian message—meaning the message of the biblical Jesus—as a good, even a sacred thing. Distressed by 9/11, I just had to know why America was swarming with fundamentalist serial killers, fraudulent evangelists, Cheney politicians, Jesus worshipping billionaires, and violent Christian cults. If I couldn't figure out why, I at least wanted to know how bad it really was.

The consistent prevalence of evil within a religion that nonetheless survived to honor a man/god like Jesus and to preserve the good message essentially intact was almost a case for the existence of such a person and for the divine protection of the texts that preserved him. I found myself defending Christianity, or at least the teachings of Jesus, with the zeal almost of a born-again against the flood of Orwellian perversion.

But I wasn't a Christian, and I knew that. What exactly was I? I was no longer comfortable calling myself a progressive Christian, and I wasn't content with being a disillusioned agnostic.

Oddly, before becoming a born-again Christian at age nineteen, I considered myself to be a Deist. During my Christian days I defended Deism with the same kind of zeal with which I later defended Christianity as I moved back into Deism. While researching "just how bad it had gotten," I also started rereading Thomas Paine. The more I read about Christian hypocrisy the more I knew I was a Deist and only a Deist.

Many articles and books contributed to my understanding of the evils of contemporary fundamentalism. But a number particularly affected me, perhaps because I read all these works very quickly one right after the other: Kimberly Blaker's well-documented exposé of the Religious Right, *The Fundamentals of Extremism: The Christian Right in America*; cult expert Margaret Thaler Singer's *Cults In Our Midst: The Continuing Fight Against Their Hidden Menace*; Dr. Robert Hare's *Without Conscience: The Disturbing World of the Psychopaths Among Us*; articles and books by theologian Karen Armstrong; *Crimes Against Nature: How George W. Bush & His Corporate Pals Are Plundering the Country & Hijacking Our Democracy* by Robert F. Kennedy, Jr.; books by Molly Ivans; Rob Boston's *The Most Dangerous Man in America: Pat Robertson and the Rise of the Christian Coalition*; Mel White's *Stranger At the Gate: To Be Gay and Christian in America* (White had been ghostwriter of many big-ticket fundamentalist books); and a large number of media and watchdog websites. It wasn't that theirs was exactly new information. It was the avalanche of examples all at once that made me realize at a deep visceral level that evil isn't just an occasional eruption but is the fundamental foundation of organized religion.

It's not that religion itself is organically evil. It's that otherwise good or at least harmless religion becomes evil when it becomes organized, because evil people realize that it's easy to exploit the naiveté and trust of inherently religious souls who assume that other religious people are honest and good, and those evil exploiters always weasel their way into positions of power.

Another problem with religion is that it doesn't prevent evil, it excuses and forgives and therefore encourages it in everyone but the scapegoat.

Numerous studies link fundamentalism with all kinds of criminal behavior. According to a 1991 Roper survey, following conversion, born-again Christians' behavior deteriorates in areas such as driving while intoxicated, illegal drug use, and engagement in illicit sex. And why not? You can always be forgiven.

In 1980, cult researchers Flo Conway and Jim Siegelman found that more than thirty of the forty-eight cult groups they studied that year "had emerged out of fundamentalist or other branches of conservative Christianity," and that those thirty "ranked higher than the most destructive cults . . . studied in terms of the trauma they inflicted upon their members."

The United Nations reported that between 1989 and 1992, of the world's eighty-two armed conflicts, seventy-nine occurred not between countries, but among religious zealots within their own countries. In the U.S., the Ku Klux Klan, Aryan Nation, Christian Identity, Neo-Nazis, Reconstructionists, the Christian Right, and another estimated 400 militia-type Christian supremacist groups stand ready, and often armed, to help enforce their version of the true faith. The white racist militia, Aryan Nation, or Church of Jesus Christ Christian, maintains heavily-armed compounds in Utah and Pennsylvania and have been linked to at least several dozen murders since 1980.

Christian Identity leader David Lane, convicted of violating the civil rights of a slain Jewish talk-show host, in addition to racketeering and conspiracy, said while in jail, "I am the symbol that is going to stop the Judeo-American murder of the white race. Killing is always justified for the preservation of your kind."

Under the influence of Christian Identity, Terry Nichols and Timothy McVeigh bombed the federal building in Oklahoma City in 1995 to protest the government's storming of the Christian cult, Waco Branch Davidians, and to avenge the shooting deaths of the Christian Identity followers, the supremacist Weaver family, at Ruby Ridge.

Christian Identity followers believe that the federal government, or ZOG (Zionist Occupation Government), is controlled by Satan and the Jews and is intent on destroying the Aryan nation. The true holocaust will occur in America during the wars of the Last Days, or Tribulation, when the Jews, who have stolen the title of Chosen People from the Aryan race, will annihilate the U.S. and the white race; there will be no Rapture. Christian Identity members have been responsible for paramilitary raids on ZOG that have killed state officials and have bombed and set fire to abortion clinics.

Another radical fundamentalist cult, Army of God, has been linked to kidnappings, bombings, shooting deaths, and the 280 anthrax threats made to abortion clinics following 9/11. *Church & State* reported that during the Army of God's 2001 White Rose Banquet, "numerous speakers called for violence against abortion clinics, approved murdering abortion providers, and made jokes about killing homosexuals." According to Army of God's Chuck Spingola, "Now, these people [gays] are vile folks . . . If you deal with these people long enough, you understand the wisdom of God when he says they should be put to death."

Most Christian militia groups mirror the Reconstructionist ideology. Reconstruction founders, Texas economist Gary North and R.J. Rushdoony, advocate "reconstructing" America into a totalitarianism based on their literal interpretation of the Bible, which would necessitate reintroduction of slavery, elimination of birth control, and imposition of a non-intervenable capitalist economy.

One Reconstructionist website, God's Order Affirmed in Love, asserts, "Christianity has historically been a religion of the white race regardless of how hard whites have tried to convert the world," and, "In addition to being grounded upon a biblical foundation, Reconstruction must be built upon preserving our families which includes the greater racial family (nation) that we were born into." These racist Reconstructionists don't know their history, or they would recall that Christianity was originally a religion of Jews and other people from the Middle East and Mediterranean areas.

Not surprisingly, Reconstructionists stress instilling absolute obedience in their children. Children must conform to their parents, and parents must conform to Reconstructionist leaders. This mentality contradicts the spirit of democratic freedom that characterizes America. Philosophically, Reconstructionism is not only cultic, but also treasonous.

Cult children grow up to be adults that bring to the outside world the racial, religious, or political intolerance they have been taught. They also bring their belief that they are chosen, elite, superior, which makes it difficult for them to be self-expressive or to form their own opinions, since they might be inferior to the norm. Like all terrorist cults, Christian Reconstructionist and militia sects link some absolute authority—in this case, their version of the Bible—with violent enforcement of their narrow ideals. Violent enforcement equals violence equals cruelty for its own sake: Violent punishment of disobedient scapegoats becomes the sadist's justification of his sadism. Justified sadism is glorified into sacred duty.

Theologians like Karen Armstrong, a foremost authority on American religious affairs, warn about the increasing militancy of some fundamentalist sects. Publications like *The Field Manual of the Free Militia* "prove" the inerrancy of the Bible and claim that being armed is a Christian duty authorized by Jesus.

In his article, "What Does the Bible Say About Gun Control?" Reconstructionist Larry Pratt, executive director of Gun Owners of America, argues that the Old and New Testaments approve killing in self-defense. Fine; but he further claims, "Christ accused the religious leaders of the day of also opposing the execution of those deserving of death—rebellious teenagers." Pratt gets away with his glaring misrepresentation of Jesus as an advocate for the execution of rebellious teenagers because his followers, who believe in the infallible Bible, don't actually check the Bible, they just blindly accept Pratt's word as gospel. Only someone who had never really read the Gospels could possibly buy Pratt's blatant lie.

Although President Obama has been in office only a few months at the time of this writing, it's disconcerting to me that he has taken no action to halt the construction of mega-churches on military bases, paid for by American taxpayers, most of whom believe that fundamentalist extremists and armaments are a dangerous combination, not to mention a violation of separation of church and state.

In *The Fundamentals of Extremism*, edited by Kimberly Blaker, Bobbie Kirkhart's essay, "Little Ones to Him Belong," documents numerous studies that have linked fundamentalism and child abuse. According to a 1974 report by H. Erlanger in the *American Sociological Review*, religious affiliation was found to be a better predictor of violent behavior toward children than age, gender, social class, or size of residence.

In "The Role of Parental Religious Fundamentalism and Rightwing Authoritarianism in Child-Rearing Goals and Practices," social psychologist Henry Danso cites extensive research that links child discipline by corporal punishment to the religious conservatism that generates the authoritarian personality type common among fundamentalists of all religions.

Although not all fundamentalist groups are cultic, all do foster ideologies that can skirt the edge of cultic extremism. In *Cults In Our*

Midst, Singer describes cult behavior in terms that fit many fundamentalist homes: "Each cult regards itself as above the laws of the land, as a sovereign state with its own superior rules . . . Often cult parents are led to regard children as creatures similar to wild ponies, who must be 'broken.'"

It's not surprising that extremist authoritarians advocate the death of rebellious teenagers, which Pratt dishonestly claims that Jesus advocated. According to Singer, "Extremely strict and punitive behavioral controls are exercised over children in many cults. Severe beatings to 'break the will, beat out the sin, overcome the demons' are accepted means of handling children. In some cults, exorcisms are performed on children to drive out evil spirits, devils, and such. These can be brutal, terrifying events."

As a top psychological expert called to testify in many criminal cases involving cult violence, Singer knows from first-hand experience that parents who have been thoroughly indoctrinated into totalist thinking can stand by and watch their own children be severely abused and even killed right before their eyes. Here are a few of the many chilling accounts that she describes in her book.

> Five-year-old Luke Stice died of a broken neck in a survivalist cult in rural Nebraska. Reportedly, his neck was broken either during a regular "discipline session" or deliberately, to force Luke's father to return because he had fled the cult leaving behind Luke and two other children. Before Luke died, the leader had made him spend most of his time in undershorts and forced him to wallow naked in mud and snow.
>
> Twelve-year-old John Yarbough allegedly was beaten to death in a Michigan cult, the House of Judah. Before his death, when John had been beaten several days in a row and could not eat or walk, the leader tried to pick him up by the ears with pliers. Another boy reported that he was burned on the face for punishment; one testified that another boy had hot coals put in his mouth and on his hands . . .
>
> In a custody battle related to a nameless religious sect in Gwinnette County, Georgia, members testified that they sing to their children and offer encouragement during beatings with wooden rods or refrigerator hoses and insisted that they didn't strike in anger. According to child welfare investigators, one girl

said "the only way she knew her daddy loved her was because he whipped her. He would tell her he loved her while he was doing it." . . .

One case in which I testified [concerned] a ten-year-old boy who was held by four grown men over the arm of a sofa and hit with a large wooden paddle 140 times, with the group calling out the count. The boy's mother stood by and watched. The cult leader was in a nearby building directing the beating over the phone. The leader of a cult in the northeastern United States had all adults carry large wooden cooking ladles and strike any child who deviated from group rules until the child "surrendered."

In fundamentalist households, as in cults, children are expected to submit, surrender, obey. The authoritarian world that fundamentalist children are socialized into is the antithesis of democratic society. Children brought up in authoritarian homes that disdain negotiation and compromise are taught to shun critical, evaluative thinking and new ideas. In some homes, independent thinking is considered sinful or demonic, which warrants suppression and severe punishment. Children learn to simply obey. In their polarized world, it's "us," the good guys in the right, v. "them," the bad guys who are wrong. These children develop anxious-dependent personality traits that include self-righteousness and paranoia regarding outsiders. Being gay, of course, is anathema. Gay children learn to bash the gay within themselves and in others. Not surprisingly, most exhibitionists are male and married, and come from strict and repressive backgrounds commonly found among fundamentalists.

Chicago Transit Authority machinist Larry Slack and his wife Constance, a nurse in a children's hospital, were strict Jehovah's Witnesses who home schooled their children; they were also rigid, devoutly religious parents who accepted child beating as biblically sanctioned practice. On November 10, 2001, when the children were unenthusiastically helping Constance find her jacket with her wallet, Larry whacked the youngest, eight-year-old Lester, with a three-quarter inch cable. During the search for the jacket, Larry observed that twelve-year-old Laree had not done the laundry, so Larry whacked Laree a few times. When she tried to squirm away, the two teenage boys were instructed to tie her face down to a metal futon frame, and Larry whacked her thirty-nine times, the biblical forty lashes minus one. Then Constance whacked

Laree another twenty times. When Laree started to scream, Larry stuffed a towel in her mouth, securing it with a scarf around her head tightened with a stick. The other children assisted in removing her clothing for the next round of Larry's thirty-nine strokes and Constance's additional twenty. Then Larry turned her over for another thirty-nine whacks with the cable. Within an hour of her arrival at the hospital, Laree was dead.

In June, 2001, five staff members of the Heartland Christian Academy in rural Missouri were charged with child abuse for what the *New York Times* called "old-time religion and old-fashioned discipline to try to save the lives and souls of its students." This was a school where "the teachers do not spare the rod . . . and they expect the children to pray." In one incident, when paddling was not effective for students who would not pay attention or who talked back to teachers, eleven kids were forced to stand in pits of cow dung at a nearby dairy farm.

Studies show that the fundamentalist male's views on the roles of women and children contribute significantly to spousal and child abuse. Incest rates are much higher among fundamentalist fathers. Noted physicians and child-protection advocates Ray E. Helfer and C. Henry Kempe report, "The assault rate on children of parents who subscribe to the belief of male dominance is 136 percent higher than for couples not committed to male dominance."

Ruth Miller, Larry S. Miller, and Mary R. Langenbrunner Miller published the findings of their 1997 study, "Religiosity and Child Sexual Abuse: A Risk Factor Assessment," which found a pronounced correlation between religious conservatism and sexual abuse by a family member: The more fundamentalist, the greater the child's risk, especially in isolated families that were less likely to participate in religious activities.

In *Characteristics of the Incestuous Family*, Jackie J. Hudson points out that although sexual abuse is typically higher among stepfathers than biological fathers, in conservative Christian families the incest rate is so high that the rate of sexual abuse by biological fathers is higher than abuse by stepfathers in the general population. Even today, the religious Right promotes traditional "biblical" sexist attitudes of male domination that are tolerant of sexual abuse. Fundamentalist wives and children have been conditioned to fear the autocratic father figure, who expects unquestioning, automatic obedience, which he is entitled to according to Old Testament mores.

Studies show that when fundamentalists adhere to the patriarchal family structure of male ownership and the traditional view that all sex is so sinful that even mentioning it is taboo, incest by a father who "has the right" is hidden in secrecy and silence.

Rampant clerical molestation stems from the same ideology of male authoritarianism that enforces secrecy to maintain power and control over those lower in the hierarchy, who are taught to listen, not speak; obey, not question; "take it," not resist. Although every state requires doctors, teachers, and other authoritative officials to report suspected child abuse, at this writing clergy are exempt from the requirement in twenty-four states, which means that if a wife or child "confesses" abuse, it can be handled internally or not at all, with no legal repercussions. The male head of the male controlled church is considered "above" the rules and restrictions that apply to the rest of us.

"Child sexual abuse has become a scandal within the Catholic Church . . . because it is embedded in the very structure of Roman Catholicism," in the opinion of Frank Bruni and Elinor Burkett, authors of *A Gospel of Shame.* That structure includes patriarchy, a priest addressed as Father, the view that all sex is sinful, the vow of celibacy, and the confessional secrecy. Believers assume the unlikelihood of sexual abuse from within the church, which itself becomes the cloak abusive clerics hide behind.

Priestly pedophilia globally has cost the Church well over a billion dollars in settlements. A report by Rev. Tom Economus estimated that up to 16.3 percent of priests are pedophiles. Over a hundred priests have been implicated in the Boston archdiocese alone.

Some child molesters claim they are acting in obedience to a commandment from God. David Koresh, for example, leader of the Branch Davidians, maintained that while in Jerusalem, he had a vision instructing him to father a child with his wife's eleven-year-old sister.

Even clean-cut all-American fundamentalists can be embroiled in sexual scandals. U.S. House Representative John George Schmitz was a Catholic fundamentalist "family values" advocate working as part of the Reagan Revolution, and his wife Mary was an antifeminist active in the Right to Life League, when a former student of John's was charged with abuse of one of her two children Schmitz had illegitimately fathered. Meanwhile, Schmitz's young daughter, Mary Kay, became pregnant, married, and moved to Seattle, where she had more children and taught as an elementary school teacher, until she got pregnant by a sixth-grade student with whom she had fallen in love.

Another fundamentalist, Susan Smith, who in 1994 drowned her two children, wrote in her confession letter, "My children, Michael and Alex, are with our Heavenly Father now, and I know that they will never hurt again. As a mom, that means more than words could ever say . . . My children deserve to have the best, and now they will . . . I have put my total faith in God, and he will take care of me." According to Smith's later statement to police, her stepfather, Beverly Russell, began molesting her when she was fifteen. Russell, county chairman of the Christian Coalition and a member of Pat Robertson's state G.O.P. executive committee, concluded a day of posting "Pat Robertson for President" posters all over town by molesting Susan. Even after the molestations became public, Russell retained his position within the Robertson organization.

During 1980 and 1981, average guy Paul O'Brien searched for an explanation for why his schoolteacher friend had murdered his own wife and three children less than a year after he had become very religious and started carrying a Bible. "My wife and children are now in heaven," the friend said on a tape he made before his execution. "I'm happy to join them now."

For a year and a half, O'Brien clipped news stories about mass murderers and serial killers from the *Flint Journal* to find out what they had in common. Eleven of the twelve reported mass murderers and serial killers had either a very religious upbringing or belief in demons and devils. O'Brien learned that mass murderers and serial killers tend to be fundamentalist and that "Most carried a Christian Bible with them at all times."

One of those eleven, Sampson Kanderayi, a Christian known as the Ax Killer, murdered more than thirty people "to appease evil spirits." Another, a frequent Bible reader, received messages from God to find women home alone and to stab them to death. Teenager David Kellers, whose "whole life revolved around church and religion," murdered his parents with a shotgun. Patricia Dueweke, a devout Catholic who had extensive religious training and had gone to a convent to become a nun, dropped her three children off a hotel balcony. Curtis Martin put his three children in a factory's steel melting pot and walked away reading the Bible aloud as his children "turned into charred ash."

A 1992 study by M.H. Medoff and I. Lee Skov, and a 1995 study by David Lester, a world-renowned authority on murder, concluded that "fundamentalism may be a cause of murder, because of the oppressiveness of fundamentalists' strict moral code." An inability to conform can result in emotional and spiritual suffering "with adverse consequences."

Studies by criminologists have revealed that anxiety, fear, and absolute dependence on faith leads to "evil imagination" expressed as hostility, judgment, condemnation, hatred, the need to punish, and violence.

It could be argued that fundamentalists use "Christianity" and biblical literalism to uphold inequality because that entitles them to exploit others, even to the extent of subjecting innocent people to the status of victims of sadistic pleasure.

Preacher Joe Combs and his wife Evangeline of Bristol, Tennessee, for instance, were just your average respectable fundamentalist parents who home schooled their children, until they were busted for the kidnapping, rape, and abuse of Elsa Garcia, their "adopted" daughter that they never bothered to legally adopt. Because the Combs family kept Elsa and the other children isolated from society, it was only when Elsa attempted suicide by drinking antifreeze that doctors discovered the scars all over her body. She fell down a lot, the good Christian Combs couple explained. Almost everybody accepted the honest word of the respected preacher.

But that explanation just didn't ring true for police detective Debbie Richmond-McCauley, who continued an investigation. After being sequestered from her family for more than a year, Elsa finally was able to reveal the truth. Besides being the Combs couple's resident slave, from the age of five Elsa was forced to have oral sex daily with the preacher, who justified his behavior by quoting Scripture such as "King David had concubines." When Evangeline found out, she beat the girl for "her" sin.

Throughout Elsa's "sinful" life, the couple beat her often with bats and garden hoses, cut her with tin can lids, burned her skin with a craft wood-burner, pulled off pieces of flesh with pliers, and on one occasion, sewed up with a darning needle the wound caused by a beating with a wooden shoe. They called her years worth of scars "the marks of the beast." State medical examiner Dr. Gretel Harlan testified that the layering and location of Elsa's 410 visible scars ruled out the possibility of accidental or self-inflicted injuries.

Science and American jurisprudence triumphed over the preacher's biblical right to have concubines and the couple's biblical right to beat slaves. It's easy to see the hidden agenda of biblical literalism and hatred of science, the courts, and everything "humanist." The Combs couple dramatically represents the "heart" of rightwing fundamentalism. According to Christian values, what you do in your heart, you truly do. The elitist "Christian" stance justifies subjugation, arrogance, and sadism. This form of Christianity is in Christian terms the "antichrist" in that it opposes everything Christ represented. The pseudo-science of the pseudo-Christian literalist perverts yes into no, love into hate, truth into biblical distortion to the point of blasphemous mockery. The abuse of the Bible in the hands of hypocrites systematically, "scientifically" sanctifies the demonic in the name of God. Behind the holy mask of biblical literalism, the devil himself smirks.

One only need think of Wichita's Dennis Rader, aka the BTK killer, so named for his modus operandi, blind, torture, kill. Rader was finally arrested in February 2005, at Christ Lutheran Church, where he had been a member for about thirty years and was president of the Congregation Council. A good Christian family man with a wife and two kids, a Cub Scout leader, a college graduate with a degree in Administration of Justice, a former employee of ADT Security Services and the current overly strict and invasive supervisor of the Compliance Department at Park City who "put down" residents' pets unnecessarily, Rader was also a sadosexual murderer of at least ten women.

The devil sneered through the wide painted grin of Pogo the Clown visiting sick kids in the hospital or appearing at charity events, or showing thirty-three young men who would become his victims one of his magic tricks using fake handcuffs that weren't fake. John Wayne Gacy's squeaky clean image was a cover-up for sadosexual murders that could possibly have been projections of his father's violent hatred of homosexuals, which he verbally and physically took out on his son, berating him with accusations of being gay and taunting him for his very real health problems—a heart condition, which continued throughout his life, and blackouts resulting from an early head injury—which his father claimed were faked for attention.

Destroying the scapegoat, or the evil nature of the scapegoat, becomes the sacred duty of enforcing the true faith that ensures one's purity. Once a believer's purity is absolutely covered, he can do whatever he damn well pleases.

Take Claude Allen, for instance.

In January 2006, conservative Christian Republican Claude Allen was interviewed by police when he left a Target store with items he had not paid for. Allen denied any wrongdoing but still resigned his position as top domestic policy advisor with the Bush administration, saying he needed to spend more time with his family. Allen was a lawyer living in a $600,000 home, so Bush was surprised when Allen was arrested in March 2006 for at least twenty-five counts of fraud in a shoplifting scam involving fraudulent refunds for shoplifted merchandise amounting to thousands of dollars. And that was just one store.

Many in Washington speculated that Allen left his White House post because he was unhappy that military chaplains were being forced to conduct nondenominational services. When Allen worked at the health department, he pushed for abstinence-only AIDS prevention programs. During his time as health administrator in Virginia, he blocked welfare payments to a rape victim wanting an abortion. Bush's nomination of Allen for federal appeals court judge in 2003 was rejected by the Democrats. While working as an aide for Jesse Helms in the 1980s, Allen helped fuel an antigay agenda that included accusing one of Helms's opponents of having ties to "the queers." More recently he contributed to the antigay language in the Republican Party's 2004 platform and has been a staunch supporter of a constitutional amendment to ban same-sex marriage. "Our desire—and Claude shares this—is for him to walk with humility and integrity," the pastor of Allen's church, Covenant Life Church, said during a Sunday service, perhaps a bit naively, if not hypocritically, given Allen's propensity for bigotry and scams.

Anyone who keeps up with the latest news or watches TV programs like Court TV or Prime Time Live has seen ample evidence of the extent to which religious conservatives commit crime. According to the Annual Statistical Table on Global Mission, compiled by Professor David B. Barrett, "Ecclesiastical-related crime, or crime in religious institutions, has grown from $300,000 annually a century ago to $3 billion by 1990. It is estimated that the year 2024 will bring $65 billion in ecclesiastical crime."

According to a more recent estimate, published April 2008 in *The Christian Century*, the cost of ecclesiastical crime, which climbed from

$5 million in 1970 to $16 billion in mid 2000, and reached $25 billion by July 2008, was projected to reach $65 billion by 2025.

While big money is paid to victims, bigger money is made thanks to willing victims.

For instance, when mega-rich prophet Morris Cerullo claimed to channel God, in fact announced that God spoke directly through him and instructed him to tell the faithful via divine afflatus, "Would you surrender your pocketbooks unto Me, saith God, and let me be the Lord of your pocketbooks . . . Yea, so be thou obedient unto my voice," suckers handed Cerullo millions.

In May 2000, John Paul Warren, a minister and former Senior Executive with Morris Cerullo World Evangelism (MCWE), filed a lawsuit against Cerullo for defrauding donors. According to Warren's lawyer, "Cerullo purports to have first met God at the age of eight. Since then, his life has apparently been one unbelievable experience after another. He says he was led out of a Jewish orphanage by two angelic beings; transported to heaven for a face-to-face meeting with God; has the ability to predict the future; can heal the sick; and has told audiences when they look at him they 'are looking at God.' He also asks them to 'give me your pocket books.'" Harry Turner, who resigned as MCWE vice-president in 1999, had previously filed suit against Cerullo for donor fraud, lies, and other grievances.

But Cerullo continued to fleece his donor base consisting of millions of trusting, gullible, uninformed American elderly, widows, and the poor, as well as suckers in third world countries. They made him mega-rich; his jet alone, a Gulfstream G4 with gold-plated interior, was worth $50 million, not including two fulltime pilots and a stewardess.

Even non-evangelicals know how to pull the fleece over the sheep's eyes, but the state, still separated from the church, is ever wary. Michigan regulators shut down IRM Corp., which solicited investors via religious television and radio programs. The sale of bogus promissory notes and limited partnerships supposedly linked to the California real estate market brought in $400 million before IRM was busted.

Sixty-five-year-old minister Gerald Payne of Greater Ministries International Church of Tampa, Florida, was sentenced to twenty-seven years and his wife Betty to thirteen years in prison on fraud charges for their $448 million scheme. The couple would not reveal where they stashed the cash. Like all prosperity evangelists, Payne cited various "Give, and it shall be given unto you" Bible verses that proved investor money would double because God said so. For the privilege of investing in "God's" cargo ships and in precious metals and diamond mines in the Caribbean and Africa, twenty thousand faithful investors were persuaded to mortgage their homes, rack up huge credit card debts, and cash in retirement funds, because God promised through his infallible Word that their investment would return to them doubled.

U.S. District Judge James Whittemore called Payne a "wolf in sheep's clothing . . . The fact that you used the word of God to perpetuate a fraud is absolutely despicable." Payne waved to his loyal supporters even as he was led out of the courtroom.

Payne's gesture reminds me of a comment made by a psychopath called "Jack" recounted by Dr. Robert Hare in his book, *Without Conscience*: "I had to steal sometimes to get out of town, yeah, *but I'm not a fucking criminal.*"

According to AP business writer Marcy Gordon, during 1998-2000, securities regulators in twenty-seven states took action against hundreds of companies and individuals that used religion to gain the trust of more than ninety thousand investors.

When the Baptist Foundation of Arizona (BFA) offered a 6.7 percent return on investments, more than thirteen thousand people, many of them elderly Baptists, invested $590 million before the foundation declared bankruptcy and was shut down by state regulators in August 1999, after the *Phoenix New Times* broke the story through its prize-winning series of investigative reports. Three of the eight accused foundation officials pled guilty to defrauding investors as part of a plea bargain to further investigations of five others charged with thirty-two counts each of theft, fraud, and racketeering. BFA became the largest fraud case involving a non-profit organization and the largest collapse of a religious financial institution in U.S. history.

IRM Corp., Greater Ministries, and BFA were all Ponzi schemes, which means that funds to pay previous investors came from payments made by newly recruited investors—a scheme that greatly enriches insiders, until the whole scam collapses.

In a news conference, Deborah Bortner, president of the North American Securities Administrators Association and Washington State's director of securities, warned about investment schemes playing on religious loyalties. Forrest Bomar, a retiree who appeared with Bortner at the news conference, served as a case in point. Bomar and his wife Lee were impressed by the salesman who came to their house. He seemed to share their values, and they trusted him. In the end, they lost almost all their $236,166 investment.

Another case in point: The Rev. Armstrong, a retired Southern Baptist minister, and his wife Lois. When they sold their home and wired the $160,000 to their BFA account, they had already "loaned" $460,000 to BFA at a high rate for promissory notes, which of course promised repayment of the money they never got back. Now the couple lives in a trailer, and Rev. Armstrong can't pay for treatments for his diabetes, cancer, and liver problems.

Investors need to be as skeptical and careful investing with a member of their faith as with anyone else, Bortner advised, pointing out that increasingly sophisticated investment schemes are on the rise. "I've seen more money stolen in the name of God than in any other way." Promoters of investment schemes based on religion often beg for financial help needed to save their church, or their pitch specifies plans to invest part of the profits in a worthy cause. Some scam artists kneel to pray with their victims.

It's worth noting that the Evangelical Council for Financial Accountability (ECFA), the self-policing, non-reprimanding evangelical watchdog group that monitors moneygrubbers, was established by Baptist Billy Graham's business manager after an embarrassing discovery in 1977 by the *Charlotte Observer* that Graham had an undisclosed twenty-three-million dollar fund in Texas that had not been mentioned in the accountings for Graham's ministry. "There are some charlatans coming along and the public ought to be informed about them and warned against them," Graham self-righteously proclaimed.

Federal law requires that all non-profit corporations, including universities and ministries, make public their five top salaries. But in 2001, the *Associated Baptist Press* reported, "About half of Baptist organizations contacted by the independent newspaper *Baptists Today* would not disclose salary information for their top executive. Three Southern Baptist Convention entities said policies allowed them to release only salary ranges." Even evangelicals who disclose salaries might receive additional undisclosed salaries for extra job titles as well as perks that can add up to millions of dollars.

ECFA is accountable only to itself, meaning its member evangelicals, not donors and other ministry supporters. In spite of its standards rating system, critics consider ECFA to be merely a sanitizing front for multi-million dollar mega-ministries seeking donors. ECFA currently boasts a membership of 1,203 organizations with a combined income of approximately $15 billion. ECFA will not release information about many of its secretive members. The outrageous wealth "earned" by top evangelists might deter some potential donors, and less money for the evangelists means less membership money for ECFA, hence their reticence.

Are these "superior" evangelists godly men, or something closer to evil?—A psychopath, perhaps? "Psychopaths have a narcissistic and grossly inflated view of their self-worth and importance, a truly astounding egocentricity and sense of entitlement, and see themselves as the center of the universe, as superior beings who are justified in living according to their own rules," Dr. Hare points out.

Even today Graham's ministry, the Billy Graham Evangelistic Association (BGEA), does not meet ECFA's criteria. In addition, the Better Business Bureau's BBB Wise Giving Alliance requested but did not receive complete information on the organization's governance and oversight, effectiveness measures, finances, solicitation materials, donor privacy, and fundraising disclosures and is unable to verify the organization's compliance with BBB's twelve standards for charity accountability. Although Graham was almost entirely disabled in 2004, his ministry listed a total income (presumably for work not performed) of $116,887,687, with total assets of $384,374,883.

Billy's son, Ned Graham, has also fallen short of ECFA standards. Besides problems with alcoholism, drug addiction, porn use, adultery, and spousal abuse, Ned's highly lucrative East Gates International, a Bible distribution company, had to deal with the resignations of most of his company's staff and board members, which he replaced with siblings and in-laws in violation of ECFA standards, which required that a majority of board members not be related by blood or marriage.

You can get all this, as I have, from the media.

But of course, "The media is ruled by Satan," according to Jimmy Swaggart, who has used television media to build his $150 million a year ministry. "But yet I wonder if many Christians fully understand that. Also, will they believe what the media says, considering that its aim is to steal, kill, and destroy?"

Snake oil sanctimony became especially dangerous during the Reagan era. TV evangelism ramped up its power and profits when Pat Robertson orchestrated his quarter of the divine-right Dominionists alliance— evangelists, rightwing politicians, major corporations, and the neocon— which brazenly violated church/ state separation and cultivated anticommunist, antihumanist, antifeminazi, antigay, anti-Muslim, antiterrorist, anti-this-and-that agendas as lucrative fund-raising hooks. Evangelism's moral tirades provided a critical red herring to deflect attention away from the rightwing Dominionists' concerted appropriation of America (in layman's terms, the enrichment of the already rich off the backs of the not rich), and it served as a symbol proving its righteousness, by which it goaded, and still goads, the sheep onto the free-market/family-values bandwagon, where they could be seduced into colluding in their own exploitation.

The original family values poster child, Newt Gingrich, and his protégé, Tom "Hottub" DeLay, both former Speakers of the House, are examples of classic dirty politicians who masterfully exploited the squeaky clean image bestowed upon them by fundamentalists. Their well-publicized womanizing and adultery were only sins, but real crimes led to public outcry and President Clinton's censure and the speakers' eventual forced resignations. Is it any wonder that faux family values Gingrich and DeLay led the Clinton-Lewinsky lynch mob? Their version of revenge was almost humorous. Gingrich was himself such a notorious adulterer that during his presidential campaign, his entire core staff resigned because of it. Gingrich and DeLay were each indicted for felonies committed against the American people and their laws, and both lost their jobs as House speakers because of some of them. Some of the worst of those crimes were committed with the active support of prominent fundamentalists.

Good Christian President "Dubya" Bush added insult to injury his first year in office when he transferred President Clinton's entire $5.6 trillion surplus—the largest in American history—to the already-rich. Every year thereafter, Bush's corporate pals pocketed trillions more of our hard-earned tax dollars—real money paid out in the form of debt against our future treasury, most of it borrowed from China and Japan. Bush shelled out over $100 billion a year in direct subsidies to the oil and other energy industries alone. In February 2006, CNN reported that a new federal investigation had discovered that $18 billion in money allocated for the Iraq War was "unaccounted for," and investigators considered that just the tip of the iceberg.

Corporate welfare for the rich fueled the Dominionists machine. Bush & co. must have been laughing at poor dumb-sheep Christians who didn't even know that subsidies (i.e. corporate welfare) consisting of *their* tax dollars were being handed out to corporations already raking in billions in profits—Exxon Mobile, for instance, posted $36 billion in profits in 2005—when many of those corporations weren't paying any taxes themselves. "American" corporations were dodging an estimated $70 billion in annual taxes by setting up shop via P.O. boxes in offshore tax havens like Bermuda or the Cayman Islands. Many corporations paid no taxes at all, while others, taking advantage of loopholes, paid a little token tax. According to economic experts, simply closing some of the more outrageous loopholes could have increased annual tax revenues by at least $110 billion.

As if being ripped off economically were not enough, after 9/11, frightened Americans willingly handed over their rights on behalf of The Patriot Act, perhaps the most unpatriotic fraud ever perpetrated by an American president. The Patriot Act covertly represented the self-interested will of corporate aristocrats attempting to appropriate America while pretending to represent America, with God's blessing. There was no war on terror. There was only the Iraq-Afghanistan War, which was a global-positioning business venture of an oil cartel acting as an independent nation—all paid for by scammed American taxpayers while our elected representatives quietly fingered their pocketed perks and next year's campaign contributions.

Good Christian President Bush told America that the war in Iraq was "making the world safe for democracy" and that his illegal invasion of that country was "maintaining stability in the region." The truth was that American invasions of other nations created instability, terrorism, and hatred of America throughout the world. The truth was that the corporate nation exploited the American military to "secure"—i.e., steal—oil from those countries. While it picked America's pocket to pay for its business venture of stealing Middle East oil, the corporate nation demonized Islam to sucker in American fundamentalists and other "Christian" bigots who could be mobilized to support "America's" destruction of the Islamic devil.

I began to wonder if America's military was purposely being weakened and our arms depleted by a corporate nation creating its own military elsewhere with the intent of conquering America and the entire world. It didn't strike me as farfetched, given that the corporate nation owned the corporations that manufactured our arms and provided the military's services, and given little hints like Halliburton's announcement that it planned to move its headquarters from Texas to Dubai—it was a Dubai corporation that Bush wanted us to sell our ports to. Was I being a bit paranoid to surmise that a corporate nation takeover of America might be in the works?

Certainly the corporate nation owned far more than the military. Much of America's infrastructure was controlled not by Americans but by huge multinational corporations. The corporate nation owned the energy that powered our cars, businesses, and homes. It controlled our natural resources, our air and water, the timber that became paper products and lumber for homebuilding, the metals manufactured into products and the machinery used to make them. It owned our airlines, carmakers, trucking companies, and railroads; the internet and phone companies, banks, media, and food producers; the tools and applications of everyday life. It was heavily invested in medical technology and owned medical facilities and drug companies. Thanks to crooked governors, large corporations were buying bridges and highways paid for by taxpayers for taxpayer use.

The Dominionist corporate alliance already owned and managed America, and America meant you and me. Presently, I thought, we were essentially serfs. Soon we would be slaves if we didn't instigate a cultural revolution to publicly "out" and overthrow Dominionism.

In January 2007, CNN's Lou Dobbs Tonight broke a story that top corporate Republican Dominionists had been meeting secretly with the presidents of Mexico and Canada with the goal of eliminating the three countries' borders and forming a North American Union. Their theme was Homeland Security and Prosperity, as the cabal nicknamed their tryst. In other words, there would be no more Mexico, Canada, or

United States, there would only be one huge continental "nation" of multinational corporate conglomerates supported by America's corporate-controlled military, otherwise known as Homeland Security.

By 2008, the Dominionist corporate alliance had become arguably the most dangerous political-religious entity to ever exist in America and potentially in the world. In essence, it was a powerful covert nation at war with America; its treasonous goal was corporate takeover. Its masquerade as "American" business abiding by "American" free-market capitalism sanctified by its alignment with religion put it beyond scrutiny and above the law. Dominionists publicly championed a "Christian nation"; behind our backs, they were surely snickering with the devil at us dumb-sheep Americans paying them large tolls to cross the bridge to slavery.

Big Brother had arrived, or so I was beginning to think. Through stealth and subterfuge, the corporate aristocracy, instigated as "America" (there's the *real* identity theft), was already executing world domination.

Money, money, money, the love of which is the root of all evil, according to the very Bible those rich rightwingers thumped to sanctify their unrighteousness as they pulled the wool over the dumb sheep's eyes.

Of course, we were dumb in part because thanks to Reagan era deregulation, rich corporations, who now owned the media, had snuffed the Fairness Doctrine, which once upheld the principle of accurate and balanced reporting, so we didn't get much of this from TV newscasters. Nor did we get straightforward facts from elected representatives who sacrificed truth to greed, fear, or "politeness."

Therefore, millions of Americans honestly believed that Bush/Cheney & co. were good Christians and wanted Bush/ Cheney & co. to institute a good Christian America. Millions of Americans jumped on the Bush bandwagon to proclaim the evils of stem-cell research, abortion, gay marriage, the Islamic threat. Millions of Americans never connected the dots between corporate greed and massive pollution that was literally poisoning our planet of very real human beings, including our and their own children.

How could that level of exploitation, how could that degree of ignorance, have happened in America, I wanted to know?

It was during the Bush years that I realized that brazen Orwellian newspeak was possible *only* because God's Big Brother stood on his big podium spouting his big lies while thumping his big Bible. People were gullible—had always been gullible. I was gullible. I, like others, had been subjugated by my own ignorance against my own will.

By the time I finally decided to write this book, two things had become clear to me: Political ignorance was spiritual ignorance, and "Christian America" had absolutely nothing to do with the actual reality of either God or America.

Although the popular religious movement of our Founders had fallen out of vogue, Deism remained, in my view, the most sensible, egalitarian, and relevant alternative to organized religion the world had to offer. What would it take for Deism to make a come-back?

What would happen, what would be rectified, if religion were suddenly supplanted by belief in the commonsense God of Deism?

Chapter 19

Education v. Indoctrination

In 1786, a decade after he penned the Declaration of Independence, Thomas Jefferson advised in a letter to George Wythe, "Preach . . . a crusade against ignorance; establish and improve the law for educating the common people. Let our countrymen know that the people alone can protect us against these evils [of monarchial government]."

The revolutionary ideals of the Enlightenment that spread throughout the world brought with them an understanding that freedom from the elitist entitlement to oppress depended upon the corrective will of educated citizens. Jefferson observed,

> There is one provision [in the new constitution of Spain] which will immortalize its inventors. It is that which, after a certain epoch, disfranchises every citizen who cannot read and write. This is new, and is the fruitful germ of the improvement of everything good and the correction of everything imperfect in the present constitution. This will give you an enlightened people, and an energetic public opinion which will control and enchain the aristocratic spirit of the government.

Jefferson believed that we the people of the new America, "especially when moderately instructed, are the only safe, because the only honest, depositaries of the public rights," and that we "will err sometimes and accidentally, but never designedly, or with a systematic and persevering purpose of overthrowing the free principles of the government."

Our Founders believed that liberty could only be assured if a liberal arts education was freely available to all American citizens, not just to a "special" few. Critics argued that the majority of people were not and would never be capable of ruling themselves, much less an entire nation. Many thought that the common man was intellectually inferior and incapable of being educated.

Jefferson disagreed. "I know no safe depositary of the ultimate powers of the society but the people themselves; and if we think them not enlightened enough to exercise their control with a wholesome discretion, the remedy is not to take it from them, but to inform their discretion by education. This is the true corrective of abuses of constitutional power."

Public education for all citizens was important enough for the survival of our fledgling nation that George Washington addressed the issue in his *First Annual Message*:

> There is nothing which can better deserve your patronage than the promotion of science and literature. Knowledge is, in every country, the surest basis of public happiness. In one in which the measures of government receive their impression so immediately from the sense of the community as in ours, it is proportionably essential. To the security of a free constitution it contributes in various ways: by convincing those who are entrusted with the public administration that every valuable end of government is best answered by the enlightened confidence of the people; and by teaching the people themselves to know and to value their own rights; to discern and provide against invasions of them; to distinguish between oppression and the necessary exercise of lawful authority.

President Washington so strongly favored the establishment of a liberal arts university that he offered to help finance one with a substantial contribution from his own wealth.

> A plan for the establishment of a University in the federal City ... I have greatly wished to see a plan adopted by which the Arts, Sciences and Belles lettres, could be taught in their *fullest* extent; thereby embracing *all* the advantages of European tuition with the means of acquiring the liberal knowledge which is necessary to qualify our citizens for the exigencies of public, as well as private life; and (which with me, is a consideration of great magnitude) by assembling the youth from the different parts of this rising republic, contributing from their intercourse, and interchange of information, to the removal of prejudices which might, perhaps,

sometimes arise from local circumstances . . . I will grant, in perpetuity, fifty shares in the navigation of Potomac River towards the endowment of it. What annuity will arise from these fifty shares, when the navigation is in full operation, can, at this time, be only conjectured.

The considerable annuity from Washington's contributed shares helped establish Washington University.

Thomas Jefferson's blueprint for a broad liberal public education warned against establishing schools that promoted the doctrines of one specific religious sect. Instead, students should be free to explore many religious traditions.

After stating the constitutional reasons against a public establishment of any religious instruction, we suggest the expediency of encouraging the different religious sects to establish, each for itself, a professorship of their own tenets on the confines of the university, so near as that their students may attend the lectures there and have the free use of our library and every other accommodation we can give them; preserving, however, their independence of us and of each other. This fills the chasm objected to ours, as a defect in an institution professing to give instruction in *all* useful sciences . . . And by bringing the sects together, and mixing them with the mass of other students, we shall soften their asperities, liberalize and neutralize their prejudices, and make the general religion a religion of peace, reason, and morality.

The goal of our early American Revolutionaries like Washington and Jefferson was not to promote the rigid belief-system of authoritarian Christianity; it was to preserve truth, security, tolerance, and liberty.

Not all religious schools educated for the sake of indoctrination. Thomas Paine, one of history's most reasonable advocates of separation of church and state, cherished the well-rounded instruction he received at a Quaker school. Even a religious education can open one's eyes to religious corruption. In *Citizen Representative*, Paine recommended quality education as the antidote to the corrupting morals of priests:

[The Quakers] are equally as remarkable for the education of their children. I am a descendant of a family of that profession; my father was a Quaker; and I presume I may be admitted an evidence of what I assert. The seeds of good principles, and the literary means of advancement in the world, are laid in early life. Instead, therefore, of consuming the substance of the nation upon priests, whose life at best is a life of idleness, let us think of providing for the education of those who have not the means of doing it themselves. One good schoolmaster is of more use than a hundred priests.

If we look back at what was the condition of France under the ancient regime, we cannot acquit the priests of corrupting the morals of the nation. Their pretended celibacy led them to carry debauchery and domestic infidelity into every family where they could gain admission; and their blasphemous pretensions to forgive sins encouraged the commission of them. Why has the Revolution of France been stained with crimes, which the Revolution of the United States of America was not? Men are physically the same in all countries; it is education that makes them different. Accustom a people to believe that priests or any other class of men can forgive sins, and you will have sins in abundance.

Education was a necessary prerequisite for the advancement of our stated ideals of life, liberty, and the pursuit of happiness for all citizens. "I do hope," Jefferson wrote magnanimously, "that in the present spirit of extending to the great mass of mankind the blessings of instruction, I see a prospect of great advancement in the happiness of the human race." Although he cautioned, "I do not, with some enthusiasts, believe that the human condition will ever advance to such a state of perfection as that there shall no longer be pain or vice in the world, yet," like all humanists then and today, he did "believe it susceptible of much improvement, and most of all in matters of government and religion; and that the diffusion of knowledge among the people is to be the instrument by which it is to be effected."

"Above all things I hope the education of the common people will be attended to; convinced that on their good sense we may rely with the most security for the preservation of a due degree of liberty," he wrote to James Madison. And in a letter to Pierre Samuel Dupont de Nemours, he commented, "Enlighten the people generally, and tyranny and oppressions of body and mind will vanish like evil spirits at the dawn of day."

The enlightenment our Founders envisioned is still to some extent an unfulfilled hope. TV evangelist Jerry Falwell expressed the sentiments of perhaps millions of his followers when he said, "I hope I will live to see the day when, as in the early days of our country, we won't have any public schools. The churches will have taken them over again and Christians will be running them." Falwell didn't live to see that day. But before he died, he raked in millions pitching his agenda.

Opposition to education and to just plain thinking is nothing new. Luther proclaimed, "Whoever wishes to be a Christian, let him pluck out the eyes of his reason." "Christ wants to slay reason and subdue the arrogance of the Jews." "Whoever wants to be a Christian must be intent on silencing the voice of reason."

Not surprisingly, many fundamentalists even today denigrate "humanists," scholars, and academia, the protectors of reason. Several outspoken evangelists are hostile to education that encourages free-thinking, imagination, scrutiny, and interpretation, and instead insist on indoctrination, often inculcated through Christian schools and home schooling, to assure obedience to their God-breathed Bible, especially interpretations of translations sanctioned by their own particular denomination, church, or preacher.

Indoctrination "teaches" absolutes revealed by God that can't be questioned. Students are molded into passive sheep taught the absolute virtues of conformity and obedience. Obedient students become obedient adults who will deny their own God-given reason, conscience, intuition, and experience to conform in obedience to the commands of their domineering teachers. If leaders teach them that good is evil, that right is wrong, that God has instructed them to sacrifice a thousand dancing virgins or to burn witches at the stake, indoctrinated adults will obey rather than risk going to hell. Indoctrination is exactly that method used by cult leaders to gain control.

To counter the push for progress, rightwing fundamentalists have become particularly adept at rewriting history to imply that until recently, public education was religious education, specifically Christian. "We're going to bring back God and the Bible and drive the gods of secular humanism right out of the public schools of America," announced presidential candidate Pat Buchanan, addressing an anti-gay rally in 1996.

Fundamentalists like Buchanan seem unaware that God and the Bible never went anywhere, and that our humanist Founders created our nation as a rejection of the controlling despotism of religion and state.

America's creators were keenly aware, as were their humanist forebears, of the danger of church merging with state to create an even deadlier version of the oppressive Holy Roman Empire.

To overcome church/state separation, fundamentalists fuse church and education and make upholding that fusion a sacred duty. Jerry Falwell warned his viewers, "The public school system is damned . . . Christian students should be in Christian schools. If you have to sell your car, live in a smaller house, or work a night job, put your child in Christian schools. If you can't afford it, home school."

Fundamentalists like Falwell teach their children that our Founders established a Christian America that must be rescued from humanist liberals.

Public education, the invention of Thomas Jefferson and one of America's proudest institutions, nurtures open-mindedness, truth, and progress; it opposes discrimination, provides accurate, up-to-date information, and facilitates exploration.

The so-called Dominionists—radical fundamentalists working to take control of America—want public education replaced with podiums for propaganda. Spokesperson Gary North sums us the extremist Reconstructionist agenda,

> So let us be blunt about it: We must use the doctrine of religious liberty to gain independence for Christian schools until we train up a generation of people who know that there is no religious neutrality, no neutral law, no neutral education, and no neutral civil government. Then they will get busy in constructing a Bible-based social, political and religious order which finally denies the religious liberty of the enemies of God.

To gain independence? To deny religious liberty? Isn't that perspective a kind of treason? By "neutrality" North implies freedom, which he opposes. His clear goal is his own elitist, dictatorial rule of slaves who will "get busy" doing his bidding.

Many other prominent leaders maintain similar positions. Robert Thoburne, headmaster of a far Right Christian school near D.C. proclaims, "Our goal is not to make the schools better . . . the goal is to hamper them, so they cannot grow . . . Our goal as God-fearing, uncompromised . . . Christians is to shut down the public schools . . . step by step, school by school, district by district."

J.M. Sutherland of The Christian Alert Network believes, "Only stupid parents would leave their children in the filthy, immoral, dangerous, public 'education' institutions for indoctrination by socialists . . . who don't seem to care about the safety of children . . . only their pay checks."

James Kennedy is another prominent evangelist that regularly bashes public education. "Not all the educators in our public schools and universities are deliberately deceitful, not all of them want to destroy this nation, but many do. The major teachers' unions certainly do," he blatantly lies. "Just a few years ago, there were as many as ten thousand Communist professors in American universities. The average person never saw any of them, and many would doubt the truth of that statistic. But I can assure you it is true." And his ignorant followers actually trust his assurance. "Teachers in many of our public schools have acceded to the policies of the liberal teachers' unions to make sure that students from kindergarten through high school will be stripped of any sense of moral or ethical absolutes. Right and wrong are non-issues in our public schools."

Having myself taught for over twenty years as a professor at ten universities and colleges and at a public charter high school, I can assure you that Kennedy's assurance is delusional.

Only blind sheep would believe that teachers' unions are deliberately deceitful and want to destroy this nation. Only blind sheep would believe that ten thousand American professors are Communists. Only blind sheep would believe that teachers' unions want to strip students of any sense of morality and ethics. Only blind sheep would believe that public schools do not address issues of right and wrong.

Well-educated James Kennedy and his well-educated colleagues are deliberately blinding the under-educated sheep via propaganda. The blinded sheep then collude in blinding their children via Christian schools or home schooling with self-indoctrinating "educational" materials. Kennedy and clan have made themselves filthy rich spewing their bunkum.

To inspire fear and fire up a witch-hunt mentality toward academics, Pat Robertson promotes a book titled *The Professors: The 101 Most Dangerous Academics in America*:

> That's just a short list of the 30-40,000 of them, they're like termites that have worked into the woodwork of our academic society and

it's appalling . . . These guys are out and out communists, they are radicals, you know some of them are killers, and they are propagandists of the first order and they don't want anybody else except them. That's why Regent University [which Robertson owns] for example is so terrifically important and why we're setting up an undergraduate program that hopefully will see shortly 10,000 students, and then from there 250,000 because you don't want your child to be brainwashed by these radicals, you just don't want it to happen. Not only brainwashed but beat up, they beat these people up, cower them into submission.

Perfect hook: Radicals beat up children; radicals, not fundamentalists, "cower" children into submission. The solution? Buy my book. Send Regent money.

Only obedient, indoctrinated sheep would nod at this typical Robertsonian snake oil.

I have to admit that some of the rationales of anti-education pundits are so ridiculous they're amusing.

While addressing the "God and Country II" rally, evangelist William Murray (ironically, the son of the famous atheist leader, Madalyn Murray O'Hair) stressed the need for in-school prayer and Bible recitations because "Young boys are on Ritalin and a lot of the problem is because we have a female-dominated educational system which tries to make little boys act like little girls."

Senator Jesse Helms warned in a fundraising campaign mailer, "Your tax dollars are being used to pay for grade school classes that teach our children that cannibalism, wife-swapping, and the murder of infants and the elderly are acceptable behavior."

What makes public schools such a problem? "Secular schools can never be tolerated because such schools have no religious instruction, and a general moral instruction without a religious foundation is built on air; consequently, all character training and religion must be derived from faith . . . We need believing people," as Adolf Hitler put it, April 26, 1933, in his speech during negotiations leading to the Nazi-Vatican Concordant of 1933.

In contrast to the Jeffersonian ideal of religious tolerance, radicals like Pat Buchanan and Pat Robertson distort nondiscriminatory openness to the ideas of all religions, making it seem anti-Christian. Buchanan told graduating college students in their commencement address, "America's public schools, we consciously deny them all religious instruction, and deny them access to that primary source of morality, God's own word. The Bible is the one book from which they are expressly not allowed to be taught."

This, of course, is untrue. The Bible can be taught as a religious or literary work at any university. It just can't be lifted up as the only source of absolute, literal truth to which all Americans must bow, which is the fundamentalists' demand.

Pat Robertson claimed on his 700 Club, "The public education movement has also been an anti-Christian movement . . . We can change education in America if you put Christian principles in and Christian pedagogy in. In three years, you would totally revolutionize education in America."

In 1993, James Kennedy amped the rhetoric to the level of a war against education: "The Christian community has a golden opportunity to train an army of dedicated teachers who can invade the public school classrooms and use them to influence the nation for Christ." Christianity still hasn't shaken its propensity for domestic terrorism.

Steven Showers, Director of The School Prayer Resource Center, Newbury Park, California, expressed his plan of attack in a letter to *The Simi Valley Star & Enterprise*, January 1, 1995: "If a local community provides for school prayer, and the children of that community voluntarily choose to participate in it, this collective decision allows God to intercede in the public dimension of that community. Restoring school prayer will allow God's angels to leap into action to arrest hellish energy patterns before they can sprout and spill over into the public square."

Of course, school prayer is not voluntary, and it violates separation of church and state, not to mention the rights of students who are Jews, Muslims, or members of other religions.

Pat Robertson hit on a lucrative fundraising strategy when he coupled education phobia with pedophilia, which he erroneously equated with homosexuality. "It's one thing to say, 'We have rights to jobs . . . we have rights to be left alone in our little corner of the world to do our thing.' It's an entirely different thing to say, well, 'We're not only going to go into the schools and we're going to take your children and your grandchildren and turn them into homosexuals.' Now that's wrong."

312 • *Born-Again Deist*

Well, it might be wrong if it ever happened. It could happen, just like a heterosexual could obtain a teaching position for the purpose of gaining access to children he or she could molest. But there has never been a reported case of a homosexual going into the schools specifically for the purpose of turning children into homosexuals. Yet Robertson dishonestly implies that this is commonplace homosexual rhetoric and, by implication, behavior. This is pure Robertsonian mythmaking generated by that extremist fear of difference called paranoia.

All the major professional psychological and medical organizations distinguish pedophilia as a separate sexual preference, as different from homosexuality as homosexuality is from heterosexuality. The pedophile's preference is not for males or females, it is for children, often of either gender. A pedophile is a child molester, not a homosexual. A homosexual is a homosexual, not a heterosexual "turned into" a homosexual. These are scientific facts denied by fundamentalists.

Fundamentalist Robert Knight also links homophobia with education. Though he would be the last person to know anything about the homosexual subculture, Knight nonetheless claims, "There is a strong undercurrent of pedophilia in the homosexual subculture. Homosexual activists want to promote the flouting of traditional sexual prohibitions at the earliest possible age . . . they want to encourage a promiscuous society—and the best place to start is with a young and credulous captive audience in the public schools." And he adds, "Homosexuals say they don't want the children, but boy they put a lot of energy into going after them."

Homosexuals say they don't want the children because they don't. Needless to say, Knight's "a lot of energy into going after them" is a lot of hot air into going after gays. Like many other fundamentalist evangelists, Knight is a master of the fallacy of false authority—himself.

The homo-pedophile frenzy is a modern witch-hunt. It's often difficult to tell if the rhetoric is motivated by genuine paranoia or if it's simply an underhanded fundraising gimmick.

In one of his direct mail letters, Don Wildmon of the American Family Association makes the preposterous claim that homosexuals recruit children to "breed." He exploits this claim to raise money, and it works. "For the sake of our children and society, we must OPPOSE the spread of homosexual activity! Just as we must oppose murder, stealing, and adultery! Since homosexuals cannot reproduce, the only way for them to 'breed' is to RECRUIT! And who are their targets for recruitment? Children!"

Thomas Jefferson must be rolling over in his grave. After two centuries of public education, an American citizen can still reach that kind of ludicrous conclusion.

Why do American citizens continue to support these clearly dishonest, reason-challenged, hypocritical TV evangelists? Jimmy Swaggart, for instance, is a self-avowed pornography addict who was more than once jailed for paying a prostitute to commit "pornographic acts," but when Jimmy shouted, "Sex education classes in our public schools are promoting incest," people cried "Praise the Lord" and sent him money. Why? Lack of education and basic critical thinking skills. Even an ass can bray like a prophet, and out there somewhere, someone will believe it.

Fundamentalist extremists like Pat Robertson are masters of pontificating the ridiculous. For instance, "The courts are merely a ruse, if you will, for humanist, atheistic educators to beat up on Christians."

Does Robertson, who holds a law degree, truly believe that the purpose of the courts is to serve as a ruse for educators; that all educators are atheist; that all humanists are atheists; or that educators have the time or inclination to "beat up on" Christians? Does Robertson honestly think that there are no Christian employees of the courts, no Christian educators, and no Christian humanists? Does he know the function of the courts? Does he even know the definition of "ruse"?

Here's the ruse. In contrast to the humanist liberal arts education of public schools, fundamentalist private school indoctrination forbids students to explore their own thoughts and feelings—unless they conform to the biblically acceptable. It devalues uniqueness and individuality. It subverts self-confidence by badgering children with their supposed incorrigible sinfulness, frightens them into believing that obedience is the means to escape hell, brainwashes them into being passive toward their "elders." It destroys their humanity.

The way legalists leash their children, and want to control the rest of us, mirrors the agenda of behavioral psychologists like B.F. Skinner, who believe that human beings are flawed machines that can be overhauled by science. Skinner demonstrated his version of a "more effective technology" by raising his daughter "scientifically" in his Skinner baby box—a large, air-conditioned, germ-free box equipped with levers that provided rewards for appropriate actions.

In contrast, anthropologists studying child-rearing among various groups around the world have documented that children given the freedom to "creep and crawl," to explore and discover the world on their own, have consistently higher IQs and are more secure and successful than children routinely restrained by anything from a mother's tugging hand to playpens (*pens*?). This is true even of groups related genetically and living side-by-side that have recently split into separate clans because of ideological differences. Grown-up creep and crawl kids have strong self-esteem and think for themselves. They learn to value freedom.

Today education has been severely constricted to teach and test only those skills subject to corporate exploitation. There's talk of extending the school day, the school week, the school year. Should this happen, the consequences will be counterproductive. Kids spend too much time cooped-up in classrooms already. The agenda to train more worker bees for long hours of work is part of a broad agenda of economic exploitation.

Instead of implementing the commonsense solution—redistribute wealth, establish economic equality, decrease the work day/week/year—we allow the weight of fat-cats to flatten us into pancake puppets. Let's just say *No!* to that agenda.

People need time to relax, to play, to enjoy life, to really get educated by reading for pleasure, taking ballet, learning to throw pots, performing in local musicals, going fishing with Walt Whitman.

A longer school and work week will only make us natives restless, frustrated, angry. The day will come when workers will rise up to snap off the fat-cats' horns and tails and raze their mocking mountaintop castles.

Free public education is an American invention intended to promote equality by giving every human being the basic knowledge and skills to think, speak, and act responsibly. Responsible action is always an independent decision reflecting personal preference. American education is founded on the process of discovery. The student learns best what he discovers for himself, which comes about with the guidance of a teacher. American education is not clichéd propaganda propagated by coercion. To *know about* is not the same as to *know*. *To know* comes about through active inquiry, willful engagement, and creative expression. Ironically, it is not public but "Christian" education that thwarts authentic soul-searching.

Instead of getting the attention they need, today's students are packed like sardines in schools and classrooms, schools are underfunded, and teachers are neither respected nor adequately paid, and it's that condition, not some evil agenda of humanists, that foments bullying, violence, illiteracy, and kids' loathing of "school."

America's Founders valued education as the means to protect liberty from forces of coercion and to ensure the continued progress that would contribute to our pursuit of happiness. The goal was that education would be liberal, guarding against the closed-field of over-specialization by providing equal access to information and skills; open-minded in allowing for new ideas and creative exploration outside the box; and public in providing equal educational opportunities for every citizen. It assumed the Aristotelian notion that people are built by God to experience pleasure and that it is wisdom attained via ongoing learning that gives the liveliest pleasure.

Fundamentalism, on the other hand, wants to confine education within its narrow box of stale histories, antiquated moralities, and juvenile sciences that reduce profound theologies and vivid representations to clichés and superstitions, none of which can be subjected to scrutiny or analysis, much less criticism.

The word education comes from the Latin *educare*, "to draw out." Socrates was such a master of "drawing out" that we call his relentless process of provocative questioning the Socratic Method. The intellectual and artistic achievement that burst from the small city-state of Athens can be attributed in large part to the critical thinking exemplified by the Socratic Method employed by Socrates himself. His process of drawing out inherent knowledge (even from an uneducated slave, as Plato recounts in his *Theatetus*) stimulated an environment in which true genius could flourish. Because each individual's revelation was brought to light from within, both ordinary lessons of common sense and profound insights of genius registered as deeply personal and long-lasting enlightenment. So long-lasting that many still revere the art, literature, and philosophy of Classical Greece as the epitome of advanced civilization.

The Socratic Method is a kind of guided freethinking; the teacher facilitates the process of learning to think for oneself. Genius can be learned, but indoctrination by rote often stifles intellectual potential.

Albert Einstein, the quintessential modern genius, provided organic proof that genius could be learned. Or rather, his brain provided the proof.

In 1911, Santiago Ramon y Cajal, the father of neuroanatomy, discovered that it was not the number of neurons that determined genius, but the number of synapses, or interconnections between neurons. Glial cells, axons, and dendrites connect other nerve cells and help transmit signals between neurons. Dr. Marian Diamond, neuroanatomist at the University of California at Berkeley, demonstrated through several famous experiments that when rats were subjected to high-stimulus environments, their brains grew in size as the number of transmitting nerve cells increased. The more stimulating toys the rats mastered, the more their intelligence increased. Conversely, rats that were given little stimulation stagnated and died younger, and their brains developed fewer cellular connections.

When Einstein died in 1955, chunks of his brain were distributed to researchers for study. Dr. Diamond's examination found a large number of glial cells in Einstein's left parietal lobe—indications that his intelligence was the result of mental exercises similar to the kinds she had provided her laboratory rats.

Following his exhaustive study of Einstein's life, works, interviews, and papers, psychologist Robert B. Dilts concluded that "instead of words or mathematical formulas, Einstein claimed to think primarily in terms of visual images and feelings . . . Verbal and mathematical representations of his thoughts came only *after* the important creative thinking was done." Einstein himself "believed that you could stimulate ingenious thought by allowing your imagination to float freely, unrestrained by conventional inhibitions."

Some of his most ingenious insights occurred to him while he was playing the violin or freethinking. He was a sixteen-year-old daydreaming when he first glimpsed what was to become his Special Theory of Relativity. In his final *Autobiographical Note*, Einstein remembers that he was wondering what it would be like to run beside a light beam at the speed of light. He kept chewing on that image. Later he imagined himself riding on the end of a light beam. According to the accepted laws of physics, you would not be able to see your reflection in a mirror. Since the speed of light was the absolute speed limit of the universe and nothing could travel faster, there would be no time left for his reflection to travel back to him; his reflection would have to travel faster than the light beam he was riding.

But that just didn't feel right to Einstein. Riding in a fast-moving train, can't we still walk at our normal pace from one end to the other? Though earth is rushing with the rest of our galaxy at 45,000 mph, and is spinning around in our own orbit at 66,000 mph, can't we still stand still? He trusted his gut instinct that he would see his reflection in a mirror that even traveling at the speed of light was still a few inches from his nose; the mirror was relative to him, not relative to some observer not on the light beam watching the light beam, and his mathematical proof of what he had intuited—the famous $e = mc^2$—revolutionized the world.

The free play of his imagination led him to a profound insight into Creation that contradicted what the experts accepted as absolute truth. Intuition transcended indoctrination.

Early in life, Einstein had begun applying the Socratic Method to himself, relentlessly asking himself questions, in daydreams, journals, letters, and conversations, that "drew out" of him solutions to seemingly trivial physical riddles that would unlock realities as vast as the universe. Einstein's method of drawing out was the opposite of indoctrination handed down from on high. When people are not encouraged to be self-manifesting, when their ideas and will and drive to know are stifled, they stagnate, mentally, emotionally, and spiritually.

Einstein attributed his scientific prowess to what he called a "vague play" with "signs," "images," and other elements, both "visual" and "muscular." He wrote, "This combinatory play seems to be the essential feature in productive thought." A free play of the imagination, not learning by rote, is what leads to authentic and often startling insights that can then be explained and made useful. "Invention is not the product of logical thought, even though the final product is tied to a logical structure."

A liberating liberal arts education, which "draws out" by encouraging authentic thought and by nurturing the free play of imagination, is the most practical antidote to set-thinking, including the close-minded absolutism of fundamentalism.

318 • Born-Again Deist

Ignorance stems from an unwillingness to step outside the Text Box into the real world of updated information and creative solutions.

If fundamentalists of all religions could be persuaded to broaden their minds to the possibility that their ultimate Text Box (Bible, Koran, Torah, pope . . .) might not be equivalent to God, and if those fundamentalists could grasp the obvious truth that knowledge and wisdom are attained through the *process* of learning, many of the world's greatest woes would vanish.

Now as in the past, common sense tells even Christians that God's truth embodies all Creation, only a minute sliver of which our dinky pea brain can grasp. Denying the validity of the monumental text of the universe in order to preserve the mystique of "exhaustive biblical knowledge" is a mistake stemming from a misunderstanding of both the universe and the Bible.

God never asks for blind obedience. It's the wolf pulling the wool over your eyes that asks you to park your brains outside the temple door.

Dominionists understand that controlling education is a key component in attaining dominion. Indoctrinate them while they're young and you'll own them for life. The quickest way to seize control over education is to privatize schools.

Privatization means that businesses would own schools. Be assured that schools, like businesses, would merge—quite possibly into a single, corporate-owned "school system." Schools would no longer be public, which means that people would have to pay to send their kids to school. The rich and their conservative patsies, of course, have no problem with this. Rich children brought up on the luxuries of corporate welfare don't think the rest of us, who foot their bills, are entitled to an education we pay for with our own tax dollars. "Where did this idea come from—that everybody deserves free education . . . It's like free groceries. It comes from Moscow. From Russia. Straight out of the pit of hell," as Texas Representative Debbie Riddle put it.

As an attempted first step toward privatization, President Bush and his Republican Congress introduced vouchers, which were meant to transfer tax dollars into private schools. Even though the vouchers bill failed to pass, federal tax dollars could still be transferred from the public schools to for-profit, non-profit, and faith-based private schools. Bush's

2004 budget included $5 billion taxpayer dollars for two voucher programs funding private schools.

As Plan B on the road to privatization, the president who famously queried, "Is our children learning?" thrust upon the nation's public schools his version of No Child Left Behind. Many children have been left behind thanks to Bush's budget, which cut public education funding by one third. He left no funding for rural education, gifted-and-talented programs, small schools, and technical education. There was so little money allocated for special education that Vermont senator Jim Jeffords abdicated from the Republican Party in disgust. Also cut were funds for educating children of parents active in the military.

No Child Left Behind was launched as a concerted scheme by the Dominionist controlled federal government to seize total control of every phase of public education (although it paid only seven percent of public education costs), allocating funds on a reward system, dictating its policies and procedures, and even determining a school's survival. Schools that didn't make the grade didn't get the money. Of course, schools not making the grade needed *more* money, not less. But they got less; and less. And as a result they "deserved" less and less. Those schools just happened to be schools already disadvantaged, meaning poor. Keeping the less-deserving poor uneducated would maintain a large rock-bottom class of lowest-paid slave labor.

Denying funds is an effective way to control the more progressive schools. In February 2003, Bush's Department of Education defied the Constitution by demanding that schools schedule time for "constitutionally protected prayer" or lose federal aid for the poor. If Dominionists were going to invest "their" money in poor schools, those schools had better crank out obedient little workers used to bowing to authority, and progressive schools had better get on board. The school prayer initiative rewarded obedient conservative "churchy" schools already programmed to produce future workers willing to salute boss man.

Dominionists understand that standardized tests lead to standardized answers lead to standardized people. Bush's purposely constricting No Child Left Behind mandated a reductive, closely scrutinized teaching apparatus consisting of focused, simplistic lesson plans that produced specific results that were judged and rewarded solely on the basis of standardized tests. Such a narrow education produces narrow minds. The champions of narrow-mindedness, of course, want narrow minds programmed by narrow habits that prepare them for obedience to Dominionist indoctrination.

To develop the habit of standardization, public school teachers have been forced to adopt a standardized teaching philosophy utilizing one teaching method that focuses on teaching to test. Educational values reduced to basic math/basic English standardized testing devalues critical thinking and programs students to see life as black-and-white right-and-wrong. The habit of absolutism makes programmed workers unable to resist bandwagon appeals to us-versus-them, "us" being "our" corporate nation. Standardized thinking allows corporations to program workers to value the entire corporate unit as "us." Even reduced to the lowest level of servitude within a corporation, the lowest-paid worker will still rally behind "his" unit. Corporations gain by the competitive spirit of bigotry, the habitual rejection of and hatred toward "them."

Privatization is the real objective of No Child Left Behind. As more and more schools economically sink, the public will respond to the crisis by gladly turning over the business of running schools to more competent hands. The school-as-business model is already being implemented. "Teaching to test" that narrows curriculum to subjects that can be easily evaluated via standardized tests is modeled on the business-driven standards-and-accountability design. "Our" corporate-purchased elected representatives are transforming our schools into training centers where kids only learn skills that make them productive laborers in the competitive global market. Even President Obama and the Democratic Congress agree with that agenda.

Large corporate publishing conglomerates have stepped in to make a killing facilitating the transition to corporate controlled education. Outrageously expensive textbooks have always been publishers' highest profit category. Now they can rake in even more peddling their overpriced teach-to-test study guides, teaching guides, workbooks, drill programs, and of course the standardized tests and testing apparatuses themselves. At Bush's January 2001 White House education summit, an old family friend, Harold McGraw, chairman of McGraw-Hill, proclaimed, "It's a great day for education, because we now have substantial alignment among all the key constituents—the public, the education community, business and political leaders—that results matters."

The truth, of course, is that parents and educators and much of the rest of the public think that education has severely deteriorated thanks to No Child Left Behind. Nobody besides the rich big guys likes its results-demanding bullying.

Most educators and most parents are against limiting a child's world to standardized math and grammar. Almost all educators and parents want kids to learn music, art, theater, dance, science, literature, creative writing, history, and critical thinking. A broad education rich in arts, humanities, and sciences creates broad-minded citizens capable of thinking and making choices for themselves. Standardized tests program standardized, homogenized, mechanical citizens who salute even a president like Bush, whose narrow vision for education assured us, "You teach a child to read and he or her will be able to pass a literacy test." If you can pass a Bush-level literacy test, you can be a product that in turn produces lots of money for a sub-literate Big Brother.

People educated to think for themselves by using good critical thinking skills rebel against blatant brainwashing and exploitation. For that reason, Dominionists aggressively work to eliminate "humanist" arts and humanities programs, and even public television. Most sciences pose a threat, because the scientific method requires close scrutiny and evaluation, and science has the dangerous habit of debunking antiquated "facts" and contemporary junk science. Junk economics fertilized with junk theology produces the junk science that savvy minds reject and often ridicule. Dominionists don't like being ridiculed; they like being saluted. Arts, humanities, and sciences, which focus on benefiting the human community, are systematically purged, and independent thinkers, especially those associated with universities, are demonized.

Meanwhile, corporations launch public relations campaigns complete with "education funds" and sentimental commercials geared toward duping their workers and the public into believing that corporations really are generous, really are green, really do care.

The only effective defense against the wolf is a good education.

Chapter 20
Taboo

Throughout this book, I've purposely left out one of the most important details of my spiritual evolution. I'm gay.

These days it probably doesn't seem odd that falling in love, having a relationship, being rejected "by necessity" by the other person, and subsequently dealing with sexual status and self-definition, not to mention emotional trauma, could catalyze a trajectory from born-again Christian to progressive Christian to disillusioned agnostic. But to delighted Deist?

Ironically, Christianity's judgmental and blatantly unloving rejection of homosexuality drove me to locate biblical support for my side, and that helped me reach the epiphany—which had been dawning on me all along—that the Bible was not God, nor was it God-breathed or necessarily a source of truth or even human wisdom. At first this struck me as a bad thing, hence the disillusioned agnostic phase. But then I realized that it was a good thing. In fact, a *great* thing! There was no gay taboo "revealed" by God.

As a child I thought taboos were just plain dumb. Kids couldn't even walk through the adult section of my hometown library. My parents, however, said their kids could read any book on the shelves, so of course I flaunted my freedom and browsed the adult section under the uptight librarian's grimace every chance I got.

In junior high a neighborhood mom reprimanded me for hitting baseballs farther than any of the boys (or even men teachers). Silly, yes, but still her judgment brought me to tears. Luckily my mom, nice as she was, called up the lady and chewed her out (which I only learned about much later via my grandmother). The lady didn't complain when she later found out that I was even better at basketball.

In high school I thought it was ridiculous that you couldn't say "hell" or "damn" except in church but you could scream "heck" or "darn" or "go to the devil" in somebody's face with fierce hate that bordered on demonic. My saintly grandmother would say "Oh murder!" at bad news, but even my free-cussing dad wouldn't dream of saying "fuck." What was more heinous than murder, except maybe rape or molestation, which you could also say? But the word that means something that everybody does and everybody likes and is the source of life itself and is celebrated by major sacred rituals like marriage and births, not to mention is the preoccupation of movies, advertisements, books, songs, gossip columns, daydreams, and day-to-day life, you couldn't even mention? Absurd.

Sex seemed like an incongruous taboo until I learned about misogyny and patriarchy's subjection of women via denial of monetary and sexual freedom. Men were men and women were property of men. Because womanly men and manly women threatened the hierarchy, they were of course forbidden, and anything that permitted the threat—sexual freedom, for instance—became shrouded in taboo.

A taboo is an arbitrary forbidding for the sake of maintaining power-over. Being a person who enjoys my freedom, I've never been one for bowing to taboos. But the gay abomination grabbed the born-again me by the scruff and gave me a good hard shake. I was nervous, maybe even a bit scared. My girlfriend was terrified. Needless to say, our closet relationship was doomed from the start. Even so, it was hard as hell to tear ourselves apart. But tear apart we did. And in the process I realized that the taboo was evil and the tearing apart an act of emotional and spiritual violence.

Most people don't have to deal with being gay. But I know many good souls who have suffered tremendous agony because they have violated—or dared not violate—some taboo imposed by their religion.

I have also known many otherwise good souls who have upheld a taboo despite doubts about its validity. Not that long ago a divorced person was considered by many religionists to be damned. Sodomy was practically blasphemous. Inter-racial romance could get lovers murdered. Homosexuality defied God's natural plan for his children, so clearly if you were homosexual, you weren't a child of God. Of course all these taboo behaviors were illegal, even for those who disagreed on righteous, constitutional grounds.

Taboos are a justification for meanness. Bullies wield taboos like bully clubs. The self-righteous paste scarlet letters on your forehead to prove their superior righteousness. The underworld promotes the forbidden as a means to get rich. Even spouses and best friends exploit taboos to keep "loved ones" in their place.

The rich and their political patsies create taboos to concentrate power and money in their own hands. In this country, it's "un-American" to critique capitalism, even though capitalism, which is driven by exploitation that's driven by greed, necessarily destroys democracy, which promotes equality and mutual benefit. Dick Cheney can get away with stealing millions (or billions) from America's Treasury, but even knowing his guilt, many Americans cringe when someone like me suggests that Cheney is a traitor who should be tried for treason. Incongruous as it is in a democracy, for many the taboo against criticizing the president (and "vice" president) is as American as apple pie.

Catholic priests are so pure it's taboo for them to marry. And look where that's gotten us. Priests by the droves are busted for child molestation and other sexual misconduct; historically priests and popes have fathered illegitimate children and committed far worse sins; many priests are trying to repress and/or hide their homosexuality. No doubt some leering priest upholds the tradition of confession as a means to vicariously enjoy taboos.

If I sidestepped the gay taboo by neglecting to mention the very critical detail of my being gay, it was only to prevent a fundamentalist or other reader from assuming that I'm bashing Christianity because I'm gay. I'm not bashing Christianity at all. My battle is with lies, fallacies, and evils, Christian or otherwise.

It's probably taboo for some fundamentalists to read this book in the first place. For them it's taboo to question cherished assumptions. It's taboo to think outside the box, to think for themselves, really to think much at all. Thinking for staunch traditionalists is really just contemplating and/or memorizing the thoughts of other traditionalists. Thoughts are controlled, feelings disciplined, difference punished. They aren't allowed to consider the thoughts of radicals like me. That's taboo.

And of course it's taboo to use the word "stupid." The evil exploit by keeping us stupid by making it taboo to point out how stupid it is to be exploited and to be kept stupid.

All these taboos seem ludicrous compared to what I view as the mother and father of all taboos: fear of death, and doubting God's goodness.

If we really trusted God's goodness, many of us would cease to fear. Some of us, of course, would fear that we wouldn't be good enough by God's standards to deserve an afterlife—a well-justified fear, perhaps, in some cases.

I believe that we all doubt God's goodness to some extent but that we're afraid to admit it. We admit being afraid of death, but most of us fear accusing God of being less than ultimately good. Even so, we feel that doubt even if we don't express it. The doubting God taboo forbids us to even think it.

Is God good when a mother watches an alligator drag her child into a lake? What about a woman told she has terminal cancer and a few months to live? Should the surviving residents of the Hiroshima bombing thank God for his goodness in granting their survival?

Questioning God's goodness is anathema. Cursing God in anger for being less than good is for most a form of blasphemy.

I shake my head at tornado victims that thank God for his goodness in sparing them, when their houses are toothpicks and their valuables strewn across three counties. For this they thank God?

Why would God do such a thing? Is God a cosmic terrorist plotting his next attack? Is God bullying us into masochistic submission to his will?

The Deist must address these dilemmas head-on, without cowering in fear, without assuming the stance of a "grateful" victim.

Why does God cause or permit (there's not much difference) bad things to happen to good people? The only answer that makes sense to me is that God has given us free will, and the will can only be truly free if it is capable of suffering unjustly and inflicting unjust suffering. We choose to rebuild our houses on a target that's been hit by tornadoes a hundred times in a hundred years. A psychopathic serial killer chooses to rape and dismember an innocent child—a deciding act that manifests and defines him as evil. The tornado victims to some extent choose to be victims by building their houses on the sand, so to speak. The psychopath chooses to be evil. The child does not choose to be a victim. It might seem insensitive to say this, but the child's suffering lasts a moment but eternal life, if it exists, lasts forever. There's some consolation in that possibility; it's possible to logically infer that eternal life is a reality.

However, we can't be free if we *know* God is judging us. We need that shadow of a doubt to be truly free to choose good over evil. If your life were perfect, and if the perfectly good God were watching you, it would be easy to be "good." But that version of good would be plastic, not organic. True goodness must be good "in spite of." Most people won't lie if they know they'll get caught, but the truly good person won't lie even if there is no chance of getting caught.

If life thrives by eating other life, is the Creator of life compassionate or brutal? To believe that the Creator is compassionate and good requires faith in the Creator's transcendent goodness. When bad things happen to us, we can curse God or choose to believe that we're in this jungle for a reason. I believe that at least one reason is to prove our own transcendent goodness.

Again, it's easy to be good when there's no reason to be otherwise or when we know other people are watching. The true test is to be good even when the universe is brutal, even when it seems like God is either evil or not paying attention, even when we have everything to lose and nothing to gain but our own goodness.

In other words, for us to be good—i.e. *become* good—we must be good not because it's the status quo, not because it's easy, not because there's a reward, not because we're under surveillance, but only because it's a free choice to be good "in spite of."

Likewise, we can choose to believe in God's goodness "in spite of." We can choose to believe in the possibility that there is a God and that God is good, and that we can transcend our expectations and demands and be good no matter what, which is the only way to be good. To be good is to just be good. Period.

This world isn't poolside in a lawn chair with a shaved ice martini and a box of chocolates. I think life is much more serious than that. We have work to do. It's a test, it's a learning process, we have a job to do—describe it as you will. But most of us have a gut feeling that there must be a purpose for existence and a purpose for suffering.

Maybe the old adage of Jesus is right—you must lose your life to gain your life. I don't think that's just a message of self-sacrifice. I think it's a simple recognition of the obvious. Every split second, your old self dies and a new self is born. You're not the same as you were in the womb, or ten years ago, or even ten minutes ago. Growth is change, which is a kind of death. Death is ultimately painful. Bad things happen because we are undergoing change. Some changes are more painful than others. We're getting older; then we're old. Old friends and relatives have suffered and died. We've loved and lost. We've accomplished like Sisyphus watching the stone roll back down the hill.

Is God mean to put us in such a body, in such a life? Maybe we really are being punished, as many have believed.

Or are we transmuting from a finite, temporal, selfish soul into something transcendent? Most of the greatest mind/souls of all time have believed that we are, in one way or another. It's true that we just have to believe in God's goodness and in the wisdom of choosing to become inherently good. That kind of free choice seems impossible. How can someone choose to change his own self to such a degree that the change is inherent, as if it were there all along? The thought is taboo: We're playing God if we think we have that much power.

But I think that kind of turning away from our own power is cowardly and irresponsible. To simply assign "It's God's will" to every tragedy is lazy. When we challenge God we recognize that God doesn't want us to suffer but suffer we must if we're to transcend ourselves. But we transcend not by suffering but by understanding that we must suffer not as passive victims but as survivors who survive by an act of free will. We must be free agents of our own souls.

Michelangelo claimed, "I saw the angel in the marble, and I carved until I set it free." If as free agents we resist passivity, we carve every moment of our lives. Our life, our life's work, our sculpture is a representation of the transformation that we have created in ourselves. We are that free. In that sense, we are created in the image of God. We are creating a godly goodness that is our highest self. There is nothing more difficult or more taboo for us than to grasp this truth about ourselves.

Chapter 21

New Deism Paradigm Shift

Perhaps the greatest pitfall of religious deconstruction is the tendency to throw out the baby with the bathwater. Letting go of the fictions and fallacies of old world "revealed" religion doesn't require giving up on religion per se. Replacing blind faith with mature respect for truth can itself be a deeply religious gesture.

Although Deism makes no claim to absolute knowledge of anything spiritual, it does acknowledge the validity of certain religious assumptions. Its most fundamental assumption is that God exists, if only because an elegant Creation infinitely/eternally in the process of becoming necessitates a Creator of transcending intelligence actively creating.

There's a reason why the religious impulse has always been at the core of human experience. The Deist assumption, quite simply, is that God exists and that we are spiritual beings in need of some kind of relationship with God. Problems arise when a person or group tries to dictate to others exactly what that relationship should be.

Deism avows unconditional religious freedom while acknowledging that religious faith rooted in truth is as necessary as air to the healthy thriving of every human being. Truth is the operative concept, and truth is reality that each individual must discover for him/herself, even if it simply involves deciding yes or no to the opinions of others. To a large extent, one's authentic decisions define oneself.

Deism is a religion rather than simply a philosophy in that it both objectively and subjectively focuses on God as living spiritual truth and experience rather than on the abstract concept "God." I believe that Deism is a universal solution to the vacuum that many people experience after shucking off their outgrown religion. The tired symptoms of alienation, depression, and despair that register the absence of God and/ or meaning vanish with the restorative vigor of Deist conviction.

Perhaps the greatest appeal of Deism is its commonsense, nature affirming approach to spirituality. Deists might agree with a traditional theological stance such as "Our intellect is led by our senses to divine knowledge," but unlike the great Catholic scholar Thomas Aquinas, we wouldn't conclude that divine knowledge includes the Trinity, which contradicts intellect (three beings do not equal one being), our senses (humans are not God, God is not human), and knowledge (Jesus-is-God is a myth).

Unlike many other religions, Deism isn't at war with "worldly" Creation. In fact, God's immanence is a critical component of new Deism: though transcendent, God is a personal Creator intimately engaged in Creation (verb and noun, or noun-verb: space-time). The Deist, therefore, accepts the stewardship of nature. Going Green is a deeply spiritual agenda.

Deism is also appealing because a religion rooted in common sense and nature is truly democratic in being equally available to everyone.

The Deist accepts the spiritual responsibility to ensure equality. "Socialism" and "collectivism" have been poisoned by rightwing denigration, but these terms represent concepts that are part of the new Deist agenda. If all men and women are created equal, then we should work to thwart violations of equality. The upper and lower classes must be replaced by a middle class that provides opportunity and security for all. Exploitation by greedy, arrogant predators must end. The capitalist façade must be replaced with small collectives that guarantee that workers get their fair share of the profits they generate. Obscene wealth among so-called "good Christians" (or Jews, or Muslims)—the Grand Hypocrisy—must be critiqued, and all upper-tier wealth the world over must be steadily redistributed to benefit the common good.

Elitism always manifests as bigotry. For the elite, everyone "beneath" them is inferior and worthy of exploitation. Big bankers who defrauded Americans by spending bailout billions on themselves should be imprisoned. We have got to stop glorifying the rich. Concept to education to action: Deists can lead the way in building an equal society, which is a giant step toward spiritual renewal.

The Deist agenda is a necessity. The threat of nuclear holocaust has shoved us to a unique threshold: We're stepping over a point of no return, the old world upheld by the rusted scaffolding of religious myth and superstition is caving in on itself, a new world is being constructed where the arrogant and the greedy can no longer hide behind the mask of righteousness. Obedient sheep are awakening to find themselves to be human, the gullible are wising-up, the passive are taking the initiative of responsibility, the religious are practicing tolerance and are exercising their freedom of choice. The time is ripe for a worldwide revolution of the soul and spirit.

Marx called religion the opiate of the people. The days of codependent addiction to old world religion are ending, if only because we're smarter and our needs and wants have evolved. We're tired of being ripped-off. We're sick of lies.

Deism is an expression of hope that we can kick the habit, clear the fog, and collaborate in the intelligent, ethical quest for the God of reality. Humanity has grown up enough to realize that organized religion is fraught with frailties and every kind of evil in spite of any good it might offer.

That true religion is not organized religion is not new information. Great writers and philosophers of Greece and Rome knew this; medieval humanists knew this; their understanding was reborn and given new vitality during the Renaissance; in every subsequent era the intelligentsia enlarged that understanding, and fresh insights of writers and artists unshackled the soul of humanity even as organized religion continued to tighten the chains.

The good news is that we no longer need to bow before false gods or conform to the dictates of religious power-mongers. In part because of the internet, even those oppressed by dictators have the freedom to explore religious possibilities and to freely choose what to believe and how to act. Technically, we Americans have always had that freedom of choice, but how rarely most of us have exercised that right—a right given to us by God, according to our Founders.

But with every right comes a corresponding responsibility. It's our responsibility to take the first step to religious freedom, and then take the next.

The first step for you is to slough off that old skin of old religion.

332 • Born-Again Deist

The next step is to establish your own working principles of faith founded on common sense and accepted as experiments: Instead of accepting principles blindly, put them to the test.

Earlier in this book I offered my own short list of working principles (working because they're subject to improvement), and I'll reiterate them here as a possible starting point for anyone interested in exploring Deism.

First, new Deism is a religion of God and only God, theologically grounded in open-minded common sense. Its fundamental tenets (beliefs) are that God exists; that God is one; that God is Creator; that God is both transcendent and immanent in Creation; that God is all-knowing, omniscient, and omnipotent; that God is good; that God is just; that God transcends the limits of human knowledge, goodness, and justice; that God spiritually engages with human individuals; and that no human or text or material or immaterial object is God or embodies God or fully or accurately represents God.

In addition to these working principles, I'd like to offer some suggestions for becoming a Deist and perhaps creating a Deist community. People that give up their old religion for Deism need not give up the best of that religion. Deists think and behave ethically; Deists pray, worship, and do good works, alone or in groups. What Deists don't do is exploit their religion for personal gain, monetary or otherwise. Rather than building cathedrals and giving priests or preachers the opportunity to get rich, Deists meet with like-minded people in homes or conference rooms or cafes or under a tree somewhere. A church is fine, but of course buildings cost money, and money can never be a central concern for a Deist.

Deism can never become a big-time organized religion—that would be a contradiction in terms. Rather, it should remain a movement rooted in simple Deist theology that can be practiced by anyone alone or in small groups or in small, self-supporting communions. I'm calling both the group and the activity a "communion."

And lest I be falsely called a communist, let me ask the reader to look up the definition of communist in any dictionary. Communion and other words derived from the same root mean something quite different, even contrary or opposite. Allow me to clarify by offering some basic Webster's Unabridged definitions.

Not to be confused with Holy Communion, regular communion can mean a group of persons having a common religious faith; a religious denomination; or, association; fellowship; or, interchange or sharing of thoughts or emotions; intimate communication or rapport: *to commune with nature;* the act of sharing, or holding in common; participation; or, the state of things so held. Communion, from the Latin version of the same word, meaning a sharing, equivalent to commun(is): common.

Think of all the positive words that share this root: communal; commune (v.); commune (n.), which has many definitions; communicate; communication; communicative; communicator; communitarian; communitas; community; commutable; commute. And so on.

I recommend both online and face-to-face communions. Talk to your friends and relatives about Deism, then maybe find a good meeting place and start a communion. Visit other communions. Invite people from other communions to visit yours. You can locate communions at NewDeismPress.com.

Articulation is a crucial aspect of spiritual as well as general personal growth. Journaling is an effective way to start figuring out exactly what you believe and don't believe. Generating a list of affirmations about your new beliefs and meditating on those affirmations as often as possible (preferably at least daily) will help clarify your new stance. (This version of meditation means thinking about/contemplating/pondering, not erasing/emptying thought or mental programming.)

Many people would probably benefit the most from discussion groups. These communions can be entirely collective or can be facilitated by one or more participants. But there should never be a designated "high priest." If someone in your group gets too bossy, get out and start a new communion. There should be as much equality as possible.

On the other hand, if one person has a skill for leading discussions, that person could keep the dialogue flowing, as long as she/he isn't overly controlling. It might be useful for each person to write questions or topics on index cards that a participant or participants would then randomly select for discussion.

Of course, if an individual Deist wants to start a discussion group or blog on a specific topic, he/she has every right to keep the discussion on track. It's your discussion, it's your blog. If some people don't like the topic or dialogue, they can start their own discussions elsewhere.

334 • Born-Again Deist

In Deist discussions, the focus is on God—one's relationship or attempted relationship with God, questions about God, things one is learning or realizing about God. But that doesn't mean that you have to say "God" every two seconds. Some people might feel more comfortable not mentioning God at all. (The Hebrews might have been wise to decide that the word for God could never be uttered or written.) God can be in the background as you address personal and spiritual growth or political and social agendas and actions. However much God is part of the discussion, remember that Deism is speculative rather than absolutist.

You might start with this basic question: What does God want me/us to do? To a large extent, you are what you do.

I believe that prayer is critical, both individually and in communions. In my view, the focus of prayer should be praise and requests for clarity; we should avoid what I call "begging and bitching." Don't ask for money; work to establish economic justice. Don't complain; work with others for others.

Most prayer is narcissistic, so it makes sense that most religion is narcissistic. If you believe in God or a God at all, or even in the possibility of God, when was the last time you thanked God for the awesome, wonderful minutia of Creation, or even just casually thought, *Hmm, life is cool, life is good!* Ingratitude is a symptom of narcissism, and vice versa. Ingratitude is both a cause and effect of wrong belief and unbelief.

The good news about Deism is that there's no human high priest to bow down to. There's no sacred text that tells you why you're not good enough. There's no huge list of thou shalts and thou shalt nots, there's only the basic humanist expectation of truth, justice, and compassion— what the Greeks called the Good.

To become a Deist, simply affirm that you are. If you've crossed that threshold, why not share your experience with others? Communicate; engage. I believe that if you do, you will experience a joy that you never dreamed possible. Born-again, enlightenment, illumination, ecstasy, or just plain peace, joy, love—call it what you will. Engage with God, and somehow God will engage with you.

SELECTED BIBLIOGRAPHY

Omission of footnotes and citations is an aesthetic choice. Because this book is not a research work but rather a spiritual memoir, facts and quotations have been offered to represent the flow of ideas and/or events in my life. I have referenced critical sources and have tried to distinguish between my own ideas and information I obtained from others. Most current information mentioned is common knowledge to those who keep up with the news, and quotes not cited have circulated widely on the internet and can be accessed via a simple online search. This bibliography is by no means a complete record of all the works and sources I have quoted or consulted. It indicates the substance and range of reading upon which I have formed my ideas, and I intend it to serve as a convenience for those who wish to pursue further study.

Armstrong, Karen. *The Battle for God: A History of Fundamentalism*. New York: Random House, 2000.

Blaker, Kimberly. *The Fundamentals of Extremism: The Christian Right in America*. New Boston, MI: New Boston Books, 2003.

Boston, Rob. *The Most Dangerous Man in America: Pat Robertson and the Rise of the Christian Coalition*. New York: Prometheus, 1996.

Boswell, John. *Christianity, Social Tolerance, and Homosexuality: Gay People in Western Europe from the Beginning of the Christian Era to the Fourteenth Century*. Chicago: University of Chicago, 1980.

Conway, Flo and Jim Siegelman. *Holy Terror: The Fundamentalist War on America's Freedoms in Religion, Politics and Our Private Lives*. Garden City: Doubleday, 1982.

Darwin, Charles. *Autobiography* (1887). Project Gutenberg, 1999. gutenberg. org/dirs/etext99/adrwn10.txt.

Ehrman, Bart. *Misquoting Jesus: The Story Behind Who Changed the Bible and Why*. San Francisco: HarperSanFrancisco, 2005.

Franklin, Karen. "Enacting Masculinity: Antigay Violence and Group Rape as Participatory Theater." *Sexuality Research & Social Policy* 1, no. 2 (2004).

Gay, Peter. *Deism: An Anthology*. Princeton, N. J.: Van Nostrand, 1968.

Hare, Robert D. *Without Conscience: The Disturbing World of the Psychopaths Among Us*. New York: Guilford, 1999.

HarperCollins Bible Commentary. Edited by James L. Mayes. With the Society of Biblical Literature. New York: HarperCollins, 2000.

HarperCollins Bible Dictionary. Edited by Paul J. Achtemeier. With The Society of Biblical Literature. New York: HarperCollins, 1996.

Haught, James A. *Holy Horrors: An Illustrated History of Religious Murder and Madness*. New York: Prometheus, 1990.

Hill, Jim and Rand Cheadle. *The Bible Tells Me So: Uses and Abuses of Holy Scripture*. New York: Doubleday, 1996.

Helminiak, Daniel A. *What the Bible Really Says About Homosexuality*. San Francisco: Alamo Square, 1994.

Hitler, Adolf. *Mein Kampf*. Translated from the German by Ralph Manheim. New York: Houghton Mifflin, 1999.

Ivans, Molly. *Bushwhacked: Life in George W. Bush's America*. New York: Vintage, 2003.

Jefferson, Thomas. *The Quotable Jefferson*. Edited by John P. Kaminski. Princeton: Princeton University, 2006.

Jefferson, Thomas. *The Writings of Thomas Jefferson*. Edited by Andrew A. Lipscomb and Albert Ellery Bergh. 20 vols. Memorial Edition. Washington, D. C.: Thomas Jefferson Memorial Association, 1903-04. Also available: Project Gutenberg, 2007. www.gutenberg.org/etext/21002.

Jefferson, Thomas. *The Writings of Thomas Jefferson*. Edited by Paul Leicester Ford. 10 vols. Ford Edition. New York, 1892-99. Etext.virginia. edu/jefferson/quotations/.

Kee, Howard Clark, Franklin W. Young, and Karlfried Froehlich. *Understanding the New Testament*. Englewood Cliffs, N. J.: Prentice-Hall, 1965.

Kennedy, Robert F., Jr. *Crimes Against Nature: How George W. Bush & His Corporate Pals Are Plundering the Country & Hijacking Our Democracy*. New York: Harper, 2005.

Krammer, Heinrich and James Sprenger. *Malleus Maleficarum*. Translated from the Latin by Montague Summers, 1928. Transcribed by Wicasta Lovelace and Christie Rice. malleusmaleficarum.org/.

Locke, John. "A Letter Concerning Toleration" (1689). oregonstate.edu/instruct/phl302/texts/locke/locke2/locket/locke_toleration.html.

Locke, John. "Second Treatise of Government" (1690). Project Gutenberg, 2005. www.gutenberg.org/etext/7370.

Luther, Martin. *Luther's Works*. 55 vols. Edited by H. T. Lehman and J. Pelikan. CD-Rom: Minneapolis and St. Louis: Fortress and Concordia Publishing House, 2002.

Madison, James. "Detached Memoranda" (1817). *The Founders' Constitution*. Vol.5, Amendment I (Religion), Document 64. The University of Chicago Press. press-pubs.uchicago.edu/founders/documents/amendI_religions64. html.

Manchester, William. *A World Lit Only By Fire: The Medieval Mind and the Renaissance*. Boston: Little, Brown, 1992.

The Oxford Bible Commentary. Edited by John Barton and John Muddiman. New York: Oxford, 2001.

Paine, Thomas. *The Age of Reason*. New York: Citadel Press, 1948, 1977, 1988. Originally published: Paris: Barras, 1794.

Paine, Thomas. *The Thomas Paine Reader*. Edited by Michael Foot and Isaac Kramnick. London, England: Penguin Books, 1987.

Remsberg, John E. Remsberg. *The Christ: A Critical Review and Analysis of the Evidence of His Existence*. New York: Prometheus, 1994. Originally published: New York: The Truth Seeker Company, 1909.

Ruether, Rosemary Radford. *Christianity and the Making of the Modern Family: Ruling Ideologies, Diverse Realities*. Boston: Beacon, 2000.

Sackville-West, V. *Saint Joan of Arc*. New York: Doubleday, 1991.

Singer, Margaret Thaler. *Cults In Our Midst: The Continuing Fight Against Their Hidden Menace*. San Francisco: Jossey-Bass, 2003.

Strauss, David Friedrich. *The Life of Jesus Critically Examined*. Translated from the German by George Eliot (1892). Reprint: Sigler Press, 2002.

Washington, George. *First Annual Message* (January 8, 1790). The Avalon Project at Yale Law School. yale.edu/lawweb/avalon/presiden/sou/washs01. htm.

Washington, George. *Letter to the Commissioners of the District of Columbia* (January 28, 1795). pbs.org/georgewashington/collection/other_1795jan28. html.

Wenger, Win and Richard Poe. *The Einstein Factor*. Rocklin, CA: Prima, 1996.

White, Mel. *Stranger At the Gate: To Be Gay and Christian in America*. New York: Plume, 1995.

Wolfson, Evan. *Why Marriage Matters: America, Equality, and Gay People's Right to Marry*. New York: Simon & Schuster, 2004.